Photograph: Christopher Deere

JULIAN MEYRICK is Professor of Creative Arts at Griffith University. He is Literary Adviser for the Queensland Theatre, General Editor of Currency House's New Platform Paper series, and a board member for Northern Rivers Performing Arts and the Council for the Humanities, Arts and Social Sciences. The son of an English father and an Australian mother, he studied politics and economics at the University of Exeter in the UK before completing an MA in theatre directing in the US. From 1990–1998 he was Artistic Director of kickhouse theatre, and from 2002–2007 Associate Director and Literary Adviser at Melbourne Theatre Company. He has a PhD in Australian theatre history and from 2008–2011 was a Research Fellow at La Trobe University and a Visiting Assistant Professor at the University at Buffalo, New York. From 2012–2019 he was Professor of Creative Arts at Flinders University, where he led the research team Laboratory Adelaide, investigating the problem of value and evaluation processes in arts and culture. He has directed over 40 award-winning theatre productions, including *Angela's Kitchen*, which he co-wrote with Paul Capsis and Hilary Bell, and which won the 2012 Helpmann for Best New Australian Work. He has published histories of the Nimrod Theatre, Melbourne Theatre Company, the Paris Theatre, the Hunter Valley Theatre and Anthill Theatre, and numerous articles on Australian culture and cultural policy. He was Deputy Chair of Playwriting Australia 2004–09 and a member of the federal government's Creative Australia Advisory Group 2008–10. His book *Australian Theatre after the New Wave: Policy, Subsidy and the Alternative Artist* was published by Brill in 2017. *What Matters? Talking Value in Australian Culture*, co-authored with Robert Phiddian and Tully Barnett, was published by Monash Publishing in 2018.

For my wife Louise and son Vincent.

AUSTRALIA IN 50 PLAYS

   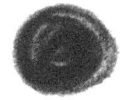

JULIAN MEYRICK

First published in 2022
by Currency Press Pty Ltd,
PO Box 2287, Strawberry Hills, NSW, 2012, Australia
enquiries@currency.com.au
www.currency.com.au

Copyright: *Foreword* © Julianne Schultz, 2022; *Australia in 50 Plays* © Julian Meyrick, 2022

COPYING FOR EDUCATIONAL PURPOSES

The Australian *Copyright Act 1968* (Act) allows a maximum of one chapter or 10% of this book, whichever is the greater, to be copied by any educational institution for its educational purposes provided that that educational institution (or the body that administers it) has given a remuneration notice to Copyright Agency (CA) under the Act.
For details of the CA licence for educational institutions contact CA, 11/66 Goulburn Street, Sydney, NSW, 2000; tel: within Australia 1800 066 844 toll free; outside Australia 61 2 9394 7600; fax: 61 2 9394 7601; email: info@copyright.com.au

COPYING FOR OTHER PURPOSES

Except as permitted under the Act, for example a fair dealing for the purposes of study, research, criticism or review, no part of this book may be reproduced, stored in a retrieval system, or transmitted in any form or by any means without prior written permission. All enquiries should be made to the publisher at the address above.

Edited by Victoria Chance.
Index by Garry Cousins for Currency Press.
Typeset by Currency Press.
Cover and internal design by Alissa Dinallo for Currency Press.

Currency Press acknowledges the Traditional Owners of the Country on which we live and work. We pay our respects to all Aboriginal and Torres Strait Islander Elders, past and present.

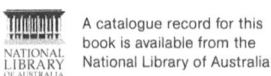

A catalogue record for this book is available from the National Library of Australia

Contents

Foreword. Play to Imagine and Learn by Julianne Schultz	vii
Acknowledgements	xiii
Introduction	1
Chapter 1. 1901–1914: Ozziewood	19
Chapter 2. 1915–1929: Unknown knowns	37
Chapter 3. 1930–1945: The real Australia	60
Chapter 4. 1945–1960: A step change	89
Chapter 5. 1961–1975: Not better, just different	119
Chapter 6. 1976–1990: The compelling mood darkens	159
Chapter 7. 1991–2005: The End (yet the persistence) of History	200
Chapter 8. 2006–2020: The return of the nation	238
Conclusion	282
Appendix	296
Notes	298
Bibliography	314
Index	325

Foreword:
Play to Imagine and Learn

Julianne Schultz

Plays, theatre, drama, entertainment, performance—call it what you will—have always had a presence in the land we call Australia. The traditions are diverse, rich and largely forgotten, thanks to a longstanding national addiction to the permanent present.

For millennia, before European sailors dropped their anchors in the intriguing bays of what they called the Great South Land, the country was alive with song and dance, storytelling and performance. The new arrivals struggled to make sense of this, but they could not ignore it. Many of those who arrived on the ships understood cultural power; they knew from their own lives at the bottom of the British caste system that performance was a special way of communicating truths and making fun.

In early summer 1788 the HMS *Scarborough*, one of the eleven boats that made up the First Fleet, approached what, by then, had been renamed Botany Bay. As they neared the vast bay, her weary passengers put on a play. After surviving nine months at sea, the convicts who had no idea what awaited them invoked a spirit of make-believe and play and entertained their shipmates.

By 1796 the first playhouse was built in Sydney town and quickly filled with a ragtag audience of officers, convicts and settlers, until Governor Philip Gidley King ordered it closed four years later and then razed the building.[1] He considered the performance of Shakespeare's *Henry IV Part One*, with its mock trials, political rebellion and raucous thieves, an affront to his authority and as soon as his governorship was

---

1   David Malouf, *A spirit of play, the making of Australian consciousness*, ABC Boyer Lectures, ABC Books, pp. 19–24.

confirmed he exercised his authority. It took several decades before another playhouse was built in the garrison town.

A century on, by the time of Federation, these unlikely antipodean colonies were among the most literate and numerate societies in the world. On special occasions these new Australians would require people of the First Nations, who they chose to consider a dying race, to perform modified versions of ancient rituals, as bit players in humiliating re-enactments.

The young nation was also home to the largest theatrical empire in history. JC Williamson was like News Corp today. As Julian Meyrick writes, it was an 'immense, tentacular organisation with money, brains and property rights behind it, pursuing activities that spanned art forms and continents'. And as the hunger for theatre, play, entertainment, drama was huge, it was also lucrative.

As World War I took and ruined lives, and later forced a recalibration of what it meant to be Australian, people continued to flock to the theatre. Between August 1914 and November 1918 more than 350 different plays were staged in Melbourne alone.

To understand what happened in the following decades you need to read this book. It is an instructive tale of creativity, expression, opposition, government control and indifference, and a changing nation. This book chronicles the ups and downs of public support, of entertainment taxes, censorship, of cultural cringe and strut, of a flowering national identity and imperial genuflection, of stages on which the most challenging and exciting ideas could be tested and explored.

***

Alfred Deakin, Australia's second prime minister, was very much a *fin de siècle* Renaissance man. His interests ranged widely, and amongst his many outputs, he also wrote well-regarded, serious plays. He had a hand in ensuring that a Commonwealth Literary Fund was created to support writers who struggled to make a living in the new nation, but he did not create a national theatre.

Half a world away, Dublin was still a city effectively under British administration, but in 1904 the Abbey Theatre was established. The theatre became a place where nationalist ideas were tested, where lives and stories were reimagined on stage, where Irish nationalism found its dramatic voice. Drama became what Meyrick calls 'a sinew of public life and debate'. It is still one of Ireland's most distinctive calling cards, drawing audiences at home and abroad with a repertoire that could not have been created anywhere else. Being in the audience and absorbing *The Plough and the Stars* or *Playboy of the Western World* is to be immersed in a distinctive Irish sensibility, and when you think about the homeland of George Bernard Shaw and Samuel Beckett, a certain Irish refraction is clear in *Pygmalion* and *Waiting for Godot*. 'National dramas do not spring up like mushrooms in a field,' as Meyrick observes. 'They are the result of repeated acts of cultural exchange.'

The Abbey Theatre was a gift in waiting for Fintan O'Toole, one of the most astute political and social commentators writing in English today, a man who has redefined what it means to write about politics as theatre. He treats the powerplays in Dublin, London and Washington with the insight that comes from close study of burlesque, tragedy, comedy and farce.

Fintan O'Toole grew up in working-class Dublin. When he was a boy his bus conductor father befriended one of his regular passengers, the Abbey Theatre's front-of-house manager. When there were tickets to spare she gave them to Mr O'Toole, who took his bookish young son to the theatre on quiet nights. 'I couldn't get over it,' he observed years later. 'A piece of theatre, even a bad one, is a very complex event—it's slippery and transient, and you have to pay a lot of attention. I think drama criticism is a good testing ground for any kind of writing in which you are trying to get behind a shifting moment and make some sense of it.'[2]

***

O'Toole's understanding of the role of the critical observer of theatre and politics is much more sophisticated than the throwaway line Australians often hear, *they treat Canberra like a game, as if it's just a show.*

As a trainee dramaturg at the Abbey Theatre, O'Toole learned that a successful performance is much more than even its complicated

---

2   Fintan O'Toole, interview, New York Review of Books, 10 June 2021 www.nyrb.com

parts—script, director, staging, music, lights, actors, audience and the short time they are all together. It is measured, planned and rehearsed, but also spontaneous, unpredictable and fleeting.

That is why O'Toole's essays pierce the carapace of contemporary politics with such devastating accuracy. His training gave him a special way of making sense of the men who walk the world's stages at the beginning of the twenty-first century. They each have what O'Toole considers 'the play of public life' as befits a polity where politics and entertainment have merged to produce 'showmen, braggarts and clowns ready to rule without real responsibility'. He distils insights from his years behind the scenes at the Abbey Theatre to help his readers around the world redefine and make sense of these troubled times, and the leaders they have produced.

Political commentators in Australia are often criticised for treating politics, particularly its performative elements in Parliament and media conferences, as theatre. And while it may be said that some in Canberra have acute and carefully honed insights, none bring the extra sensibility of really understanding the construction and execution of stage drama to the task. *Australia in 50 Plays* shows that this closeness is not merely rhetorical, much is shared. A better understanding of theatre may help political editors make more sense of what they are observing—the big picture, human frailty and hubris, consequences for the public and the nation, refracted in the moment. The best critics know the history and have an acute understanding of psychology, so they can get below the carefully constructed surface and define the real meaning. Theatre teaches us how to truly see.

As Meyrick reminds us in this fine book, plays are unlike other art forms. 'They exist both in the domain of thought and in the physical world. They are both timeless and timely … [D]rama's temporal compression into a few hours, and its style of public address, give the knowledge it offers special impact.'

It's a big claim, but it is one that I find persuasive. That drama is a sinew of national life, not an adjunct, but a creator of its real meaning. Often it is on the stage, in a performance, that ideas and stories that struggle to be heard or make sense in the churn of public life take root and grow. Those sitting in a dark room for a couple of hours are forced to suspend judgement, empathise, to put themselves in the shoes of the actors before them, to imagine another way of being, to explore ideas that are challenging and revealing.

This is one of the reasons theatre is more than entertainment, though entertainment is its essential mask. Theatre is one of the few places where ideas can be tested, indeed where, over time, the very idea of the nation can be reworked. This has a long tradition in Australia, but is one that is rarely celebrated.

The very notion of national identity has become the last refuge of marketers and scoundrels. But everyone comes from somewhere and has, as the price of citizenship, an (unstated) obligation to try to make it a better place. The Uluru Statement from the Heart described this as, 'a fuller expression of Australia's nationhood', and Julian Meyrick argues that the theatre still has, as is had in the past, a special role in this mission.

Imagining an Australia that is fit for purpose in the twenty-first century demands that we know the past but look forward to a new future. Sometimes it is easier to do that in a small space with living actors who take you somewhere else. It can even be life changing. It is always profoundly different to a screen-mediated experience. In an age where screens are ubiquitous, the immediacy and intimacy of theatre, performance, play, drama, may be easy to overlook, but it is more important than ever.

For theatre to contribute to a fuller expression of Australia's nationhood, the challenge will be to find ways to revive and reimagine the repertoire. To find the support that makes it possible to continue to create new works that speak to the contemporary circumstances and recalibrate the past. This book provides an aid for that process, helping theatre goers, actors, directors and producers to understand more of this Australian theatrical 'somewhere' better. Not to relive it but to learn from it.

Julianne Schultz AM FAHA is Emeritus Professor of Media and Culture at Griffith University, the founding editor of Griffith Review, *and the author of* The Idea of Australia, A search for the soul of the nation *(Allen & Unwin)*.

Acknowledgements

This book was conceived, researched, drafted and published during the 2020–22 global pandemic. It is a strange thing to write about Australian drama at a time when its flow has reduced to a trickle, and often stopped altogether. At the start of 2021, I was remounting one of my own theatre shows for a national tour that had been twice cancelled in 2020. Almost immediately, Covid forced rehearsals online. A few weeks later, we lost our Brisbane dates when south Queensland went into a snap lockdown. In retrospect, we were lucky, given the havoc the Delta variant was shortly to unleash, that we got to perform at all.

Because of Covid restrictions, I received help from a more than usually large number of people in writing this book. I was on staff at Griffith University throughout, and could not have completed it without the support of my faculty and school leaders, particularly Scott Harrison, Gerry Docherty, Jamie Carson and Sue Trevaskes. Susan Forde and the Griffith Centre for Social and Cultural Research provided invaluable assistance, and enabled me to employ the wonderful Sue Jarvis to critically review the historical dimension of the book. When I began writing, the late, great Professor Stuart Macintyre generously gave me an inscribed copy of the fifth edition of *A Concise History of Australia*. He is a profound loss to Australian history, and Australian theatre in particular, as he was researching the New Theatre League at the time of his death.

Decisions about which plays to include and on what basis continued until the moment writing stopped. I am grateful to theatre and drama colleagues who contributed to these discussions, helping me avoid more mistakes than I have otherwise made. I would particularly like to thank Veronica Kelly, Rachel Fensham, Robert Reid, Maryrose Casey, Chris Hay, Meredith Rogers, Paul Rae, Jonathan Bollen and Robert Walton for their play suggestions. John McCallum, more familiar with Australian drama in the twentieth century than I will ever be, provided detailed feedback on my initial list of plays, and read the entire manuscript when it was in draft.

I am grateful to AusStage, the leading live performance database, and its long-time manager, Jenny Fewster. The database is an irreplaceable resource for theatre historians doing research of scope. From its data, Peter Beaglehole was able to compose a graph of the Australian plays professionally staged during the 120 years this book covers.

I am fortunate to regularly communicate with a group of eminent scholars from a variety of disciplinary backgrounds. From it coalesced the foundational ideas shaping this synoptic account of Australian drama, in particular the positive conceptions of 'nation', 'national life' and 'nationhood'. Julianne Schultz, Justin O'Connor, Anna Yeatman and Richard Maltby, and my dear colleague, Tully Barnett, are researchers whose views I seek on a daily basis. Which is not to say they will agree with every view I put forward here, only to acknowledge the invaluable assistance they give me by expressing their own.

Though I am less involved in directing theatre now than formerly, I write for a sector of which I am proud to be a part. Over the past two years, conversations with Emily Goddard, Brigid Gallacher, Darcy Kent, Mark Seymour, Justin Gardam, Ella Caldwell, Fiona Symonds, Natasha Marich, Keziah Warner, Jane Bodie, Glenn Shea, Peter May, Ann Tonks, Stephen Curtis, Neil Pigot, Naomi Rukavina, Tom Healey, Emily Collett, Lisa Mibus, Alysha Watt, Christina O'Neill, Dushan Philips, Samuel Rowe, Lee Lewis, my wonderful agents Anthony Blair and Lisa Fagan, and Meredith Rogers (again), enriched this book in countless ways. Chris Mead, then Literary Manager at Melbourne Theatre Company, advised me at length on Australian drama in the 2005–2020 period. Glace Chase, the last playwright I discuss, generously gave me access to the unpublished script of *Triple X*, permission to quote from it, and invaluable guidance on its interpretation. Though they may be unaware of the signal impact they have on me when I wear my historian's hat, the theatre artists with whom I work provide the heart and context for all my scholarly research.

Finally, I am grateful to my publisher, Claire Grady, and editor, Victoria Chance at Currency Press, who supported me psychologically and practically through the most challenging writing project I have as yet undertaken. Their suggestions on every aspect of the book, from core arguments and play inclusions, to ordering and layout, were indispensable as it evolved in the short time available: a symbolically ominous nine months. My debt goes beyond the professional. I feel I am part of the Currency Press project that Katharine Brisbane and Philip Parsons began in 1971, as their acolyte, satellite and legatee. This book coincides with Currency's 50th anniversary. It is an honour to mark the occasion with a contribution I hope is in keeping with a publishing vision that not only recognises Australian drama, but actively calls it into being.

When the present moment is paralysed, it is a relief to turn to the past and be reminded, among other things, that 2020–21 are not the only years of hardship Australians have endured. The past is closer than we think, especially in drama, where play scripts channel the voices of the artists who first fashioned them. John McCallum calls plays the teeth and bones of theatre history. For me, they are more like books of spells, which, when necromantically incantated, summon up once-imagined worlds to live again. They are devices for joining the present and the past, and thus for defeating time. Unlike novels or poetry, their re-enactment requires the creative coordination of an extensive group of people. Perhaps the real magic lies in us, when we reach back in history in this crafted way, and allow the plays of the past a place in the precarious and precious zone of apprehension we call 'the now'.

During the pandemic, both my mother-in-law and my own mother died. Locked down in Melbourne for long periods, it was impossible for my wife or me to visit either of them save sporadically, and then right at the end. The pandemic has—or should have—made us conscious of the miracle of family. For me, this is supplemented by knowing what mine had to endure in someone obsessively writing a book such as this. 'It's like living with a teenager,' my son, just turned 18, complained. 'You never come out of your room.' I was struck to the quick, but kept writing, an impertinence I hope Vincent and Louise will eventually forgive. I dedicate this book to them because the beauty of their lives—both are visual artists and designers—is a constant source of wonder and inspiration for me. If they could see themselves through my eyes, they would know how true it is. We are a family in which words and pictures struggle to combine in optimal fashion. What could be truer to the spirit of theatre?

Introduction

> If writers with the knowledge which Barbara Baynton, Henry Lawson and Tom Collins possess of Australian life had the trained dramatic faculty, we would have a distinctive drama, which would be a refreshing change from the flashy stage-plays we have dumped down here from England, America and France.
>
> Leon Brodsky, 1904

The (theatrical) life of the nation

In *A History of Australian Drama*—a book now nearly half as old as the 120 years this one will cover—the historian and critic Leslie Rees describes journalist Leon Brodsky's despair at the time of Federation at the lack of connection between Australian theatre and Australian national life. He comments,

> The relation of the theatre to national life! This *was* a new note. The term 'national life' was itself new, for the Commonwealth, embracing in its fold the six previously self-governing states and offering to visionaries the chance of a loftier conception of Australianism, had been constituted for only seven years. But before quoting further from Brodsky's vigorous article, it may be as well to remind the reader that… there had been one or two theatrical revolutions on a world scale that completely altered the approach to theatre and drama, both from behind the footlights and on the part of the more discriminating public.[1]

---

1 For sources of direct quotes and play edition details see Notes on page 298.

Brodsky was a friend of Australia's second prime minister, Alfred Deakin, himself a playwright of the heavy-set literary kind that attracted rare recognition and rarer reward in a theatre scene dominated by commercial potboilers, operetta and spectacle.

In 1904, Brodsky founded the Australian Theatre Society, 'first of the groups committed to a serious Australian drama'. It fizzled out after a spate of play readings, mostly of work from abroad. The interest in 'theatrical revolutions' was understandable. These were the years when Harley Granville-Barker and George Bernard Shaw were exploding British theatre from within, while in America, groups like the Theatre Guild and the Provincetown Players were paving the way for Eugene O'Neill, Clifford Odets and Thornton Wilder. In Europe, the shadows of the two colossi of modernist drama, Henrik Ibsen and August Strindberg, loomed larger with each passing year. By contrast, as late as 1947 Allan Aldous was protesting that

> … Australia which has given the world great novelists, actors, actresses, scientists and painters, has not produced a single good playwright. No Australian play (Australian in setting and mood) has appeared on a London or New York stage in the past quarter-century… There has been no playwright of the consistent competence of a Priestley, a Sherwood, a Behrman, an Odets or a Rattigan.

Complaints about the lack of 'real' Australian drama are so common among critics of the twentieth century they qualify as a core characteristic of the art form. Australian drama, it can sometimes feel, exists as an object of aspiration or lament, to be exhorted into being then tasked with measuring up to 'world standards' over which local artists have little say and less control. These standards emanate from 'mature' cultures (how? why? in what way 'mature'?), leaving Australia to 'catch up' with London or New York lest the country 'lag behind', this admonition left deliberately vague, and all the more daunting for it. Brodsky and Aldous are good examples of this long-established FOMO, which in 1950 the critic AA Phillips—himself a drama-lover with considerable theatre experience—skewered in the phrase 'the cultural cringe'. Like Donald Horne's 'the lucky country', the maxim soon took on a life of its own, recruited to a pugnacious nationalism. Now there were two choices for local artists. Either they could try and meet international expectations (whatever these might be) or they could assert their own uniqueness and refuse any comparisons. Phillips would have shaken his head. The 'cultural strut' was as bad as the cultural cringe so far as he was concerned. He wanted 'a relaxed erectness of carriage' as a 'cure for our disease'. Wisely, and with the empathy of the great schoolteacher he essentially was, he advised, 'there is no short-cut to the gradual processes of national growth… The most important development of the last twenty years in Australian writing has been the progress made in the art of being unselfconsciously ourselves'.

How do historical currents like these inform Australian drama now? What should be said to someone wanting a big-picture summary more than a century after Brodsky's fledgling efforts, of what today is a vast and diverse body of work? In truth, it always *was* substantial. From the 1860s onwards, the quantity of theatre in Australia was considerable, both in absolute amount and per capita. At the time of Federation, the country was home to the largest theatrical empire in history, JC Williamson's, *aka* 'The Firm'. Like Pixar or Disney today, this was an immense, tentacular organisation with money, brains and property rights behind it, pursuing activities that spanned art forms and continents. Elisabeth Kumm comments:

> Between 1880 and 1911, The Firm employed leading international stars, as well as negotiating the rights to thousands of plays, musical comedies and operas from London's West End, Europe and New York's Broadway, and touring them throughout their vast network of Australasian theatres. The company's strength lay in its geographic spread and its ability to give the public what it wanted. Employing many of the country's leading performers, designers and technicians, the quality of The Firm's productions was second to none… During the period August 1914 to November 1918, more than 350 different plays were staged in Melbourne, some 200 being performed for the first time. By far the most popular

genre was drama, which constituted more than half the plays produced, followed by comedy, musical comedy, pantomime and revue.

Numbers like these do not suggest a nation uninterested in theatre. But it was not the kind the catcher-uppers had in mind, which had to supply 'drama of poetry, drama of psychology and character and ideas, drama in which the author's literary capacity and understanding of life are unquestioned'. In the decades after Federation the name of this coveted type of theatre varied—'repertory', 'non-commercial', 'Little', 'pro-am', 'alternative', blending into today's more familiar 'independent' and 'small to medium'. Beneath the changing labels, however, the aspiration remained the same—a theatre 'Australian in setting and mood' that would approach 'the ideal state that real theatre-lovers dream about'. From this perspective, the fact that the Firm was so successful was galling. For all its polish and professionalism, its boatloads (literally) of stars, its full houses and full pockets, it produced *theatre of the wrong kind*. It produced only 'theatre in Australia', not the more elusive but nationally vital, theatre 'Australian in setting and mood'.

Any overview of the history of theatrical production in Australia, however modest, has to start with this paradox. On the one hand, there has often been plenty of it. On the other, its most staged playwright is William Shakespeare. Australian drama is a subset of Australian theatre in a way that British drama is not a subset of British theatre but its apotheosis and *raison d'être*. This fundamental de-centredness reflects the violent dislocations of the white colonisation of the country, and the fact that successive waves of immigrants from Europe, and later Asia, brought histories and habits that displaced those of the oldest continuously existing culture in the world. First Nations peoples have their own autochthonous performance forms entirely different from post-1788 theatrical conventions.

As theatre, 'Australian in setting and mood' sought a place in the nation growing up around it, it has had to acknowledge the facts of British invasion and the consequences of 230 years of white occupation. 'The ideological weight of Shakespeare's legacy is nowhere felt more strongly than in the theatre', note Helen Gilbert and Joanne

Tompkins in their seminal book *Post-Colonial Drama: Theory, Practice, Politics,* 'his work is still widely seen as the measure of all dramatic art, the ultimate test for the would-be actor or director, the mark of audience sophistication, and the uncontested sign of "Culture" itself'.

Already, it is possible to see that the main reason why the history of Australian theatre is not straightforward is because the history of Australia is not straightforward. The ready correlations some nations might make between their social development and their cultural development do not hold for the jangled roil of aggression, theft, invention, cruelty, curiosity, fellowship, discrimination and hope that characterises the colonisation of Australia, and the final outcome of which remains uncertain. Indeed, lack of certainty is a noteworthy quality in Australian drama as it began to appear over time. For if the consolidation of the art form did not happen as quickly as Brodsky and Aldous wanted, it was established enough for Rees to publish a 435-page book about it in the early 1970s, and a hurried sequel a few years later.

In the intervening years, the Firm sank from sight in a sea of red ink, while there emerged from the unsteady efforts of successive federal and state governments, and from practitioners themselves, the structure of the Australian theatre we see today, with its small number of 'flagship' companies surrounded by a more numerous flotilla of small-to-medium-size ones. If at the time of Federation, Australian theatre was a matter of visionary promise and imaginative potential, it now seems as solid as any other area of contemporary life. It is easy to forget that promise and potential still provide its animating spirit and creative life. The arts centres that dot the country like miniature cathedrals are less important than the faith of the people inside them. It is important not to assume, yet it is easy to assume, that theatre advances in the same way as our computers and washing machines advance, that it *upgrades*, so that the Australian theatre we have now is superior to the Australian theatre of a hundred years ago because the technology around it is more sophisticated. On the other hand, many would argue there has been an overall betterment in the lot of the art form. The question then arises—and it is the first key question for this book—*what* exactly changes in Australian theatre, and how can we assess its (growing) contribution to Brodsky's 'national life'?

In histories of a conventional kind, culture is often portrayed as the tertiary expression of more fundamental forces. This pyramid model of history is described by the historian Robert Darnton as making '[the assumption that] one can distinguish levels in the past: that the third level (culture) somehow derives from the first two (economics and demography, and social structure); and that third-level phenomena can be understood in the same way as those on deeper levels'. In effect, this is a version of Maslow's famous Hierarchy of Needs. The wide, bottom level of the pyramid represents our material requirements—for food, shelter and warmth. The middle level represents our social requirements—for security, community and shared identity. The small triangle at the top represents the things we want after we get the things we actually need. These include cultural pursuits like theatre, which provide symbolic meaning and value.

Does it need to be said that this conception is also a product of white Australia? That it pertains to a view of culture held in the West, and then only for a short period, though its distorting influence is still felt today, particularly at a government level? No nation, ancient or modern, takes this schematic view of its collective life. Our desire for symbolic meaning and value is not something that we pursue only when our bellies are full. It is nonsense to imply, as the pyramid model of history does, that a nation's culture is just the precipitate of material and social forces. If that were true, countries similar in these respects would have similar cultures. A quick flip through SBS's World Movies catalogue shows that is far from the case. Of course, economic and social forces *condition* culture, but then the reverse is also true, that cultural forces condition economic and social systems. The question is—another key one for this book—*how* are they related? To what kind of 'national life' do they contribute? And where does Australian drama come into the picture?

Before addressing these questions, it is helpful to consider the different 'cultural history' approach that Darnton himself takes in his marvellous book on eighteenth century French life, *The Great Cat Massacre*:

> Anthropologists may have overworked the concept of culture-as-language, but it provides a tonic to historians.

For if culture is idiomatic, it is retrievable. And if enough of its texts have survived, it can be excavated from the archives. We can stop straining to see how these documents 'reflect' their social surroundings, because they were embedded in a symbolic world that was social and cultural at the same time… [T]his kind of cultural history should not be subjected to the same standards of evidence that rule in the history of international relations or politics. World views cannot be pinned down with 'proof'. They are bound to be fuzzy around the edges, and they will slip through the fingers if one grabs at them as if they were pages from the *Congressional Record*.

Two things are important for this style of history. First, it must take *all* the activities of life seriously, where going to the theatre is as ubiquitous as going to the shops. Second, it must be sensitive to 'world views' and what drama (for example) can tell us about the social conditions in which it occurs (as we will see, it is a great deal). Finally, eschewing 'standards of evidence that rule in the history of international relations or politics' is a reminder to cast our net widely and look for unexpected connections: to use the surprises and radical otherness of our cultural past as a whetstone to sharpen our grasp of Australia's bumpy ride into the present.

Professional, cultural and political perspectives

Now that I have complicated the idea of Australian theatre, and rejected a simple notion of cultural progress, we are in a position to consider the connections between individual plays and Australia's national life. We might identify three types of relationship, generative of three different, but interdependent perspectives on Australian drama:

1. *Drama as a creative practice, with its own internally generated rules and norms.* I will call this the 'professional' view of Australian drama.

2. *Drama as a symbolic activity embedded in a range of symbolic activities that face similar expectations.* I will call this the 'cultural' view of Australian drama.
3. *Drama as a social function managed by governments using negative sanctions and positive incentives.* I will call this the 'political' view of Australian theatre.

All three perspectives are needed to understand the impact of a play. The sort of drama that Brodsky wanted in the 1900s had no reality in Australia *culturally*, despite the fact that the Firm was producing a large quantity of theatre *professionally*. The Entertainment Tax that governments levied on theatre between 1914 and 1953, and the censorship laws they applied until the early 1970s, conditioned *politically* what plays appeared on stage and what playwrights could *culturally* say in them. Conversely, individual plays sometimes changed the cultural expectations around them, like Ray Lawler's *Summer of the Seventeenth Doll* (1955), David Williamson's *Don's Party* (1971) and Jane Harrison's *Stolen* (1998), all of which I will examine. Arguably, *Stolen* changed the politics of Australia too, because it highlighted Indigenous history and the signal contribution of Indigenous theatre artists.

In October 1994, Prime Minister Paul Keating launched Australia's first national cultural policy, *Creative Nation*, which sought to bring the three perspectives together (see Chapter 7). Whether the policy was successful or not is less important than the fact that, 93 years after Federation, the government had reached a point where it could view Australian culture in a fuller way.

My life in drama: a personal story

To illustrate these distinctions, let me briefly set them within the context of my own work in Australian theatre. In 2002, I was appointed Literary Adviser and Associate Director at Melbourne Theatre Company (MTC), and given a windowless office next to the set construction workshop. This compelled me to wear industrial-strength ear defenders while engaged in my chief occupation: reading plays. In my first year alone, I read nearly 300, getting through them at the rate of four a day. Later, I employed paid readers to assist me, while I focused on running Hard Lines, the company's playwright development program. My successor as Literary Adviser, Chris Mead, ran a three-tiered scheme, supported by donors, trusts and foundations. In 2017, MTC launched a $4.6 million five-year Next Stage Writers' Program. As of June 2021, it had seen three new plays selected for 'slots' in the company's seasons, 31 playwrights under commission, and 11 playwrights in residence. This 'slate' reflects a balance of 'emerging', 'mid-career' and 'established' writers, as well as projects devised in a more collaborative way, or by practitioners who do not consider themselves as playwrights primarily.

When a theatre company plans a season, it considers not only the actual productions it will mount, but how the slots in which they sit are distributed. The number of available slots, and the type of drama to which these are tied—overseas, classic or Australian plays—is of crucial importance. I will have more to say about this during the course of the book. Slots are much more than vacant holes in a theatre program. They are virtual categories of dramatic anticipation that must exist prior to any individual play being programmed in them.

To talk like this is to talk like a theatre professional, in my case a literary manager. In 2005 I travelled to the United States and Britain to meet my counterparts. I discovered we shared the same outlook and used the same terms. These reflected the nature of the tasks that filled our daily lives: reading scripts, working with playwrights (and those adamant they weren't playwrights) and attending to the abiding issue of which plays, out of many hundreds, should be chosen for production. Working as a theatre professional—the same holds true for directors, designers and actors—is not usually a self-reflexive activity. It is something you *do* rather than think about. The language that grows up around its core tasks is a practical one which aims to assist practical decision-making. As such, it creates what physicists call path dependency. Judgements about what plays 'work' are based on knowing what plays worked in the past. A playwright's track record, while it isn't everything, certainly matters.

Of course, literary managers should be aware of the inertial drag on their thinking, and allow for it. But given the rough and tumble of the theatre business, and the expense of putting on shows, it is easy to ignore. As a result, plays can have a strained relationship with the professional structures that surround them. However, they have one remarkable advantage: they typically outlive the people who first read them, remaining available for future production and retrospective rebuke. This is certainly true of revivals of Patrick White's *The Season at Sarsaparilla* in 1976, and *A Cheery Soul* in 1979, and arguably of the revivals of Dorothy Hewett's *This Old Man Comes Rolling Home* in 1990, and Louis Nowra's *The Golden Age* in 2016. In all four cases, original critical judgements were confounded, and the plays elevated to a new prominence. Plays may be 'the thing', but they engage assessment processes shot through with human frailty. After his dismal experience with *Night on Bald Mountain* in 1964, White remarked that 'for the first time I have enjoyed writing a novel, so at least the theatre has done that for me'. Only when we consider plays in the context of their production do they take on proper life. But this may come later than the playwright originally intended, or even after they have died.

In the ten years prior to joining MTC, and in the ten years after I left it in 2008, I was undertaking research into Australian theatre history. I wrote two long books and two short ones, which were the outcome of very different daily activities from those of a literary manager. Typically, I was buried in the archives of a library, or interviewing practitioners about their relationships with their craft and each other. As a result, I discovered that the story of Australian theatre is situated in a broader cultural narrative. This led me to investigate other art forms and influences.

For example, while researching the Nimrod Theatre, an important Sydney company of the 1970s, housed in what is now Belvoir Street Theatre, I examined: the history of Australian theatre venues, especially the Sydney Opera House; the relationship between Australian opera, dance and theatre in the 1950s and 1960s; the establishment of the National Institute of Dramatic Art (NIDA); and the influence of British companies such as Theatre Workshop and the Royal Shakespeare Company on Australian artists. I also researched changes in social outlook associated with the intellectual movement known as the Sydney Push and the counterculture of the 1970s. I concluded that during this period the status of Australian drama fundamentally altered. Whatever the quality of individual plays on offer, perceptions of their general value grew. My book on the Nimrod Theatre sought to describe how and why this happened, and its connection to the events in Australian society at the time.

In the public domain, plays exist in a web of cultural expectations at once diaphanous and powerful. Many early Nimrod shows—and this is also true of its Melbourne equivalent, the Australian Performing Group (housed at the Pram Factory)—would not have passed muster with the literary managers of an earlier era (or me). But cultural expectations set the ultimate parameters for the meaning and value of a live theatre experience: how people react to what they see. When audiences flocked in droves to the 'rock pantomime' *Hamlet on Ice*, staged in 1971, despite the fact that it had few discernible literary qualities, they delivered a binding public judgement. Professional norms live at the grace and favour of cultural ones, which can upend seemingly settled questions regarding what makes a 'good' play, or even what makes a play at all. Occasionally, these are so decisive they change everything happening in the art form thereafter. At these times does Australian theatre *lead* these transformations in the nation's soul, or does it merely *reflect* them? The fact that it is even a question makes theatre a socially explosive art form and vividly illustrates the flaws in the pyramid model of history.

From the mid-1990s onwards, like many theatre practitioners as they get older, I began to take an interest in matters of administration and governance. I sat on arts boards and attended meetings of peak bodies. As I was running my own theatre company at the time, I learnt the basics of grant finance and legal incorporation, and how to manage relationships with Australia's three levels of government—the local, the state and the federal. Other countries have similar tripartite polities, but Australia's feel particularly challenging. It is as if they are pieces from different jigsaw puzzles inadvertently thrown into the same box. Applying for a venue permit from the Fitzroy Council, or for support for a play reading from Melbourne City Council, felt profoundly different from developing a business plan for the state government, or applying for a project grant from the federal agency the Australia

Council for the Arts. This political understanding of Australian theatre has its own language too and, at first glance, appears to be mostly about money. The three levels of government dispense different types and amounts of subsidy to practitioners to make theatre. On closer inspection, though, there is more at stake than just cash.

From time to time in my research I would come across references to government policies. Shortly after Federation in 1908 the Deakin government set up the Commonwealth Literary Fund (CLF), to assist writers who had fallen on hard times (using a criterion of 'indigence'). In the 1930s, without changing its name or its mission statement, the CLF gave the young writer Vernon Knowles a grant to work in England (using a criterion of 'merit'). After 1945, there was pressure on the government to establish a national theatre to tour the country with popular plays and sell tickets cheaply (using a criterion of 'democratic culture'). In the 1980s, the Australia Council developed programs for artists and audiences from non-English-speaking backgrounds (using a criterion of 'cultural democracy').

These policies changed not only the way Australian theatre was supported from the public purse but the way it was conceived in the public mind. The distinction is crucial. The relationship between Australian theatre and Australian national life is not just a pecuniary one. It is also a matter of social recognition. Barry Andrews, writing about the Labor government's 1973 decision under Prime Minister Gough Whitlam to double financial support for the arts, titled his research, 'Enter Gough, the Fertility God'. Every so often, arts ministers are accused (or praised) for being 'arts czars', as Senator George Brandis was in 2015 when he took a slice of the Australia Council's budget away for a new funding body that he controlled. His successor, Senator Mitch Fifield, was condemned for the opposite reason: for dropping out of view, and letting government concern for culture disappear with him.

The events that have shaped Australia's 'cultural policy envelope' are almost as complex as those that formed Australian theatre. Like a soccer match, however, it is a game of two halves. For the first 50 years after Federation, government policy towards theatre was mostly a matter of prohibition. This included stipulating where and when plays could be staged, and how much they would be taxed for the privilege. A 'wowser' attitude is discernible, one that saw going to the theatre as frivolous, coarse or corrupting. What happened on stage was the subject of censorship in respect of subject matter, language and appearance (especially nudity). Of the plays considered in this book, Sumner Locke Elliott's *Rusty Bugles* was heavily expurgated when it was first staged in 1946, while the director and actors in Alex Buzo's *Norm and Ahmed* were prosecuted in 1972 in both Queensland and Victoria. If Sir Rupert ('Dick') Hamer had not become Victorian premier when he did, it is possible the latter would have gone to jail.

After 1950, however, the government discovered a different way to manage theatre—by funding it. The establishment of the Australian Elizabethan Theatre Trust in 1954 marks the beginning of serious arts grant-giving. In 1968, the Trust was superseded by the Australian Council for the Arts, which in 1975 became the Australia Council, a statutory body operating at 'arm's length' from the government of the day. This distance was conceived as a way of foiling direct ministerial control over culture. At the same time, censorship ceased to be enforced in the same black-letter-law way.

Yet these changes have not led to a depoliticisation of Australian theatre. Which artists and companies should get government support, on what basis, and for how long, constitutes a heated contemporary debate. Within the theatre scene, there is intense discussion about the features of individual plays. Concerns with subject matter, language and appearance have not gone away. Their framing might be different—nudity might be viewed as 'exploitative' rather than 'unwholesome' or offensive words as 'sexist' rather than 'immoral'—but the political dimension remains. Do non-Indigenous playwrights have the right to portray Indigenous characters? What about drama that tackles situations of which the playwright has no personal experience? To what degree can imagination stand proxy for reality? Where does the world end and theatre begin?

Questions like these are a reminder that Australian theatre is as irradiated by politics as ever; and that this is expressed in government policies, in the views of practitioners, and in the grey area between the two. Having political forces against you can be a terrifying experience.

But having them on your side can be liberating. The extraordinary flowering of Indigenous drama in Australian theatre over the past 25 years reflects not only the talents of the artists involved, but also the capacity of the nation to recognise and reward them.

What is a play?

Now that it is clear that plays are simultaneously professional, cultural and political objects, and draw their meaning and value from any or all of these dimensions, we can ask: what is a play? So far, I have used the terms 'theatre', 'drama' and 'play' as if they were interchangeable. Whole books have been written about the distinctions between them. I do not intend to add to that *oeuvre*. We may agree that 'theatre' is a general term for live performance of which 'drama' is a particular kind (other kinds are 'cabaret', 'stand-up comedy' and 'new circus'). 'A play' is a textual embodiment of 'drama', and its chief characteristic is the one I mentioned earlier: it is written down and you can read it.

Terminological distinction-making may be wearisome, but some observations around what qualities make up a play will be useful. First, a play is a blended combination of two different art forms—literature and live performance. Drama proper began in ancient Greece 2,500 years ago, coinciding with the emergence of writing. Writing enables drama to escape the laws of time and space imposed on live performance. Being recorded in some way allows for the acts of future repetition and interpretation that give plays their uncanny double nature. On the one hand, they are historical artefacts, performed at certain dates, in certain places, for certain people. On the other, they exist on a timeless plane of creative pertinence. We could—and do—pick up plays written hundreds of years ago and stage them as if they had been written last week.

It is the double nature of plays—literary and timeless yet theatrical and historical—that makes them so compelling. They come from the past, but potentially exist *now*. They are viral creatures, looking for human hosts to inhabit and come alive again. But they are also unstable. Many of the qualities that define a play can be found in other mediums. Films and television programs have dramatic action and dialogue, digital games have dramatic characters. There are many crossover art forms: dance-drama, music drama, performance art, immersive performance, cos-play, historical re-enactment. If the list isn't endless, it is certainly long. As digital technology has impacted traditional media, it has expanded the range of performance forms and reconceived the notion of 'a play' in seemingly limitless ways.

Or has it? Do we hyper-focus on technological change and assume this changes drama's double nature, unwittingly succumbing to the upgrade view of culture? As anyone who has shopped in a modern supermarket knows, the appearance of diversity can be deceptive. It is what is in the packet, not on the label, that counts. Without minimising the impact of intermediality in theatre today, it is important that plays are not swept into claims of global transformation before due investigation. We must ask *what* exactly is changing. Plays continue to be written down, or recorded, in ways that permit the repetition–interpretation process. If drama's qualities are now found in digital media, does this represent its supersession or a widening of its influence?

A second important characteristic of stage plays is the way they combine their elements in an intellectually concentrated way. This stems from the literary side of drama's legacy, which draws on the devices of classical rhetoric. The dialogue in plays takes its form, aims and values from the *agon*, an ancient Greek term for the contention of two equally persuasive but opposed points of view, an attitude towards dispute resolution that underpinned the Athenian legal system. This makes drama a superb vehicle for broaching issues of public interest. *The Oresteia*, the oldest complete play on record, is full of arguments about the horror of war, the complexity of families, the sterility of revenge, the importance of justice. These themes are as relevant now as they were when it was first presented in the fifth century BCE. The capacity of drama to engage debates like this makes it conceptually powerful.

Plays are an important delivery mechanism for new ideas. They are cost-effective too. Compared with the equipment needed by any and all digital technology, a few bits of paper (if that) and warm bodies in space are available anywhere. Although there are theatrical productions where no expense is spared, many plays are staged quickly, with minimal overheads. Such ready accessibility of means allies drama to another form of expression with its foot in the political realm: street protest. Throughout the twentieth century, Australian plays were used by political movements to convey their beliefs and goals. This continues today, both with plays that contain self-conscious political messages, and in street protests, such as Extinction Rebellion, that shape themselves in a consciously dramatic way.

The paradox of 'theatre in Australia' versus theatre 'Australian in setting and mood' can now be seen for what it is: not a contradiction but a tension. Plays exist in the domain of thought and in the physical world. They are both timeless and timely. When we examine the Australian drama of the last 120 years, we are not rootling through a collection of discarded historical objects. We are listening to a past that is speaking to us still, aware that the present moment will be subsumed in the same historical stream, and all our cultural achievements of which we are so proud, will eventually join it. When we can see the past as 'the now' and ourselves as 'the past' then we are humbled, but also ready to properly consider the plays that make up the Australian drama repertoire.

The plays selected

If you write a book called *Australia in 50 Plays* you better have a way of deciding which ones to choose. The Australian drama repertoire resembles a range of mountain peaks (see Appendix, page 297). At the time of Federation and for 30 years afterwards, there are only a few plays of note by Australian authors. Beginning with the work of the non-commercial Little theatres in the 1920s and 1930s, the volume of Australian drama increases, and some significant works make their appearance. From the late-1960s onwards, the peaks lengthen. The 'New Wave' of drama associated with companies like the Nimrod Theatre, La Mama, the Australian Performing Group, Troupe Theatre, the Hole in the Wall, and others, populates the repertoire. After 2000, the number of new plays increases further, though not smoothly. The shape of this book follows the same trajectory. Its eight chapters, each dealing with 15 years, contain uneven numbers of plays and are of different lengths. This is unavoidable. The problem of picking plays from the 40 years after Federation is a problem of discovery. The problem of picking them from the last 40 years is a problem of choice.

Thankfully my book is not a history of Australian drama *per se*, it is about the history of the nation seen through the lens of some of its plays. There is not the same constraint to be fully representative, nor the same intention of offering a summative account. The works I discuss are a lively raid on the repertoire for explanatory purposes, not an Olympian verdict on an entire body of work. Still, there was a winnowing process of sorts. An initial long list of 120 plays was assembled. I sought advice from historians, literary managers and reviewers about which to include or rule out. An eclectic range of factors informed these discussions. Where and when did a play first appear? What kind of audience was it written for? Is it the first of its kind or the best? What sort of inner or outer world does it explore? Plays are singular creative artefacts. Any rule used to group them together for critical purposes must necessarily be of the loosest kind. I applied my tri-dimensional professional/cultural/political rubric, giving individual plays maximum scope to recommend themselves for selection. I strove for gender balance, though this was hard to achieve given the skew towards male playwrights in the middle decades of the years under examination.

More personal considerations assisted the cut of the final 50. To be selected, plays have to exist in a form that makes them available for future repetition and interpretation. One-off dramatic events, however significant, are not included. Adaptations are also excluded, but there are exceptions if these are versions of earlier dramas and they exist in repeatable–interpretable form. Finally, and most personally of all, I have not chosen plays that I developed or directed. This eliminates six or seven works from the long list that I am proud to have had a hand in, but circumvents the dubious challenge of critically examining my own creative work. There is one exception to this, *Ned Kelly* (1944), the importance of which is overriding.

How are the plays approached in the chapters that follow? They are discussed more or less in chronological order, as history unfolds chronologically. By way of background, I draw on two standard, readily accessible historical accounts, Stuart Macintyre's *A Concise History of Australia* and, to a lesser extent, Manning Clark's *A Short History of Australia*. Federation marks the moment when Australia becomes a separate nation (sort of) and Covid, at the time of writing, has been the latest significant event to impact on Australians as a whole. In between lie the collective experiences of the tumultuous twentieth and twenty-first centuries: World War I; the Depression era; World War II; the Reconstruction period; the Menzies years; the Whitlam years; the Hawke and Keating era; the Great Moderation of the mid-1990s to the mid-2000s; the Global Financial Crisis of 2007–8. Then what? Then ready-made labels are harder to come by. As the flow of Australian drama increases, the number of mental containers to put it in falls. History doesn't feel like history when you are living it. It eludes consensus description and lurches ahead, unconcerned with the needs of historians who want to write manageable narratives about it. What can we say about Australia from 2010 to 2020? Were these years of growth and advancement or stagnation and decline? Time, not us, will do the telling here.

But if life as it is being lived escapes the historian's grasp, it does not slip the dramatist's gaze. In Nathaniel Hawthorne's wonderful phrase 'the soul beholds its features in the mirror of the passing moment'. The passing moment is the supreme concern of drama, and playwrights make the most of it. No other art form is so sensitive to the rips and eddies of everyday change, none so capable of giving it immediate, forceful expression. The life of the nation and the drama of the nation are like two planets circling around the historical events that provide their shared solar centre. Sometimes the orbits grow close or eclipse each other. Other times, they occupy positions seemingly far apart. Yet ghostly gravitational fingers hold them fast together. They may be separate bodies, but they are part of one system of intellectual order. To study the plays of the nation is to study the nation. Let me admit here the curiosity, courage and chutzpah needed for this exhilarating task.

1
1901–1914: Ozziewood

On Our Selection **(1912)**. *The Time is Not Yet Ripe* **(1912)**.

> Australians know little and care less about the origins of their nation. Historians have commonly encouraged them in this response by depicting [it] as a business deal... [But] the people who devoted themselves to the creation of the federation regarded it as a holy or noble or sacred cause... The petty and provincial concerns of colonial politics—the struggle over roads and bridges, the endless deputations to ministers begging favours—would be replaced by a politics that dealt with a national life and the fate of a whole people.
>
> John Hirst, 'Federation: Destiny and Identity'

On 1 January 1901, the six individual states that had hitherto comprised the British colony of Australia became a self-governing dominion—the Commonwealth of Australia—with its own written constitution and bespoke balance of powers. On Thursday 9 May, the first federal parliament opened in Melbourne with considerable fanfare on the occasion itself and extended celebrations thereafter. From a distance, these have the aura of a school fete—inclusive, slightly wobbly festivities, with visiting dignitaries, colourful processions, earnest speeches and cheering crowds. That weekend, a parade of floats of mind-boggling variety and weirdness snaked its way through town to the Exhibition Building in Fitzroy, where the recently arrived Duke and Duchess of Cornwall and York were installed in an octagonal pavilion painted red, white and blue for the occasion. An *Argus* journalist covered the parade (and the royal response to it) in microscopic detail:

The first large float... was... a richly decorated car, beneath the canopy of which were half-a-dozen figures representing the Rechabites of old... [while] [a] black-bearded man swallowed constant draughts of cold water from a golden goblet presented by a handmaiden ... [Then came]... six girls, handsomely attired in classical costumes form[ing] a ring... while in the centre of this ring, raised on high, stood Britannia in a golden chariot. On each corner of the float was a stalwart young man with bare arms, mailed and helmeted like a Roman warrior. Closely following was a second float representing King Harold... Lines of hundreds of white hooded Druids marched behind, and... a very small boy riding a tricycle, and attired as Father Time... [Finally] [came] the Sons of Temperance, who had fitted up on a lorry a bit of Australian landscape snatched from the bush. Kangaroos, emus, and other fauna of the land were shown, browsing peacefully among a quartet of bushmen. Ferns rose from the ground, eucalyptus and wattle branches spread above them, while at the rear of the lorry rose a high rockery, down which a miniature waterfall dripped ceaselessly. The whole picture was redolent of Australia, and the spectators were quick to acknowledge the originality of those who conceived the idea.

Compared with other nation-defining events—Britain's Glorious Revolution, France's Tennis Court Oath, America's Declaration of Independence—Australian Federation has a decidedly holiday feel. Perhaps this was because it had taken so long to achieve. From 1891 onwards, the states haggled over the terms of their union, voting in separate, successive referenda whether to proceed with it or not. A note of burlesque can be detected. Sir Henry Parkes, initially an obstructer of Federation, became its champion. In the first round of plebiscites, only three states voted 'yes', while two would not participate. As the joke has it, the people must keep voting until they get it right.

Federation Celebrations, 'The Chinese Procession', Corner Spring and Bourke Streets, Melbourne, May 1901. The festivities were a spectacular way to mark the founding of the new nation. The Chinese float included traditional Chinese dragons and music. The Riverine Herald commented: 'the two dragons were wonderful and marvellous constructions, hundreds of feet long and wriggling a most diabolical manner, with mouth open and the ears flapping to and fro'. Source: Museum Victoria.

After a decade of quarrelling and prevarication, collective agreement was finally reached. But there were some surprises. New Zealand, which as part of 'Australasia' had been expected to join the Commonwealth, chose to become a dominion in its own right, its 770,000-plus population almost a quarter of the size of the new nation 'across the ditch'. Western Australia, long adamant it would not be included in any federal arrangement, changed its mind at the last minute and voted to join it, a decision aided by thousands of Victorian miners who had migrated to the Kalgoorlie region to prospect for gold. Interstate negotiations had a monetary ring. If the aim was political union, it would only be acceptable if no individual state lost out economically.

Thus was Australia as a (semi) independent nation born: not in the rifle's mouth, but the drawer of a cash register. Yet for all the lack of a sense of grand occasion, Federation was a moment of profound national self-definition. Macintyre writes,

Those plebiscites were all important. They installed the people as the makers of the Commonwealth and popular sovereignty as its underlying principle… [T]he people themselves would elect the makers of a new federal arrangement, the people would adopt it, the people would be inscribed in its preamble and included in the provisions for its amendment. This was a uniquely democratic achievement. In the words of one celebrant, it was 'the greatest miracle of Australian history'.

How was the historical miracle memorialised in the theatre? What theatrical performance(s) marked the triumph of the people's will? 'Woman and Wine is proving a big-draw at the Royal, and on Saturday evening there was another excellent house', noted the *Herald* in the week the new parliament opened. 'The drama abounds in exciting situations, the steeplechase scene, where a field of horses take the jumps in full view of the audience, being particularly thrilling; whilst the Japanese ball and the duel scene in the flower market are exceedingly good.'

With its spectacular visual effects, stock characters and ludicrous plot, Arthur Shirley and Ben Lanseck's *Woman and Wine,* produced by the irrepressible 'King of Melodrama', Bland Holt, is an archetypal stage vehicle of the late Victorian era: theatrically innovative but dramatically inert. *The Bulletin*, a feisty nationalist newspaper that first appeared in 1880, took gleeful aim at the manifold absurdities of such popular fare. These by-the-numbers crowd-pleasers were purchased abroad, in London or New York, sometimes with costumes and props attached, then onsold to producers in remote parts of the world, especially to the third of it coloured pink on the map—the territory of the British Empire. 'On Saturday a number of 'chasers jibbed and toppled over, bringing some of the scenery down with them', noted *The Bulletin* sardonically. 'If the same unreliable steeds are going to appear every night, the members of the orchestra… will probably be buried beneath an avalanche of horseflesh before the week is out.'

In its affectionate but unrelenting excoriation of these plot-creaky, over-the-top shows, *The Bulletin* was undertaking a ground-clearing operation. For Australian drama to live, a serious intellectual place would need to be found for it in a theatre scene then at the height of its commercial powers. Clustered around the behemoth of the Firm were a number of other production companies, chancing big money on a global touring circuit more extensive than any before or since. Veronica Kelly in *The Empire Actors* describes the workings, industrial and human, of this gigantic entertainment machine that I call 'Ozziewood' to give a sense of its scale and organisational capacity. She comments,

> In the activities of significant entrepreneurial 'empires' like JC Williamson's, Meynell and Gunn, Harry Rickards, Fullers, Hugh D. McIntosh, William Anderson or the Tait brothers, Australasia formed an international command base and major touring territory… Global managerial carve-ups for purposes of leasing or selling monopoly rights over theatrical properties might or might not overlap with physically contiguous regions, but in the case of [Australia and New Zealand] the legal and geographic more or less coincided… Companies… would travel readily to population centres from Invercargill to Charters Towers, Sydney to Perth. The cultural life of Australia and New Zealand at the start of the new century was scarcely a site of provincial belatedness. The new nations were as much initiators of modernisation as followers. Constitutional and political developments launched them towards independent paths, though with British strategic interests still eager to monitor where these paths might lead.

The beginnings of Australian drama were as impromptu as the political arrangements around it. No bold statements of new artistic purpose are observable, as in Ireland's Abbey Theatre or France's Théâtre Libre, no declarations of unique history or language. Rather, Australian drama was calved from the profit-making monster of British imperial theatre in the shadow of which local dramatists had to live and work for the next 60 years. Sometimes this relationship served them well, providing career paths, resources and audiences. More often, it imposed, dictating formats and values, and aggressively insisting on the 'standards' that 'professional' theatre required. Yet even at its most overbearing it remained of use. Australian playwrights—let us leave aside for a moment what sort of people might fill this category—watched the commercial plays put in front of them and took both what they needed and what they could not avoid.

If drama arises, as Kelly says, in places that are 'intractably regional', it draws on the larger frame of cultural reference dominant at any one moment in time. It is what theatre artists *do* with that larger frame which is of interest: how they apply it, subvert it, bend it to their own purposes. Whatever else Australian drama may be, it is not pure. It is pointless to look for an exact moment of national inception. Australian drama grew demotically, incrementally, ineluctably, until one day it bent the imperial frame of reference around it sufficiently to claim it as its own. In looking for 'difference' we blind ourselves to a complex process of cultural individuation that occurred in combination with one of colonial domination. National dramas do not spring up like mushrooms in the field. They are the result of repeated acts of cultural exchange. The history of the development of Australian drama may look fragile, partial and hesitant compared with other countries. But it could not be stopped, any more than Federation could be reversed.

The comedies *On Our Selection* by Steele Rudd and *The Time is Not Yet Ripe* by Louis Esson both premiered in 1912. As sometimes happens in the national repertoire, they make a neatly contrasting pair, one rural, working class and reliant on physical comedy, the other urban, upper class and propelled by witty dialogue. Their audience receptions also contrast. *On Our Selection* toured extensively until 1928. In that time, over one million Australians saw it—25 per cent of the population. *The Time is Not Yet Ripe* had a run of a few weeks only, and was patronised largely by the type of wealthy professionals it was satirising.

Despite the disparity in their commercial impact, however, *dramatically* their influence is the reverse of what these numbers suggest. For all its wild popularity, *On Our Selection* marks the end of a certain kind of creative endeavour. *The Time is Not Yet Ripe* points forward to the plays that would come next. Many of these proved no more profitable than *The Time is Not Yet Ripe*. But in pursuing a national drama, box-office success is a misleading hare to chase. Plays can have an impact beyond their audience numbers and sometimes, as in the case of Douglas Stewart's *Fire on the Snow* (1941) even before they are staged at all. In a very real sense, people do not make drama. Drama makes a people. It is the internal logic of their connections, not the outward markers of their reception, that shapes the plays of a nation into a cohesive body of work.

On Our Selection is four acts' worth of rural vignettes held together by clever comic craft and the memorability of its main characters, rather than by an overarching narrative. Based on a series of short stories by Arthur Davis *aka* Steele Rudd, originally published in *The Bulletin*, they were adapted for the stage by Frank Beaumont Smith and the actor-manager Bert Bailey (among others), who was then running the Anderson acting troupe. This troupe was 'the only major professional Australasian company that, however, sporadically, nurtured an ensemble of writing talent and performed original material'. Its treatment of the Steele Rudd source material illustrates the subtle but decisive shift involved in repurposing an established theatrical genre towards a new dramatic end—a shift from working *to* a formula to working *with* one.

At the heart of *On Our Selection*'s story (such as it is) is Dad Rudd, a 'selector'. No Australian in 1912 would have needed this term explained. It referred to a small-hold farmer provided with an official parcel of land by the government; enough, it was believed, to be self-sufficient, usually around 160 acres (65 hectares). His erstwhile rivals and foes were the early colonial 'squatters', who had laid claim to considerably larger properties for sheep or grain, and removed, subdued or killed the original Indigenous inhabitants. The struggle between selectors and squatters was one of the main political tensions at the time of Federation, when Australia was emerging from a severe depression. Global agricultural prices had collapsed, sending the balance of payments into the red and igniting fiery industrial conflict.

Dad, his two semi-useless sons, Dave and Joe, his entirely useless brother, Uncle, and the more competent wives and sisters who make up the Rudd clan are in dispute with their neighbours, John and Jim Carey, father and son, the former grasping, ruthless and manipulative,

The cast of first production of On Our Selection. *From back row, left to right: Lilias Adeson as Lily, Queenie Sefton as Mrs White, E Duggan as Maloney, Guy Hastings as Sandy, Alfred Harford as Billy Bearup. Arthur Bertram as Joe, Alfreda Bevan as Mum, Bert Bailey as Dad, Mary Marlowe as Kate Rudd, Fred Macdonald as Dave, Laura Roberts as Sarah and Willie Driscoll as Uncle. Proportional to population,* On Our Selection *remains the Australian play seen by the highest percentage of Australians.*

the latter silver-tongued, immoral and selfish. Although the Careys aren't called squatters in the play, they obviously are. The odium attached to them indicates the widespread feeling in Australia at the time not only against sharp commercial practice, but against any accumulations of wealth perceived to be egregiously unequal. Dad, irascible and indomitable, has all the makings of a patriarchal tyrant… bar the fact that no-one seems inclined to obey him! His store of wisdom begins and ends with the land he has hard-scrabbled for more than 40 years. His main quality is endurance, and it is endurance-as-virtue that animates the comedy of the play and provides it with deeper moral resonance.

When Kate Rudd returns from an unsatisfactory sojourn in Brisbane—that sinkhole of urban iniquity teeming with every kind of vice ('fine clothes, theatres, suppers and amusements' 59)—she rhapsodises on the rustic simplicity she sees around her, one passing into Australian legend even as it fixed fast as a national ideal:

KATE: Oh, to be with everyone I love again. Nothing is altered.
The old dray with its broken shafts still unmended.
The water cask on it too. The broken panel still in the
Corner, the same old hole in the roof of the barn.
It's just the same dear old place…
But you don't ask why I've come back?…
MOTHER: Why should any of us? We only know you're here by
Your Mother's side with the rest of the children. I thank
God for it and pray you may never wander away again.
(50)

While John Carey schemes to filch Dad's land and livelihood, Jim Carey sets about seducing Kate. Fortunately, Kate has a protector and would-be suitor, Sandy, a nearby selector, whom the Rudds befriended when he arrived on his own block of land with nothing but the clothes on his back. At this juncture, the play splits in two. One half remains anchored in the terrain of nineteenth century melodrama. A murder plot involving Jim, Kate, Sandy and a mentally impaired day-labourer, Cranky Jack, uses the familiar soap-opera devices of misunderstandings, wrongful accusations and (seemingly) dashed hopes. The other half develops into what we would now call a 'drama of character'. Here, story makes way for social and psychological insight into the dilemmas of the lives portrayed. These are neatly encapsulated in a speech by Dad at the end of Act 1 when, in typically underhand fashion, John Carey presses a debt and sequesters his cattle. Dad remains defiant:

DAD: For years I have faced and fought the drought and the
fires and floods of this country. I came here and cut a
hole in the bush when I hadn't enough to buy a billy can
with or a shirt to put on my back. I've worked hard and
honestly living on dry bread, harrowing me bit of wheat
in with a bramble, but I never lost heart for one single
moment. Sometimes me few head of cattle would famish
and die out there before my very eyes, and the roof go
from over my head with the wind, but me spirit was never
broken. Do you think you can break it now? By the Lord,
no. Take me bits of things, take the bed from under me,
take me few head of cattle and go.
CAREY: You talk about spirit. The drought has got your crops.
I've got your stock. Now, what can you do?

DAD: What the men of this country with health, strength, and determination are always doing, I can start again. (41)

One gauge of a play's popularity is if its individual scenes acquire names of their own. In *On Our Selection*, there is 'the kangaroo skin' scene, the 'parson's egg' scene, the 'courtship conversation lolly' scene and so on. They involve comic business of a highly skilled kind—the sort JC Williamson himself demonstrated as an actor when he founded his empire in 1870. But these *scènes très drôle* are not the play's most striking feature. Rather it is the Rudd family itself, who generate an emotional engagement deeper than the events that happen to them. They persist as compelling characters long after the historical conditions that gave rise to them have passed away. This has a universal resonance to it, the observation, within the play, of general truths.

The centrality of work to life is one such observation. Everyone in *On Our Selection*, man or woman, adult or child, works a long day, and that work is hard, unremitting manual labour—clearing, cleaning, digging, fencing, mending, herding, planting, harvesting: an endless list of chores from sunup to sundown. While work isn't valorised as spiritually ennobling, avoiding it is the mark of lesser persons, such as the loafer Uncle, or the loathsome Jim Carey. Shared work is the foundation for an egalitarian community.

The selectors in the district stick together in the face of adversity and, in Act 4, unite to defeat John Carey in his self-entitled run for parliament. Instead, they elect 'a man… [to] talk straight, and tell 'em what's right and what ought to be done' (90): Dad Rudd. This outcome—unimaginable in a British drama of the same period—sounds a progressive note for a nation founded on the male franchise and the majority of the female franchise, and that voted a Labor government into power years before other countries. The 'dimmycratic' feeling that soaks the play like the life-giving rain for which the farmers pray, makes the Rudds the progenitor of the hard-pressed but worthy families in Australian drama to come, striving to keep their errant members together in the face of external threats and internal disarray.

To turn from *On Our Selection* to *The Time is Not Yet Ripe* is to go from the country paddock to the city salon, from the world of work, to the world of talk. The comparative neglect of this pitch-perfect comedy, with its startling contemporary feel (it is at times laugh-out-loud funny), indicates the cultural barriers facing early Australian dramatists, however well they learnt their colonially controlled professional craft. In his excellent introduction to the 1973 Currency Press edition of Esson's first significant stage work, Philip Parsons observes:

> It is astonishing that a play so beautifully written, so ebullient... and above all, so popular in its appeal, should have been laid aside after its production by the Melbourne Repertory Theatre under Gregan McMahon.... The opening (in the presence of the prime minister, Andrew Fisher) was hugely successful, much critical acclaim followed and the play went into print—but not into the commercial theatre, where it obviously belonged. It is ironic that Australian managements, willing to gamble only on proven success, should have been too busy scouring the overseas market to pick up a proven success on their doorstep. (xiii)

Gregan McMahon, and the two companies he founded, the Melbourne Repertory Theatre (established 1911) and the Sydney Repertory Theatre (established 1921), were key to the production of Australian drama in the years after Federation. McMahon presents as the first modern Australian stage director in much the same way as Esson appears as the first modern Australian playwright. That is, they were *self-consciously* Australian theatre artists, psychologically distant from the British imperial touring circuit, with its glittering career opportunities and cultural dead-ends. Esson went on to found the short-lived Pioneer Players in 1922, with the writers Hilda Bull, Vance Palmer and Stewart Macky: the first company to stage exclusively Australian drama. This flopped monumentally, even as McMahon veered away from his commitment to local plays. These twin events create one of those gaps in the national repertoire that give it the appearance, in Peter Fitzpatrick's apposite phrase, of 'a history of beginnings'. The year 1912 presents as perhaps the first of these beginnings.

The plot of *The Time is Not Yet Ripe* is as clever and convoluted as *On Our Selection*'s is perfunctory. Sir Joseph Quiverton is the prime minister of Australia, an able and successful politician. Which is to say, he can talk at length without saying much, make promises without committing to concrete outcomes, and argue the need for new ideas while ensuring none are put into effect. He is a Liberal—politically, from the Centre Right—perhaps based on Alfred Deakin, one of the architects of Federation and Australia's second prime minister. At the start of the play, his daughter, Doris, wants his permission to marry the Socialist firebrand Sydney Barrett, who, despite being a wealthy pastoralist himself, is determined to bring about Change with a capital C:

> BARRETT: Here am I after a four years' absence, returned to my native land, full of a fine enthusiasm, to find the country stagnant, decadent—and the young Australian, with his bright, fresh mind, untrammelled by the traditions of the past—that is the current phrase—repeating all the popular superstitions, from beer to bishops, of his fog-bound ancestors. Australia is an outer suburb of Brixton… We prate of progress, and what is Australia's chief contribution to civilization? Frozen mutton and the losing hazard… Things can't go on like this. But where are our leaders? Look at your worthy father. He certainly seems troubled about many things, but he goes on uttering empty phrases, meaning nothing, suggesting nothing –
> DORIS: Yes, I know. Father is very tiresome. But what are you proposing to do?
> BARRETT: Everything. I propose change, disorder, revolution. We will have to make a fresh start. I attended the Socialist Congress tonight.
> DORIS: That explains your behaviour.
> BARRETT: We had a stormy meeting. I was accused of being an intellectual. There was nearly a split in the party. That shows how earnest we are. We are going to do things. You must give up this empty life, Doris. (11–12)

Doris, of course, has no intention of giving up her life, which she finds far from empty. As Quiverton fights with (and loses to) his imperturbable daughter, Barrett steps forward as the Socialist candidate for the federal seat of Wombat. Caught between conflicting loyalties and swept along by events, Doris finds herself standing against him as the Anti-Socialist League's Good Woman nomination.

Where *On Our Selection* ends with a parliamentary election, *The Time is Not Yet Ripe* begins with one. Arguably, their internal motors thrust them in opposite directions. Steele Rudd's play, excluding its melodramatic flourishes, shows a slow-moving world that finally opts for radical action—voting Dad into parliament. Esson portrays a frenetic society constantly dashing about but never getting anywhere. Events have a habit of returning to their point of origin. Realising they are standing for the same seat on competing platforms, Barrett and Doris call off their marriage. But when Barrett is defeated by his fiancée, Doris immediately resigns, and the marriage is on again. She is more interested in Barrett than Barrett's politics, her feelings of love stronger than the talk that comes out of his mouth, which is shown to be as windy and ill-defined as his erstwhile partisan opponents.

If the time is not yet ripe for the socialism Barrett wants, it is in part because he cannot articulate what socialism that actually is. On the hustings, he regales the crowd with confusing and contradictory statements:

> BARRETT: It is not my intention to talk politics. I don't believe in politics.
> FAT MAN: Give us your programme.
> BARRETT: I haven't got one. I believe in all the things you are too stupid to understand.
> OLD MAN: Do you believe in Immigration?
> BARRETT: No, why bring in agricultural laborers. Haven't we sufficient dullness of our own! Australia doesn't need workers—it needs idlers—it needs Egyptologists, and biblical critics, metaphysicians and Italian tenors, and it needs them very badly.
> FAT MAN: Talk sense.
> OLD MAN: You don't represent the working men.
> BARRETT: Of course I don't. That's why they should vote for me. Remember it is not your business to teach me—the proletariat is always the most Conservative element in Society—it is my business to teach you…
> OLD MAN: Talk practical politics…
> BARRETT: Haven't you had enough of practical politics? … the curse of this country, and every other country, is the plain practical common sense man with his low standards

and narrow outlook. We want poets, dreamers, builders of ideals. The national need is for a thoroughly unpractical man. (49–50)

At the time his play opened, Esson was a regular contributor to *The Bulletin* and *The Socialist*. He was certainly familiar with 'practical politics' and, as his freelance journalism attests, his own views were considerably more developed than Barrett's. In sending up politicians and political activists of every creed and stripe, he was operating as an adroit insider deflating puff and pretention, rather than a cynic dismissing politics altogether.

Politics is present in the play, but runs along gender lines. The well-heeled 'Toorak Village set' who first saw it would have been aware of Justice Higgins's 1907 Harvester judgement, when the newly created federal High Court decided that:

> wage levels were… to be based not on profits or productivity but on human need [and] premised on the male breadwinner, with men's wages sufficient to support a family and women restricted to certain occupations where they were paid only enough to support a single person.

Women contested the dual standard for the next sixty years.

The Commonwealth of Australia took a socially progressive approach to fixing what became known as 'the basic wage', ensuring the working classes were not subject to the rapacious exploitation evident in other capitalist countries—but only if the worker was a man. Women were *legally* paid less because the presumption was that they were caring only for themselves or their husband's wage would supplement their own.

From this perspective, the Good Woman 'wowser' platform in the play does not look so ridiculous, its anti-pleasure agenda aimed predominantly at *male* pleasures (drinking, gambling, smoking) and returning men to the families they should rightfully be supporting. On the hustings, the forthright Miss Perkins, Doris's campaign manager, lays out her uncompromising feminist-cum-conservative policy aims:

MISS PERKINS: We are fighting for Social Reform and the Purity of the Home.

CHEEKY YOUTH: Are you in favour of hobble skirts?

MISS PERKINS: I am not in favour of small boys smoking cigarettes.

Laughter.

The prohibition of tobacco and alcohol would make you a better man… It is time women took their proper place in our National Assembly.

Cheers.

In Finland and Norway women have asserted their right to legislate as well as vote. I am informed that in Denmark, women act in the capacity of police constables.

Laughter.

Why should Australia lag behind Europe? We will show tomorrow what we can do. I ask every man and woman who values home life to vote for and support Miss Quiverton—the Good Woman candidate. (39)

The quality of Australian drama in the Ozziewood years after Federation is not often high. But it had a meaning and value that a century on is important to recognise. The Anderson troupe was responsible for staging many local plays. These include: *The Squatter's Daughter* (1907), about the rivalry between two outback sheep stations that featured real sheep, kookaburras, shearers, wood choppers, whip-cracking, sheep dogs, a waterfall and a fight between a man and a kangaroo; *The Man from the Outback* (1909) where the picturesque hero (played by Roy Redgrave, Vanessa Redgrave's grandfather) foils 'a gang of cattle duffers, aided by his dog who comes down his hut chimney to rescue him from a bushfire set by the villain'; and *White Australia or The Empty North* (1909) which climaxed in a semi-prescient invasion of Sydney Harbour by the Japanese navy, gallantly beaten off by the early Australian air force (a self-propelled dirigible balloon).

These plays may not pass my repeatable–interpretable test with flying colours. The level of playwriting craft involved in them does not go beyond the artisanal. But they are revealing of the nation's history. Veronica Kelly calls *White Australia* 'a crash course in complex political and nationalist passions'. She is referring to the Anglo-Japanese Naval Treaty of 1902, concluded by Britain without consulting dominion governments, which in the minds of many left Australia vulnerable to foreign aggression by allowing Japanese imperial expansion in the South Pacific. Military alarmism and racist politics ('the yellow peril'), brought to the point of hysteria by the prime minister, Billy Hughes, coloured Australia's involvement in the Versailles peace treaty of 1919. Japan, which had been an ally of Britain and France during World War I, found itself disadvantaged in the new Four-Power Treaty of 1921, and drifted into the arms of an aggressive and resentful Nazi Germany in World War II.

Thus, in its own way, *White Australia* was responsible for stoking the passions that fed the politics that informed the decisions that brought about the very actions it presented as fanciful melodrama. In June 1942, three Japanese midget submarines did, indeed, enter Sydney Harbour and attempt to sink Allied warships. Later the Japanese fleet that launched them attacked the ports of Sydney and Newcastle. Today, at a time when Sino–Australian relationships are deteriorating in a similar way, a switch of Japan for China, airships for aerial bombers, makes *White Australia* not so much a piece of Ozziewood baloney after all.

Reading the repertoire

A general point before going further. When reading the Australian drama repertoire, it is possible to fall into a number of traps. As these affect every play discussed in this book, they are worth identifying here. The first is anachronism, looking at plays from the perspective of present concerns and values only, while ignoring their original context and the audience knowledge they assumed. Careful attention needs to be paid, for example, to the fact that telephones are in regular use in *The Time is Not Yet Ripe* and do not need explaining, while 'wireless telegraphy'—the early version of radio transmission—is new, and so does. In *On Our Selection*, the 'coach' that Kate catches to Brisbane is clearly pulled by a team of horses, and while automobiles are unremarkable in the Melbourne of *The Time is Not Yet Ripe*, they are sufficiently few for Doris to have 'every car in the city painted red, white and blue with dear little Union Jacks, rushing all my supporters to the polls' (55). Details like this tell us much about the world outside federation theatre that conditioned what happened inside it.

The second, but opposite trap is imagining we can read these dramas 'as originally intended'. What conditions a play's meaning is in part what its creators and spectators cannot yet imagine. In 1912, the tragedy of the twentieth century lay ahead for Australia. The carnage of World War I, the catastrophe of the Great Depression, the abyssal revelations of the Holocaust, the horror of the nuclear bomb. Today, these events are impossible for us to un-know. There is no easy entry into the febrile innocence of Rudd's and Esson's plays. Whether their ingenuous charm was justified even in 1912 is a matter of opinion, but what is undoubtedly true is that the optimism of early federation drama vanishes from the repertoire for the next half century. Not until the 1970s do Australian plays engage again an energy so ebullient, open and hopeful, and then for very different reasons.

A third trap is to fixate on the surface novelty of a play's plot, characters or language and fail to acknowledge the enduring lines of continuity that hold the repertoire together across decades. It is a short hop from *The Time is Not Yet Ripe* to *Utopia*, the contemporary ABC television comedy poking fun at modern bureaucracy. The whacky faddism of Working Dog's Nation Building Authority is the direct descendant of feckless Quiverton–Barrett politics. Its deadpan dialogue, fast-paced yet going-nowhere action, and clever sprays on government, have a similar impact to Esson's play a century ago. Discussions about genre will not fully illuminate this impact, as literary terms apply to only one dimension of a play's onstage existence. Similarly, talk of 'dramatic structure', as if plays were miniature buildings made of words instead of bricks, is also misleading. Drama is a type of understanding that arises when different creative elements combine to generate a shared mode of performative inquiry. The type of understanding that conjoins plays of different periods and styles changes slowly in comparison with their surface details. Reading the repertoire requires forensic skill to plumb the invisible slots (categories of dramatic anticipation) on which dramas rest like an air cushion, and a degree of humility in seeing that while we may now fill a slot with a different play, it is not a different kind of slot.

The fourth trap is the most challenging: to discover in a play what its creators and spectators may have known all too well, but chose to understate or ignore. This is not the same as identifying the issues plays do not address. Obviously, that is an endless list. But plays throw a shadow. At the edges of their positive form is a fugacious zone of 'unknown knowns', of matters that reside within their generated mode of inquiry but which, for whatever reason, do not attract explicit attention. In exploring this liminal zone from today's standpoint, it's important to be aware that we have unknown knowns of our own. Reading the repertoire is a matter of comprehending ourselves as much as the play in front of us, managing our own partiality as well as the exclusions and occlusions of the past.

2
1915–1929: Unknown knowns

The Touch of Silk **(1928)**. *Brumby Innes* **(1929)**.
Gallipoli Bill **(1926)**.

> We found the old No-Man's-Land simply full of our dead...
> The skulls and bones and torn uniforms were lying about
> everywhere.
>
> CEW Bean, 1918

> STIFFY: Tell me have you done anything heroic?
> MO: You ask me, if I've ever been a hero?
> STIFFY: That's what I want to know.
> MO: Yes, I've been a hero!
> STIFFY: Then tell me all about it...
>
> Stiffy & Mo sketch, *The Sailors*, 1927

On 4 August 1914, George V of the House of Saxe-Coburg-Gotha (later changed to the House of Windsor), King of the United Kingdom and the Commonwealth Realms, Emperor of India and King of the Irish Free State, declared war on his cousin, Wilhelm II, Emperor of Germany. Therefore, so did the 88 million people who counted as British subjects, including those in Australia. The British Foreign Secretary Sir Edward Grey made his sad remark that 'the lamps are going out all over Europe, we shall not see them lit again in our lifetime'. After years of rising military tensions, a complex system of interlocking alliances meant dozens of countries were plunged into a conflict of unprecedented scale and ferocity.

News of war's outbreak quickly travelled to Australia via undersea telegraph cable, but the import of it took a while to sink in. 'Bidding was very slack even for the best of animals at... the annual draught stock parade', complained a lead article in the *Argus* the following day. 'Many lots were passed in, bidding being as low as 50 per cent of the owners reserve.'

Politicians fell over themselves to show support for Britain, debating the form this should take, a citizen militia or a professional army. A typical federation compromise was reached: a force of volunteers who could be deployed abroad. The first troops embarked for Egypt by the end of 1914. Winston Churchill, the First Lord of the Admiralty, had devised a plan to force a passage through the Dardanelles and thereby break the bloody deadlock of trench warfare on the Western Front. 'On 25 April 1915 members of the Australian Imperial Force (AIF) landed on Gallipoli in Turkey with troops from New Zealand, Britain, and France', notes the Australian War Memorial on its website. 'This began a campaign that ended with an evacuation of allied troops beginning in December 1915.'

Gallipoli was a military disaster. Of the 16,000 Australian and New Zealand soldiers who disembarked on the peninsula that first day, 2,000 were dead or wounded by nightfall. Yet it was also a collective myth-maker. The actions of the Anzacs became a central motif in Australia's self-perception. If it had a basis in factual courage and suffering, it was woven into myth by the sylvan words of journalists like Keith Murdoch and Charles Bean, the latter of whom became the official war historian after the war. 'You could imagine nothing finer than the spirit of some Australian boys—all of very good parentage', wrote Murdoch in his famous *Gallipoli Letter,* 'who… deserted their posts in Alexandria out of mere shame of the thought of returning to Australia without having taken part in the fighting on Anzac's sacred soil'.

Growing up in England as the son of a British father and an Australian mother, and coming to Australia when older, I have been struck by the contrasting attitudes of the two countries. In England, memories of the Great War (so called because there was not supposed to be another like it) have a bleak, sinister feel to them. It is mourned rather than celebrated, the two minutes silence observed on Remembrance Day not only a tribute to the millions who died, but acknowledgement of the futility of the cause that took their lives. In Australia, while there is pain in the recollection, there is also an indispensable item for any new nation: the image of an idealised national character. 'For Bean, the archetypal Anzac was strong, resilient, inventive, good-humoured, laconic and duty-bound', comments Sarah Midford. 'This is not too far removed from the archetypal Australian bushman of the late 19th and early 20th centuries'. Thus the old was preserved in the new, even as the 'Anzac legend' was greeted as a unique event.

For those soldiers who were *not* strong, resilient, inventive and good-humoured, however, who were traumatised by being shipped to Flanders and used as shock troops in horrific battles of uncertain aim and tragic end, the legend was a poorer fit. In July 1919, Hugo Throssell VC, son of a premier of Western Australia, led a victory parade through his hometown. The speech he made afterwards shocked his listeners:

> Nearly five years ago I rode through the streets of Northam in charge of eighteen men, who were among the first to enlist… Of that eighteen, seven [are] lying either in Gallipoli, Palestine, or France. … The war has made me a socialist. I have seen enough of the horrors of war, and want peace. After four years of [fighting], after the loss of nearly 8,000,000 lives, with a total of 18,000,000 wounded, of whom 6,000,000 are permanent wrecks … [how is it] still possible for individuals to make colossal fortunes by the manufacture of armaments?

World war did not settle any issues in relation to European geopolitics or the British empire. If anything, more questions were being asked about their moral and political values. But doubts were drowned out by the frantic pace of post-1918 life. 'So far from strengthening a common purpose', writes Macintyre, '[the war] weakened the attachment to duty: to live for the moment was a common response to the protracted ordeal'. As Australians continued to move from the regions to the cities, new suburbs sprang up to accommodate them. There was a boom in domestic house construction, while new electric fridges, washing machines, razors and vacuum cleaners appeared to fill them. 'The cigarette replaced the pipe, the beard gave way to the clean-shaven chin, the long skirt to the light frock. New forms of packaging and advertising promoted a wider range of consumer goods—soap, toothpaste and tooth powder, cosmetics, processed food and brand confectionery.'

The word 'leisure' acquired fresh meaning as the Steele–Rudd world of 24/7 work receded (though not for everyone). Public works increased. In 1925, the building of the Sydney Harbour Bridge began. In 1928, the first solo flight between England and Australia was completed, the same year that Warner Brothers' *The Jazz Singer* appeared, the first sound film. In 1922, another Australian legend was born: the savoury spread Vegemite. Over all this hung an atmosphere of panicky recreation: horse races, bike races, dances, 'the talkies', beach culture and 'surf bathing', once morally unacceptable, now promoted as the epitome of good health. The theatre adjusted its position in national life. John Rickard writes,

> 'Going out' usually meant either to the cinema or dancing. The 1920s saw the building of grand picture palaces in the capital cities, temples of architectural pastiche which were called 'theatres', and, indeed, often retained a theatrical component with a live orchestra, Wurlitzer organ and stage acts. The 'legitimate' theatre was now an increasingly middle-class preserve, specialising in musical comedy; vaudeville, however, survived and was still capable of producing a comedian with the popular appeal of Roy Rene 'Mo', whose humour represented an extraordinary fusion of Australian, English and Jewish elements.

Nothing exemplifies the distracted atmosphere of the 'roaring twenties' better than what came to be known as 'the six o'clock swill'. During the war, as an austerity measure, pubs were closed at 6 pm. After 1918, the measure was retained—with predictable consequences: 'drinking now became primarily an after-work social activity for men who, after frantically drinking against the clock in pubs which resembled large urinals, then surrendered themselves to home, family and evening tea'.

It is often assumed that the rise of cinema undermined the Firm's grip on Australia's entertainment industry. This is not the case. In 1913, JC Williamson died, and the suave and intelligent Sir George

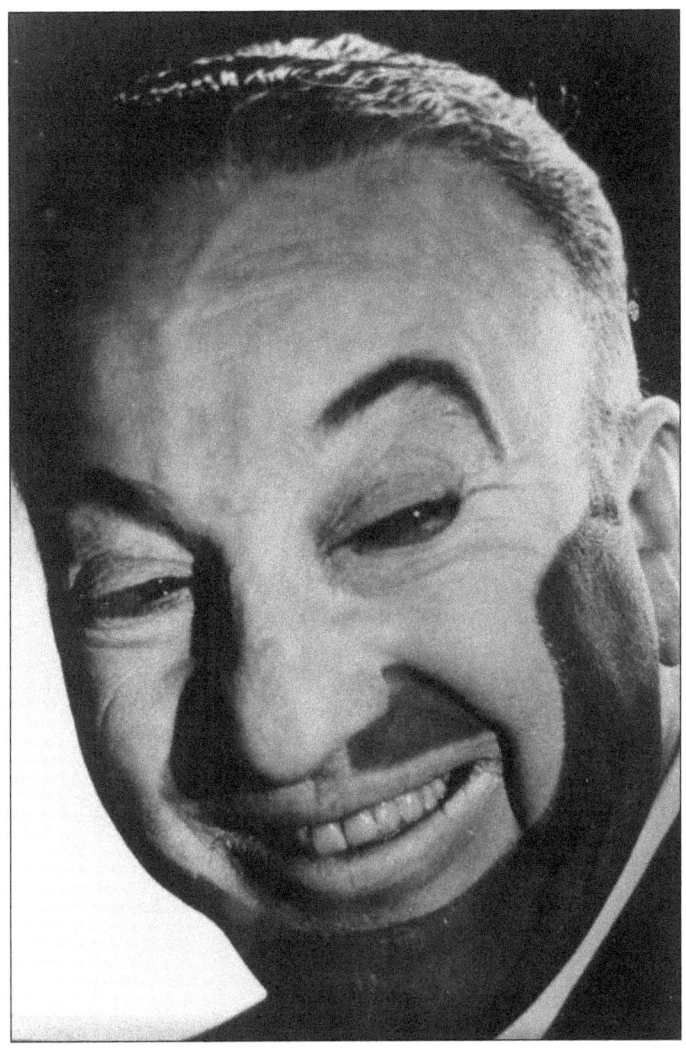

Roy Rene in his make-up as 'Mo' McCackie in the 1920s. A comic genius, Mo's face became an icon for the New Wave artists of the 1970s, especially for the Nimrod Theatre. Source: National Library of Australia

Tallis succeeded him as managing director. In 1920, he joined forces with J&N Tait ('the Tait brothers') who dominated live concert music. Together, they moved into radio, securing the licence to operate 3LO in Melbourne and, through Tallis's relationship with Frank Thring senior, bought an interest in a number of cinemas. JC Williamson's was at the height of its commercial might in the 1920s. In an interesting, if unsuccessful example of reverse colonialism, the Firm even tried to extend its theatrical activities to London's West End.

The Touch of Silk by Betty Roland and *Brumby Innes* by Katharine Susannah Prichard are plays that appeared close together, in 1928 and 1929 respectively. Like Rudd's *On Our Selection* and Esson's *The Time is Not Yet Ripe*, their production histories are very different. *The Touch of Silk* was immediately produced by the Melbourne Repertory Theatre, and revived frequently thereafter, albeit in Little theatre seasons and on radio. *Brumby Innes* had to wait until 1972 for its first production. In 1929, it was considered brilliant but too disturbing to stage. Louis Esson called it 'terribly daring' and warned an audience 'will get the shock of their lives when it is played' (xv). The years between 1915 and 1928–9 were momentous ones for Australia, and this is reflected in a change in the form and content of its drama. Later I will consider the implications of this change which involve dealing with the trap I described at the end of the last chapter: what plays touch on, but do not elaborate; what they suggest, but do not—or cannot—openly face.

In *The Touch of Silk*, Jim Davidson is a returned soldier from World War I married to Jeanne, a French woman. They are settled on a small (arid) block of land in north-west Victoria. At the start of the play, they have been in Australia for some time (the original stage direction, significantly excised in the 1973 text, sets the action 'ten years after the Armistice' xxi). It is a hard, unrewarding existence, scrimping and scraping to keep the farm going. Living conditions are basic, while dust, drought and loneliness are constant. These are magnified for Jeanne, who the local community treats as an interloper, a stereotypically 'loose' Frenchwoman. Jim's mother, Mrs Davidson, especially, misses no opportunity to put Jeanne down and make it clear she believes her an unsuitable companion for her son.

The opening scene is set in the draper's shop of a nearby town. Jim has come to beg the owner, Alexander Ritchie, for an extension to a vital loan, while Mrs Davidson looks for trimmings to brighten up an old hat. Jeanne appears midway through and the contrast between the two women could not be starker: the mother-in-law—narrow in her tastes, vocabulary and opinions, incapable of seeing beyond parochial concerns, the only ones she has ever known; the wife—exotic and glamorous despite the grinding poverty she must endure, bearing an air of personal freedom from which the prejudiced community around her instinctively recoils. The collision between Mrs Davidson and Jeanne is usually seen as the driving force of Roland's play. Jonathan Shaw, in the Currency edition (a reprint of the original text), says,

> It is Jeanne's play… but not without a struggle… Although subjected to the indignity of funny hats and trivially vulgar preoccupations, [Mrs Davidson] … dominates the spiritual life of the town as surely as the elder Ritchie controls the financial… All other interactions in the play are secondary to the conflict between Mrs Davidson and Jeanne. Even Jim's anguished jealousy at the end of Act Two is subsidiary to Mrs Davidson's realisation at that point of the impact of her words on him. Unusual anywhere, the central importance given to stresses between female characters surely makes this play extraordinary in the literature dealing with rural Australia, where so often relationships between men dominate to the exclusion of so much. (xvii–xviii)

This was also the critics' view when the play opened in 1928. By such a measure, *The Touch of Silk* is a tragedy of the outsider. Jeanne, representing the 'Other', is harried to the point where her mistakes compound and disaster results. Foolishly, if understandably, she spends her last £6 on silk underclothes to remind herself of the European way of life she has lost forever. When a desperate Jim, refused further leeway on his loan by Ritchie, asks her for this money, she is forced to admit she spent it at the behest of Clifford Osborne, the draper shop's new assistant and Jim's childhood rival.

That night, Osborne drives Jeanne home from a local dance. Jim assaults him, Osborne is killed in an awkward fall, and Jeanne finds herself cast as a faithless wife—the role the community had always seen her in anyway. Though nothing illicit has happened, Jeanne decides to testify to an affair with Osborne to give Jim a plausible motive for his attack, thus sacrificing her own reputation to save that of the man she loves.

The only problem with this interpretation of *The Touch of Silk* is that it is wrong. While the rivalry between Jeanne and Mrs Davidson certainly informs the action, at its heart is a triangle of relationships with Jim at the main vertex. Jim is the issue the women fight about, especially the recurrence of what Jeanne calls '[his] old pain… and… fear' (36). For what is obvious to any reader now is that Jim has post-traumatic stress disorder (PTSD), which shapes his behaviour and leads to the violent outcome of the play. Nor is Jim's PTSD an incidental plot detail. It is the focus of every scene in which he appears. His symptoms, and the reasons for them, are discussed by Jeanne and Mrs Davidson at length, and Roland provides compelling descriptions of Jim's haptic presence on stage. A good example is the start of Act 2, scene 2, when Jim is waiting for his wife to return from the dance she ran off to after they quarrelled earlier in the day:

Eleven o'clock that night.

The curtain rises on Jim alone in the little kitchen. It is dark and a single oil-lamp gives the only light. He is dressed in shirt and trousers, as in the last scene, his sleeves rolled up and his collar open at the throat. He is seated at the table, gazing straight ahead. He grips a side of the table in either hand, but even this is powerless to stay his violent trembling. Every line and movement reveals intense nervous strain. He gives a start as the clock commences to strike. He waits until it stops. (63)

In Jim's backstory he suffered a mental breakdown after his return from France, and was sent to an asylum. In the play's present, it is clear to everybody that he is showing signs of paranoia and instability once again, though they disagree on what to do about it. For Mrs Davidson, Jim should see a doctor. For Jeanne, that is the last thing he needs: only she knows what Jim went through in the war and can help him. For Ritchie, the voice of the obdurate, hyper-judgemental local community, 'every other man who was at the war had to go through it, too. Most of them came out all right, the ones with the weakness gave way. Jim has been under strain again… and he has been unable to stand it' (78). Typically, Mrs Davidson attributes all of Jim's problems to Jeanne, whom she calls 'Jan', refusing to use her proper name. As the police are taking statements after the assault, she laments:

> Oh, poor Jim!... my poor boy! Never did I think I'd see a day like this. He was such a gentle little fellow when he was a baby, constable. I remember how we used to laugh at him because he cried if anything got hurt, and I've seen him turn as sick as anything if he saw a rabbit in a trap... Doesn't it all go to show the difference a woman can make to a man. If only he'd gone and married one of our own girls, he'd never have felt like he did and nothing would have happened. He was crazy about Jan. There's something not quite decent about a man's loving a woman the way he loved her. It isn't *good* for him! (71)

Jim is not the only returned soldier in the play. Osborne is a veteran too, and while his reaction to the war is different from Jim's, he is also clearly disturbed—he cannot stay in one place, and is constantly flitting from country to country, from job to job. When Jim and Osborne fight, it is the confrontation of two damaged men for whom the memory of World War I is overwhelmingly painful.

Jeanne decides to say that she had an affair with Osborne, to prevent Jim from being incarcerated for an unlimited period of time in a psychiatric facility, not to save his good name, a matter to which she is indifferent. She makes her admission in the hope that she will get Jim back, and their marriage will survive. 'It's my chance of 'appiness and I've got to take it', she tells the local doctor, who is aghast at her intention to implicate herself. 'No-one dies of broken 'earts... and Jim and I will get on... some'ow' (89). PTSD is thus central to *The Touch of Silk*'s story, characters and dialogue. Why did it not feature in any of the reviews? Not simply minimised, but *not mentioned at all?*

The most compelling explanation is that in 1928, with 60,000 Australian soldiers dead and a further 156,000 wounded, gassed or taken prisoner—over half of the 416,809 men who enlisted—trauma over World War I was not confined to those who fought it. An incapacity to process the loss that had occurred is evident, a collective disattention to the returned soldiers who did not conform to the heroic narrative of resilient Anzacs, and an ignoring of the costs of modern warfare on those sent to fight it.

This was *again* the situation in 1975 with the Vietnam War, when the play was staged in Sydney in a revised edition, with Australia going through *another* period of denial about the hurt inflicted on a fresh generation of combatants. All the rewriting Roland completed for this later version of the play to dampen down its supposedly 'melodramatic' elements—Ritchie's predatory lending practices, Jim's unmotivated one-punch attack, the bone-deep prejudice of the community—effaces the theme of PTSD in the original. These changes now read as an attempt to normalise Jim's condition for a post-1945 audience, for whom the portrayal of looser sexual mores was acceptable but the calamitous effects of war were (still) not.

War, the damage of war, and the impact of the damage of war: these are the unknown knowns of *The Touch of Silk*, and alert us to the need to address the Australian drama repertoire as a living body of work, not a repository of inert data. The features of *The Touch of Silk* ignored in 1928 and 1973 are those likely to be prominent today. Australia's forgetting of war trauma has been replaced, hopefully, by a more honest, empathetic and informed view—a vital shift for a country that has been almost continuously at war in one part of the globe or another since 2001.

Brumby Innes by Katharine Susannah Prichard is an example of a type of Australian play that became depressingly common in the course of the twentieth century—an outstanding prize-winning drama that could not attract theatrical production. Gregan McMahon, one of the judges of the play competition that Prichard's script topped, wrote, 'I consider *Brumby Innes* to be in a class by itself. In originality of subject, atmosphere, characterization, virility and technique, it is a very remarkable work, comparative to some of the best of Eugene O'Neill's, and it is, moreover, essentially Australian' (xiv).

He tried to follow through on his good opinion. He presented *Brumby Innes* to the members of the Sydney Repertory Theatre as a play reading, and led a company debate afterwards about whether it should be staged. This was a decisive moment for Australian drama. Discussion would have been imbued with political as well as artistic significance. It is a mistake to think of Australia's interwar Little theatres as composed of well-meaning but ineffectual amateurs. As

Christine Comans amply demonstrates in *La Boite: The Story of an Australian Theatre Company*, these companies attracted powerful professional and society patrons. In a theatre scene dominated by British commercial imports, they were a countervailing force in our national drama. Not until three years after Prichard was dead, did Australian audiences get to see *Brumby Innes* in the theatre. What would be the story of Australian drama now if the Sydney Repertory Theatre had staged it in 1929?

Brumby Innes is compact: three acts of less than 50 pages. Short Australian plays were beginning to appear in numbers in the 1920s. The unsuccessful Pioneer Players seasons of 1922 and 1923 contain several of them. But Prichard's play is deceptive. Its substance belies its length. Act 1 is a carefully described ceremony by Indigenous characters whose identity and tribal language are precisely rendered. The 1974 Currency edition of the play carries an appendix by Carl von Brandenstein, a specialist in Australian Indigenous languages. He comments that Prichard

> gives the name of the tribe as Gnulloonga, which becomes in modern transcription *Ngaala-warngga*, meaning the language (*warngga*) which uses the word *ngaala* to express the pronoun 'this'. The tribe speaking the *Ngaala* dialect is known to linguists as the South *Pandjima*. They form a link between the *Pandjima* proper in the north and the *Paljgu* in the east. Turee Creek, the station [Prichard] visited in 1927, is in the heart of South Pandjima territory. (101)

Prichard, then, did some research for her play, and this reflects not just a concern with ethnography, but a political commitment to portraying her Indigenous characters as individuals rather than stereotypical 'blacks'.

The high point of the ceremony is the appearance of the narloo, a figure at once Dionysian (and thus sexually potent) and sinister (and thus morally suspect):

> *From the darkness beyond the firelight,* SPIDER *as the narloo comes hopping. He seems to come from the horizon,*

a crouched figure, hopping low, like a frog, all his bones outlined with white, a huge face of white bark over his head. A fearsome figure, he hops and crouches right up to the fire, peers at the women and children. Still singing, their voices quivering with fear and excitement, they watch him, beating their stick. NARDADU'S *voice shrills out as she steps forward and threatens the narloo with her stick. Singing of the women vibrates to the charm they are trying to use against the narloo. The narloo wavers before the old woman's threatening figure and upheld stick. He retreats backwards, thwarted, intimidated and hops off into darkness across the plains again while the singing of the women takes on a tone of derision and triumph…*

WONGANA [*clicking and singing*]: Narloo, narloo… gindoo bun abbie.

WOMEN: Narloo, narloo… gindoo bu abbie.
Warieda munga murnda bun abbie. (55)

Crashing through the sacred tribal gathering comes 'Brumby' Innes, mad drunk, and looking for a young Aboriginal woman, Wylba, to carry off and effectively rape. Which he does, threatening to shoot, or actually shooting, anyone who gets in his way.

The next day, after sleeping off his intoxicated rampage, and with the tribe arriving to punish him and rescue Wylba, he is entirely unrepentant. In fact, all shades of moral feeling seem to be entirely absent from Brumby. He is a cannonball of unrelenting violence and aggressive male sexuality. His default modes of interaction are to bully, threaten or wheedle, especially the first and second. The only thing he respects is physical strength, and his needs reflect a brute order of immediacy. He is, in the words of Jack Carey, Brumby's aging and near-blind stockman, 'rough as bags' (96). He is also a remarkable bushman, a master of the harsh north-western Australian landscape in which he resides, and kin to the animals he musters, breeds, or, when occasion presents, steals. Hence his nickname: 'Brumby boss-horse' (97). He never lets up, never shows a softer side, except, perhaps (and barely) with his Indigenous mistress, Polly, who drifts through Brumby's mud-brick homestead treating the other women he attracts with queenly disdain.

In Act 2, Brumby's neighbour, John Hallinan and his niece, May, pay him a visit. John is the owner of the adjoining cattle station, trying to retrieve stock that Brumby has been helping himself to with increasing impunity. May is attracted to Brumby like a moth to a dangerous flame. Her uncle tries to warn her away, but it is no use. The Act ends with a seduction of sorts, with Brumby baldly stating his desires and May either incapable or unwilling to repel him (or both):

> BRUMBY *rises, goes to the shelf for some cartridges and reloads his revolver.* MAY *is alarmed.*
>
> MAY: What are you doing that for?
> BRUMBY: You never can tell when it may be useful.
> MAY: But I thought the abos up here were all so quiet?
> BRUMBY: They are. But sometimes one gets over the fence; or a sulky fellow comes in from the bush.
>
> *He thrusts the revolver into the leather case on his belt, and goes to the bench again. Pouring sugar into a tucker bag, he spills a good deal.*
>
> MAY: Here, you're spilling it, I'll hold the bag for you.
>
> BRUMBY *pours the sugar as she holds the bag, staring at her, with glowering fascination.*
>
> BRUMBY almost in a whisper: I want you.
> MAY [*startled*]: What? What did you say?
> BRUMBY [*moving between her and the door*]: You're like water on a dry stretch to a thirsty man.
> MAY [*scared*]: Oh– …
> BRUMBY: I've knocked round with gins all me days: gins and bullocks, blacks and brumbies. Born in the Breakway country. Never been to school. But I want a white woman. How about staying here? … [*throwing an arm round her and holding her.*]
> MAY: I'll scream the place down.
> BRUMBY: Scream away. They wouldn't hear you at the yard… even if I let you.
> MAY [*struggling but yielding*]: Oh you…
> BRUMBY: I like 'em thoroughbred and buckin' a bit at first. (83)

The politics of *Brumby Innes* run along gender, class and race lines. Brumby Innes is white. He is also working class, and that had particular significance for Prichard, who was a co-founder of the Communist Party of Australia and a committed left-wing activist all her life. The Indigenous characters in the play treat Brumby with a mixture of ridicule and hate, as if he were, like the narloo, a symbol to be respected for his potency and feared for his malice. If he stops short of being a hundred per cent evil figure, his amoral energy, like Shakespeare's Iago or Richard III, tilts towards tyranny and oppression. His abusive behaviour receives no check.

In Act 3, Brumby is prosecuted for sexually assaulting the underage Wylba. But John Hallinan perjures himself, Brumby gets off, and the Indigenous men go to prison for attacking *him*. When May, now married to Brumby and carrying his child, wants to leave the homestead with her uncle, Brumby beats him to a pulp. The play ends with Brumby's three 'mares' on stage, Polly, May and a now-reconciled Wylba, Jack telling May to accept the situation as 'Brum ain't unkind to his women'. (95)

For a contemporary audience, if Brumby Innes is a symbol of anything, he is a symbol of white male violence. This hardly needs to be demonstrated beyond a simple description of the action, and the indictment implicit in the harshness of Brumby's character is almost certainly the main reason those who read the play in 1929 were confronted by it. All the more remarkable, then, that Leslie Rees in *A History of Australian Drama* gives it less than a page, concluding that *Brumby Innes* 'shows insufficient theatrical technique, but remains a vivid exposition of the primitivism of one kind of northern life, not unmixed with a little private admiration for the roaring bull that is Brumby'. He draws a number of bizarre conclusions: that 'May hates men'; that the play is 'too brutal and bare'; that 'there is needed a filling-out scene' (filling out what?). His focus is on Brumby's 'virility' and whether it is a plausible portrayal of male–female sexual relations.

He is not alone in seeing the play in this way. In a 1973 article for the Australian literary journal *Meanjin*, the eminent theatre historian Margaret Williams argues '*Brumby Innes* is not first and foremost about white exploitation of black, but about the nature of sexual relationships, and is really a hard-headed demolishing of the whole concept of romantic love as a basis for sexuality'. This opinion, like that of Rees, is unlikely to be accepted now. It does not hold up when the play is considered in a more historically informed way. Brumby's rapacious sexuality is not something that can or should be distinguished from his displays of despotic authority.

The French philosopher Michel Foucault coined the term 'biopower' to indicate that sexual practices and practices of social control should not be seen as separate, but rather converge in a politics of biological propagation. In 1909, a new Aborigines Act gave so-called 'Protectors of Aborigines' the legal right to remove Indigenous children of 'mixed blood' from their birth families. Macintyre writes,

> Earlier humanitarians had… proclaimed a duty to smooth the pillow of a dying race. Now as Darwinian science displaced evangelical Christianity and natural law as a source of authority, the scientist provided new confirmation of this forecast… New agencies, usually called protection boards, were empowered to prescribe their residence, determine conditions of employment, control marriage and cohabitation, and assume custody of children… [A] practice of expelling people of mixed descent from reserves began in Victoria in 1886 in the expectation that they would be absorbed into the community… In sharp contrast to other white-supremacist settler societies, there was no uncrossable barrier between black and white, for Australia's policy inverted the logic of racial separation that operated in the United States. All of this was premised on the elimination of Aboriginality, the abandonment of language, custom and ritual, and the severing of kinship ties so that the absorption would be complete.

Seen from this politico-legal perspective—one the members of the Sydney Repertory Theatre would certainly have known about, and some may have been involved in—the known unknown of *Brumby Innes* is Australia's near-genocidal treatment of its Indigenous population. That this is a main driver of the play is made clear by Prichard in her preface to the published text in 1940 (reproduced in the 1974

Currency edition). Of the opening ceremony, she wrote, 'The corroboree... is used to give something of the dignity, beauty and mystery of a primitive people in their natural surroundings: against their appearance under the conditions of a vanquished race' (51). The absence of explicit (playwright-flagged) condemnation of Brumby, the sparseness and brutality of the action, should not be read as approval or acceptance of it. Quite the reverse. Such intense depiction allows audiences to engage with Prichard's political themes in a fully responsive way. This is the value of serious drama. It provides rich experiences, not pre-digested messages, inviting spectators to participate in a process of making emotionally intelligent judgments about them.

The Sydney Repertory Theatre's failure to stage *Brumby Innes* in 1929, like the ignoring of war trauma in *The Touch of Silk*, has broader significance. If Australian drama remained for so long 'a history of beginnings', that is in part because there was a reluctance to proceed to the next step. Even Rees saw this. 'Why didn't somebody produce this play? Had a theatre made a success of it, even a *succès d'estime*, Katharine Prichard might have worked on more plays. Where was Gregan McMahon?'

Both *The Touch of Silk* and *Brumby Innes* can be related to the Australian plays that come before and after them. The farm that Jim tries so desperately to maintain is similar to Dad Rudd's in *On Our Selection*, while Mrs Davidson might be a less benign Ma Rudd. May might be a fuddled Doris Quiverton from *The Time is Not Yet Ripe*, and John Hallinan, the pastoralist Sydney Barrett 20 years on, *sans* socialist ideals. But an optimistic vision of the world has given way to a darker view. The Rudd farm prospers over the three acts of *On Our Selection*. Jim's doesn't, and this reflects another grim historical fact—that most of the soldier settlements the Australian Government parcelled out as a reward for war service failed. *The Time is Not Yet Ripe* ends with a marriage that is happy and heaven-blessed. *Brumby Innes* ends with one that is exploitative and hellish. *On Our Selection* and *The Time is Not Yet Ripe* are comedies of recognition and reassurance. *The Touch of Silk* and *Brumby Innes* are dramas of criticism and conflict. For the Australians of the late 1920s, life has not turned out the way that federation playwrights once imagined.

The Touch of Silk and *Brumby Innes* also point ahead. The character of Brumby might be an early version of Roo in Ray Lawler's *Summer of the Seventeenth Doll* (1955). Prichard's play ends where Lawler's begins: with the extolling of male physical prowess as a supreme virtue. [BRUMBY: A brumby boss-horse don't allow his mare to be took off… MAY: Until another shows him he is not the boss he thought he was? BRUMBY: That's right. (97)] Mrs Davidson is the progenitor of Miss Docker in *A Cheery Soul* (1962), whom Patrick White described as the embodiment of 'the destructive power of good'. Jeanne prefigures Michael Gow's Barbara, whose melancholic sophistication in *Europe* (1987) also evokes a way of life at once desirable and foreign. And Jim foreshadows the damaged World War II veteran Les Harding in John Romeril's *The Floating World* (1974), the damaged Vietnam War veteran Eric in Patricia Cornelius's *The Berry Man* (2010), and the Iraq War veterans who actually performed in Daniel Keene's *The Long Way Home* (2014).

Every character in a play steps on stage twice, once as a singular individual, once as the representative of a general type. Like the invisible 'slots' of anticipation that plays occupy, and which change more slowly than we imagine, so character types develop over long periods of time, coalescing in a collective understanding that makes them important repositories of social insight. This is another way in which the national repertoire is a living body of work, its surface details forever in flux, its internal spirit producing emotional constants and ongoing concerns.

That this does not apply to every stage work, that 'theatre in Australia' is *not* the same as theatre 'Australian in setting and mood', is shown by turning to the third play under consideration in this chapter, *Gallipoli Bill*. This appeared a few years before *The Touch of Silk* and *Brumby Innes*, in 1926. Written by journalist and author Arthur Adams, a one-time literary manager for JC Williamson's, it was first performed by the actor-manager Tal Ordell, then optioned by Bert Bailey, who toured it to suburban theatres and country towns in scratch productions. The script has an odd early federation feel to it, as if the innocent outlook of Steele Rudd could be transposed holus-bolus to war-bloodied Australia. Like *On Our Selection*, it is more an expedient string of comedy skits than a fully developed narrative. Richard Fotheringham comments in the introduction to the play,

> The story of *Gallipoli Bill* could not be simpler: two Australian soldiers, Bill and Jim, recuperating from war wounds, are invited to stay at a stately home in the English countryside, where Bill confounds the host family with his colloquial speech and (lack of) manners and Jim woos their daughter [and] Bill her coincidentally Australian friend. The fact that the uneducated former Queensland farm labourer, Bill, has been promoted to Lieutenant while his mate the farm owner's son, Jim, is a private, challenges the more rigid class assumptions of English society, where military rank was based on class and wealth. The play does not just contrast England and Australia but also records the clash of generations. (5)

Fotheringham is generous. Adams's reliance on stock comic devices is working to a formula rather than with one. Blustering lords, imperturbable butlers, amorous aunts, and foppish Hoorah Henrys supply one-dimensional characters with few surprises to them. There are a number of humorous exchanges around the 'manner' of Australian soldiers and their 'magnificent physique' (28), while poking fun at an England struggling to cope with the demands of industrialised warfare. But it is a stretch to see these as a 'challenge' to the imperial order. True, Jim gets engaged to Alice Loveday, Lord and Lady Halstead's 'modern' daughter, who works in a munitions factory and even has a working-class friend (though she turns out to come from Sydney so is perhaps 'class neutral'). However, it is revealed that, despite being only a private—which in the AIF is as good as being a general—Jim is heir to a large cattle station and in pole position to bail out the crumbling Halstead Hall.

The wrap-up, with the entry of the Halsteads' son, Clive, is at once bathetic and predictable:

> CLIVE: What's all the trouble? [*Starts and recognises* JIM] Why, that's the Anzac that saved my life in France!
> ALICE: It's Jim, Clive. My Jim! There, I knew he was a hero!

CLIVE [*crosses to* JIM *and salutes*]: Stand easy, please. [*Looks closely at* JIM] By all that's amazing, it's the Anzac that rescued me in France…
ALICE: There now, everything's turned out all right.
CLIVE: So he's the chap you wrote to me about? Well, you're lucky to get him, Alice! […]
LADY: But, Charles, it's very nice of you to approve of Mr Blake, but … well, we must be sensible, for their sakes. You know how we're situated financially…
CLIVE: By the way, is your name Blake—James Blake?
JIM: That's me.
CLIVE: I've got a telegram for you, addressed here. The station-master gave it to me to give to you. [*Produces telegram*] Here it is.
JIM [*opening it*]: What's this! It's from my Dad in Australia…
ALICE: Good news, Jim?
JIM: It says here that my Dad has retired from Merriwinia for good. He's handed over the whole caboose to me! Well, what do you think of that?
LADY: Does that mean to say, Mr Blake, that you're a rich man?

Enter BILL, *downstairs…*

BILL: My oath! Cripes, Jim, you're a millionaire twice over! (104, 106–7)

The historical associations of *Gallipoli Bill* are as off-kilter as its humour. A reference to Pozières places the action after the Battle of the Somme, in 1916. Both Jim and Bill are obviously recovering from 'Blighty wounds' and while they show no taste for Flanders mud, they are keen to return to the trenches and help 'win the war', a phrase repeated no less than nine times during the course of the play. The Jim of *Gallipoli Bill* is as unlike the Jim of *The Touch of Silk* as it is possible to be, while the dialogue shows little awareness of the moral significance of the events it evokes for comic purposes. At Pozières, the Australian army suffered 23,000 casualties in less than seven weeks, a rate of loss comparable to the whole eight months of the Gallipoli campaign the previous year. While it is possible to imagine productions of *The Touch of Silk* and *Brumby Innes* now, or adaptations of them, it is much harder to envisage a contemporary staging of Adams's play. Yet if *Gallipoli Bill* is unsatisfactory as a written text it is not necessarily so as a theatrical experience.

Prichard wrote a play for the Pioneer Players, *The Great Man* (1923). Although Roland did not, and the authors of this company are not examined in this book, they shared similar values and aspirations. They were all *literary* playwrights of the sort Alfred Deakin considered himself to be. They were well educated, well read and well travelled. Their relationship with Australian theatre was not a matter of the daily round. They worked in it, not for it, and if not on their own terms, then not at all.

This is very different from actor-managers such as Bert Bailey, Bland Holt, Tal Ordell and JC Williamson, for whom Australian theatre was first and foremost a source of income and employment. Their talents were of the non-literary kind, and while Bailey might brag about being 'the author' of *On Our Selection*, in reality he brought to its skeletal script the skills of the consummate stage performer. These lie at the heart of drama as a live performance event. Even a piece of flim-flam like *Gallipoli Bill* can be made to 'work' given the opportunities it provides for actors to demonstrate their comic proficiency.

The literary turn that Australian drama took with Roland, Prichard and the Pioneer Players brought powerful intellectual resources to bear on the task of playwriting. The quality of the dialogue of these plays is incomparably better than the popular fodder of the stock and touring companies of the period. Nevertheless, a rift now opens up between literary values and performance practices that will dog Australian drama in the decades to come, as if these are opposite poles of theatre production instead of complementary skill sets.

It also sent the national repertoire in a decidedly realist direction. Whatever else *On Our Selection* and *Gallipoli Bill* might be, they are not naturalistic plays. They reflect a constraining commercialism in one way, while in another, their loose-limbed theatricalism bears vague kinship with the non-realist Modernist drama then emerging from Europe and the United States. But having discovered stage realism later than their overseas counterparts, Australian playwrights held on to it for longer. In the 1920s, a 'good' Australian play, was a literary play written in the realist 'strain'. As Australian drama faced

Betty Roland. A prolific writer and tireless political activist, the two aspects of Roland's life came together when she helped establish the Melbourne branch of the New Theatre after her return from the USSR in 1936.

the unprecedented—indeed, unimaginable—challenges of the 1930s and 1940s, this stylistic dominance held it back from discovering its full imaginative potential.

The character spectrum

Roland and Katharine Susannah Prichard knew each other. It would be inaccurate to call them good friends, but they were certainly close acquaintances. When Prichard travelled to the Soviet Union in 1933 to report on the activities of the Bolshevik government, Roland, then married to the Marxist intellectual Guido Baracchi, was also there. They shared a room in Moscow. Later, Prichard returned to her native Western Australia and started the left-wing Writers League, while Roland came back to Melbourne and co-founded the New Theatre movement, whose communist-inspired work I touch on later (see Chapter 4). Both women were prolific writers. Roland wrote radio dramas for the ABC, then an important art form. Prichard wrote short stories and novels. Both felt a strong attachment to the theatre which did not bear proper fruit. If asked, they might have said that as playwrights, success eluded them. In truth, the kind of theatre in which they might have been successful failed to materialise.

Prichard lived out her own version of *The Touch of Silk*. In 1919, she married Hugo Throssell, who continued to be an outspoken socialist and pacifist. The Australia of the time was unable to cope with his views or with what had happened to engender them. He was shunned by his community and committed suicide in 1933. In 1999, Prichard's son, Ric Throssell, also a playwright, also left wing, also ostracised for political reasons, likewise committed suicide.

The valorisation of men and masculinity is reflected in the drama of this time. Yet it is not a straightforward matter. There is one kind of man Australians seem markedly less interested in: the broken kind. There is a character spectrum, with Brumby-style apex predators at one end of it, and Jim-style walking wounded at the other. This imbues the male characters in Australian drama with a palpable sense of internal conflict, if not in every play, then certainly as a regularly observable phenomenon in the repertoire. There is, one might say, something *unsustainable* about Australia's masculine ideal, as actual flesh-and-blood Australian men faced the hope and heartbreak of the twentieth and twenty-first centuries.

In the same way, characters such as Ma Rudd, Doris Quiverton, Miss Perkins, Mrs Davidson and May Hallinan show an ambiguity about whether women are *critics* of the existing order of power or *guardians* of it. A number of positions are available. There are women who want whole-hearted change in social and gender relations, like Roland and Prichard themselves. There are those in support of the current order but not its outcomes, like Miss Perkins and the 'wowser' women of the early federation era, who prevailed on some issues, such as the mandatory closing of pubs at 6 pm. There are Lawrencian women like Doris and May who eschew party politics and look to sexual relationships as the authentic expression of human life. Finally, there are the Mrs Davidsons of this world, who present as formidably conservative figures. Here, too, there is a spectrum of internal conflict available for future Australian drama, with Mrs Davidson–style System Maintainers at one end of it, and Jeanne-style Free Spirits at the other.

What characters in Australian plays represent when they appear on stage, and where they stand in relation to each other in an ecology of general types, is a crucial theme for the rest of this book. Australian drama is often discussed as if its most distinguishing features lies in its narrative dimension ('Australian stories'). This is a limited view. As a mode of inquiry, all the elements of a play are important in generating drama's unique type of understanding. As the national repertoire evolves, this integrative capacity only gets stronger.

3
1930–1945: The real Australia

Men Without Wives **(1938).** *Fountains Beyond* **(1942).**
Morning Sacrifice **(1942).** *Lady in Danger* **(1942).**
Ned Kelly **(1944).**

> The great air-liner stood at the end of the runway, ready for the journey right across the world to Australia... John sat beside Daddy and Alison was in the seat in front, next to a tall sunburnt gentleman... 'Are you a real Australian?' [she asked]. 'As real as a kangaroo', he replied with a grin. Alison looked at him with new interest and then turned round to Daddy. 'This gentleman is a real Australian', she said.
>
> *Flight One—Australia*, A Ladybird Book of Travel Adventure

The Ladybird Book imprint dates back to 1914, but the first pocket-size hardbacks (4½ by 7 inch)—reading staples for decades of schoolchildren—appeared in 1940. The Travel Adventure series included imagined family holidays in Canada, the United States and India. Australia, the first trip, was published in 1958. Lawrence Zeegan, author of *Ladybird by Design*, comments, 'through the 1960s we weren't well travelled, we had a particular view of our place, our standing in the world. We had won the Second World War, and the British Empire was still fairly intact. The colonies were where they were, and we had... a rather condescending view of other civilisations... [It] reflected a particular understanding of the rest of the world'.

Zeegan's 'we' are people living in the United Kingdom. 'The rest of the world' includes Australia, initially part of the British Empire, but from 1926 'the British Commonwealth of Nations'. After 1949, with

India a republic, and the dominions more independent, this became just 'the Commonwealth of Nations', a voluntary association informed by principles of 'consensus and common action, mutual respect, inclusiveness, transparency, accountability, legitimacy and responsiveness'.

Britain decolonised over the course of the twentieth century, a process which accelerated after World War II. Australia's Federation was an important early step. The Commonwealth was a shopfront designed to ease the passing of old political relations and facilitate the rise of new economic ones, providing shared symbols for a post-imperial age. Yet it would be a mistake to regard its pronouncements as having no weight, just as it would be a mistake to imagine that, because a government adopts a new agenda, the underlying beliefs of its citizens immediately change to reflect it.

During the 1930s and 1940s, there was continuing acceptance by most Australians of the country's status as 'the rest of the world', with London the natural centre of it. A sense of subordination can be more enduring than its ostensible cause. After 1945, London might be swapped out for New York, Los Angeles, Tokyo or Paris. The conviction that 'real' culture lay elsewhere and that Australia was peripheral to it remained.

For Australian artists this cult of national inferiority was both baffling and infuriating. The low value accorded Australian art was not the *cause* of AA Phillips's cultural cringe. It was the *result* of it. There was ongoing, insidious disavowal of Australian books, plays, music and paintings. It was *this* that had to change. To have a better national culture, Australia needed a better idea of what a national culture was. Between the wars, this conversation began in earnest among Australia's critics and artists.

In 1932, Miles Franklin, celebrated author of the semi-autobiographical novel *My Brilliant Career* and an early champion of Australian culture, returned to the country after 26 years abroad. She joined the Fellowship of Australian Writers, established in 1928, which included nationally minded writers such as Katharine Susannah Prichard, Nettie Palmer and Dymphna Cusack. The Contemporary Art Society, established in 1938, included Australianist painters Arthur Boyd, Sidney Nolan and Albert Tucker. In 1940, John Reed, tireless promoter of Australian art, was elected its president. In classical music, the Melbourne Symphony Orchestra (established 1906) and the Sydney Symphony Orchestra (1908), were joined by the Western Australia Symphony Orchestra (1930), the Adelaide Symphony Orchestra (1936), and the Queensland Symphony Orchestra (1947). On 1 July 1932, the Australian Broadcasting Commission (later Corporation) was launched with the goal of ensuring all Australians had access to high-quality local radio services.

The ABC quickly became a fixed feature of Australian life. A number of playwrights discussed in this book—Betty Roland, Max Afford, Sumner Locke Elliott—were successful radio dramatists; in Afford's case, writing 30 full-length plays, 100 play adaptations and 800 episodes of the mega-popular radio serial *Hagen's Circus*. Australian drama changed: there was now more of it. Or, more accurately, since the issue of the country's cultural detachment from Britain remained unresolved, there were more artists willing to see their work through a national lens. This offered a tempting reversal. Rather than Australia being peripheral to other countries, perhaps these countries were peripheral to Australia. Maybe the rest of the world was the rest of the world. Perhaps Australia was its own centre, with views and values that should take precedence ahead of overseas ones. Rather than *embracing* 'foreign' culture on (apparently) unequal terms, perhaps Australia should be trying to keep it *out*.

This raises an uncomfortable question: who has the right to consider themselves a part of the Australian nation? Are only those born in Australia 'real' Australians? For a population that, even in 1930, was 30 per cent migrants, this is a narrow criterion. What about those born in Australia but who spend most of their life abroad, like Miles Franklin? Or Indigenous Australians, whose existence in the country predates non-Indigenous colonists by many thousands of years? For the Jindyworobak movement, established in 1938 to 'free Australian art from whatever alien influences trammel it', Indigenous culture was the primary one, the first time it had been so seen in Australia's white history. Or perhaps the problem relates to 'where' rather than 'who'. Is the 'real' Australia to be found in the town or the bush? In the lives of its elites or its 'ordinary' men and women? In the events that happen to the nation outwardly or their inner implication? Is the 'real' Australia located in the emotions of its people rather than the contours of its landscape?

After Federation, an answer of sorts to these questions was provided—but it was an ugly and self-defeating one. 'Real' Australians were white people of Anglo-Celtic descent, whether they were born in Australia or not. If they were immigrants, they came from other white countries. This was written into law in the *Immigration Restriction Act 1901*, more widely known as the White Australia Policy, and remained in force until 1958, while its underlying spirit lingered for far longer. It is important to understand, not just deplore, the mentality that produced the policy. Federation Australians were as committed to separating out racial groups as we are to encouraging a multicultural society today. Australian workers supported the White Australia Policy as necessary for maintaining job security and the basic wage. Australia's professional class—including Australian artists—supported it as necessary for ensuring racial harmony and social progress. Manning Clark acidly notes, 'the men who believed that the unity of labour was the hope of the world united with the apostles of the Christian civilization to preserve Australia for the white man'. As with the forced removal of Indigenous children from their families, the implementation of the policy was both harsh and disingenuous:

> The method was simple. Under Section 3... any person who failed to pass a dictation test of fifty words in a European language could be declared a prohibited immigrant. Any immigrant resident for less than five years could also be given the test and, on failure, be deported... [A]ll Pacific Island labourers who had migrated to Queensland were to be deported by 1905... [B]oth Commonwealth and State legislations discriminated against Asiatics, Pacific Islanders and Aborigines... Under Section 4 of the Commonwealth Franchise Act of 1902 no aboriginal native of Australia, Asia Africa or the islands of the Pacific except New Zealand were entitled to have [their] name placed on the electoral roll... Section 16 of the Invalid and Old Age Pensioners Act of 1908 excluded

Asiatics (except those born in Australia) and aboriginal natives of Australia, Africa, or the islands of the Pacific from a pension.

The government could set the dictation test in any 'prescribed language', including Gaelic, which in 1934 it did for Egon Kisch, a communist writer it wanted to keep out of the country for his anti-fascist activism (it failed after a High Court challenge). There were many people of colour in Australia prior to the Immigration Restriction Act and many remained afterwards. 'Australia for the white man' was as much of a lie in practice as it was immoral in precept. For Australian culture, however, it had two pernicious consequences. First, it identified Australian national life with the category of race, thus racialising (and reducing) the idea of a national culture. Second, it anchored that national life on a principle of exclusion, an all-purpose xenophobia that looks from a distance very much like an inverted form of the cultural cringe. Australia's default response to situations of national vulnerability was to protect itself by closing its borders and, along with them, its collective mind.

The tendency to isolationism intensified in moments of crisis. One of these occurred on 29 October 1929, when the American stock market collapsed, sending shockwaves around the globe. Australia's unemployment rate skyrocketed from an already high 10 per cent in 1929, to 20 per cent in 1930, to an unmanageable 32 per cent in 1932. Immigration ground to a halt. In 1927, net overseas migration (immigrants arriving in the country, minus permanent residents leaving) was 41,401. In 1929, it was 10,087. From 1930 to 1934, it turned negative, more people leaving Australia than coming into it. For the rest of the decade, it was very slightly positive. Not until 1948 did the figure substantially increase again, with passage-assisted 'New Australians' immigrating from the Baltic countries to redress the nation's acute labour shortage. By then the government had learned that keeping the rest of the world out was as financially unsustainable as it was culturally depriving.

None of the plays examined in this chapter touches directly on the White Australia Policy or the Great Depression. None explores the bitter sectarian disputes of World War I either, when Roman Catholics under the leadership of Archbishop Daniel Mannix opposed the military conscription demanded by Australia's angry wasp of a prime minister, Billy Hughes. These antagonisms continued through the 1920s. With economic catastrophe in the 1930s, they compounded. At one end of the political spectrum were militant unionists and an increasingly influential Communist Party. At the other were returned servicemen in paramilitary organisations such as the New Guard, some with quasi-fascist views.

It is important to understand this environment on its own terms. Interwar Australian politics were fluid and contradictory. Adela Pankhurst, for example, youngest of the Pankhurst sisters, leaders of the suffragette movement in Britain, was a co-founding member of the Communist Party of Australia in 1920. In 1941, she helped establish the far-right Australia First movement, and in 1942 she was interned for advocating peace with Imperial Japan. In the run-up to World War II, appeasers on both sides of the political spectrum wanted nothing to do with another disastrous conflict in 'decadent' Europe. After hostilities broke out with Japan in 1942, Australia's new prime minister, John Curtin, a bitter opponent of conscription in 1916, had the flinty task of legislating it in the face of resistance from his own Labor Party.

The years 1930 to 1945 were filled with turmoil, trouble and change. Australia was an increasingly divided country, and these social and political divisions supplied the gridlines for the plays of the time. Even if Australian dramatists did not address the issues of the day directly, they could not avoid the bigger questions hanging in the air about the 'real' Australia. Because the volcanic politics of these years have passed, it is easy to miss the intellectual pressures that informed them. In 1942, with Australia facing military defeat in both the Middle East and Southeast Asia, the playwright Vance Palmer wrote an essay, 'What is Significant in Us will Survive':

> If Australians had no more character than could be seen on its surface, it would be annihilated as surely and swiftly as those colonial outposts white men built for their commercial profit in the East… But there is an Australia of the spirit, submerged and not very articulate,

that is quite different from these bubbles of old-world imperialism… Sardonic, idealist, tongue-tied perhaps, it is the Australia of all who truly belong here… And it has something to contribute to the world. Not emphatically in the arts as yet but in arenas of action, and in ideas for the creation of that egalitarian democracy that will have to be the basis of all civilised societies in the future. This is the Australia we are called upon to save.

In statements like this from Australian artists—and they were increasingly forthcoming—can be found a more confident conception of Australia's national culture. Yet the light of this was darkened by the shadow of a racially based national*ism*. Palmer's appeal to those 'who truly belong' in the country was a restricted one. He was an unrelenting opponent of fascism, but also a supporter of the White Australia Policy. It is in the crux of this disturbing paradox that the Ladybird Book image of a 'real Australian' was born.

The bush. Again.

Looking at the plays of the 1930s and 1940s a contemporary reader might be forgiven for thinking that most Australians lived in the outback; that their houses were rudimentary and amenities non-existent; that the land around them was sparse, dry and empty; that their working lives were filled with unrelenting toil and their emotional ones exiguous. Again and again, settings similar to that opening *Men Without Wives* are described:

> *The dining-room at Kooli Crossing homestead, towards evening. The curtain rises on a bare room, with walls of corrugated iron, painted an uncompromising shade of green. A few coloured supplements from periodicals are fixed up on the walls. There is an open brick fireplace, right, with a smoke-blackened mantlepiece of rough timber. Two weather beaten cane armchairs crouch towards the log fire. A large bare deal table occupies the centre left of the stage. Various chairs of the kitchen variety stand about, left a door, centre back, closed. No windows showing.* (12)

Henrietta Drake-Brockman's play premiered in 1938, ten years after *The Touch of Silk* and *Brumby Innes*. At first glance, it occupies similar geographical and dramatic territory. John McCallum comments,

> In play after play the setting is the interior of a simple bush hut, with walls made of hessian, rough timber slabs or kerosene tins and a few pathetic attempts to enliven the room… There is usually a gun somewhere, to be used on the marauding kangaroos (or escaped convicts in historical plays), and which an intruder sometimes turns on the inhabitants of the lonely dwelling… When the drought breaks at the end of the play, as it tends to do, the rain pounds on the tin roof, and a slow curtain falls on the defeated, but sometimes, newly hopeful characters.

Sure enough, *Men Without Wives* finishes with a rainstorm and a flooding river. The ending is ambiguous, however. The leading character, Mrs Bates, 'a hard-bitten northerner', has discovered she is dying: a point of despair. But the impassable river means she cannot be taken to a hospital in the south: a point of hope. 'Yet no man living has ever done me a better turn nor God has done ternight', she cries ecstatically at news of the flood, 'I'm that happy I could sing' (101).

Such compound emotions become more common in Australian plays after 1930. Even where professional skill is lacking (by some standards), their cultural reach is greater. The bush setting may be ubiquitous, along with melodramatic flourishes to the action. But the creative worlds are richer, invoking a wider swathe of ideas and experiences. Not quickly, and not without backwards steps, yet indisputably, the gap between Australian national life and Australian drama that Brodsky lamented in 1907 had started to close.

The location of *Men Without Wives* is northern Australia, the same as Prichard's *Brumby Innes*, and Mrs Bates is described with the exact same phrase: 'rough as bags' (26). At the start of the play, 'a young woman from the south' (11) who has married Jack Abbott, the owner of a large cattle station, is coming to take up residence there with the same oblivious self-centredness May Hallinan displays when she pursues Brumby to a disastrous end. Act 1 takes place at Kooli

Crossing, an obligatory way station for all travellers heading up or down the country, where Mrs Bates and Mrs Abbott narrowly miss meeting each other. Mrs Bates and Lovatt, the old boot of a station manager, discuss the marriage. Mrs Bates is sceptical the young bride will withstand the isolated existence awaiting her. When Mrs Abbott turns up, she seems to confirm those doubts in full. 'All day I felt as if we were driving across the setting of some exciting Hollywood drama', she breathlessly announces to the cluster of seedy men around her, who are, from the play's perspective, representative of white Australia in the north. With Mrs Bates gone to tend a prospector on his deathbed, they wonder how to tell Mrs Abbott what life there is really like:

> MRS ABBOTT: Kooli is an aboriginal word, isn't it? Has it a pretty meaning?
> LOVATT: Don't know about pretty, missus, but near enough the truth to be a sort er warning. Means to 'pour water'. We're on the bank of a sizeable river here, hence the name …
> MRS ABBOTT: A river! That dribble?
> LOVATT: Too right a river! She goes a quarter mile wide and fifty feet deep in the wet season. She has a pretty habit of running sudden, too…
> MRS ABBOTT: What you call running a banker, isn't it? Too thrilling!
> LOVATT: We're not thrilled. Cuts us and the back country right off f'r days at a time. A damned menace…
> MRS ABBOTT: Don't you ever get tired of people dropping in on you?
> LOVATT: Don't take that much notice. We're on the track in. They all stop here.
> MRS ABBOTT: Oh. Shall we have lots of visitors, John?
> ABBOTT: 'Fraid not, Kit. Erriba is off the track to anywhere…
> MRS ABBOTT: We'll ask people for the week-end. [*The men look rather startled.*] (24–5)

In a mostly male environment Mrs Bates stands out, not only because she is a woman, but because she has the strength and heart to endure a life of constant challenge and privation.

Act 2 is set a couple of years later, and Mrs Bates and Mrs Abbott have still not met. The latter's renovations to Erriba Station are the talk of 'the spinifex wire'. Clara and Lulu, Mrs Bates's daughters, present a contrasting pair. Clara, falling under the spell of Mrs Abbott, is desperate to go south and live a life of imagined glamour, while her sister, a true northerner, is 'sick to death of Mrs Abbott… She's a rotten silvertail and I'm tired of hearing her name' (45).

While the girls bicker, the plot revelations that drive the play to a climax kick in. Mrs Bates's husband, Joe, wants to purchase life insurance for his family. He is won over by the sales patter of Bob M'Kee ('Forty. Florid. Fat. Always trying to be funny, but a very successful insurance agent' 60). M'Kee turns up at the Bates home with a young doctor to administer a routine health check prior to processing the paperwork. But Mrs Bates refuses to be examined, and does her belligerent best to talk Joe out of insuring her. As she has been surreptitiously swallowing pain-relief medicine since the start of the play, it is clear something is wrong. When Lulu catches her mother in the act, she persuades her to see Dr Jones, and the truth comes out: Mrs Bates has a malignant tumour.

These sensational revelations, however, are less interesting than the equivocal moral atmosphere in which they occur. All the characters in *Men Without Wives* are flawed, if we mean by 'flawed' that they are lonely, sometimes weak, with dubious pasts and uncertain futures. Most of the white men are sleeping with Indigenous women, and Mrs Bates's attitude to this, and to their behaviour generally, is an interesting blend of reproval and acceptance. She does not condone what she sees—she has some sharp insights into white–black relations—but she understands where it comes from. She reserves her sternest judgement for Mrs Abbott. In Act 3 the confrontation between the two women that is the core of the drama finally occurs. The setting is again Kooli Crossing, as Mrs Bates and Mrs Abbott wait for the boat that will take them south—in the former's case certainly, and in the latter's probably, for the last time. Undone by northern Australia, Mrs Abbott's attitude is the reverse of Act 1, hating it with bitchy intensity. Mrs Bates, by contrast, dreads leaving it.

> MRS BATES: They'll plant me in some dark, shut-in cemetery, not out in the open, decent, like I've always lived. Nor'll you be back, either, I'll bet. You an' me, we're the only

white women here ter make a bit er home life. [*She turns and regards* MRS ABBOTT *with a kind of aggressive contempt.*] But you—you ain't got the guts ter stick by Jack. He's too good fer you. Ain't I seen it all happen? I s'pose you can't stand the heat—and the flies—and the loneliness. [MRS ABBOTT *starts*] …

MRS ABBOTT: Couldn't Mr Bates go with you? Couldn't you all go?

MRS BATES: What? Sell out? [*She laughs.*] You don't know what it feels like ter carve out a place—you with yer money and big companies. Joe'd eat out his heart anywhere else. And all the kids but Clara'd mope something terrible. No thank you, I'm not making the whole family miserable fer my sake. I'm finished. Whether north—or south.

MRS ABBOTT: Don't say—

MRS BATES: You be quiet with yer don't says! If yer can't say what yer darned well likes in the little time what's left before yer die, when can you? Listen, Mrs Jack Abbott, it's the likes er you what hinders the north. Won't there be discomforts and loneliness as long as the women won't stop ter make life better? (97)

The women reach a *rapprochement* and the rain comes. Mrs Abbott chooses to stay in the north and Mrs Bates gets to die in it.

Taken by itself, the play illustrates Macintyre's observation that the main division in Australia at this time was between north and south; between different regions with different outlooks, values and ways of life. However, two features of Drake-Brockman's writing are significant for Australian drama as a whole. The first—unmissable—is that the dialogue of *Men Without Wives* has a resonant quality to it that is at once richly colloquial and powerfully lyrical. When Clara is accused of getting 'dressed up like a sore finger' (47), when Joe says about his wife's reluctance to get insured 'he'll word her tonight' (72), and when Mrs Bates tells Mrs Abbott 'that when I heard Jack had married a flash tart from the south, I says, You mark my words, she'll not stop long this means the end er Jack' (89), both choice of phrase and rhythm of delivery exemplify the Australian vernacular in its unique combination of concision, humour and expressive force. The language of *Men Without Wives* is the language of Ray Lawler's

Summer of the Seventeenth Doll, of Jack Hibberd's *Stretch of the Imagination*, and of Patricia Cornelius's *SHIT*.

The second feature is the mood of the play. The melodrama of the plot is at odds with the inner lives of the characters, ones that reflect their ambivalent relationship with the land around them. This is only lightly explored by Drake-Brockman, but it hints at something decidedly modern: a mood of sustained irony.

Four years after *Men Without Wives*, with Australia now at war with Germany and Japan, two plays appeared that took that ironic mood further: Dymphna Cusack's *Morning Sacrifice* and George Landen Dann's *Fountains Beyond*. In December 1941, Curtin wrote his famous lines saying that 'Australia looks to America, free of any pangs as to our traditional links or kinship with the United Kingdom'. In February 1942, the British fortress of Singapore, which Australia had relied on to protect it from the threat of invasion, fell to the Japanese. Fifteen thousand Australian soldiers were taken prisoner, most without firing a shot. Interned under appalling conditions, fewer than half survived. General Douglas Macarthur, the American general sent to take command of Allied forces in the Asia-Pacific region, told Curtin 'you take care of the rear, and I will take care of the front'. In the same month Japan bombed Darwin, killing more than 200 people.

Over the next three years, one million American troops shipped to Australia to train before fighting in Burma, the Philippines and Indonesia. Australia became part of the war effort in a way it had not envisaged: as a military base, a munitions factory, and a source of vital provisions. As more men were conscripted, women entered the workforce in greater numbers. After World War I, Australia had remained a predominantly agricultural economy, which left it vulnerable to the worst of the Great Depression. Now, under the pressure of another global conflict, it rapidly industrialised. Australians lurched from the hedonism of the 1920s, to the privations of the 1930s, to calls in the 1940s to embrace a spirit of self-sacrifice and common endeavour. No wonder their drama was becoming more complex.

Where Drake-Brockman writes about men without women, Dymphna Cusack focuses on women deprived of men. *Morning

Sacrifice takes place in the staff common room of an upmarket all-girls high school, over three bleak mid-winter days. In many ways it inverts the norms of the bush play. Its environment is cloistered rather than expansive, the timeline concentrated rather than extending into years, its characters urban and talkative rather than rural and taciturn. If the bush play is haunted by a sense of social and spiritual isolation, *Morning Sacrifice* is oppressed by the opposite: a sense of enforced physical and emotional intimacy. Over three acts and five scenes, the play shows the teachers on their breaks from class. Most of the action occurs during six hours on the first day. As a school, Easthaven aims to show its pupils 'how to be ladies' (88) in the Miss Perkins–like belief (*The Time is Not Yet Ripe*) that 'the future of social morality is in the hands of women' (163).

Beneath the crust of snobbish aspiration, however, is a rigid system of hierarchical control that imposes on staff an endless succession of dreary tasks and petty rules. Miss Carwithen, the most rebellious of the teachers, refers to 'Easthaven's three Rs—Ruthlessness, Repression and Results' (44). What Aristotle calls the 'inciting incident' of the play involves a transgression by Mary Grey, a star pupil, whom the audience never gets to see. Indeed, it is only well into the second act that we discover what she has done. Thus, there is ample opportunity to study the dispositions of the nine teachers in a detached way, without knowing the stakes. Although the tensions evident in the common room suggest they are high.

Looking at the names of the characters in *Morning Sacrifice* reveals another odd fact: only one appears to be married. Eight are listed as 'Miss', as if they were students at Easthaven rather than teachers. This crucial detail is Cusack's real object of dramatic concern. It stems from another aspect of Australia's dark historical past: the marriage bar. Perhaps difficult to believe now (or not), Australia, while one of the first countries to extend the vote to women, also imposed draconian restrictions on their employment. The marriage bar legally required a woman working in the public service—as a teacher, for example— to leave her job when she married. The justification was that the demands of a professional career and the responsibilities of raising a family were—for women—incompatible.

It is not hard to discern behind this flimsy argument the sexist inequities of the Harvester judgement and the gender-discriminatory 'basic wage'. A public service manual published in 1942 opined that women 'are more adaptable to monotonous work than men... and their retirement upon marriage is still an important factor ensuring rapid turnover, thus mitigating the problem of blind-alley employment'. Faced with a system where the choice is to stay single and employed, or get married and leave the job for which they have trained, the teachers in *Morning Sacrifice* are trapped in lives of evasion and duplicity. This does not create solidarity, but rather the opposite, what Susan Pfisterer, in her introduction to the play, calls 'the horizontal hostility between women [that is] a barrier to female emancipation'.

The Easthaven common room is a snake pit of rumour, slander and misinformation—of friending, flaming, shoulder surfing and bash-boarding *circa* 1942—where the possibility of collective action is undercut by status competition between the women and the sexually repressed, morally punitive atmosphere in which they interact. These divisions are brought into sharp focus by the problem of having to decide Mary Grey's fate after she has been caught kissing a boy at the school dance.

At the top of the Easthaven pecking order is the deputy headmistress, Miss Portia Kingsbury. She is perhaps the most fascinating character in Australian drama to this date. Cusack introduces her thus: *'Miss Kingsbury is... a middle-aged woman of great beauty and dignity, with an exquisitely modulated voice. Her clothes are well-chosen, fashionable and expensive, in contrast to those of most of the other teachers'* (14). Miss Kingsbury's rule over the teachers reflects the school's life more broadly: all care and concern on the surface, all egotism and exploitation underneath. She wields protocols and procedures like a cattle prod, controlling her staff by using 'standards of conduct we once regarded as absolute' (54) to suppress dissent, especially anything that smacks of liberal thought or behaviour.

From the start, Miss Kingsbury has Miss Carwithen in her sights, so it is no surprise when she eventually ousts her from the school. Caught in the crossfire, however, is Miss Ray, once Miss Kingsbury's most adoring student, now her youngest teacher and protégée. Here, there is a problem within a problem, for Miss Ray is Mary Grey's protector, while Miss Kingsbury wants her expelled. This would ruin Mary's prospects of a scholarship to study medicine at university but take Miss Kingsbury one step closer to the position she covets and for which she has sacrificed her personal life: headmistress of Easthaven. It is the seamless combination of charm and harm that makes Miss Kingsbury such a compelling dramatic creation. On the one hand she is intelligent, articulate and emotionally insightful. On the other, in Miss Carwithen's words, 'she is the most thoroughly evil woman I've ever met… a spiritual vampire' whom Miss Ray is 'letting suck [her] blood' (57).

Fountains Beyond is also set in a confined location, a coastal Aboriginal settlement, and the majority of the action is compressed into a period of just two weeks. A sense of brutal hierarchy is likewise apparent, though in this case it is a racial one. Kooreelba is a regional Queensland town that is expanding towards the sea. Standing in the way of the plans of the local council and attendant property developers, however, is a satellite community of 'coloureds' who have lived on the land they occupy for thousands of years. As Mr Watson, a local powerbroker with ambitions to be Kooreelba's mayor explains, 'That may be—but civilisation advances, you know. Up till lately there's been no objection to you Abos living here. But the town is growing rapidly. We'd no idea it would spread in this direction. It was all planned to go the other way—along the river front—but the modern craze for surfing's upset that' (43).

Like *Morning Sacrifice*, the action of George Landen Dann's play draws on an unsavoury part of Australia's past—the continued repressive treatment of its Indigenous population. In the 1930s, a more enlightened view of Indigenous culture seemed to be taking hold at a government level. But this did not change the policy of forced assimilation. In a note to the play, Susan Davis explains that 'The *Aboriginal Welfare: Initial Conference of Commonwealth and State Authorities* in 1937 advocated for the protection of "full-bloods" in generally isolated communities and the "absorption" of half-castes into the "ordinary community". There was limited support for Indigenous people living outside the mission system and the plight of fringe-dwelling settlements was dire' (8). In other words, though now taking advice from anthropologists rather than religious leaders, the government doubled down on its 'dying race' theory of Indigenous Australians, and became even more dismissive of their demands for equal treatment.

Kooreelba's Aboriginal community has a spokesperson, however. This figure is as dramatically compelling as Miss Kingsbury, but with the opposite moral charge. Vic Filmer is the first leading Indigenous character in a modern Australian drama, and he is a memorable creation. Dann based him on a real-life person, Freddy Ross, whom he met while travelling around Australia's remote townships. Dann's description of Freddy captures the essence of Vic too:

> He is a medium-sized man, very strong and active and rather handsome with his black curly hair and finely cut features. His personality is a thing you can't resist and he possesses into the bargain a sympathetic understanding towards others and an ever-ready willingness to lend a hand… When he begins to talk everybody listens… An expert axeman… [h]e cuts through a log as evenly and as straight as if it had been sawn… His fishing feats and sea adventures can be vouched for by any resident of the Urangan district… He has the knack of being able to adapt himself successfully to almost any outdoor work. His one aversion is snakes. He is very much afraid of them. (12)

Though an ordinary country town, Kooreelba gets a visit from Miss Harnett, a celebrated English travel writer, who has been commissioned to write a book on Australia but has no time to go north and see '[the] way real coloured people live' (33). In Act 1, Watson brings her to Vic's shack, where he lives with his young wife, Peggy. The age gap between the couple is significant because it signals not only that Peggy is susceptible to the charms of the amiable but scheming Wally (a 'handsome looking fellow of the larrikin type' 20), but that she does not have the experience to see through the offer Watson puts to Vic: to organise a corroboree for Miss Harnett, 'a fair dinkum Australian affair' (37). When Vic won't help, Watson explodes, refusing to accept Vic's

A day of signal protest. On 26 January 1938, about 100 Aboriginal men, women and children gathered at Australian Hall (Sydney) to commemorate '150 years of misery and degradation imposed upon the original native inhabitants by the white invaders of this country. The Australian Aborigines League was established in 1932. The Aborigines Progressive Association in 1937.

argument that 'corroboree is… [a] sacred thing to blackfellas. White people make fun all time they watch' (44).

Vic sees what Watson barely bothers to hide: that the council wants the land the settlement stands on, and the money raised from the corroboree will go to funding a children's playground to replace it. Vic makes Watson a counter offer: he'll help with the corroboree if Watson will guarantee the settlement can stay. But Watson is evasive, saying only 'I'm out, naturally, to see justice and rights are upheld for all sections of the community. But I have also to consider the advancement and the betterment of the town' (45). Such weaselly statements are typical of the white characters in Kooreelba—and similar to Miss Kingsbury's manipulative style. Even when they mean well, they act in ways that irreparably damage the lives of the Indigenous folk.

In Act 2, Miss Harnett, who has seen through the town's canting hypocrisy, and is appalled at the travesty of a corroboree that Wally lazily throws together, tries to help ('I thought there'd have been a hush of—of reverence over it all. A respect for old traditions—like at a grand ceremony. Instead, well, no third-rate vaudeville show could have been worse' 59). Watson now tries to buy Vic off, to get him out of the way while he makes his run for mayor. He offers Vic a plum job and a four-room house on a cattle station 'right out west' (72). For Peggy, it is a dream come true. But with Miss Harnett's promise to throw her support behind a campaign to save the settlement, Vic turns Watson down. Again, Watson is enraged, but the cynical horror of the situation is that he is not really against the Aboriginal settlement. He just cannot afford to endorse it if he wants to become mayor. Hand in hand with racial prejudice comes electoral expediency—an accurate portrayal of the tawdry politics of the time.

In Act 3, Watson is elected mayor; Miss Harnett fails in her attempts to help the settlement; and the homes the Indigenous characters have lovingly constructed over the years are razed to the ground. Miss Harnett visits Vic for the last time.

> VIC: You goin' back to England now?
> MISS HARNETT: At the end of the week. I've stayed in Australia much longer than I intended. I travelled here as a sort of holiday away from travel. But heavens! I've done more of it than I've ever done before in any country!
> VIC: You been lots of places, eh?
> MISS HARNETT: All over the north and half of the central district. I had to go there after all. [*She laughs.*] There's no telling what I'll do when I get bitten by an idea and my ink pressure is high. I felt I simply couldn't complete my book until I'd visited those places and seen the conditions of the natives for myself...
> VIC: What name you call your book??
> MISS HARNETT: I haven't quite decided—but I think the title will be 'Fountains Beyond'.
> VIC: 'Fountains Beyond' ...? [*Shaking his head.*] I not see no sense in that name. What them fountains beyond?
> MISS HARNETT: Tragedy ... Tragedy, cruelty, misunderstanding—and the greatest of these for white people to overcome and make amends for, to the black people, is misunderstanding. Only when that has been remedied will there come a hope for the salvation of the Aborigines. (84)

Miss Harnett is Dann's mouthpiece in the play, and at times there is a polemical feel to the dialogue. But his message is prescient, looking ahead to the land rights campaigns of the 1970s and 1980s, and the Mabo decision of the High Court (see Chapter 7). 'Salvation will come when tracts of land have been set aside for [the] sole use [of Indigenous peoples]', Miss Harnett tells Vic. 'There must be places where white men cannot go into… There they must be allowed to follow their own customs without interference' (85). *Fountains Beyond*, which faced considerable controversy when it was first staged, is a good example of Australian drama leading, not just reflecting, debate on a matter of significant public concern.

Beyond melodrama

From the point of view of a literary manager, one indication of a play's nature is where it places its climax. All plays have beginnings, middles and ends. At a minimum, this is imposed on them by the temporal nature of live performance. Audiences arrive. They watch what is put on stage in front of them. Then they leave, re-entering the world beyond the theatre. Melodramas locate the peak of their action towards the end of this timeline, and their plot devices are familiar ones. The last-minute reprieve. The final reveal. The lover's kiss as the curtain falls. Privileging narrative energy over character response, melodrama has limited capacity to investigate what more far-reaching genres are interested in: the nuances of human behaviour. It is a crude generalisation, but a useful one, to say that, from 1940 onwards, the climaxes of Australian plays happen earlier and earlier. There is thus more time for playwrights to probe the implications of the action they portray. Where *Brumby Innes* and *Men Without Wives* finish soon after their last major plot reveals, both *Fountains Beyond* and *Morning Sacrifice* have subsequent encounters of great dramatic power, in the case of Cusack, a whole new scene. The effect is to prolong the emotional states provoked by the main action—not to release the audience into the night 'satisfied' with a neat resolution, but to keep them pressed up against what they have seen, perhaps uncomfortably so, and insist they consider its deeper meaning.

Both *Fountains Beyond* and *Morning Sacrifice* transcend melodrama and embrace a genuinely tragic sensibility. This is a professional achievement as well as a cultural one. Dann and Cusack are writers capable of sustained exploration of the uneasy territory that arises in the wake of the climaxes of their plays. In Act 2 of *Morning Sacrifice*, Miss Kingsbury rounds on her disciple, Miss Ray, accusing her not just of misconduct, but of moral corruption—of being responsible for Mary Grey's 'debauchery' (137). The consequence is Miss Ray's suicide, reported in Act 3, which hangs over the final scene like the sword of Damocles, even as Miss Kingsbury is confirmed as Easthaven's new headmistress. In Act 2 of *Fountains Beyond*, crushed by Vic's refusal to take the cattle-station job and confused by the politics around her, Peggy has an affair with Wally. When Vic learns what has happened in Act 3, he goes after Wally with his gun. Peggy tries to stop him, the gun goes off, and she is killed. Henry, an Aboriginal Elder enters, and the two men try to make sense of what has happened to their community, before leaving in Henry's boat, with the implication the men are going to their deaths. In both plays, the weight is thrown off the narrative *per se*, and onto the consequences it has for the characters, with corresponding focus on their inner lives and motivations. Needless to say there are no easy answers, and audiences are left on a vertiginous emotional edge, with endings that bear witness to the full complexity of human behaviour.

Lest it be thought that transcending melodrama always involves a 'serious' play engaging problems in realistic fashion, *Lady in Danger* by Max Afford is a reminder that drama contains a wide range of forms and registers of understanding. Afford died in 1954, at the age of just 48. Had he lived he may well have achieved the merger between Australian drama and commercial theatre of which his contemporaries thought him capable. During the 1940s, JC Williamson's produced two of his plays, with *Lady in Danger* becoming the first Australian drama to open on Broadway. Afford was a brilliant comedy writer, and his facility for witty dialogue, razor-sharp characterisation and absurd situations, makes him the inheritor of both Rudd's *On Our Selection* and Esson's *The Time is Not Yet Ripe*. Unlike Adams's *Gallipoli Bill*, his writing works with, rather than to, a formula, and the fact that he embraced the norms of commercial theatre should not count against him any more than it counts against Steele Rudd. '[T]he commercial theatre and the embryonic nationalist drama were pursuing essentially the same material', says McCallum, 'despite their different motivations and a great deal of mutual antagonism'. Perhaps because of his success as a writer for radio, Afford paid little attention to the concocted division. *Lady in Danger* is both a signal contribution to Australia's national drama *and* a play for the commercial stage.

Afford's comedy teeters on black, but never fully embraces the macabre—perhaps it might be called 'dark grey'. The plot centres on a newly married couple, Bill and Monica Sefton. At the start of the play, Bill has lost his job as a journalist for speaking out against his boss, Sir Charles Redmond, and Monica is trying to make up the shortfall in their income by writing a bestselling murder mystery. For this, she is researching different poisons, and subjecting her husband to surprise tests to see how someone might react to, for example, finding his dead wife's body stuffed in a linen cupboard (the *coup d'theatre* that opens the play). As luck would have it, the flat next to the Seftons' is occupied by Dr Gresham, a police psychiatrist. Monica invites him round for supper to pick his brains about how to 'plan perfect murders' (27). Suddenly, there is an interruption: a black cat is on the windowsill outside. Monica scoops the cat up and, to the consternation of both her husband and Dr Gresham, insists on keeping it. Thereafter a succession of half-hilarious, half-disturbing narrative twists and turns ensues. Monica's manuscript goes missing and a real dead body turns up in her linen cupboard. She is arrested for murder, while Bill, fellow journalist Andrew Meade, and his droll, long-suffering wife, Sylvia, Monica's best friend, attempt to exonerate her.

Like all rapid-fire situation comedies, *Lady in Danger* makes use of recognisable character types. In Afford's play there is a goodly array of tight-fisted landladies, dim-witted policemen and malformed henchmen. Dr Gresham, it turns out, has framed Monica to take the fall for an assassination involving a cat with poisoned claws—the same cat that Monica rescued only a few nights before. Removing her from jail and bringing her to his private nursing home, Gresham mixes up a potion to kill Monica and make it look like suicide. When Monica, investigating Dr Gresham's office, accidentally pulls a dangling drawstring, curtains open to show *'a full-length portrait of Adolf Hitler, a glorified Fuhrer, brooding and evil'* (109), all is revealed.

> GRESHAM *stiffens suddenly, clicks his heels together and bows. Then, very deliberately, he puts the glass on the table and turns to* MONICA.
>
> GRESHAM: How much do you know?
> MONICA: Everything! You're the head of a Nazi group in this city. Sir Charles Redmond was one of your men. Because he couldn't hold his tongue, you killed him.
> GRESHAM: Go on.
> MONICA: You tried to put the blame on me. And because you know you could never prove anything, you plan to kill me, probably hoping that the police will think it suicide because I couldn't face up to the trial!
> GRESHAM: I have already said that you are a remarkably quick-witted young woman, Mrs Sefton. May I repeat the compliment. As you say, it is to look like suicide.
> MONICA: And do you think the police will believe it?
> GRESHAM: They will when they find your confession ...
> MONICA: But—why do this to me? I've never harmed you ...
> GRESHAM: Mrs Sefton, when we burn a rotted log, do we enquire about the emotions of the insects that perish in the flames? When we blast a rock that stands as an obstacle in our way, do we pause to consider the feelings of the worms that crawl beneath? [*His voice rises, trembling with fanatical fervour.*] My dear child, don't you realise that you are privileged to sacrifice your life for the greatest cause in the whole history of civilisation—the rebuilding of a grand and splendid New Order from the ruin and misery of a decadent and outmoded democracy! (113–4)

The tongue-in-cheek humour of Afford's writing—the same irony at work in Dann and Cusack's plays—allows *Lady in Danger* to transcend its stock-comedy origins. The polished ease of the dialogue—at its most charming when it is most intimate, as in the scene where Monica and Sylvia discuss their imperfect relationships with their husbands—holds the story, by turns political and farcical, at an unthreatening distance, keeping the focus on the characters' impulses and dispositions. The story propels the play forward, but the drama belongs to the human beings in it. It might be said that the real danger in which Afford is interested is not the murderous intentions of Nazi doctors, but the travails of modern marraige.

Lady in Danger is not location specific. Nominally, it takes place in wartime London. When it opened on Broadway, it was set in Sydney, with German spies becoming Japanese ones. But geography is incidental to the action. And while the language of the play reflects the rhythms of Australian English, it is not self-consciously vernacular in the manner of *Men Without Wives*. Afford is concerned not with capturing a local way of speaking but with crafting a verbal resource to animate his play in a certain auditory range. Its smoothness is a writerly effect, not an exercise in ethnography. It is significant, therefore, that *Lady in Danger* is dedicated to Sydney Tomholt, Australia's first expressionist playwright. The wrought intensity of Tomholt's plays—Leslie Rees calls them 'an electric wire stretched almost, if not quite, to breaking point—would seem to be the opposite of Afford's hyper-affability. But on examination, the contrast evaporates. Rees describes Tomholt as a kind of dramatist who

> Without bothering to establish more than the mere basic outline of a physical environment and without giving more than a few facts about his personages, proceeds at once… to illuminate the life of the emotions… He illuminates unusual phases not only through a study of the relationships of people but through the evocation of a significant and compelling mood… In such a play there is poetry, spirituality, the worrying consciousness that the understanding of life waits just round the corner, eluding human grasp.

This describes Afford's plays as much as Tomholt's, and with good reason. Both, in their different ways, are anti-realist playwrights. Afford is part of Australian drama's poetic trajectory that blossomed after the war in the plays of Patrick White, and later, in those of Dorothy Hewett, John Romeril and Jack Hibberd. *Lady in Danger* is a reminder that when investigating Australian drama we must not be satisfied by classifying like with like, but must look beyond standard critical categories to study the workings of plays that have imaginative affinities more wayward than often supposed. Although the surface of Afford's play is naturalistic, its 'compelling mood' is not. From now on, I will use Rees's phrase 'compelling mood' to describe this overall quality of a play's impact.

1942

In 1943, Dolia Ribush, a Russian-speaking Latvian theatre director of medium height and considerable charm, made an illegal trip to Sydney from Melbourne—interstate travel then, as during Covid in 2020–21, being restricted—to persuade Australia's leading poet to collaborate on a stage play. Even more remarkably, his ally in this endeavour was none other than the critic AA Phillips, both a close friend and the business manager of his theatre company, the Ribush Players. Douglas Stewart was the poet in question. In 1942, his verse drama *Ned Kelly* was broadcast by the ABC as a radio play. Getting hold of a copy of the text, Ribush was convinced it could be adapted for the stage. He won over not only Stewart, but also Stewart's admirer and supporter, the artist Norman Lindsay, who agreed to design the show. Thus in October 1944, exactly 11 years before *Summer of the Seventeenth Doll* appeared in the same venue, *Ned Kelly* opened at the Union Theatre, on the campus of the University of Melbourne, in a production that involved some of the country's most accomplished—and self-consciously Australian—artists.

Phillips, still six years shy of publishing his influential cultural cringe essay, was actually *in* the production, taking the part of an anguished preacher, Reverend Gribble. Although the play's season was a short one, it had a profound impact on those who saw it, including a 16-year-old schoolboy named Manning Clark. Twenty years later, the historian wrote to Rosa Ribush, Dolia's widow, saying, 'one of my sources of inspiration to write *A History of Australia* was seeing the production of *Ned Kelly*. It was an event in my life which made me pose the question: why are we as we are?'; then, 'Permit me to add that in moments of despair, and they happen all too often, my mind takes comfort from recalling that night in Melbourne when your husband's work got me thinking about what Australia stands for'.

Costume sketches for 'the drunkards' in the Jerilderie bar scene in Ned Kelly. *Norman Lindsay's drawings and model for the 1944 production are on file in the State Library of Victoria archives. The UTRC's 1956 production of the play had backdrops designed by another famous Australian painter, Sidney Nolan.*

Ned Kelly is one of the most undervalued plays in the national repertoire. In part, this stems from its form as a seemingly outdated verse drama. Viewed from the perspective of theatre's past, however—some 2,500 years—the ascendancy of prose drama is less than a tenth of that span. In the 1930s and 1940s, verse drama enjoyed a modest revival. In the United Kingdom, TS Eliot, Stephen Spender and WH Auden, and in the United States, Maxwell Anderson, fused their talent as poets with their mastery of dramatic structure to write plays that, if not regularly revived, are at least acknowledged and read. Perhaps, like *Ned Kelly*, they await a time when prose drama has less of a hold on audience tastes than it does now.

Just as its verse form gives Stewart's play a misleading *passé* look, so its radical sensibility is easy to miss. In 1997, I directed *Ned Kelly* in one of its few professional productions. Spruiking the show to audiences, I heard many times that people 'already knew the story'. But when I asked what they knew, they were often at a loss to give even the basic facts. They felt they knew the Kelly story, but they did not. This combination of a firm belief that the past is known, yet ignorance of the events that actually make it up, fuels Australia's 'history wars'. So Stewart falls into a historical black hole as well as a theatrical one. A nation dismissive of its past dramatic forms, is also dismissive of its past. Reclaiming *Ned Kelly* as an object of proper consideration for the repertoire is therefore more than its disinterment from the sarcophagus of neglected plays: it is an act of intellectual reclamation whereby Australian history is made available as a dramatic resource and drama is validated as a mode of historical inquiry. Of the famous Australians that Geoffrey Dutton discusses in his 1982 book *The Australian Heroes*, many have appeared as serious stage characters: Ned Kelly, 'Breaker' Morant, Nellie Melba, Truganini, Caroline Chisholm, Lola Montez, Ern Malley, Albert Namatjira, Daniel Mannix, Les Darcy and Henry Lawson. But only *one* was before 1940 (Colonel Light, in *Awake My Love*, a play about the founding of Adelaide, written by Afford in 1936).

Ned Kelly has a feature unusual in drama but not uncommon in great poetry: the more you read it, the more disturbing it becomes. Presented in four acts, at a time when three was the norm, it is biblically epic in the scope of its action. Its long slabs of speech vary between describing the vast emptiness of the bush, and exhaustively examining the morality of the deeds of the bushrangers. Even today, these prompt divided responses. For some Australians, the Kelly gang were cold-hearted killers who deserved their bloody end. For others, they were victims of the historical injustice inherent in the convict settlement of the nation and its legacy of colonial repression and abuse. The fact that Ned Kelly and his brother, Dan, were Irish by blood and background is also an important fact, evoking the exploitation of Britain's first colony, Ireland. Although Ribush staged *Ned Kelly* when World War II was at its height, his production still attracted its full share of bitter comment and rebuke.

The language of *Ned Kelly* is incomparable. Though grand and sweeping, rather than stylish and urbane, it is kin to *Lady in Danger* in eschewing realism for larger poetic effect. More so than Afford, Stewart's rhythms anticipate Patrick White's in *The Ham Funeral*, *Season at Sarsaparilla* and *A Cheery Soul*. Like White, his view of humanity is an uncomforting one, at times even chilling. Though little is *shown* in *Ned Kelly* and much is *said* (in keeping with its origins as a radio play), violence drips from every page. This is not the reassuring redemptive violence of melodrama, where villains get their just deserts and heroes walk into an upbeat future, but an unholy crush of hostility, brutality and slaughter that covers the action like an ash cloud. In Stewart's vision, it is as if violence is stitched into the Australian national character. This is voiced directly by Reverend Gribble—the role played by Phillips—in speeches of turbulent, agonised power. Act 1 is set in the country town of Jerilderie, where the gang hold up the bank and corral the population in the pub, threatening to shoot the bank manager until the preacher intervenes:

> GRIBBLE: Laugh at me if you like,
>   That's better than brooding murder. When you laugh
>   at the bar
>   It's hard to imagine those terrible shots in the mountains,
>   The cries, and the blood on the ground, and on your
>   hand...
>   In England even the words, the fields, and the rivers,
>   Like the churches the Normans built, ivy and stone,
>   Have a sense of grace and order, a long tradition
>   Of labour and love and patience against the weather.
>   Australia's the violent country, the earth itself
>   Suffers, cries out in anger against the sunlight
>   From the cracked lips of the plains; and with the land
>   With the snake that strikes from the dust,
>   The people suffer and cry their anger and kill.
>   I have come to understand it in love and pity;
>   Not horror now; I understand the Kellys. (147)

Like the fall of the House of Atreus in Aeschylus's *Oresteia*, the end of the Kelly gang is foretold. A supernal doom haunts the play, not least because Ned and his fellow bushrangers know they are going to die. This imparts a dense, almost unbearable claustrophobia to the action. Despite the gang roaming over miles of bush, the emotional terrain they occupy is cramped and ever-reducing. As they run out of time, they run out of space. Queensland dangles as the promise of escape, just as for Drake-Brockman's Mrs Abbott the south seems to be where freedom lies. But it is an illusion. The gang aren't going anywhere but the graveyard.

Against the heaviness of this predetermined tragedy, Stewart counterpoises a different sensibility in the characters who surround the

Kellys. These fall into three groups: active sympathisers from the working class, head-shakers from the professional class, and the gang's mortal enemies, the police ('the traps'), three of whom Kelly murdered before the start of the play. In both the Jerilderie pub scene in Act 1, and the hotel scene in the Victorian town of Glenrowan in Act 4, when the gang plot to derail a police train and kill its 70-odd occupants, including Aboriginal trackers, the atmosphere is a hellish mix of the merry and macabre. Aside from Gribble, no-one condemns what the Kellys are doing, either because they do not believe it is wrong, or because they are afraid for their own skins. Tarleton the bank manager, Elliot the schoolteacher, Brett the squatter, Cox the hotelkeeper, Rankin the merchant, Harkin the storekeeper and Reardon the railwayman, all seem indifferent to the ethical questions raised by the gang's actions. Even the traps adopt an amoral attitude, as if their hatred of the Kellys arose from a struggle for power and control, rather than censure of their criminal behaviour.

In *Ned Kelly* the irony detectable in *Men Without Wives*, *Morning Sacrifice*, *Fountains Beyond* and *Lady in Danger*, reaches new saturation. Ambiguity and amorality create the play's compelling mood. All the characters, with the exception of Ned Kelly himself, behave in a self-interested way, as if moral judgement of the gang's actions were unimportant, something that could change depending on who is in charge, or how many drinks have been downed. Ned tries to act out of conviction. But he lives in a colonial society with little integrity, so his resolve to be a man of principle leaves him even more isolated than the killings he commits. The play ends with the famous image of Ned Kelly in his armour, fighting the police who have surrounded the hotel, an outcast because of his defiant attitude as much as his murderous deeds:

> NED: Yes, it's Ned Kelly! You want me, don't you, you traps?
> Then come and get me. Or wait and I'll come and get you.
> Shoot, go on, why don't you shoot me down?
> ... You can't do it!
> Now I'll go where I like and do what I like.
> Come out from behind the tree if you think you can stop me.

>   You're thirty to one. Isn't that how you like it?
>   Stand up and meet me then! You asked for this:
>   You drove me out of my home, you made me an outlaw,
>   You sent your traps against me, you paid my friends
>   Blood money to give me away; you hunted me down
>   Like a dog with your black trackers. I'd have killed you all
>   Tonight if I could have; I'll kill a few of you yet.
> VOICES: Fire at his legs! Below the armour! Fire!
> NED: You wouldn't let me alone; then come and fight me!
>   (235–6)

Although first staged in 1944, *Ned Kelly* was broadcast two years earlier, the same year that *Fountains Beyond*, *Morning Sacrifice* and *Lady in Danger* premiered. In Australian theatre's history of beginnings, 1942 must therefore take its place as a year of fundamental change. The plays considered in this chapter imparted new substance and significance to the term 'Australian drama'. The theatre historian's eye is drawn to the 1950s, with the premiere of *Summer of the Seventeenth Doll*, as the watershed decade, yet the 1940s were decisive in both enlarging the kind of drama that playwrights wrote, and the capacity of their plays to convey complex philosophical, political, social and psychological insights. As a result, not only did Australian drama grow in professional craft, so did the cultural imagination of the nation it addressed. The Ladybird concept of a 'real Australian' was challenged, both in respect of present reality (who was included in the nation and who was excluded from it, or neglected), and with regard to its history (what had happened in the past to make Australia thus). Furthermore, it is noteworthy that this new growth—Phillips would have said, new maturity—occurred not at a time of collective confidence, but the opposite: when Australia was at its most vulnerable, troubled and alone. That the challenging experience of war should give rise to a consolidation of our national drama is another indication that it is more than an exercise in confirmation bias, echoing views and values we already hold. It is a powerful engine of collective discovery, that in 1942 achieved new heights of expression when the country's circumstances were at their worst.

4
1945–1960: A step change

Rusty Bugles **(1948)**. *The One Day of the Year* **(1960)**.
Summer of the Seventeenth Doll **(1955)**.
Here Under Heaven **(1948)**. *Sky Without Birds* **(1952)**.
The Shifting Heart **(1957)**. *The Day Before Tomorrow* **(1956)**.

> No future without a past.
>
> Gordon Bennett, Untitled work on A4 paper, 1998

As we approach the middle year of this book—1960—a new problem emerges for those interested in the historical development of Australian drama. It has both quantitative and qualitative dimensions. The first is easy to state: there is a clear increase in the number of Australian plays staged which starts in the 1960s and rises significantly thereafter. In the decades immediately following Federation discernible jumps in the data occur. After 1965, however, Australia's commitment to the national repertoire undergoes a sea change. But it is hard to fully capture because it is so diffuse, expressed by different people in different ways. This is the qualitative problem, the change that took place internally, transforming the self-perception of Australian playwrights and their sense of what they could accomplish.

A national repertoire does not need a well-established body of work to be an object of allegiance. Quite the opposite. If it does not exist, it can be pursued by artists determined that it *should* exist. But at a certain point in a historical trajectory—when enough has been achieved to boost belief in what can be done next—something like a cultural take-off may occur. The year 1955, when the Union Theatre Repertory Company (UTRC, now Melbourne Theatre Company) staged Ray Lawler's *Summer of the Seventeenth Doll* (the *Doll*) to national and international acclaim, is often treated as the ground zero of Australian drama. Leslie Rees dubs the *Doll* 'The Breakthrough' and John McCallum 'the most famous Australian play ever written or produced'. Peter Fitzpatrick titled his 1979 study of Australian drama *After the Doll*. There is no doubting the historical impact of the *Doll*, even if there remains debate about whether *The Torrents*, the Oriel Gray play that shared first prize with it in the same competition, is of equal merit.

Lawler was certainly fortunate. He was Artistic Director of the UTRC at the time, and reluctant to program his own play. John Sumner, the founder of the company, was working for the government's new arts agency, the Australian Elizabethan Theatre Trust (AETT). Free to direct one play a year for the UTRC, he was determined it would be an Australian one. Hugh Hunt, the AETT's classically trained director, agreed. But neither of these men, both recent British migrants, had deep knowledge of Australian drama. So where did the *Doll*'s success come from? From the genius of Lawler? Or was it just sheer good luck that a play appeared in 1955 that tapped into the life of the nation for the first time since *On Our Selection*?

Neither explanation is adequate. While the *Doll*'s status as a cultural catalyst is important, the environment that conditioned its production and reception was the achievement of prior artists. The *Doll* may look like the start of the Australian drama narrative, but it is the middle of it, the reward for the steady creative toil of post-federation theatre. Borrowing the observation of Indigenous artist Gordon Bennett, by the 1950s, Australian drama had enough of a past to conceive a future. That this past was—and remains—largely unacknowledged, reflects the difficulty Australia has of owning its past generally. In my Conclusion I consider how our negative view of nationhood is preventing proper understanding of the role and value of Australian drama. Here, it is enough to point out that the lull in Australian plays in the early 1960s may not be due to a failure to capitalise on the *Doll*'s success in the 1950s, but of the waning energies of the 1940s. Social critic Humphrey McQueen describes the 1950s as 'forever amber', years of apparent idling and indecision. 'Some Australians may have been chomping at the bit to join the rest of the world', he writes in *Social Sketches of Australia*, but 'expectations were held in check by the Cold War, and even more by financial shackles'.

When World War II ended the country found itself broke again. Stuart Macintyre has written about the attempts by the Curtin and Chifley governments to haul the country's economy and social outlook into a more progressive era. But the Reconstruction program came to an end when Robert Menzies won the 1949 election and became prime minister for a second time. His new Liberal Party formed a coalition with the Country Party that then remained in power for 23 years.

Menzies was an inertial figure in many ways. For a nation with no meaningful conservative tradition, it is difficult to think of him as a truly conservative politician. But he certainly disliked radical change. Paradoxically, this assisted the legacy of Reconstruction, as Menzies adopted many of the policies of his erstwhile Labor opponents, particularly the commitment to full employment. This in turn fuelled 30 years of steadily rising living standards and industrial growth.'The postwar settlement reconciled capitalism with democracy', Macintyre comments. 'Economic progress secured voters' acceptance of a market economy, while governments in turn accepted a responsibility to intervene in markets and correct their outcomes in the interests of their citizens.'

The new government attitude to market intervention had consequences for Australian culture, and for the performing arts in particular. Calls for a publicly funded national theatre were heard immediately after Federation, and enjoyed another rhetorical outing in the 1920s. They returned more insistently in the last years of World War II. The Council for the Encouragement of Music and the Arts (CEMA), was founded in 1943 as a peak body. It had similar aims to the British CEMA which was chaired by the intellectual titan of Depression recovery and founder of macroeconomics, John Maynard Keynes. Keynes had an Australian equivalent too—Herbert 'Nugget' Coombs, also an economist, who was Director-General of Post-War Reconstruction under Chifley, and later, Governor of the Commonwealth Bank (now the Reserve Bank). Unlike Keynes, Coombs did not succeed in persuading his prime minister to commit to the public provision of arts and culture in 1945. However, he was the driving force behind the establishment of both the AETT in 1954, and its successor body, the Australian Council for the Arts (later the Australia Council) in 1968.

A step change in attitude towards culture by the government was matched by a step change in organisation among artists. The collective action that led to the founding of a string of arts advocacy bodies in the 1930s morphed into a new policy activism the following decade. Australia's CEMA became a 'hub' for a network of nationally minded artists and cultural institutions. This did not include JC Williamson's, which continued to adhere not only to a commercial theatre ethos, but to the limited faith Williamson himself had shown in local plays. Thus the expansion of soul that transformed 'theatre in Australia' in the postwar period into theatre 'Australian in setting and mood' passed the Firm by. This was to have significant consequences when JC Williamson's collapsed in 1976, leaving the fate of commercial theatre in Australia unresolved.

In the 1940s, the leadership gap was filled by the repertory theatres, together with the New Theatre League. Founded in 1932, the New Theatre was affiliated with the Communist Party and soon had branches in every major Australian city. Its record of dramatic achievement is important in its own right, but its influence went beyond the productions it staged. The company's motto 'art is a weapon' lent playwriting a militant edge, highlighting drama's political potential. In the 1930s, the New Theatre's program consisted mainly of overseas plays, such as *Waiting for Lefty* by New York socialist playwright Clifford Odets. During the war, however, with foreign scripts harder to come by, Australian drama became a staple of its seasons.

When the New Theatre joined with the repertory theatres to pursue CEMA's national theatre objectives, the first fruits of the alliance were modest but the long-term impact was profound. Cultural policy in a contemporary sense was born, and moral and artistic, if not financial, leadership of the theatre profession passed to the non-commercial theatres. Their aims were quite different from those of the Firm, as can be seen by reading the archived minutes of a CEMA meeting held in 1946 to discuss the proposal for a national theatre. These espoused the democratic values that underpin cultural policy today. Thus the new commitment to Australian drama had two outcomes: a creative one, leading to the staging of more Australian plays; and a policy one, leading to closer linking of Australian culture to the political, economic and social agenda of the government. It is in this sense—and *only* in this sense—that we can say that Australian theatre became 'more professional' after 1945. It achieved a higher degree of recognition from Canberra as a public good. From this flowed more support from the Treasury purse, and increased investment in the infrastructure that is the bedrock of the Australian cultural sector today.

Was the 'professionalisation' of Australian theatre an unqualified benefit? Certainly John Sumner thought so when he arrived in Melbourne in 1952. His memoirs are caustic about the 'amateurism' he saw in local theatre at the time. Had he come ten years earlier he might have formed a different view. However, as non-commercial theatre received more support from the government, and became better remunerated as a career choice, it also became more male dominated.

Until 1950, Australian theatre shows a high proportion of female artistic leaders. Playwrights such as Betty Roland, Katharine Susannah Prichard, Hilda Bull, Henrietta Drake-Brockman and Dymphna Cusack, and directors like May Hollingworth (the Metropolitan Theatre), Doris Fitton (the Independent Theatre), Catherine Duncan (the New Theatre) and Barbara Sisley (La Boite) are the prophets and pathfinders of Australian drama, their creative and management talents transforming it into a serious cultural force. Yet this decisive contribution is habitually overlooked. Michelle Arrow is dismayed by the 'manwashing' of the Australian drama narrative, noting the role of the New Theatre especially in fostering female artists. Of the period 1928 to 1968, she comments, 'the women playwrights who rose to prominence during this forty-year period have effectively been upstaged by their younger, brasher counterparts in the 1970s'.

There is something deeply dispiriting about the absence of women from key roles in Australian theatre as it 'professionalised'. It takes nothing away from the achievements of male artists to observe that their dominance as a gender excluded women in a way that mirrors the racially exclusionary aspects of Australian culture. A national culture does not *have* to be exclusionary. But Australia's has sometimes clearly been so. Whenever exclusion manifests, there is a loss of momentum and creative potential. This may also explain the lull that followed the *Doll's* success in 1955. From the 1980s onwards women playwrights and directors return in numbers to the national repertoire; the operative word being 'return' rather than 'arrive'.

Memory and loss

One harsh measure of reality is the discrepancy between the world as we imagine it, and the world as we discover it to be. The gap between belief and experience can manifest in different ways. It can be an 'out there' gap, a confusion about the physical or social world around us, its problems and limits. Or it can be an 'in here' gap, a misperception of the interior world, of emotions and thoughts. Reality is a double helix of what we witness with our eyes and ears and what happens in our own minds: of action and response, events and their consequences. Always interested in where reality lies, regardless of whether they write in the realist style or not, playwrights usually focus on either the world out there or the world in here. Occasionally, however, they set up shop on the elusive boundary between the two, exploring how external and internal phenomena intertwine. If successful, audiences get to see the social environment, the 'big picture', and the human beings in it, the 'small picture', at the same time. There is a solidity to these plays that changes in critical fashion cannot diminish. They 'just are' in the same way that certain paintings or pieces of music just are. The wellspring of their existence lies in the complex reality they embody as well as reflect.

Sumner Locke Elliott's *Rusty Bugles*, Alan Seymour's *The One Day of the Year* and *Summer of the Seventeenth Doll* are the three great pillars of mid-twentieth century Australian drama, evenly spaced in their premieres. Each has features that make them original. Yet the plays also have interesting similarities, and in many ways reference each other, as if they were echoes of one great shout into a shared cavern of creative possibility. Each owes a debt to the past of Australian drama even as it pays that debt forward, creating a platform for playwrights yet to come. They also share a compelling mood—one of loss, flecked by anger, heartache and regret—despite their different concerns and structures. Hope is not a conspicuous feature, though it is not entirely absent, only kept at a distance while more immediate feelings are examined. If there is a nostalgic quality to them, it is one we impose. Taken straight, shorn of retrospective romanticising, these plays are as stark as a mathematical formula and as confronting as a nighttime look in the bathroom mirror.

The *Doll* is the most traditional of the three, in that its construction resembles plays of an earlier period. Its long, utterly surprising Act 3, however, following the violent climax of Act 2, shows Australian drama continuing to progress from its melodramatic roots. *Rusty Bugles* and *The One Day of the Year* demonstrate a fluidity of incident and image that presages playwriting in the 1970s. *Rusty Bugles* is the first Australian play to do without a plot as such, to throw its entire emphasis onto character and language. Behind one story always lies another, however, so that the discarding of a dominant through-line releases other stories to be seen and heard. *The One Day of the Year* uses split staging techniques and switches of time and location to similar end.

Another common feature of the plays is the difficulty of saying who are the lead characters. Relationships, rather than individuals, are their focus, both the ones we see and those we only hear about. The representative function of dramatic character is evident. Locke Elliott evokes the lives of all Australian soldiers with those he shows on stage. Lawler's cane-cutters are indicative of all Australian seasonal workers, and Seymour's generational divide emblematic of every generational divide. In the critical scholarship, this is sometimes referred to as the plays' 'universal significance'. This is suggestive, but inaccurate. Rather, it is an effect caused when characters are successfully portrayed on external and internal levels simultaneously ('out there' and 'in here') and we gain insight into a larger social configuration through a small number of relationships shown directly. That three Australian plays so successfully achieved this delicate effect within a few short years, is one sign that Australia's drama was starting to leave a mark on its national life.

Rusty Bugles is a series of bittersweet vignettes about Australian army life, set on a remote outback equipment depot in 1944. The soldiers spend their days in boring tasks overseen by their NCOs, who either revel in the tyranny they can inflict, or treat their rank with the same indifference the men show them. Locke Elliott wrote that *Rusty Bugles* was 'a documentary… not strictly a play' (vii), happy to claim the label that David Williamson vehemently abjured for *Don's Party* 25 years later. The two plays are similar, however, in being streams of seemingly minor incidents that gradually coalesce into a substantive drama.

At the start of *Rusty Bugles*, long-awaited relief troops have arrived in the camp—there were supposed to be hundreds, but only five turn up—including the well-spoken (that is, middle-class) Rod Carson. The world he enters might be made up of bits of past Australian plays. Like *Brumby Innes*, it is set in the Northern Territory; like *Men Without Wives*, it is an all-male environment; and like *Morning Sacrifice* it is a world of petty rules and regulations. The difference lies in the atmosphere, which is cheery despite the dreadful conditions in which the men live, fearful of 'the wet' (October to April), when the heat becomes unbearable and the humidity shoots up to 90 degrees. Like May Hallinan (*Brumby Innes*) and Mrs Abbot (*Men Without Wives*), Rod is a newbie from the south who must learn what life in the north is like. This involves mastering the tricks and dodges devised by a group of egalitarian-minded Australian soldiers to subvert the obdurate military hierarchy that attempts to control their lives. War, it is said, is long periods of boredom punctuated by brief moments of terror. In *Rusty Bugles*, the terror is left out, and for audiences in 1948 recovering from the horrors of global conflict, this would have been a welcome choice. By fashioning his play as a pastoral comedy, Locke Elliott can explore the themes of the war play while letting war itself fade into the background.

The most central theme is friendship, or in 1940s Australian parlance 'mateship'. The lack of a dominant narrative in *Rusty Bugles* allows a collation of eccentric individuals to swim into focus: the big-boned Gig Ape, whom the men wrestle to the ground on every occasion; the hyperactive Ot, forever into the latest fad; the older Keghead, always having his hat pulled from his head and trampled; and Andy Edwards, 'a minute little bloke but cocky with the deliberate assurance of the

The recreation hut in Rusty Bugles *from the 1948 Independent Theatre production. Michael Barnes as Ken Falcon, Ralph Peterson as Keghead Stephens, Lloyd Berrell as Darcy McClure, Ronald Frazer as Rod Carson, John Kingsmill as Des Nolan and Frank Curtain as Bill Henry. Like the Doll, Locke-Elliot's play toured extensively around Australia, although it did not travel overseas except to New Zealand (where its irreverent humour met a muted response).*

very small' (8). Camp life revolves around the Armco huts in which equipment is endlessly unloaded, itemised, then loaded up again; the recreation building, with its battered, out-of-tune piano and meagre selection of books; and night watch, where the soldiers guard stores in a land so vast and empty they wonder who could ever find them there, let alone steal anything.

Underneath the unvarying routine, life's not-so-little catastrophes continue: marriages collapse, leave is cancelled for the nth time, people go mad. Rod comes into conflict with another soldier, Vic, who takes against him from the beginning. One night, they are both on guard duty, and the reason for his hostility emerges:

ROD: What's the matter with you?
VIC: The way I feel about the whole place... about the army and life in general.
ROD: You mean you hate it.
VIC: I dunno that I hate it any more than I would be out of

it. But I'm just not one of those jokers that can make the best out of things that are just a racket—and the army's a racket. The whole war's a racket... same as anything else.

ROD: Same as everything?

VIC: Yep. I haven't had any chances like you.

ROD: I don't know that I've had so many chances.

VIC: Don't give me that. You've had a good education. I can tell that by the way you talk and the sort of things you read.

ROD: I don't know that education counts for much these days.

VIC: You've had a good job, haven't you? You're a writer aren't you? ...

ROD: What's your grudge? The world?

VIC: Far as I can see it's all a lot of empty damn promises. By the time we get out of this mess the jobs will be gone anyhow. You see, I've never really got anything out of it. I never got what I wanted out of the war. I never wanted to get stuck up in an Ordnance dump like this. My cobber is up at Lae right now getting stuck into the Japs... Two years here... two bloody years and I'm not even a returned soldier when it's over. (48–9)

From the date that Locke Elliott wrote these words to the opening of *The One Day of the Year* was less than a dozen years. Yet in the latter, it feels as if the war has already become an unwanted memory, a ghoul at the feast of modern Australia. Hughie Cook is a university student from a working-class background at a time when less than 2 per cent of the population went on to further education. His father, Alf, wounded at the Battle of Alamein, is an obsessive observer of Anzac Day, which in practice means getting blind drunk, behaving in a boastful way and attacking anyone who disagrees with his inflated view of himself and of Australian men. Not that Alf needs to be inebriated to do this. Peter Fitzpatrick calls him the archetypal Awful Australian, a figure Barry Humphries would remorselessly satirise in coming decades. Alf is a master of the rant—a form of speech that is decidedly unpleasant when it occurs in real life, but that can be a lot of fun on stage. He is opinionated, bigoted and crude. But his explosive jeremiads have undeniable bombastic power. Here is the one that closes the play:

ALF: I'm a bloody Australian and I'll always stand up for bloody Australia. I seen these jumped-up cows come and go, come and go, they don't mean a bloody thing, what did they ever do for the country, they never did nothing. It's the little man, he's the one goes out and gets slaughtered, we're the ones they get when the time comes, we're the ones, mugs, the lot us, mugs. He said that. He said it. Did my son say that? Did he say that about me and my mates? That's good men he's talking about, men who give their all, that's decent men. I'll show the little cow. Someone's gotta show these kids. I'll show him, I know what he thinks, I'm nothing, but I'll show him, I'll show the lot of 'em. I'm a bloody Australian and I'll always...(96)

Alf's rancour is a carbon copy of Vic's in *Rusty Bugles*, and his prejudiced speeches reflect what Fitzpatrick calls 'the representative terms of Hughie's dilemma'. The collision that occurs between father and son is not specific to the Cook family. It is symbolic of the dilemma facing the Australian nation as the Depression and World War II passed into the history books, with Hughie and his upper middle-class girlfriend, Jan, wanting to forget them, and Alf and his mates holding on to their memory because it defines their lives. Alf is a lift attendant. He operates an elevator in a department store, mechanically taking people to different floors, all day, every day. Hughie, by contrast, is studying for an economics degree and is upwardly mobile. Anyone familiar with the Reconstruction program will know that economics was the 'hot' discipline of the day, akin to software engineering or data science now. This creates a double bind for Alf and Hughie. Both want Hughie to study hard and do well. Yet the more he excels in a middle-class world, the further he drifts from his working-class roots.

Hughie is a keen photographer. Disgusted by the boozy antics of Anzac Day, he publishes a photo-article with Jan for their university newspaper showing the debacle the 'one day' has become. When Alf sees the article, he hits his son. But the generational conflict does not end there, because Hughie feels ambivalent about both his family and the war. On the one hand, Anzac Day is, in the words of the *Honi Soit* piece that inspired Seymour to write the play, 'a yearly pageant of national necrophilia' (16), the celebration of a military blunder and the human waste it involved. On the other hand, the march itself strikes Hughie as 'Serious as anything... sort of proud but... Not military. Not aggressive' (66).

Over the course of the play, Hughie veers between puzzled respect and noisy rejection of Anzac Day. His father's opinions can be set aside as the outbursts of a man who has not got what he hoped from life (and never will). But those of his mother, Dot, and Alf's best friend, Wacka, are not so easily dismissed. The unassuming Wacka fought at both Gallipoli and Alamein having 'put me age up to get into the First World War and down to get into the Second' (46). When a violent row splits the family, Wacka says little to Hughie, and nothing at all to Jan, whose class-based condescension he recoils from. But in a play full of words, it is the silent moments that count. An example is the early morning of Anzac Day in the Cook household. Alf has left for the dawn service. Hughie has refused to go and stayed in bed. Then,

> *Light fades in again, held down very softly. The sky behind the house has traces of pink through it. Very gradually it begins to lighten. In* HUGHIE's *bedroom some slight movement. He lights a cigarette, lies back, hand behind head. Then he flicks radio on. Its small light flows softly in the dark. Steps are heard approaching. The front door opens,* WACKA *is silhouetted against light from sky spilling through door. He comes in, leaving door open to give himself some light. Crosses to lounge windows, quietly pulls up blinds. Dawn light comes in. He looks around, moves quietly back to door. He is about to close it but a sudden quickening of light all through the sky stops him. He takes a step outside, looks up at the sky. It is dawn. He stands very still as though listening for something.* WACKA *turns, comes back to door. Stands another second or two then shrugs, laughs quietly to himself. But still he stands, looking out and up. There is absolute silence.*
>
> WACKA [*to himself, so quietly it can hardly be heard*]: It was now.
>
> *He stands still, remembering. And out of the silence comes, soft and distant, the sound of a trumpet playing* The Last Post. (61)

Irony and ambiguity supply the tone for *Rusty Bugles* and *The One Day of the Year*, just as they did for *Fountains Beyond*, *Morning Sacrifice* and *Lady in Danger*, the 1942 plays discussed in Chapter 3. Locke Elliott's soldiers endlessly attempt to escape their tedium-filled days on a 'leave draft'. Yet when Vic does get to go, he touches the side of his hut saying, 'It's going to seem sort of funny not having the old blokes around… the old bull going on at night' (84). When a squad of veteran soldiers returns to the camp unexpectedly, it is obvious everyone is extremely pleased to see each other. Ot, chronically depressed since receiving a Dear John letter from his fiancée, cheers up when faced with his old enemy, Mac. Underneath the constant complaining and swearing, the soldiers display a marked fragility and need for companionship.

At the other end of the spectrum, although Wacka condemns Hughie and Jan's article, his judgement of Anzac Day itself is equally damning: 'Ballyhoo. Photos in the papers. Famous. Not worth a crumpet' (73). He rejects both sides of the generational divide when he says to Alf, 'He's got a right to think and say what he likes. Any fightin' we ever did, you'n'me, in any wars, it was to give him that right. And if we don't agree with what he thinks—well, it's his world. We've had it. He's got it all ahead of him' (94–5).

Both Locke Elliott and Seymour deal with memory worlds. One way of looking at this is through the lens of gender. Jonathan Bollen and his co-authors offer some penetrating insights into the drama of the period. Noting that masculinity 'does not describe a reality but is a conflation of myths, stereotypes and caricatures', their book, *Men at Play: Masculinities in Australian Theatre Since the 1950s* (2008) aims to 'expos[e]… assumptions about Australian masculinity to public recognition'. These are the heroic-ideal ones of physical strength, resilience, willpower, self-control and mateship.

It is true that *Rusty Bugles*, *The One Day of the Year* and, as we will see, *Summer of the Seventeenth Doll* explore Australian masculinity in the so-called 'angry years' of the 1940s and 1950s when it was undergoing a crisis. But a focus on gender alone is not sufficient to grasp the meaning of these plays. In particular, it downplays the concept clearly uppermost in the minds of the playwrights who wrote them: social class. Class does make an appearance in *Men at Play*, but a lesser one, which reflects, perhaps, Australia in the twenty-first century. An exclusive concern with issues of gender and sexual identity obscures what was most striking for audiences at the time: that all three plays focus on working-class characters, investing them with a depth of feeling and a capacity for expression that in other nation's drama was reserved for middle-class ones. When the critic Ken Tynan reviewed the *Doll* in London in 1957 and wrote of its 'respect for ordinary people', he meant that it escaped Britain's rigid class assumptions. Fewer Australian playwrights see the world through a class lens now (Daniel Keene, Katherine Thomson, Debra Oswald, Angus Cerini and Patricia Cornelius being marked exceptions). *Rusty Bugles*, *The One Day of the Year* and the *Doll* challenge us to remember that a class-divided world is one in which the lives of rich and poor are very different.

The *Doll* is the one Australian play that a book on Australian drama can expect its readers to know—if they are Australian. The play has little presence outside the country, and this reflects not only the inferior status of postcolonial drama, where British classics are 'our' classics yet not the other way round, but also an ineluctable performance truth: that the Australian accent is hard for non-Australian actors to capture. Indeed, during the *Doll's* first rehearsals, Lawler worried that even Australian actors of his time, usually asked to adopt 'RP' (Received Pronunciation, a British accent variant) had forgotten how to sound like Australians on stage. Nor was this the only barrier to his play's success. The fact that it was a prize-winning drama meant nothing. Most thought the shoebox was its likely destination. Once programmed, no-one imagined the play would run beyond its two-week graveyard October slot. An inner-city milieu was unusual for an Australian play, and designer Anne Fraser's Carlton terrace set, which looks quaintly old-fashioned now, was confronting in its urban realism in 1955.

Yet on opening night something unexpected happened. Niall Brennan, manager of the Union Theatre where *Ned Kelly* had been staged 12 years before, and Jack Hibberd's *White with Wire Wheels* would be staged 12 years later, recalled:

Some strange conversion took place in the minds of the Australian theatregoers… and I remember saying to one of the usherettes…. 'I think this play is going to be a *great* success'. None of us could understand it. The jinx [on Australian plays] had just gone. They clapped the house curtain when it went up, and they clapped the set. They clapped every actor who came on and the roars which greeted Ray's own entrance were tremendous. When the curtain came down at the end, the theatre almost shook… It was the first Union Theatre Repertory play ever to play to an extended season. They took it to Sydney, then on Australian tour, then booked it into London. They sold the film rights to an American organisation. Ray stood, puzzled but pleased, in the floodtide of royalties. I met him shortly before they left for London. He was wearing a new suit. I said to him 'Ray, be careful lest all this go to your head. Success is a transient thing.' He replied with a grin 'I know. Seventeen dolls don't make a Summer.'

The plot of the *Doll* need be only briefly sketched. Roo and Barney are two Queensland cane-cutters who have been coming down to Melbourne for the off-season, the 'lay off', for 16 years (anchoring the backstory in 1938, the world of *Men Without Wives*). Here they meet up with Olive and Nancy to blow their money and enjoy the high life before returning to back-breaking labour up north as winter comes.

The nature of the relationship between the four characters is what an older generation would have called 'unconventional'—that is, the couples are not married. It says a great deal about 1950s Australia that this aspect of the play was accepted by its audiences as unsensational. A flight to Melbourne had also become routine. In *Fountains Beyond*, there is one reference to an aeroplane, but boat is the usual mode of interstate transport. In the *Doll*, Hughie Cook's modern Australia has arrived, with its readily available entertainments and its loosening of morals and behaviour (so Esson's Miss Perkins and Cusack's Miss Kingsbury would think). How meaningful is this material abundance, or this endless cornucopia of gaiety and fun? It is easy to imagine Roo and Barney as two of Locke Elliott's soldiers. They are the same generation, the same class, the same mix of pride and need. And while they do not rant like Alf, give them a few more years and they might start.

Like *Rusty Bugles* and *The One Day of the Year*, the world of the *Doll* is haunted by the memory of Depression and the war, voiced directly in the play by Emma, Olive's tight-fisted, clear-eyed mother. The fleetingness of health, wealth and happiness is not confined to particular characters, however, but is stamped on every moment of the action as through a stick of Brighton rock. This is what makes the *Doll's* ending so crushingly complete. Every line in the dialogue points to what Elizabethan playwrights called 'mutability' as the truth of human existence, the sense of loss that postwar Australia was both conscious of and determined to forget.

Before the start of the play, Nancy has left the couples' unconventional arrangement to marry a bookseller. Her place is taken by Pearl, who looks and sounds like a 1950s version of Betty Roland's Mrs Davidson. Pearl is to pair off with the silver-tongued Barney, while Olive continues her longstanding romance with taciturn Roo. But nothing goes right. Roo, 'ganger' of a squad of cane-cutters, has fallen out with them over their newest recruit, Johnny Dowd, whose youthful strength is a challenge to his top-dog status. In the play we learn that while in Queensland, Roo engaged in an unwise test of cane-cutting prowess with Dowd, and lost. As Olive, Pearl, Barney and Roo vainly try to recapture the love and glory of past lay-offs, the squad arrive in Melbourne, lurching from pub to racetrack while trying to arrange a reconciliation between Roo and Dowd. The compelling mood continues to deteriorate, however. At the end of Act 2, Barney and Roo have a fight (a 'blue') when it emerges that Roo lost the cane-cutting test not because of a bad back, as he previously claimed, but simply because of his age. The exchange between the two men is heavy with self-loathing:

> ROO: Did you hear that? No strain, nothin'. Dowd did a better job than me because he's a better man than I am…
>
> *He shoves* BARNEY *forcibly from him and the smaller man spins around on the floor, grasping his arm and crying out from an indefinable sense of loss and repentance.*

BARNEY: You damned fool—do you think I would have told them?

ROO: Well, it's about time they knew what they was dealin' with anyway, a coupla lousy no-hopers! Yeh—you, the great lover that's never had a knock back. Tell 'em how lucky you've been lately –

BARNEY [*almost pleading*]: Don't, Roo.

ROO: This is gunna be good! How about the two waitresses at the Greek café?

BARNEY: I never went near them…

ROO: You did, they told me. And laughed fit to kill themselves. A fine performance that must have been!

BARNEY: They lied about it…

ROO: Yeh? And I s'pose Mrs Kelly lied when she had you thrown out of the Royal pub? 'N' the cook at Adam's, she was lyin', and the little New Australian woman, and Skinny Linton's missus. All of them lying, and you're still the best there is—like hell you are!

BARNEY [*tearing himself free, blazing*]: That's enough, Roo.

ROO [*towering above him*]: And Nancy—after seventeen years, you couldn't even hold Nancy!

BARNEY: You dirty rotten swine! (100)

Act 3, however, set the morning after the blue, is the source of the *Doll*'s indelible power. Olive has taken down all but one of the kewpie dolls that decorated the terrace house walls, and Pearl is leaving for good. As Emma chides Roo for the chaos of the previous night, Barney arrives. Roo announces he has made an important decision: he will not go north for the next season, but will stay in Melbourne. When Olive appears, he offers her what he thinks she has always desired: marriage. But to his astonishment—and ours—this is not what Olive wants at all. She wants the one thing no-one, certainly not Roo, can give her: the past back again, the undoing of their 16-year affair. 'You give it back to me—you give me back what you've taken…' (125), she screams at Roo. In the profound shock of his new awareness, Roo destroys the seventeenth doll, 'smashing and tearing at it until it is nothing but a litter of broken cane, tinsel and celluloid' (128). The play ends with Barney leading his mate away saying 'Come on, Roo. Come on, boy' (128), to a future where the halcyon days of the lay-off are forever gone.

The incendiary force of the *Doll's* ending elevates it from well-constructed realism to full-blown tragedy. It rests on Lawler's choice of a key playwriting device. In a narrative drama, playwrights typically drive the action forwards with the mechanisms of revelation and reversal. These were identified by Aristotle in *Poetics*, the first book on dramaturgy, in 335 BCE. A revelation (*anagnorisis*) is a disclosure of previously unknown information that changes our understanding of a play in the present. Examples in the *Doll* include the revelation that Roo fled Queensland to escape Dowd, that Barney's sexual charms have waned, and that Nancy foresaw the end of the lay-off arrangement when she left to get married.

A reversal (*peripeteia*) has a deeper impact. It changes not only our grasp of the present, but our view of the past as well, by showing that what we assumed to be the case is not actually true. Finding out that Olive's affair with Roo is over is not a reversal. Discovering their whole relationship is a lie, that the golden times Olive tried to persuade Pearl existed were, in Pearl's words, 'a day-dream' (104), is a toppling insight that turns the world of the *Doll* upside down. The reality Lawler's characters have carefully built up, year by year, memory by memory, collapses like a dynamited building. This is what makes live drama such a potent mode of inquiry. It puts on stage not just the depiction of loss, but the experience of it. Exposed to the same negative epiphany as Olive and Roo, we, the audience, have no option but to feel their pain as well.

A final observation about *Rusty Bugles*, *The One Day of the Year* and the *Doll*: they each made the media headlines, becoming part of Australian history in their own right. In the case of the first two plays, this involved a struggle with censorship. The profane language of the original *Rusty Bugles* script was watered down for its 1948 production, yet even the restored 1984 version is a pale reflection of what Locke Elliott likely heard while on military service and pre-emptively kept out of his dialogue. *The One Day of the Year* was due to open at the first Adelaide Festival. After word escaped about its controversial content, however, it was forced out of the program by a clique of conservative Festival governors and the backstairs influence of the Returned and Services League. The *Doll* met a different reception, feted from the moment it opened. Even so, it did not lead to a significant improvement in opportunities for Australian playwrights. This is demonstrated by the careers of the three writers after their plays opened. By 1961, all three had left the country.

Enter the 'Other'

In the *Concise History of Australia*, Macintyre discusses Australia's postwar migration program. It was a massive venture, not easy for the country to undertake—or for a Labor government, long committed to restricting immigration to white and British (or at least Anglo-Celtic) subjects, to implement. Arthur Calwell, the first federal Minister for Immigration, ordered the deportation of wartime refugees in 1947 and uttered the infamous words 'Two Wongs do not make a White'. 'Yet it was Calwell who coined the term "new Australian" to encourage the assimilation of unfamiliar newcomers', writes Macintyre. 'He set a target of a 2 per cent annual increase in the current population of 7.5 million, half of which was to be contributed by new arrivals'. Most of them were from non-English-speaking countries in Europe. By the end of the 1960s, together with their children, they had driven Australia's population up to more than 12 million. The narrow goal of assimilation rather than integration, though, remained in place:

> 'Our aim', Arthur Calwell had laid down… 'is to Australianise all our migrants… in as short a time as possible'. Although his Liberal successors relaxed the opposition to foreign-language newspapers and ethnic organisations, that aim continued. 'We can only achieve our goal through migration', the new minister declared, 'if our newcomers quickly become Australian in outlook and way of life'. On the ships, in the holding centres and migrant hostels, in English-language classes and naturalisation ceremonies, through 'Good Neighbour' committees and other voluntary bodies, they were

introduced to an Australian way of life that was open to all. The depiction of Australia as a sophisticated, urban, consumer society had clear Cold War implications… A gap between expectation and reality was there from the beginning.

Our next four plays, Mona Brand's *Here Under Heaven*, Oriel Gray's *Sky Without Birds*, Richard Beynon's *The Shifting Heart* and Ric Throssell's *The Day Before Tomorrow,* all deal with outsiders coming into a closed social order and threatening its dominance and collective identity. In the first, a Chinese war bride, in the second a Jewish refugee, in the third a family of Italian immigrants, and in the last Australians as their future selves, provide the impetus for a protracted struggle around acceptance and social inclusion. But these struggles do not originate with the 'Other'. Rather the different perspectives they bring expose pre-existing tensions that have previously been hidden. Their hostile receptions prompt heartfelt discussion which, after some retrograde steps, brings about broader change. That is, not only does the Other meet with greater tolerance and respect, but the 'real Australians', initially unfriendly, indifferent or rejecting, are liberated from their fears and prejudicial views. In the words of Martin Luther King, the plays hew out of the mountain of despair a stone of hope. Even *The Day Before Tomorrow*, unrelentingly bleak as befits a post-apocalyptic drama, ends with the possibility of human redemption.

On a professional level, the narratives of these four plays are unsatisfactory in many ways. They end abruptly (*Here Under Heaven*), sentimentally (*Sky Without Birds*, *The Shifting Heart*) or melodramatically (*The Day Before Tomorrow*). They are monothematic, exploring a single underlying idea, and have a one-act-drama feel, even when they use a three-act format (*The Shifting Heart*). Two are by New Theatre playwrights (*Here Under Heaven*, *Sky Without Birds*) and contain slabs of socialist proselytising designed to be uplifting, but that come across now as dull and sanctimonious. It is as if Australian playwrights, having mastered the craft of telling stories about Australian characters, must learn anew what is involved in telling them about anyone else. For this reason, the plays are less likely to be revived than *Rusty Bugles*, *The One Day of the Year* or the *Doll*. Yet their significance is greater than their production history suggests. For if the population of Australia was expanding, so too was the population of Australian drama. Without abandoning the bush completely, these four plays show an array of alternative settings. Let's briefly compare them:

Here Under Heaven:

> *Mingana, a sheep station in Southern Queensland. The room is simply but solidly furnished. A staircase leads to bedrooms. There are lounge chairs, a cocktail cabinet, a small table and reading lamp, a telephone. On one wall is a painting in oils of a pioneer, John Hamilton.*

Sky Without Birds:

> *The [Koorora] post office... beside the railway line across the Nullarbor Desert... small and built of fibro. A low counter runs along the left side and continues, L-shaped, along the back wall. About halfway along the wall, it stops short and gives place to a door, which opens onto a section of verandah.*

The Shifting Heart:

> *Collingwood, which once composed most of the early city of Melbourne and since has steadily decomposed. The last of a terrace row... The yard is untidy with a large garbage can down L[eft]... The whole is bound tightly by two paling fences—one on either side of the stage.... A side-entrance runs upstage and out of sight to the front of the house.*

The Day Before Tomorrow:

> *The Jacksons' home... The walls are smoke-blackened and torn from top to bottom by a great jagged crack. Strips of plaster hang from the ceiling. Part of the window has been blasted in, leaving a ragged edge of brickwork. Outside there is a panorama of utter devastation, the ruins of a residential suburb.*

More (and different) people, in more (and different) places, providing the occasion for more varied drama.

'Art is a weapon', the New Theatre slogan. With its streamline black and white design and forceful representation of muscular power, this company poster fuses a Modernist aesthetic with a Marxist belief in the heroic role of the working class. It is an emancipative vision of the working class that disappears almost entirely from Australian drama after 1990.

If *Here Under Heaven*, *Sky Without Birds*, *The Shifting Heart* and *The Day Before Tomorrow* seem outdated now, their action clunky and tame, this was not the case when they were first staged. Their impact lay not only in what they showed directly, but in the implied claim for wider scope for *all* Australian plays. This was especially true at the New Theatre. Its commitment to revolutionary Marxism and the class struggle meant its productions were often interventions in fiery political debates. Until the 1970s, the company's work was subject to legal repression by those in power who feared what would happen if its 'subversive' views were aired. This is another aspect of the struggle of Australian theatre against censorship. Because live performance involves a live crowd, and these are capable of direct action, the line can blur between the world of the stage and the world of the street—as this anecdote from a 1936 New Theatre production demonstrates:

> *Till the Day I Die* [was] an anti-Nazi play first performed in Sydney. The German Consul General in Australia protested to the federal government who, through the NSW Chief Secretary, banned the play from performance. The group revived *Waiting for Lefty* for the first half of the programme then proceeded to perform an 'un-named play'. The police who were there in force attempted to stop the play mid-scene, whereupon the audience were asked directly 'Do you want to see this show?' 'Yes!' they shouted, and the play proceeded without interruption. Even more amazing scenes occurred in Melbourne [where]… all halls and theatres had been instructed that the play was not to be shown on their premises. There was a storm of protest that hit the front pages. Finally, the Mayor of Collingwood found a loophole and granted the use of the Town Hall on the grounds of it being a private club performance: a crowd of around three thousand people turned out for it, along with hundreds of policemen. Some club! … Three years later the Australian government was declaring war on the country whose reputation and ruler it had taken such pains to avoid offending.

The stories of *Here Under Heaven*, *Sky Without Birds*, *The Shifting Heart* and *The Day Before Tomorrow* all develop in a similar way. A location is established and a situation, ripe with tension before the action begins, is discovered. In *Here Under Heaven*, set in 1942, the upper-class Hamilton family are about to celebrate the centenary of their ownership of the land they violently settled. Mrs Hamilton—like Mrs Davidson in *The Touch of Silk* before her, and Mrs Dawson in *Inside the Island* to come (see Chapter 6)—is an upholder of traditional values. These are race, class and gender based. All are challenged when it is revealed her eldest son has married a Singaporean Chinese woman, her second son has fathered a child by a local Indigenous woman, and her third has fallen in love with a Land Army 'jillaroo' from a humble background. In *Sky Without Birds*, set in 1952, a German Jewish refugee who has survived the horrors of a Nazi concentration camp, arrives in a remote Western Australian town to work as railway engineer. His appearance sets off a chain of events that puncture the insularity, immaturity and inertia of the local inhabitants. In *The Shifting Heart*, set in 1957, the Bianchis, a family of Italian migrants, meet with hostility from their inner-city working-class neighbours, in part because they think these New Australians will take their jobs, in part because they are just different. As the Bianchi children, Gino and Maria, try to assimilate to Australian life, a tragedy reveals the deep prejudice they daily confront. Finally, in *The Day Before Tomorrow*, set in a catastrophic future, Australia has 'othered' itself. In a cordoned-off city that nuclear war has reduced to rubble, the diseased inhabitants have turned savage, determined to survive at any cost. They are seen by those living beyond the cordon as little better than animals. As a result, that is how they behave. The challenge for an audience is to recognise that the Jacksons, a 'real Australian' family, have become refugees in their own country.

The foreign characters in the four plays leave a lot to be desired. They are little more than stereotypes. In the 1970s, in the hands of New Wave artists challenging the predicates of stage realism, 'the stereotype' became a sophisticated dramatic device (see Chapter 5). But Lola Hamilton (*Here Under Heaven*), Heinrich Schafer (*Sky Without Birds*) and Pappa and Momma Bianchi (*The Shifting Heart*) do not belong in this superior class. In her introduction to the 2007 republication of *Sky Without Birds* and *The Day Before Tomorrow*, Katharine Brisbane comments, 'The plays… were just too early to embrace [overseas] innovations in form, but do reflect the accelerated aspiration to play a more sophisticated part in the affairs of the English-speaking world…

It is notable... how little vernacular there is in these plays, compared with the language of the first flush of AETT plays' (vi).

These are fair observations, and fit *Here Under Heaven* too. The dialogue in all the plays is serviceable at best. But it would be wrong to compare them too harshly with *Rusty Bugles*, *The One Day of the Year* or the *Doll*. They are interested in other things. This becomes obvious when looking at the Australian characters in them, who, far from being one-dimensional, are sophisticated creations. An interesting and important fact is that, out of the 37 characters in all four plays, only two are unsympathetically drawn. The other 35 characters are complex individuals grappling with divided loyalties and difficult decisions. It is here that these works make their original contribution, and further illustrate how drama is a mode of inquiry into a nation's collective life.

Let me take *Here Under Heaven* as an example. Mona Brand's Mrs Amelia Hamilton, the mother-matriarch of the family, is described in terms near-identical to Dymphna Cusack's Miss Kingsbury: '*She is fifty, proud, stately and well-dressed. A kindly woman by her own standards, she is, however, somewhat humourless*' (148). Over the course of the action which spans two days, Mrs Hamilton behaves in an appalling way. Her eldest son, John, who is fighting in Singapore, has smuggled his wife out to safety in Australia. But when Lola arrives at Mingana, '*a good-looking Chinese woman, dressed in the type of Cheon Sam worn in Singapore just before the war*' (167), Mrs Hamilton does all she can to hide her presence there, and tries to move her on to Brisbane as soon as possible.

An Aboriginal camp has set up on the family property, near the river that continues to run despite the ongoing drought. Mrs Hamilton demands that Richard, her third son, and Reynolds, the overseer of the station, drive them away. When they flatly refuse, saying it would be tantamount to murder, she refuses to have one of the camp's sick children in her home. This, it turns out, is the daughter of her second son, Peter, and his Indigenous lover, a relationship she deliberately broke up, forcing Peter into a sterile marriage with Iris, a feckless heiress.

Finally, she keeps Richard, crippled in one leg by a bout of polio, from having a life of his own, though he is nominally 'the man of the house' (200). When Richard shows an interest in the jillaroo, Jill Ramsay, his mother is rude, condescending and dismissive towards her, making her class prejudices plain. In respect of her *behaviour*, then, Mrs Hamilton seems a villain, someone who thwarts the happiness of those around her in pursuit of the family 'honour', which is little better than a glossed-over story of a vicious colonial land-grab.

But Mrs Hamilton has a different side to her. She is a loving mother, bossy but far from overbearing. She treats the household servant, Rosie, with exasperated tolerance. She cares deeply about her 14-year-old daughter, Helen, and struggles with 'the generation gap' Seymour later made his focus of attention in *The One Day of the Year*. She worries constantly about her sons. She is never deliberately cruel, but is limited by the values she thinks she should uphold, despite the fact that they no longer reflect the changing world around her. Though driven by fears she cannot articulate, she is more than the sum of those fears.

The contrast between who Mrs Hamilton *is*, potentially, and what she *does*, in actuality, is the piston driving the play forward. It comes to a point of contradiction after Lola is revealed to be pregnant. By this time, Peter's Indigenous child has died, and Helen has witnessed the death. Mrs Hamilton has blood on her hands, if indirectly. The compelling mood is one of guilt and remorse. The stage direction reads: '*At the news of the child's death,* RICHARD *has moved from the window and now tries to look at his mother, but she avoids his glance, fussing about the room, collecting papers, patting cushions etc.*' (203).

Lola, coming from nursing the child in the shearing shed, now delivers the news Mrs Hamilton has been dreading: John has been killed fighting in Singapore. She leaves Mrs Hamilton to read a last letter written by him. It says, 'Tell mother not to fret about me. Tell her that I love her dearly. Tell her that to no-one else in the world would I entrust the precious burden of my wife. Her heart is so big that there will be room there for you too. You might find the outside world strangely unfriendly at first—we're still rather backward about race questions in Australia, I'm afraid—but you will find a home and shelter at Mingana' (208). With this description of her potential self delivered thus by her dead son, Mrs Hamilton changes for the better.

The last line of the play is: 'My mind is clear. I must do what John says. I must go to Lola. She may be needing me' (208).

Here Under Heaven demonstrates the difference between melodrama (or, in television, 'soap opera') and drama. As with narrative, so with character: while the former works *to* a formula, the latter works *with* one. Mrs Hamilton is, in part, a representative social type. The audience comes to the theatre with expectations about her already in place. Perhaps they recognise her 'type' from other plays (*The Touch of Silk*, *Morning Sacrifice*) or from the world outside the theatre. But she is also an individual creation with a unique outlook—what Elizabethan actors called 'personation'. This means she cannot be 'read off' entirely against type, but within the confines of the play, has a degree of freedom. As a consequence, an audience must engage with her in an active way as the story unfolds. They cannot presume her course is set because each decision she faces could go either way, reflecting the interplay between the expectations raised by her social type, and the fact that she has an individual life of her own. Nor will audiences passively wait for Mrs Hamilton's decision-making to reach an end point. They will infer from the decisions she does make, the ones she *should* or *could* make, forming judgements about her intelligence, capacities and level of responsibility.

Plays like *Here Under Heaven* therefore go beyond the literal information contained within them, joining with spectators' imaginations to create a new horizon of intellectual and emotional response. Mrs Hamilton is not a villain. She *behaves* in a villainous way but, given a final opportunity to mend her ways, she takes it. Mona Brand develops her in such a way that her ultimate redemption is coded into the foregoing action (in other words, she is a sympathetic character). The play asks us to remain focussed on the different decisions from which, at any moment, she might choose. This will be a different mental experience for each spectator. Yet it will also be something an audience does together, noting common reactions and the compelling mood on stage. In this respect, we can say that drama is a creative act accomplished as much by those watching a play, as by the artists presenting it.

What is true of *Here Under Heaven* is true of *Sky Without Birds* and *The Shifting Heart*: an ocean of decisions is revealed through which the characters must plot a course as hazardous as any Odysseus faced returning to the island of Ithaca. In *Sky Without Birds*, Heinrich is attracted to Nereia O'Hara, wife of Rick O'Hara, the union shop steward. They have an affair, and Heinrich becomes the target of local animosities, fomented by a quasi-Nazi shopkeeper (one of the two non-sympathetic characters in these four plays). Rick's reaction to his wife's infidelity is 'against type', however. He tolerates and understands it, as she is younger than him. What he does *not* do is forgive Nereia because, as he explains to her when he thinks she is leaving with Heinrich, 'It's your choice—it's your right. Everyone's choice is their right' (141). In the event, Nereia stays with Rick, realising her marriage is a 'real, practical love' (p141), and finding a new maturity that parallels the emotional growth of the community around her.

In *The Shifting Heart*, the learning curve is steeper. Maria is married to Clarry Fowler, a 'real Australian' of conventional type who employs her brother Gino in his scrap metal business. When Gino is stabbed at a local dance, Maria blames her husband's underlying reluctance to be seen working with 'a dago… a wop' (36) and, by implication, being married to her. Clarry is easygoing, affable, humorous and unreflective—a kindred spirit to Lawler's Barney. He is also emotionally withheld, and in Poppa Bianchi's eyes not a complete person because he can't, or won't, cry. When Gino dies from his wounds, Maria rounds on Clarry in words as searing in their naked anger now as when they were first uttered in 1957: 'Take your hands… let me go… go… let me… take your… you killed him… KILLED HIM. YOU… KILLED… HIM' (81). Clarry is held accountable for the racism and violence of the postwar Australia through which he obliviously moves. Overwhelmed by his feelings at the savage physical attack on Gino, and the savage verbal attack on himself, Clarry's heart does indeed 'shift'. His habitual emotional distance gives way first to outrage, then bewilderment, then awareness that immigrants are 'the same as us; bad makes the mistakes, who pays? It's the good, same as us. You hear? Just THE SAME AS US!' (104). The stage direction reads: '*Now the full realization of this last statement strikes home*'.

Ric Throssell's *The Day Before Tomorrow* would seem to depart from a concern with character agency. What could be less amenable to human will than the after-effects of nuclear devastation? The lives of the Jackson family—Alan, the hapless, once-bookish father, Mary, the anxious, dying mother, and Carolyn, the cunning, amoral daughter, who prostitutes herself for food—appear locked in a downward spiral of depravity and starvation. The few people confined in the radioactive Urban Zone are mad, despairing and prone to violence. What social types exist to judge such characters by? What decisions can these victims-cum-monsters possibly make?

The answer lies in the masterstroke that opens the play. Alan Jackson's memory is defective. Each morning when he wakes, he has forgotten all about his grim, dystopian existence and believes he is in the normal world. He must discover again—along with the audience, who are equally ignorant—the ruin that nuclear conflict has wrought. Prior to nuclear catastrophe, the Jacksons were a typical Australian family. The play explores what happens when they fail terribly in the expectations of their own behaviour. A Relief Committee visits the Urban Zone, distributing much-needed food but treating with suspicion the people they are charged to help. These fears seem justified when it is discovered that Carolyn helped three desperate youths to break into a store on the perimeter and half kill a guard in the process. Misunderstanding compounds with the murder of a member of the Relief Committee, and Carolyn is accidentally shot by one of the accompanying soldiers.

As the play ends, Alan is left with the knowledge that the grief he feels at hearing of his daughter's death he will feel again and again, as each morning he forgets what happened the day before. In 1956, with the Cold War between the United States and the Soviet Union at its height, both with large arsenals of nuclear weapons trained on each other, and British nuclear tests happening at Maralinga in South Australia (dramatised in the 2020 ABC series *Operation Buffalo*), Throssell's challenge to his audience is stark: decide for nuclear disarmament today or risk the fate of the Jacksons tomorrow.

The achievements of *Here Under Heaven*, *Sky Without Birds*, *The Shifting Heart* and *The Day After Tomorrow* are not singular, pertaining to these plays and none others. They created new norms and possibilities for future drama. This is because, thematically, plays tend to cluster. Anyone who has wondered why Netflix has, at any one time, so many quirky murder mysteries or bromances will have witnessed the murmuration that occurs in dramatic writing. When characters are created, they join an ecology of general types that expands exponentially if, as is the case with the four plays here, these are subject to intensive creative exploration. Playwrights coming later thus find at their disposal new repositories of dramatic expectation—new character types—that they can reproduce, subvert, spin, deflect or supplement.

This is why it is not only at the level of narrative we should focus our attention if we want to understand why the Australian repertoire sticks together as a collective body of work. Language, image, compelling mood, ideas and arguments and, above all, character, provide stage plays with depth and dimensionality. We know without requiring further proof of it that the same story can be told in different ways. Viewed as a mode of inquiry, narrative is the carrier of meaning in a drama but not the prime generator of it, which is the job of other elements. Mrs Hamilton, Nereia O'Hara, Clarry Fowler and Alan Jackson are therefore more than additions to a 'who's who in the (Australian theatre) zoo'. They are points of navigation in the moral imagination and artistic purposes of our national drama as a whole.

5
1961–1975: Not better, just different

A Cheery Soul **(1963)**. *Private Yuk Objects* **(1966)**. *The Legend of King O'Malley* **(1970)**. *Norm and Ahmed* **(1967)**. *The Chapel Perilous* **(1972)**. *Don's Party* **(1972)**. *A Stretch of the Imagination* **(1972)**. *The Floating World* **(1974)**. *The Cake Man* **(1975)**. *Crossfire* **(1975)**.

> Common forms are continually breaking into brilliant shapes. If we will explore them.
>
> Patrick White, *Riders in the Chariot*

In 1965, Katharine Brisbane became the first, and to date only, national critic in Australian theatre. Given a generous travel allowance by her employer, *The Australian* newspaper, she was able to fly from city to city seeing a range of shows that other reviewers—HG (Harry) Kippax at the *Sydney Morning Herald*, Geoffrey Hutton at Melbourne's *Age*, Peter Ward at the *Adelaide Review*—could not. In 1971, together with her husband, theatre academic and dramaturge Philip Parsons, she established the first performing arts publishing house in Australia, Currency Press. It was directly associated with the explosion of New Wave plays being staged by large and small theatre companies around the country. To many, it felt that the cultural cringe was at last fading. Describing the changed status of Australian drama in 1971, Brisbane called it 'not wrong, just different' (later, the title of her book on theatre criticism). It was a phrase that signposted a fork in the road. Henceforward, Australian drama would be an independent entity, beholden to its own values and expectations. Its relationship to drama happening overseas would be one of creative equality. No longer would London and New York set the *desiderata* of artistic success; or at least not in the same way. Australia (however defined) and Australians (whoever they might be) would be the focus of Australian drama.

Brisbane's words captured the surging confidence of the theatre scene around her at the time. From this has arisen the common view that awareness of cultural difference liberated Australian artists in the 1960s and 1970s from the oppressive colonial relationship that hobbled their predecessors. With the New Wave another beginning was begun; this time, a *real* beginning. It is here that the upgrade model of culture unhelpfully asserts itself. For it is easy to look back on the six decades of Australian theatre after Federation and imagine one sees an overarching teleology, to think that, unconsciously, it was laying the ground for the theatre that came afterwards. The purpose of pre-1960 drama is post-1960 drama, which is more creative, more courageous and more compelling—in a word 'better'—in comparison. Past Australian plays may be interesting historical artefacts, but they are of limited dramatic use.

The problem with this view is that it is half right. There *is* a sense of progress flowing across different time periods of Australian drama, an arc of growth in its creation and delivery (albeit, one susceptible to challenge). A national repertoire does evolve as a holistic body of work if it excavates a larger space of imaginative possibility and adds new features and formats. But this is a separate issue from applying a retrospective notion of excellence, ignoring the lifeworlds from which plays arise and for which they were originally intended. So this chapter starts with a rejig of Brisbane's memorable words, and a warning: Australian drama after 1960 is not *better* than the drama examined so far, just *different* from it.

Inevitably, this clashes with the claims some New Wave artists made to ground-breaking originality. History puts a check on totalising opinion. Judgements about stage plays are not entirely relative, but they are always particular. Inarguably, Australia advanced as a nation after 1960. It became a more self-aware, open-minded, inclusive and energetic society. Yet there were parts of its collective life where that did not happen, parts that even went backwards. The phrase 'New

Wave' declares a radical cultural caesura that was widely accepted by the Australian theatre of the time. This declaration must be treated with caution. It may be a guide to how artists *felt* about the past, but it is not a guide to the past itself, especially for a country so prone to gaps in its collective memory. We must not confuse a changing nation with an improving one. The hubris of the upgrade model of culture reduces awareness of this vital distinction. Australian plays after 1960 must be treated in context—the same way I have treated Australian plays before 1960.

What, then, is the context for this chapter? Each year brings a clutch of notable events, but 1961 seems particularly fateful. In January, JF Kennedy was sworn in as the youngest ever American president; South Africa left the Commonwealth to pursue its policies of aggressive racial segregation ('apartheid'); and Adolf Eichmann, the SS officer in charge of the Auschwitz concentration camp during World War II, went on trial in Jerusalem for crimes against humanity. In April, the Soviet Union put the first man into space, Yuri Gagarin, for a flight lasting 108 minutes; in Cuba, armed exiles failed in a bid to overthrow Fidel Castro's Marxist government in the invasion of the Bay of Pigs; and Portuguese Angola and French Algeria erupted in rebellion against their European colonial rulers. In June, the man who gave the world the term 'the collective unconscious', Swiss psychoanalyst Carl Jung, died; the Soviet ballet star Rudolf Nureyev defected to the West while transferring flights at a French airport; and Berlin, a city politically divided into Russian and Allied zones of control since 1945, was physically split by the erection of a giant, militarised wall. In December, the United States established a Commission of the Status of Women that found widespread discrimination against women in every walk of contemporary life.

In Australia, a bill to give full voting rights to Indigenous Australians, sponsored by the Deputy Leader of the Opposition, Gough Whitlam, failed in the Upper House, while the Coalition government won another a term of office—but only just, kept in power by the support of the anti-communist Democratic Labor Party. 'Rocket Rod' Laver won the Wimbledon men's tennis singles finals in a record 56 minutes, Tulloch became the first Australian racehorse to earn more than

£100,000, and Miss Joan Barry, age 26, pleaded not guilty to offensive behaviour for wearing a bikini on Bondi Beach. The *Chronicle of the Twentieth Century* is a fount of facts like these, although it was not always the ones making headlines that turn out to be the most fateful. On 22 December, specialist James Davis became the first American soldier to be killed in Vietnam. The United States stood on the brink of war with the Viet Cong. Therefore so did Australia, its willing ally.

The year 1961 may not be one of signal transformation for Australian theatre, but it is important for two reasons. First, Patrick White's *The Ham Funeral*—kept out of the Adelaide Festival, like *The One Day of the Year* before it, by a risk-averse board of governors—received ten performances at the Adelaide University Theatre Guild. The following year White's *The Season at Sarsaparilla* premiered, the year after that, *A Cheery Soul*, and in 1964, *Night on Bald Mountain*.

These four plays mark the entry of Australia's then most famous fiction writer into theatre. They represent a turn away from the naturalism that had dominated Australian drama in the interwar and postwar years, and they attracted some influential supporters: anti-censorship campaigner and publisher Max Harris, author and Australian cultural historian Geoffrey Dutton and, most importantly, Harry Kippax. Even by the high standards of twentieth-century theatre criticism, Kippax is an outstanding contributor. His introduction to Penguin's iconic *Three Australian Plays* and his *Meanjin* article 'Australian Drama Since *Summer of the Seventeenth Doll*' are two impressive long-form essays on the development of Australian drama. In these, Kippax outlined an alternative path for the national repertoire, one that eschewed realism in favour of more imaginative approaches. This entailed situating Australian playwriting in a historical vista looking less to Britain and America for creative inspiration, than to Europe and its parade of bold, modernist theatre innovators—playwrights like Maurice Maeterlinck (symbolism), Ernst Toller (expressionism), Federico García Lorca (surrealism), Bertolt Brecht (epic theatre), and Eugene Ionesco (absurdism). For Kippax, White is the first Australian dramatist in this mould. While he is respectful of plays like the *Doll* and *The One Day of the Year*, he saw Australian theatre's future as lying with White's experimentalism. He was both right and wrong. Realism was to remain an important and flexible genre for Australian playwrights. But from 1960 onwards, it was increasingly joined by other dramatic styles.

This points to a second noteworthy occurence, one exemplified by the new imaginative space White's four dramas carved out: the very idea of what a play could be started to expand. Those familiar with the diversity of 1960s and 1970s theatre might wonder where its fecundity sprang from. Despite Kippax's desire to recast Australian drama within the trajectory of European modernism, it manifestly did not come from overseas. Nor did the talents of Australian playwrights increase *sui generis*. While both these things occurred to some degree, they do not explain the force of the national eruption.

Perhaps the best way to conceive of the change is to recall that drama is a fusion of two art forms: literature and live performance. Until the mid-1950s, the controlling perspective (and the status) lay with literature. Esson, Roland, Cusack, Stewart and Gray were *writers* first and foremost, and held a literary conception of drama that JC Williamson, rightly or wrongly, considered unappealing to Australian audiences. After 1960 this changed. A 'turn' to the performative meant not only new sorts of plays, but a new understanding of how to create them. This had profound implications, as many of the elements that seemed indissolubly linked to drama as an art form—narrative, character and language—were peeled away to reveal a more fundamental theatrical charge. Plays are written to be performed, and performance is the ultimate measure of a play's meaning and value. After 1960, Australian dramatists can be distinguished from the general category of Australian writers as a cohort apart. It is one of the many ironies of Australian theatre that the man associated with the birth of the autonomous view of the Australian playwright, Patrick White, is also one of our greatest *litterateurs*.

Changes taking place at a creative level were matched by shifts in play programming, the slots of dramatic anticipation by which the now-ascendant repertory companies chose their annual programs. As singular art works, plays aim to meet or challenge audience expectations, as per their authors' intentions. The seasons in which they jointly appear, however, aim to manage them in a more indirect way. Play programs curate a diverse selection of drama, attempting to balance different tastes and desires over time. Thus, in any one season, one might see: a number of comedies and family dramas; a seasonal pantomime or children's show; a musical (expensive to stage but likely to be popular); and a new experimental work (less expensive to stage but with niche appeal) and so on. The individual plays a theatre chooses will change every year. The slots they fit into change far more slowly.

It is therefore of profound significance when new program slots appear allowing for more Australian drama even before any actual Australian plays have been chosen. Slots can change for different reasons. Funding bodies such as the AETT may commit to co-producing local work; or supply-side incentives, like play competitions, boost the pool of available plays. In either case, programming is the decisive end point because it is here that companies commit concrete resources to concrete outcomes. When the programming *habitus* of companies changes, it impacts more than the fate of a few plays. The whole direction of Australian theatre changes.

An important disclaimer: after 1960, Australian plays of professional, cultural and political significance become more numerous. The act of choosing a few for a book like this therefore is more personal. The 'not better, just different' caution applies to the plays I have selected too, acknowledging they are a small and potentially unrepresentative part of a large and dazzling creative constellation. In no way do they reflect 'the best' Australian drama, a criterion I have tried to show is comparatively meaningless (New Wave theatre artists rightly treated the term with derision). My hope is that each play examined will spark an interest in its origins and background, alerting the reader to the wider field of dramatic endeavour around it. To this end, I have imposed another rule on my choices: to discuss only one play by each individual writer, though many Australian playwrights after this time produce a number of outstanding stage works. This does nothing to assist the gender imbalance mentioned in the previous chapter. More than any other period, Australian drama from the early 1960s to the mid-1980s feels male-dominated. It is progressively less true after 1990 and leading up to the present day. This is reflected in the increased proportion of women playwrights in later chapters, but does not entirely compensate for the earlier historical skew.

Towards 1970: Act 1 concludes

Patrick White's *A Cheery Soul*, Alan Hopgood's *Private Yuk Objects*, Alex Buzo's *Norm and Ahmed,* and *The Legend of King O'Malley* by Michael Boddy and Bob Ellis are like steps along a path to a freer conception of Australian drama. The last two plays are often discussed as key New Wave works, while White is feted as an influential progenitor. To go from *A Cheery Soul* to *The Legend of King O'Malley* is to witness a sea change in play construction. Although stylistically different to the *Doll*, *A Cheery Soul* still resembles it in some ways. It has a bounded story, recognisable characters, and dialogue that is conspicuously literary. The term 'poetic' captures the unique aspect of White's drama—the striking language that freights a heightened view of the world, a singular lyric vision.

By contrast, *The Legend of King O'Malley* is associated with adjectives such as 'provocative', 'irreverent', 'energetic' and 'partisan'. The word waiting in the wings to describe this febrile mix of qualities was 'larrikin' and it was much used by theatre critics in the period. It is as good as any other. The important thing is to note the shift from a drama that hovers above the characters it portrays in a god-like way, to one earthily connected to them—a drama less concerned to express a higher understanding of existence than to directly engage with it. This function of Australian drama—as a tool for social change—stemmed from Australian artists' desire to transform the nation in which they lived.

'What do they know of theatre who know only theatre?' asks the American theatre critic Eric Bentley. It is a sentiment that applies to the New Wave from first to last. In the 1960s, Australian drama did not change because it became more 'professional' in a JC Williamson sense, or more modernist in a Kippaxian one. It changed because Australian life changed, beginning with the 60,000 soldiers the government sent off to a disastrous war in Vietnam. Many of these were conscripts drawn from the New Wave age cohort. This unilateral executive action—another blot on the historical record of the nation—galvanised theatre artists in a way nothing else could. *The Legend of King O'Malley* while making no explicit mention of the conflict, breathes with anti–Vietnam War sentiment. Its loose construction, miscellaneous songs, and discontinuous action made it a perfect vehicle for expressing political dissent. Yet it was also, as its audiences quickly realised, great fun. Fun is not a conspicuous feature of White's plays. So the shift from *A Cheery Soul* to *The Legend of King O'Malley* also marks the rediscovery of drama's entertainment value, a dimension lost in the longstanding disaffection between Australia's commercial theatre and the more socially committed repertory companies.

By 1965, Patrick White had had enough of 'the slithery snake dance of Australian theatre' and had returned to creative fiction. *A Cheery Soul*, the third play of his early playwriting period, was produced by the Union Repertory Theatre Company two years before, directed by John Sumner. The fact that the director associated with the realism of the *Doll* in the 1950s was also a champion for quasi-expressionism in the 1960s is revealing. Kippax thought that White's drama was a challenger to the dominant naturalism of the Australian theatre of his day. But it can also be seen as its complement.

The first thing to observe about Miss Docker, *A Cheery Soul*'s central figure, is that she is 'about 60' (189), making her the same age as the century in which she appeared at the time of her creation (1962), and a walking-talking symbol of post-federation Australia. 'No doubt to pluck a message from the prickling ambiguities of [this] play is to oversimplify [it]', warns Kippax. No doubt. White's Nobel prize–winning talents create a multifaceted dramatic jewel glittering with allusive meaning. Other Australian plays to this date have great moments. But only the *Doll* bears comparison with *A Cheery Soul* in the wrought intensity of each line, the compositional balance of the whole, and the transcendent vision of human frailty that infuses every aspect of its unfolding.

That said, Miss Docker is also a memorable, flesh-and-blood character. Her vigour—and the horror of her vigour, the way it undoes those around her, particularly those trying to do good (but weakly)—has a brutal inevitability to it, like a runaway steamroller. Writing about the 1979 revival of the play, Andrew Fuhrmann comments, 'Miss Docker cannot be read only in her baleful aspect; there is, too, her restorative power. She is the agent of a creative daemon that can reclaim and renew only by virtue of destruction, a powerful figure of life who emerges as an aesthetic reality through the chaotic ordeal of the sublime'.

The only misleading word in this perceptive insight is 'read'. It is when a great actor *performs* Miss Docker on stage (in 1979 it was the 36-year-old Robyn Nevin) that her power becomes apparent. Developing from dramatic moment to dramatic moment, though Miss Docker may act badly, like Mrs Hamilton in *Here Under Heaven*, she can never be written off. She always teeters on the edge of redeeming self-knowledge, and despite her vulgarity, insensitivity, intrusiveness and ridiculousness (or, perhaps, aided by them), seems more genuinely alive to life's possibilities than the play's other characters caught up in the inertial world of 1960s suburban Australia. Ultimately, this makes her a figure of hope, and deeply so.

A Cheery Soul takes place over three acts (ten scenes): the first in the small(ish) house of Mr and Mrs Custance who, in a soon-regretted act of charity, invite Miss Docker to stay as a lodger; the second in the Chinese Room of the Sundown Home for Old People, where Miss Docker imperially imposes on the faded residents; and the third in various locales that include the study of the local clergyman, Reverend Wakeman, and the church in which he preaches and, thanks to Miss Docker's relentless criticism, dies ('You don't mind me telling the truth. Someone has to' 246).

The ending of the play is deliberately anti-climactic. The dregs of federation melodrama drain away, replaced by a Samuel Beckett–like scene where Miss Docker tries to befriend a mangy dog who urinates on her leg, leaving her to wonder whether it is God's judgement on her, or—worse—whether there is a God at all. Like Winnie from *Happy Days*, she carries on nonetheless. 'I'll pray… and if it isn't answered… then, I'll… pray… [*She goes… old, shattered, holding down the brim of her hat*]' (264). This is Miss Docker's last and most effective assault on the audience. Having spent two and a half hours mocking and deploring her, we are made to feel, in this final parting, an inescapable compassion for her.

In both structure and language *A Cheery Soul* reflects not so much hostility to stage realism as indifference to its predicates. The sense is of an author writing in a way that pleases him, rather than consciously 'rejecting naturalism'. *A Cheery Soul* floats across places and periods, now in the present portraying the present, now in the present recounting the past, now in the past portraying the past. It also slips easily from external to internal reality, so that it is sometimes hard to say whether the action being presented is literal or metaphorical. White expertly switches between different levels of audience apprehension. Just when we think the play has strayed permanently into poetic reverie, he offers an exchange of sharply observed social interaction—usually Miss Docker doing something appalling, or getting her squirm-worthy comeuppance.

White's *milieu* is the invented suburb of Sarsaparilla, which recurs in his other plays and stories. Sarsaparilla captures a world marked by a falling away from active belief—from religion, from politics, from collective life altogether. Imaginary though the suburb might be, it is clearly emblematic of 1960s Australia. In Sarsaparilla, the nation has shrunk back into itself, like the folding petals of the plants in the Wakemans' gardens that Miss Docker violently lops (MRS WAKEMAN'S VOICE [*very stern*]: Miss Docker, do you know you have pruned *Crimson Glory* to death? MISS DOCKER'S VOICE: I only pruned the rose as a gesture. And nobody knows for certain it didn't die a natural death 241).

In the setting of the play, White abandons naturalism altogether. Props are to be mimed and locations indicated. A note at the beginning of the play reads, *'Only three of these scenes amount to "scenery". The rest of the action takes place in front of a gauze or on an empty stage with rostra'* (182). Plot mechanics are slack—like *Rusty Bugles*, *A Cheery Soul* is a collection of incidents held together by authorial will—while characters expand to universal resonance. Here, another sort of 'representativeness' is on offer, based not on social type but psychological distillation. Borrowing the vocabulary of Carl Jung, we can identify Miss Docker as a psycho-physical archetype, a character who exists partly in external reality, partly in our own minds. Like Alf from *The One Day of the Year* and Barry Humphries's Dame Edna Everage, she is another Awful Australian. Her destructive behaviour has an allegorical quality that makes her a case study in national character.

Perhaps *A Cheery Soul*'s most strikingly non-realist feature is its use of a Chorus. This is composed of the ladies from the Sundown Home for Old People, who move out of their individual roles to provide commentary on the play's action as a group. In keeping with the traditional multitasking function of the chorus in ancient Greek drama, they offer a range of services: insight into the mind of the protagonists; useful filling-in of backstories; and delivery of warnings from the gods about the transience of human existence. Their first appearance is in Act 2, describing the travails of old age:

> CHORUS *of* OLD LADIES *forms up forward in a frieze, leader* MRS HIBBLE. MISS DOCKER *and* MRS LITTLE *absent.* CHORUS *lit from footlights.*
>
> MRS HIBBLE: Nothing to get worked up about, however.
> CHORUS: So ordinary, everyday. It comes in with the morning tea. It goes out with the supper tray. It comes and goes as quick and light as you spill the egg on the sheet.
> MRS HIBBLE: Sometimes the sheet tightens and twists. But it's nothing to get worked up about.
> CHORUS: Nothing to get worked up about. Nurse is so kind, the doctors love her. One's thoughts are worse than the touch of her hand. But the sound of brass will drown one's thoughts at twilight if one lets it.
> MRS HIBBLE: Mercifully we are often deaf. We can lie and watch the pictures…
> CHORUS: … the flick of the silent pictures.

The Chorus then give an account of one of their number, Mrs Millicent Lillie, whose husband Miss Docker nursed after he suffered a paralysing stroke. Millicent and Tom Lillie are classic riches-to-rags no-hopers (MRS LILLIE: 'We drained a fortune to the dregs, and I loved every penny of it' 217). Miss Docker's ministrations of Tom in penurious old age were typically inept and intrusive:

> CHORUS *disperse L. and R. They line sides of the stage.*
>
> MISS DOCKER *and* MRS LITTLE *are shown on rostrum [centre], either side of the bed,* MISS DOCKER *seated,* MRS LILLIE *standing. The form of* TOM LILLIE *in bed.* MRS LILLIE *trembling in her palsy.*

MISS DOCKER [*explaining to* MRS LILLIE, *though absorbed in the patient's face*]: I'm talking to him. You never know with a stroke. You might get through to them. [*Looking directly at* MRS LILLIE] You don't mind, now do you, dear? I have what they call an intuition. I've been telling him about the process of digestion, which I read about in a medical journal, in a doctor's home, where I was invited recently.

She is fanning the patient with a rolled-up newspaper.

MRS LILLIE [*helplessly*]: I must do… *do!* I can see the hate in his eye. Only *I can see*. (220–1)

The colours mentioned most often in *A Cheery Soul* are black (for the Chorus) and brown (for Miss Docker). It is as if all other hues have been leached from this land of material hyper-stability. People not emotionally alive are dying ahead of time, so the inhabitants of Sarsaparilla, save for its perennially cheeky children, seem to be easing themselves into an early grave. There is a sense of finality everywhere; of things declining, concluding, disappearing in time, space and memory.

A Cheery Soul thus marks the ultimate expression of certain preoccupations in Australian drama over its first 60 years. The tone of irony and ambiguity found in plays from the 1920s is brought to perfection by White's craftsmanship. The catastrophic events of the twentieth century are present but also, in the minds of his fading suburban characters, erased there. By contrast, while Miss Docker may be a monster, she is self-aware, and has a chance at an active inner life. She continues to evolve while the Sarsaparilla around her remains in stasis, an object of satire or nostalgia, or both. It is as if White is putting a full stop at the end of half a century of collective endeavour. *A Cheery Soul* is more than an elegy to Australia's past. From the perspective of its national life, it is also a paean to letting it go.

Private Yuk Objects is not a play that has enjoyed much historical attention and it is easy to see why. Having said that 'the best' is a term with little application in drama, there can be no doubt that *Private Yuk Objects* is a cruder article than *A Cheery Soul*, less well written and less well constructed. In many ways, it bears comparison with Adams's *Gallipoli Bill* as another war-themed comedy of manners that now feels superficial and overly flip. The play centres on Hoth Yuk, a young, hillbilly character who might have walked directly out of *On Our Selection* into the 1960s. Conscripted to fight in the Vietnam War, he descends from his Mount Baw Baw farm to Melbourne, where he is to billet with the McKay family. Hoth's father, Daddy Yuk (identical to Dad Rudd) is a VC-awarded soldier who saved the life of Henry McKay on the Kokoda Trail in World War II. Henry is now a prominent businessman and conservative politician—how often the two phrases go together in Australian drama!—outspoken in his support of the current conflict. He has two sons and a daughter. One of the sons, Peter, is away fighting; the other, Tony, is thinking about burning his draft card.

Tony and his father quarrel about the morality of the war, but Henry can put forward no substantive arguments to justify it. The absence of any such arguments is the main feature of the play, the problem at issue behind the laughter. For Henry, the war comes down to the fact that 'wiser heads than [Tony's] have faced the question of Vietnam, and *they* have decided, not only are we right to be there, but the only way to be there in sufficient numbers is to conscript' (12). Later, he talks about how 'the Commos' want 'to gain minds' and 'turn allies against allies' (49); so Australia needs to 'fight the Commos at their own game' which it 'can't do by giving them Vietnam as a present' (50). In the last act, his position devolves further into the need 'to keep our civilization going' otherwise Tony's generation will 'have to accept… a yellow god, totem or a new manifesto' (66). Henry concludes by saying to his daughter, Jeannie, who is now having an affair with Hoth, and is reluctant to see him go off to war, that 'if you spend all your time criticising and resisting… you may never have a chance to control anything' (66).

Private Yuk Objects was staged in September 1966, when Australia's presence in Vietnam was just four years old. Initially, the number of boots on the ground was small, the first conventional troops being sent in mid-1965. The drafting of young men began in November 1964, and Australians were beginning to divide over conscription when Hopgood's play premiered. In 1968, after the Viet Cong's militarily disastrous but politically successful Tet Offensive, anti-war protests accelerated. Yet Australia never officially declared war on North Vietnam. It was only ever 'involved' in this questionable campaign, first providing jungle warfare 'advisers', and later 'assistance' in the form of RAAF squadrons, infantry battalions, armoured personnel carriers, and support services. Australian soldiers were in Vietnam from 1962 to 1972, making it the longest external conflict in our history until the country's involvement in Afghanistan (2001–2021). Stuart Macintyre writes:

> Australian casualties mounted. Of 50,0000 who had served in Vietnam by 1972, 500 were killed and they included nearly 200 conscripts. Conscription for an unjust war was the primary concern of a peace movement that began with the lonely vigils of the women's group Save Our Sons and swelled into noisy protest by radical students until by 1970 it filled city streets with a nationwide demonstration, the Moratorium, in numbers not seen for decades. Horrifying images of children with napalm burns, television footage of street executions and reports of village massacres combined with the bizarre ritual whereby young Australian men were required to register for national service and then face selection by drawing birthdates from a barrel in a 'lottery of death'. A generational divide widened between government ministers who sought to justify the war and those they sent to fight it.

Private Yuk Objects was probably the first anti–Vietnam War play in the world. Judging by the accounts of both Macintyre and Clark, the arguments advanced by the Coalition government to support the conflict were little better than Henry McKay's. His shabby rodomontade accurately reflects the level of official rhetoric at the time. After it ended, the response of Australians, in true Sarsaparillian fashion, was to try to forget about it as quickly as possible. Not until *Away* in the mid-1980s is it possible to find an Australian play mentioning the Vietnam War in a direct and serious way.

In fact, it is astonishing that *Private Yuk Objects* exists at all, that in 1966 Australia was capable of viewing its military commitment in a dramatically critical way. Hopgood's comedy does not sparkle. Its

Australian soldiers trek through the Vietnamese jungle. Between 1962 and 1973, over 50,000 Australian troops were sent to Vietnam (including my uncle), and over 500 died there, 200 of them conscripts. Until Australia's recent involvement in Afghanistan, it was our longest war. (Photo: Australian War Memorial COL/67/0126/VN. Photographer Michael Coleridge)

structure is workmanlike, with predictable switches of location (the well-appointed McKay home/a village in South Vietnam), unsubtle dialogue and broad-brushstroke characters. Yet its *message,* and its resolve to deliver it in a *direct* way, heralds the New Wave drama to come. Here is the paradox of value in drama: that under certain circumstances *Private Yuk Objects* may be a 'better' play than *A Cheery Soul*. For all the brilliance of the latter, for a country engaged in a war and, as it turned out, destined to lose it, the former may have more to offer.

There is in Hopgood's play one prescient speech fired at the audience, flat and low, like a rifle bullet. It comes at the end, when the fractious Peter, a captive of the Viet Cong, is interviewed for a last time by the civilised Vo Lai, who informs him he will be returned to his own lines. Peter's view of the war is on the same sub-rational level as his father's, and he explodes. What has been the point of his lengthy interrogation then?

> VO LAI: Captain… it has answered a question for me. And I needed to have it answered. You see, I felt our two brains could at least come together to find some understanding.

> That if nobody else will come to the conference table, at least… we two small, insignificant units of this chaos… could… learn from each other. But I have concluded, finally, that understanding is an empty solution. No matter how much you learn about us, it will not change anything. Because your much-lauded plea for humanity is convenient humanity… white humanity… the white race will be humanitarian when and if it suits them. So this is what we face in the future. Not just one Vietnam. But many more Vietnams. All over the world. As the inferior races struggle to reach the surface, they will be met… not with understanding… not with honoured agreements and pledges… but only with repression, destruction and hate… Until you forget that there can be one set of rules for you and another for us, what we know of one another will never alter anything. (61)

How is a play to be judged? By its overall 'quality', or by the power of a single moment it fully achieves, delivering a truth that, until then, has not been heard? It is a conundrum with no pat solution, useful to remember when we are tempted to pronounce a final verdict on drama that has the immediate world, not historical opinion, in its sights.

It is also a good introduction to the remaining plays in this chapter. I begin with *The Legend of King O'Malley*, before backtracking to *Norm and Ahmed*. I treat David Williamson's *Don's Party*, Jack Hibberd's *A Stretch of the Imagination* (*Stretch*), Dorothy Hewett's *The Chapel Perilous*, John Romeril's *The Floating World*, Robert Merritt's *The Cake Man* and Jennifer Compton's *Crossfire* as a job lot. These plays are better known than some I have discussed so far, and a number have received multiple productions in Australia and overseas, for example, *The Floating World* in Japan, *Stretch* in China, and *Don's Party* in England (to which my mother took my father to introduce him to her country. Predictably, he was appalled). They were written by playwrights with little interest in abstract standards of excellence or the hypothetical judgements of future generations. They were written for the moment. Their force and appeal is because of this fact not despite it. Some are of good literary quality, but literary brilliance is not their *raison d'être*. Grasping this avoids some obfuscating distinctions that have troubled scholars in recent years, notably between 'text-based' and 'devised' stage work, as if these were different species of drama. They are not. In the New Wave we find both kinds of creative endeavour. Often, they are by the *same* playwrights, who move unselfconsciously from a 'knit-one-purl-one' theatricalism to high literary craft. The same existential challenges face all stage work, however it is created, whatever its chosen form.

The Legend of King O'Malley (*O'Malley*) is often seen as a point of origin for the New Wave. Premiering in 1970 in a season of experimental plays at Sydney's Jane Street Theatre, a number of its key artists then founded the Nimrod Theatre, which went on to produce a string of local plays in a miscellaneous range of styles until its collapse in 1985 (leaving two venues as its legacy, the Stables in Kings Cross and Belvoir Street in Surry Hills). Its Melbourne counterpart was the Australian Performing Group, or APG, which grew out of La Mama Theatre in Carlton, before moving into its own building, the Pram Factory in the same suburb. Like Nimrod, it staged a significant number of Australian plays during its life from 1970 to 1981. The histories of these companies is seminal to the development of Australian drama but have been written-up elsewhere, in the case of the Nimrod by me, in the case of the APG by Gabrielle Wolf.

O'Malley is a coat-hanger of scenes, songs, and comedy sketches illustrating the life of a federation-era Texas-born preacher, huckster, and Australian politician. King O'Malley helped to select Canberra as the site for Australia's national capital city, founded the Commonwealth Bank, and was responsible for dropping the letter 'u' from the name of the Australian Labor Party (for anyone who ever wondered, it is a deliberate misspelling and, typically for Australian politics, has a long story behind it). The script comes with notes from the writers about how it should be staged that reveal an interesting tension. On the one hand, *O'Malley* exists as a unique performance event, and so each production is unguidable. On the other hand, it is a repeatable text that must be interpreted in a certain *spirit* to be successful. 'The bourgeois crap concepts, "Good Taste" and "Artistic Sensibility" are dead', the authors joyously assert, 'let us dance on their graves' (xxvii).

The notes are designed to stop producers and casts from getting the wrong end of the New Wave stick. Staging is to be spartan (platform and catwalk), costumes 'like a cartoon' (xxiii), and live music ubiquitous. 'The finale should be romantic and full of hark-backs to patriotic and symbolic finales which were seen so much in the days of the Tivoli shows. If you cannot parade out of theatre through the audience, then parade on stage' (xxi). Having fun is crucial. If *O'Malley* isn't fun— and this goes for many New Wave plays—it isn't anything at all. The line between the theatre and the world outside is to be deliberately blurred. In the Jane Street premiere, the authors write 'we specified side-shows for the foyer with a barker who runs the whole interval bit. Snake-charmer, fire-eater, Punch and Judy, man–woman. These lead naturally into Act 2, and provide the audience with lots of fun' (xxiii). If instructions like these seem concerned mostly with the externals of production, the notes on character reveal what is really at stake:

> This is a legend. We are working from fact. The facts of [O'Malley's] life are true. Everything else that happens in the play is pretty sure to be true. All the legislation that O'Malley talks about is real. Hansard has been used. Everything that Hughes does is true. With this solid basis in fact as a jumping-off point, we can fly anywhere. Working from fact into fiction means that you can liberate the audience's imagination… The characters are simple, larger than life, epic. The confrontations are the same, almost child-like. From this we come quite close to the truth. (xxiv)

The distinction between what is *real* and what is *true* lies at the heart of the difference between the realist strain in Australian drama *pace* the *Doll*, and the poetic strain *pace* White. *Some* reality is required in even the most anti-realist play if truth is the aim. But the true is of a different order of understanding to the real, and justifies the freest treatment of form. This is what makes *O'Malley* and plays like it (Michael Boddy and Ron Blair's *Hamlet on Ice,* Jack Hibberd and John Romeril's *Marvellous Melbourne,* the collectively devised *Betty Can Jump*) more than theatrical romps. They address the Australia around them *truthfully* regardless of choice of narrative, approach to character or style of language. Donald Horne writes in *O'Malley*'s Foreword that it gives an audience 'a chance to know what fraud and vision can really *feel* like', (viii, original emphasis). He goes on, 'the fact that [the play] use[s] forms so banal as those of revivalism and vaudeville [is] fitting to its subject' (that is, Australian politics).

In the early 1970s, heated discussion about the role of 'the stereotype' in New Wave drama blew up, pursued by Margaret Williams in three important *Meanjin* articles. These were a *riposte* to the realist misconceptions of theatre critics at the time, particularly Harry Kippax. But in relation to characters like O'Malley the term is misleading. If we substitute 'archetype' for 'stereotype' then we have a concept that both illuminates what New Wave playwrights were trying to do, and a link back to the drama of previous decades—a link that gets effaced when focussing on just the novel aspects of the movement.

No selection from *O'Malley* can be representative of the entire play, but Act 2 scene 13 illustrates the argument I am making here. World War I makes a burlesque appearance earlier in the Act (scene 10). '*A wild bugle call rings out... Band plays quick march time "Colonel Bogey" tune... Emphasise that war is fun*' (83). Fifteen pages later, O'Malley gets to his feet in a circus-like depiction of federal parliament to oppose Billy Hughes's demand that Australia introduce conscription:

> O'MALLEY: To me it makes no sense to fight for freedom against Prussian militarism if we have to become Prussians to do it.
> To me it is not freedom if we can be dragged out of our beds and flung into jail because exercising our freedom of speech is treason.
> To me it is not freedom if our lives are to be drawn out of a barrel on Tattersall principles and blow (like spit) in the face of the Kaiser because his is the tyrannical system and ours is not.
> To me it is not freedom if men are not free to choose the freedoms they will die for.
> To me it seems there will soon be no freedoms left worth fighting for.
> How does it seem to you? (98)

The most significant thing about this speech is that O'Malley never gave it. A sheepish postscript in the 1987 reprint of the play 'confesses to one allowable fiction' (xxvii). On the matter of conscription O'Malley was a fence-sitter. However, 'for the purposes of this play... [he] just had to represent and summarise what all the anti-conscriptionists were thinking, both in 1916 and 1970, whether in real life he deserved to, or not'.

Here is an example of Australian drama using the resources of history. A war that could not be portrayed directly could be couched in a metaphor. To find one, the playwrights turned to the story of Federation (the birth of the Australian nation in a moment of hope), ransacking the events of the past to address those in the present, a strategy also adopted by the APG in *Marvellous Melbourne*, its 1890s–1970s reworked melodrama. Professionally, *O'Malley* is more successful in its clever artifice than *Private Yuk Objects* in its gauche directness, but it is noteworthy that Boddy and Ellis chose this circuitous route to express their oppositional views. Why? The answer is revealing: because Australian drama and Australian national life had collided, and playwrights had to watch their words very carefully. No play better illustrates this *political* confrontation than the early production history of *Norm and Ahmed*.

In 2009, on the anniversary of the Melbourne premiere of Alex Buzo's first play, Graeme Blundell, one of its original directors, wrote: '*Norm and Ahmed* quickly became known in newspapers as "that word play" after the actors who uttered it during the next two years were prosecuted. After its 1969 Brisbane season, magistrate WC Barlow convicted actor Norman Staines... on a charge of using obscene language in a public place... I directed the play in Melbourne later that year and was hounded through the courts by Victoria's infamous vice squad and was eventually found guilty in the County Court of "aiding and abetting obscene language in a public place"'.

Buzo's play was not alone in facing legal suppression. Overseas books and films were regularly banned from entering the country, while Adam Carr calls 1969 'a vintage year' for theatre, with *Hair*, *O Calcutta!*, *I Love You, America Hurrah!*, and *The Boys in the Band* all ending up in court alongside *Norm and Ahmed*. Carr comments, 'Australia had always had one of the most rigid censorship regimes in the western world, and authors, publishers and theatre people had long chafed under its strictness, illogicality and unpredictability... In the 1920s and 30s, it was mainly political in intent... In the postwar years, however, censorship was increasingly directed at sexually explicit or suggestive material'. The switch in focus permitted governments to claim they were not *banning plays* but *protecting the public*. The result was the bizarre spectacle of Vice Squad detectives attending opening nights, notebooks in hand, to jot down any 'obscenities' that needed prosecuting.

The history of censorship in Australian theatre is beyond the scope here. I have touched on it elsewhere and I examine the premiere of *Norm and Ahmed* in *Australian Theatre After the New Wave* where I call it 'the symbolic beginning of alternative theatre in Australia'. The phrase 'alternative theatre' refers to companies similar to the Nimrod and the APG that sprang up in many Australian cities in the 1960s and 1970s to challenge the hold of the repertory theatres as once these challenged the dominance of the Firm. Blundell offers a pithy summary of *Norm and Ahmed's* slender action (the 1999 reprint is just 17 pages long):

> Buzo's play dramatizes a late-night encounter between a middle-aged ocker Aussie and a young articulate Pakistani university student... At the start of the play, Ahmed, walking past a bus stop near a city construction site, is asked for a light by the slightly under-the-weather Norm, holding up a cigarette. For the next 45 minutes, he plays cat-and-mouse with Ahmed, and the audience, in what is almost a private rhapsody. No-one is sure of his intentions, or the style of the play. Is Norm a racist, threatening violence, or an elderly suburbanite, a lonely widower? Is the play an extended Barry Humphries– style revue sketch working off contrasting accents or a delicately structured, polished dramatic piece with a political conscience? At the end, Norm wishes Ahmed well, and offers his hand... [He] then punches him, grabs his head and bashes it against the nearest post, then flings the limp body over a handrail. 'F...kin' boong', he says.

While *The Legend of King O'Malley* can be considered an example of 'hot' New Wave theatre, all high energy and fast-paced action, *Norm and Ahmed* represents the 'cool' variant: just one location, only two characters, and a single real-time exchange. Again, there are echoes of the drama of the past. Norm could be a clone of Lawler's Barney from the *Doll* or, better yet, of Beynon's Clarry from *The Shifting Heart*. It is not difficult to see him as one of Henrietta Drake-Brockman's creepy station hands, or Locke Elliott's squaddies, older now but still living a tedium-filled life. The language of the play that Kippax described as composed of 'satirical flights of eloquently patterned dialogue' is not so different from White's or, for that matter, the tempered exchanges in Afford's *Lady in Danger*, or the controlled humour of Esson's *The Time is Not Yet Ripe*. Which begs the question of what, exactly, is new about *Norm and Ahmed*?

The answer lies in the way its elements come together to a new dramatic end. It is always difficult to pinpoint the origins of a decisive change in cultural sensibility, in the compelling mood of a nation. But if a moment in Australian theatre has to be identified when twentieth century modernism tips into another order of creative possibility—into late modernism, 'liquid' modernity, postmodernism, call it what we will—the opening night of *Norm and Ahmed* is surely a contender. For it takes the qualities of the drama that preceded it—the eye for social detail, the irony and ambiguity, a sensitivity to the idioms of spoken Australian English—and fashions a work that breathes with meaning every minute it is on stage yet entirely resists definitive interpretation. Here is a section of the play that occurs a few pages before Norm's assault on Ahmed, when their friendship seems at its most assured:

> NORM: I get a little lonely, you see, being all alone. I like to get out and do something, meet some people. I like to have a nice chat with a bloke, find out how he's getting on in the world. A bloke like you, for instance, Ahmed. A visitor to our shores. A young citizen from the south-east Asian sub-continent.
> AHMED: Well... I hope I can... I mean... if I can be of... any... that is, I...
> NORM: Step over here a minute, will you?
> *Pause.*

AHMED: What?

They look at each other.

NORM: Just step over here for a minute.

Pause

AHMED: Why?

NORM: What's the matter, Ahmed? Come here?

AHMED *moves warily closer to* NORM.

Over here. Under the light.

AHMED *moves closer.*

AHMED: What do you want?

NORM *surveys* AHMED.

NORM: Just as I thought. [*Pause.*] You haven't really got such a dark skin have you?

AHMED: A dark skin? What do you mean?

NORM: I mean you're not a black, are you? You could pass for a Greek or a Turk. You've got more of an olive complexion.

AHMED: What are you getting at? I fail to understand…

NORM *laughs. He moves out from the shadows.*

NORM: Don't get upset, Ahmed. Don't do your block. I was only thinking that if you didn't have a dark skin you'd be all right. I mean, it'd be all right for you to stay here, like, get a job and stay in this country. (253)

The menacing-yet-alluring experience of *Norm and Ahmed* involves inviting an audience into a fully realised stage world, then depriving them of the instruments to semantically navigate it. It is 'ironic'. But about what? Its ending is 'ambiguous'. But what alternative readings, exactly, are on offer? To borrow a phrase of cultural critic Mark Fisher, 'the words are little labyrinths, enigmas with no possible solution—the appearance of enigmas perhaps'. In its depthless lapidary style, the play illuminates like a star shell a more abstract realm of dramatic understanding, calling for a self-aware spectator to assay it. It does this not by *rejecting* the theatrical past, but by *subsuming* it to its new purpose. In the impassable void between *Norm and Ahmed*'s action and the stable meaning it flatly denies, a strange silence accrues in which a more dynamic conception of Australian drama is born.

After 1970: Act 2 begins

In the following analysis of six New Wave plays together I will adopt the 'holon' as an organising concept. This ancient Greek word was introduced into contemporary cultural criticism by Arthur Koestler in his 1967 book *The Ghost in the Machine*, as a way of transcending the dichotomy in Western thinking between 'part' and 'whole'. According to this reductive division, phenomena are *either* to be massed together in one great system (such as 'world drama') *or* broken down into the smallest available units (such as 'single plays'). The holon—a structure that both has individual integrity and forms part of a larger structure in which that integrity is reflected—allows part/whole relations to be understood in a more nuanced way. Holons are arranged not in an order of supervenience but in a 'holarchy', which philosopher David Spangler describes thus:

> In a hierarchy, participants can be compared and evaluated on the basis of position, rank, relative power, seniority, and the like. But in a holarchy each person's value comes from his or her own individuality and uniqueness and the capacity to engage and interact with others to make the fruits of that uniqueness available.

Holarchic relations are characterised by repeating, intertwined and overlapping patterns and processes. There is no 'top' or 'bottom', 'up' or 'down'. Instead, there is a type of intermediate clumping that Koestler calls 'subwholes', which roughly correspond to the realist/poetic strains in Australian drama I have been discussing. The concept of the holon gives us a way of looking at the national repertoire that respects the creative singularity of individual plays, yet allows them to be situated within larger assemblages of creative effort.

Each of the next six plays has a critical literature around it, and most have been on the school syllabus at one time or another. Although only a few Australian dramas are regularly revived, these works are better known than some others, so detailed description of them is unnecessary. A quick sketch of the plots, and a sample of the dialogue will show their differences and, more importantly, what they have in common.

Summary of the plays

The Chapel Perilous (*Chapel*), the first of the plays to be performed (premiere January 1971), follows the journey of its central character, Sally Banner, from her beginnings as a rebellious schoolgirl educated by nuns in Widgiemooltha, a small-minded town on the Western Australian plains (shades of Koorora in *Sky Without Birds*), through her time as a talented but wayward university student, to becoming a committed communist, to 'finally and irrevocably [being] responsible for [herself]' (88). The setting is non-realistic: an altar, a collection of rostrums, some giant masks, and a stained-glass window '*discovered later to contain a figure of* SALLY BANNER' (4). The action is a pell-mell hurtle through Sally's anarchic sex life with four different lovers, each worse than the last (the second makes a return appearance later in the play, when he behaves even more badly than the first time round). For the repressed Australia around her, including her ultra-bourgeois, uncomprehending parents (shades of the Custances from *A Cheery Soul*), Sally is 'a dirty little whore' (17) or later, when she becomes a party activist, 'a dirty Commo' (62). Early on she describes herself thus:

> SALLY: I am sixteen years old. I am a Gemini. I am pretty but I am something more than that. All I want is to be a great actress and a great writer. Sometimes I sing, too, and I spend a lot of time drawing women with slanted eyes and long tousled hair. People do not approve of me but I fascinate them. My teacher calls me a poseur and the girls think I am trying to be different. Some of them think I am a genius and so do I. …
>
> FIRST GIRL: Sister, Sally Banner takes off her black stockings and meets a man with a violin at the school gates every night.
>
> SECOND GIRL [*giggling*]: What does he do with his violin?
>
> FIRST GIRL: He plays 'Souvenirs' off-key when the sun goes down.
>
> SECOND GIRL: And he's actually *twenty-two*.
>
> FIRST GIRL: He's a Catholic so he only feels her breasts.
>
> AMPLIFIER [*man's voice, breathing hard*]: I might take your chastity but I'll never take your virginity.
>
> *Schoolgirl giggles.* (18–9)

Chapel Perilous, *New Fortune Theatre, Perth 1971. Note the stain glass window of Sally, centre, and the outsize masks either side. The New Fortune, with its intimate and flexible thrust stage, was one of Dorothy Hewitt's favourite venues, and saw the premiere of* This Old Man Comes Rolling Home *in 1967 and* Catspaw *in 1974.*

As *Chapel* moves from the 1940s to the 1960s, and Sally matures, her faith in herself to 'walk naked through the world' (86) is sorely tested. At the end of the play, she repeats the verdict delivered on her by a much-hated teacher at the beginning: 'I was a rebel in word and deed. The latter usually tones with time' (26/89). Is it a moment of awakening or acquiescence? According to Hewett's introduction to the play, it is a bit of both.

The next three plays were all originally APG productions. *Don's Party* (premiere March 1971) is set on what, for its first audiences, was the night of the previous federal election: 15 October 1969. Kath and Don are 30-something professionals hosting a party for their 30-something friends, most of whom are left-leaning (though not all of them, the source of both humour and conflict later on). The action is on a micro level and mostly involves the men—Don and Don's friends, gloomy Mal, newly separated Mack and appallingly sexist Cooley—trying to seduce women to whom they are not married: the Liberal-voting Jody, the beautiful but insecure Kerry, and the stripper-cum-arts student, Susan. The best that can be said of their advances is that, for the women so targeted, the men are marginally more appealing than the ones they are married to. The dialogue is shaped to reveal beneath the comic veneer the vulnerability that haunts the characters now they are no longer young, and life has seemingly flatlined. The sex talk that so appalled my father is explicit. An argument between Don and Mal and their wives, Kath and Jenny, in Act 2 gives the flavour of it:

> KATH: You won't stop 'em now. They're into the mutual admiration stage.
> JENNY: Twelve glasses?
>
> KATH *nods*.
>
> MAL: Mindless people following mindless rules.
> KATH [*to* DON]: Why don't you lick his arse?
> DON: That's not very nice! I'm not ashamed of the fact that out of all the people I know Mal is one of the two worth listening to.
> MAL: I've said exactly the same thing about you—[*Sharply.*] Who's the other one?
> DON: Bob Hawke.
>
> *Pause.*
>
> The trouble with you two is that you never question the social institutions around you.
> MAL: Marriage for instance. It would be very difficult for man to conceive a more boring social institution than marriage.
> JENNY: Boredom's not what's wrong with our marriage.
> MAL [*challenging her*]: What is?
> JENNY: The size of your prick.
>
> MAL *is deflated*. KATH *is interested*.
>
> KATH: What's wrong with the size of his prick?
> JENNY: Nothing. He's got an obsession about it.
> DON: Still?
> JENNY: Still.
> MAL [*wounded*]: If you don't mind.
> JENNY: Well, God Almighty—
> MAL: If it's just an obsession then how come you never have an orgasm?
> JENNY: How can I have an orgasm when I'm worrying about you worrying about the size of your member? (69)

As the evening dissolves into a drunken shambles, the Coalition is voted back into power with the help of the DLP. Priapic antics are replaced by a mood of sombre disillusion. 'There's a fucking great world full of people out there who don't give a stuff about little Donnie Henderson', Kath chides her self-pitying husband, 'boy wonder, prematurely retired. Whizz kid. Adolescent genius, full grown bomb out. Fizzer. Squib' (74).

A Stretch of the Imagination premiered at the APG a year later (March 1972). The lone character in it, Monk O'Neill is the ultimate old curmudgeon into whom all the Awful Australians from past dramas are drained as if into a theatrical slurry pit. Like Miss Docker, he is symbolic of the twentieth century. As he yarns about his life, the decline of his aging body seems to parallel the destruction of the world that modernity has wrought. The setting, 'a small hut, dilapidated, built form old corrugated iron' (3) is surrounded by the debris of ruined civilisation: an old alarm clock, a tattered umbrella, a tin drum serving as a toilet, an open grave for when Monk's moment of expiry finally comes. The action is composed of Monk's half fanciful, half all-too-real memories wherein the hubris of Western culture is comically assaulted:

> MONK: To imagine that as a young beard I dined at the most select restaurants in Melbourne. A youth of breed and starch—dapper, punctilious, well-kidneyed, etiquette itself. Knew the wines too. Must have an 1876 Chateau Carbonnieux with the basted salamander, anything else would be unspeakably yan yean, eh Jeremy? Waiter! [*Annoyed*]. Tongs, please. Pluck that slug from the endive. Thank you, Boris. Oh, could you impeach a less bumptious volume from the fiddler this evening? Now, for mains may I in all impudence suggest you plump for the hot Shlong Arabesque a la Crème, set off by a Bordeaux? ... Exquisite. Garcon! This table napkin is much too stiff. Another. It must adapt to the undulations of the lap, not rasp and chaff the Savile Row, you ox... You call that coffee, *cameriere*, it's squid piss! Summon the manager. At least the saxophonist is in tune. (18)

Everything Monk touches suffers destruction—usually because he destroys it. His hut in the middle of nowhere sits on top of One Tree Hill. When he moved in, his first action was to chop the tree down, whereupon 'every cockatoo, crow, emu and rosella in the kingdom [took] to the heavens filling them with spleen and indignation. Lesser men would have regarded this as a harbinger and knelt down in supplication. Not me' (41).

The Floating World (premiere August 1974) is the third play discussed here to come from the APG. Like *Chapel* it is scenically and stylistically super-fluid, moving across locations and aesthetics that are, from a realist point of view, discordant, but coexist quite naturally within the splintered mind of the protagonist, Les Harding. Les is a returned serviceman from World War II. Captured by the Japanese he was forced to work on the infamous Burma–Thailand railway. The play takes place on a passenger ship, where Les and his wife Irene are taking a Cherry Blossom Cruise to Tokyo for a two-week holiday. As the trip continues, Les's long-repressed war memories bleed into his current reality and the action becomes a surreal wash of tortured past and unbearable present. In the final pages, Les recounts in nightmarish detail traumatic incidents from his time as a POW:

> LES: Acute appendicitis. I was lucky. They still had some anaesthetic. I came to the hospital compound. They were all dying there. You could tell that. None of 'em would eat. An English boy was taking weeks to die… He had eyes you couldn't look into. Trembled whenever he heard a Jap voice. I was the only one recovering. Eighteen and he's seen the lot. I watched a blow-fly crawl out of his arse. Slowly. All the time in the world. And he lay there in a coma with his mouth open and another one crawled out his mouth. Along his tongue. Feeding on him. I told 'em to eat. Eat like the Jesus. Just rice. They couldn't hold anything down. Bring it near them, they'd chuck. Chuck nothing. Pus and bad air. The sweet stench of—I made myself eat. No matter what. And the bloke next to me gurgled a bit… I took a look and kept eating. He'd died. I turned over and ate. And later I took his boots. I had none. (86)

Les is a mix of Jim Davidson from *The Touch of Silk*, a man shattered by war, and Alf from *The One Day of the Year*, one turned into a racist bigot by it. But it is impossible to separate the monster from the victim, or apportion blame. 'It's not that human beings cannot bear too much reality', says Harry, the dead comrade who accompanies Les in his descent into madness that is also a recovery of self. 'It's that reality is too much to bear' (93).

The Cake Man is the first play examined in this book to be written by an Indigenous Australian. It is not, from the perspective of Euro-Australian theatre, the first full-length Indigenous play. That honour belongs to *The Cherry Pickers* by Kevin Gilbert (1968). But it was the first to be given a professional production (premiere January 1975). Like *Don's Party*, it is set in the recent past. It opens with a parabolic playlet about the white invasion of Australia, in which three allegorical figures—the Priest, the Soldier and the Civilian—offer an Aboriginal family they encounter a bible, coloured ribbons and a cake. Then the Soldier shoots the Aboriginal father dead. His corpse metamorphoses into Sweet William, the father of a 1960s Aboriginal family living on a mission station. Sweet William is as hopeless and confused as Wally in *Fountains Beyond*. It is his wife Ruby, living in virtual destitution and under the thumb of the mission's white manager, who holds the family together. Their 11-year-old son, Pumpkinhead, is the heart of the drama. Lacking pastimes or toys, Ruby tells stories to entertain him that are fusions of Christian myth and Aboriginal Dreamtime:

> RUBY: Long time ago, when Dreamtime's ending, Jesus, he sent the Cake Man over to the sea to find the Kuri children. And he come…
>
> PUMPKINHEAD: With the cake. With the cake Jesus put to carry in his heart. Plenty!
>
> RUBY: He come, with the cake, the cake that was love from Jesus, and he's lookin' round then for good children to love and give cake to…
>
> PUMPKINHEAD: Only the bad men stuck a stick in Cake Man's eyes!
>
> RUBY: That's the truth, the bad men, the wicked men done that…
>
> PUMPKINHEAD: And then the Cake Man lose his way, and

>   can't see because his eyes is blind, and he can't see the Kuri boys, only the gubba kids he kin see ever since them bad men done that! Cake Man's a blind man…
> RUBY: Yes, and all the time since then, the Cake Man been walkin' around the bush lookin' for something' he's forgot about what it was…
> PUMPKINHEAD: But he still got all the cakes, and we gotta find him and tell him!
> RUBY: He still got all the cakes, that's right, but he don't know any more about who Jesus told him to give 'em to…
> PUMPKINHEAD: He forgot! He don't even know he *is* the Cake Man! His eyes gone blind, and he forgot even who is s'posed to give the cakes to, and he forgot about havin' to do it. He don' know who he is… gotta tell him!
> RUBY: Pumpkinhead, who's tellin' this story? [*Pause.*] Well then, what we got to do, we got to wait for him, got to keep lookin', till we see him there, and then we tell him about the cakes that Jesus sent to Kuri children, make him know himself, remember he is the Cake Man…
> PUMPKINHEAD: Got to stick him in the heart with a spear! Story says that… a spear! (21–22)

The ending is double-edged. Sweet William leaves for Sydney to find work, but is arrested for being drunk and disorderly—even though he isn't. Mr Peterson, a contemporary version of the Civilian, who has been pursuing Pumpkinhead for filching his coal ('the little black bastard' 39), is changed when he sees what life on the mission is actually like. The stage direction reads: '*He moves a hand abruptly to his chest, as if a pain has struck him there. They all look at him and he looks at* RUBY' (47).

Crossfire (premiere March 1975) is the most structurally ingenious of these six plays, co-occurring across two time periods—1910 and 1975—but in one location, 'the living room of a rather large, gracious old house which is at the same time the real thing and the lovingly restored house of a stockbroker and his wife' (5). The action, and some of the roles, are doubled, so that characters from the two eras occupy the same set simultaneously, and the actors, especially the men, play related parts in both.

The theme of *Crossfire* is women's rights, but less the questing sexual emancipation of Sally Banner in *Chapel* than the dogged egalitarian activism of Miss Perkins in *The Time is Not Yet Ripe*. Cilla Onslow is a conflicted feminist and wife of a successful stockbroker, Sam. His income allows her to champion women's causes, which she does by taking into her home an unwed mother, Mim, and pursuing an interview project about a historical manuscript she has discovered in her house. This was written by Jane Onslow in 1910 (the names of the characters in the two eras deliberately echo each other). We see a slice of Jane's life too, as the closeted wife of a tea merchant desperate for a freedom that the society around her cannot even imagine, let alone allow. There are moments when the eras briefly but powerfully touch. The first, in Act 1 scene 2, is when Janie, a hard-line feminist, agrees to portray the manuscript's author for one of Cilla's 'faction' interviews. It is in the middle of being recorded when suddenly,

> JANIE *stands. She is talking for* JANE. CILLA *is caught off guard. Everyone is surprised.*
>
> JANIE: I died very young. Thirty-six. I thought I was going to have a child. I was so happy. But instead it was some sort of growth. My doctor—oh, they didn't know much then or care much and he didn't pick it up until it was too late. It wasn't a child. It was my death.
>
> CILLA: What are you doing, Janie?
>
> JANIE *sits.*
>
> JANIE: I don't know.
>
> CILLA: You've ruined it. That ending. [*She waves to stop the tape.*]
>
> SAM: That was the only part that was true to the manuscript.
>
> CILLA: How would you know, Sam? You've only ever flicked through it. Oh Janie, now we'll have to start all over again.
>
> JANIE: Not today. I've got to take the new account to lunch.
>
> CILLA: Oh, all right. I'll ring you about how we get on this afternoon.
>
> JANIE: Not today. I told you I had to take the new account to lunch.
>
> CILLA: We were going well, but that ending! … I liked the first part, Janie—you showed her up for the fool she was,

> but I want this to be hard-hitting. I want to shake women out of it.
>
> SAM: Shake them out of what? (21–2)

Like *Don's Party*, though for more explicitly political reasons, gender relations in *Crossfire* fray in an atmosphere of indecision, perplexity and mixed messaging. Both Cilla in 1975 and Jane in 1910 want, or think they want, a child. Yet neither can conceive. 'The more I think the more confused I get', says Cilla at the end of the play (65). 'I wanted to be a real woman and have everything we should have. I'm so tired of being stuck in the middle and caught in the crossfire… Both sides look like the enemy' (67).

Analysis of the plays

Perhaps the most striking feature these six plays have in common is that they are all, without exception, preoccupied with the past (or a sense of the past). Three are set in the past (*The Chapel Perilous*, *Don's Party*, *The Cake Man*), two recount stories from the past (*A Stretch of the Imagination*, *The Floating World*) and one exists simultaneously in both past and present (*Crossfire*). For dramas that are supposedly about 'the now', like *O'Malley* they step back in time to frame it. Certain moments in the life of the nation I have flagged as important assert themselves as ripe for dramatic exploration: the post-federation years, in which one half of *Crossfire* is set, and is a source of reminiscences for *Stretch*; the 1940s, the starting decade for *Chapel*, and the point of return for *The Floating World*; and the 1960s which provides the baleful Sarsaparillian environment for *The Cake Man* and *Don's Party*.

Certain themes repeat themselves across the plays and echo those of earlier decades: the theme of religion (especially *Chapel*, *The Cake Man* and *Stretch*); the theme of race (especially *The Cake Man* and *The Floating World*); the theme of love (all plays), and the physical body, its needs, limitations, fragilities and self-betrayals. There is frequent talk of the mechanics of sex—of copulation, ejaculation, menstruation, birth, abortion; and of illness and disease—getting sick, being sick, getting old, dying, death. The level of thermal comfort is a matter of comment; characters are too hot or too cold; seasonal changes are remarked. Two of the plays are usually classed as comedies (*Don's Party, Stretch*), two as political message dramas (*The Cake Man, Crossfire*) and two as cross-genre blends (*Chapel, The Floating World*).

Using my own classification, two can be seen as examples of 'hot' New Wave theatre: *Chapel* and *The Floating World*. These use a medley of theatrical techniques and a steady infusion of songs, skits and poetry to drive their action forwards (*Chapel*, like *O'Malley*, has a musical score at the back of its script). By contrast, *Crossfire, Don's Party* and *Stretch* are examples of 'cool' New Wave theatre, and share *Norm and Ahmed*'s one location, single set of characters, and restricted time period(s). *The Cake Man* is harder to characterise. A 'warm' play, it glows with a pellucid light reflecting both ends of the New Wave spectrum.

Superficially, the genres of the plays announce their provenance. *Don's Party* and *Crossfire* are the most naturalistic, easy to trace through the *Doll* back to the drama of the previous half century. *Chapel* and *The Floating World* belong to the realm of poetic expressionism, with their Whitean use of a chorus and Douglas Stewart–like scraps of verse. *Stretch* and *The Cake Man* tread the line between realism and anti-realism, blending the two strains in equal proportion. But these lineages must not be taken too seriously, as blending (and bending) genres is a feature of all six works. The detail in the plays is instructive. A careful reader will note that phones are ubiquitous and pawpaw is rare; that medical care is expensive and no-fault divorce has yet to arrive; that television sets are portable but 'radiograms' still a stock item of furniture; that tax offsets are available to male wage-earners for their non-working wives; and that coal is burnt in winter to keep warm. For works that, bar one, were by writers under 30 years old, they contain an impressive array of older characters (Les, Ruby, Monk) or ones grappling with the dilemmas of aging (Sally, Don, Cilla), disproving the assumption that New Wave plays are all about 'youth'.

The social context in which the plays were performed is vital, and in that respect, this 15-year period contains a red-letter day in Australian political history. On 2 December 1972, federal Labor finally returned to power, and Gough Whitlam became the new prime minister. After two decades of conservative rule, the country shot forward like a cannonball with rapid carriage of a raft of liberalising legislation that transformed the life of the nation. The government's first term in office involved changes to almost every area of portfolio responsibility. 'Whitlam extended the ambit of national government further than any peacetime leader before or since', Macintyre writes. The list of what he accomplished in a short period of time is breathtaking:

> In the first month the government withdrew the last troops from Vietnam, ended military conscription, established diplomatic relations with China, announced independence for Papua New Guinea and the ratification of international conventions on nuclear weapons, labour conditions… Assimilation was abandoned as incompatible with an increasing diversity that was celebrated for its enrichment of national life… Women finally achieved the full adult minimum wage… and more was promised to give practical effect to that formal equality: maternity leave and child-care centres for working women along with women's health centres and refuges, and simplification of divorce… A new Australianism, 'femocrat', captur[ed] the novel role of those who sought to reconcile their duties as public servants with their loyalties to the women's movement in regulatory affirmative action. Similar strains were apparent in the new Department of Aboriginal Affairs where Aboriginal administrators answer to white superiors as they established a range of activities, including a medical service and a legal service, tailored to the particular needs of their people… A Schools Commission provided the charter for Commonwealth support of… schools on the basis of need; there was increased university funding and the abolition of tuition fees. A health inquiry created a scheme of universal medical insurance. A commission of inquiry into poverty expanded the welfare system. Another commissioner prepared recommendations for the legal recognition of Aboriginal land rights in the federal territories… A Department of Urban and Regional Development assisted

state and local government to improve urban amenities and funded the acquisition and development of land for housing.

Just as World War I and the Depression form the backdrop to the plays of the 1930s, so Whitlam's 'vision splendid' and the years that led up to it, which Horne calls 'a searching for liberty and equality, and for more democratic modes', provide the backdrop to the New Wave.

Yet if this is a nation running bravely towards the future, it is one haunted by memories of the past. If Australians are now part of the permissive society then these plays suggest they are uncertain about what that means, the benefits it offers, and the power relations it involves. Old lines of structural disadvantage, dating back to Federation, have not disappeared. If anything, there is greater awareness of their entrenchment. But Old Left–style class antagonisms have gone. The plays' mix of hope and despair conjure up stage worlds that are not so much ambivalent about the new life on offer, as constantly changing their perspective on it. Turning and turning again, they present their action from multiple perspectives, refracting their characters from ever-new angles, making ever-more penetrating judgements—yet never a final one. They leave their audiences with the feeling that there is always more to be said.

Stylistically, the plays are eclectic, raiding with impunity the techniques of vaudeville, melodrama, musical hall, the classroom, the courtroom, church services and stand-up comedy, then combining them in energised performance structures that critics of the time readily dubbed 'filmic'. These are plays profoundly interested in the traditions and conventions of theatre—but not in conforming to them. Their professional touch is sure. All six are products of advanced dramatic craft—are 'good' plays that 'work'. But beyond the matter of skill, they are also furiously engaged with the world outside the theatre and, like *Private Yuk Objects*, intent on delivering their message(s) to that world. It is therefore redundant to ask which of these plays is political. *All* New Wave theatre is political as a matter of primary commitment. This is a drama intent on absorbing the social experience of Australians, fracturing it, and examining it imaginatively on stage. This is a drama intent on thinking for a nation.

Structurally, the plays overlap and repeat each other in holarchic fashion. Cilla and Sam Onslow in *Crossfire* might be guests of Don and Kath in *Don's Party*, and vice versa. Les Harding in *The Floating World* might be one of Sally Banner's early lovers in *The Chapel Perilous*, before he goes off to the war, destined never to return, at least not as the same person. *The Cake Man's* Pumpkinhead might be a kid stealing vegetables from Monk O'Neill's garden in *Stretch of the Imagination* (if he lived a little closer). Monk might be a garish passenger on board *The Floating World's* Cherry Blossom Cruise. There are myriad connections with earlier plays. Sally Banner might be one of the girls from *Morning Sacrifice's* Easthaven school. Indeed she might be Mary Grey herself, facing expulsion for kissing a boy. Ruby might be the daughter of *Brumby Innes's* queenly Polly, or a friend of the impulsive Peggy in *Fountains Beyond*. It is easy to see Monk as one of Sarsaparilla's faithless parishioners, while his physical comedy routines resemble those in *On Our Selection*. In fact, *Stretch* is quintessentially a bush play. It may mock the genre at every moment, but it relies on a century of audiences staring at drab outback huts to achieve its full effect. The hopeless men in *Don's Party* might be younger versions of the hopeless men in *Rusty Bugles* or, for that matter, in *Men Without Wives*, now married, but still hopeless. Jane Onslow might have walked out of *The Time is Not Yet Ripe*, turned serious, and wandered into *Crossfire*. It may be a reach to see *Ned Kelly* in *The Cake Man*, but when Mr Peterson calls Pumpkinhead a 'blasted… delinquent black baby-bushranger' (40), the parallel is there.

Connections also exist on the level of language. The dialogue in *Don's Party* has a quick, slick Max Affordish feel to it. *The Floating World* is full of idioms particular to Australian soldiers, like *Rusty Bugles*. *Chapel* inserts Mona Brand–style observations of class-bound Australia into its anti-parable of personal liberation. *Crossfire's* twin-era dialogue produces an inter-temporal 'kinetic stuttering' (37) that might come from *A Cheery Soul*. Parts of *Stretch* might have been written by Ray Lawler; parts of *The Cake Man* by Katharine Susannah Prichard; parts of *Don's Party* by Patrick White; parts of *Chapel* by Douglas Stewart; parts of *Crossfire* by Dymphna Cusack.

What is new in these six plays? Like *Norm and Ahmed*, the answer lies not in their individual elements but the way these combine to create a new type of dramatic understanding. This is clearest when looking at their endings. None end happily. Yet each gestures to a future not without hope, even if the present in which the characters are mired precludes immediate redemption. There are no precedents for their endings in the plays of the past. Neither the 'strong' finish of the *Doll* nor the ironic conclusion of *A Cheery Soul* provide a template for how these plays resolve. As a dramaturgical species, I would call them 'endings of possibility'. They reach out to the audience as if to ask, 'what will *you* do now?'

Two examples from perhaps the less well-known plays will show what I mean. The last scene of *Crossfire* overlays an angry row between Jane and her husband in 1910, with a fight between Cilla and her husband in 1975 (the actor playing Sam/Samuel being the same in both eras). The two women are oppressed by their gender roles, but in different ways. In both times—and this is a crucial point—their husbands are loving. Neither Cilla nor Jane is physically or emotionally abused or explicitly controlled in their marriages. They both have considerable autonomy within the home and, in Cilla's case, outside it as well. But this only makes their politically inferior status more unbearable. What chance of an authentic life when structural discrimination permits no scope for equal relations? This is more obvious for Jane than for Cilla, who has a lifestyle in Whitlam's permissive society that the former can only dream about. But it is there as an undertow and, once Cilla is caught in it, she cannot escape. Both women, Nora-like, are trapped birds in a (shared) gilded cage. The ending sees Cilla sobbing uncontrollably, unspooling the tape of her interview with Mim (in 1975), while Samuel holds the autobiographical manuscript Jane has despairingly thrown in the bin (in 1910). The last stage direction and line reads:

> SAMUEL *reaches for a whisky, but the decanters are not there. He remembers where he put them and goes into the box room. He comes out with the empty sherry decanter. He sits in the armchair.* CILLA *finishes unthreading the tape. She looks at* SAMUEL *and meets his eye.*
>
> CILLA: There.
>
> *Lights down.* (71)

The Cake Man ends twice: in a final scene, then in an epilogue to it. The former is perhaps one of the loveliest in the Australian drama of the period—of any period. Struck to the quick by what he has seen of the mission, Mr Peterson is waiting for Pumpkinhead when he sneaks back to return the coal he has stolen earlier. Together, they then go to Ruby's house with a box of Mr Peterson's provisions and a huge cake. The last line and stage direction read:

> PUMPKINHEAD [awed]: Awwww! You d'Cake Man! ... Noelie! Cake Man! Robbie! Come on, come an' see what's in here. The Cake Man!
>
> MR PETERSON, *looks puzzled, smiling, at* RUBY. *She shrugs. They both look to the door, and kids come streaming in the door one after another as* PUMPKINHEAD *shows them the cake, the big, beautiful cake, and the 'Cake Man', who has trouble embracing all those kids as they run to him.* RUBY *gives him a knife. He gives cake to all the children.* (56)

Immediately after this, Sweet William is arrested. In the lockup, he tells a story about a 'eurie-woman', a spirit he saw when working on an outback sheep station. It is a vision both disturbing and full of wonder. 'She was always there in front of me... her hair shinin' and swirling like it was made out of water, an' her skin like black lightnin'... so beautiful she coudn' ever be bad' (59). The 'gubba' Sweet William works for, however, sees nothing:

> SWEET WILLIAM: He said, come on, William, ain't no eurie-woman... come back to reality.
>
> *Pause.*
>
> Exac'ly what that eurie-woman was sayin' to me...
>
> *Pause.*
>
> Two realities.
>
> *Pause.*
>
> An' I've lost one. [*Pause.*] But I want it back... I need it back.
>
> *Pause.*
>
> Not yours... mine. (59)

The endings of *Crossfire* and *The Cake Man* are characteristic of New Wave drama in their fusing of professional skill, cultural resonance and political messaging to create final images of haunting beauty and power. As white light is made from all the colours of the spectrum so these last scenes synthesise patterns found earlier in the action, bringing them to a new point of intellectual and emotional intensity. To appreciate how revolutionary this was for Australian drama as a whole, not just the six plays I have discussed, let me make a final observation that within this bolder imaginative landscape, the realism/anti-realism division no longer holds, and *will* no longer hold, in the same way, from this time on. New Wave playwrights internalised the division as a *productive tension,* drawing on both strains as required in pursuit of their different dramatic aims. Thus, the endings of these plays are both 'real' in a realist sense and 'true' in a poetic one, signalling the development of Australian drama beyond the boundaries of these genre labels—a creative expansion that occurred in parallel with its greater social acceptance as authoritative inquirer into Australian national life.

6
1976–1990: The compelling mood darkens

The Blind Giant is Dancing **(1983)**. *Diving for Pearls* **(1990)**.
Inside the Island **(1980)**. *No Sugar* **(1985)**. *Away* **(1986)**.
Call of the Wild **(1989)**. *The Forty Lounge Café* **(1990)**.

> Australia is a lucky country run mainly by second-rate people who share its luck.
>
> Donald Horne, *The Lucky Country*

Donald Horne's book *The Lucky Country* was published 50 years ago (1962), and has gone through countless reprints since. Its title captured the hopeful mood of the late 1960s, replacing AA Phillips's 'the cultural cringe' as the *mot juste* summing up a nation. The second part of his observation—that it was 'run mainly by second-rate people who share its luck'—is less often quoted, while his 1976 follow-up volume, *The Death of the Lucky Country*, is universally unread. The tone of this short polemic is one of biblical wrath. Gone is the avuncular social psychologist of *The Lucky Country*, replaced by a furious Jeremiah hurling scorn at the 'second-rate people' who had just triggered Australia's worst political crisis since Federation. 'What happened?' Horne thunders, before immediately answering his own question,

> This: The Governor-General secretly made a decision, the effect of which was to support the political plans of the Liberal and National Country Parties. Against all contemporary practice he did not discuss that decision with the government that was then in power. But having

contemplated the decision secretly he secretly got for it the support of the Chief Justice, a person of no more constitutional significance in this matter than you or me, but one whose respected office could seem to give extra authority to what the Governor-General had decided. The Governor-General then mounted a time-tabled operation, for which the phrase 'constitutional *coup d'état*' seems a useful description. It was an operation which had the general effect of leaving the Prime Minister with a false sense of security, then, without discussing any alternatives, kicking him out of office, installing the minority leader as Prime Minister, then dissolving Parliament. It all happened so quickly that no preventive action could be taken.

On the afternoon of 11 November 1975, Sir John Kerr sacked Gough Whitlam and the Labor government he led. Many parts of Australia's history suffer from not being remembered in sufficient detail. Truth is the casualty of neglect. 'The Dismissal' however suffers from the opposite problem. The tsunami of books, articles and websites offering in-depth accounts of the events that fall under the umbrella of this infamous heading make it difficult to discern where their real significance lies.

Immediately after the sacking, the Coalition (the Liberal and Country parties) went into overdrive to justify the quasi-legal actions that had occurred. Malcolm Fraser, the Leader of the Opposition, had talked openly about wanting to get rid of the Whitlam government. This was difficult to square with the Coalition's commitment to traditional values and the conventions of the Westminster system. Although Whitlam left office as instructed, and the Coalition was elected to it a few weeks later, the harm done was long lasting. Australian democracy was brought into discredit by those whose job it was to keep it safe.

The rivers of ink spilt since on whether Kerr's actions were 'appropriate' given the 'constitutional crisis', obscure the basic fact they should not have happened—that the Dismissal was, like the White Australia Policy, the removal of Indigenous children and conscription for the Vietnam War, an immoral act, damaging to the self-conception of the nation as one able to transfer power in a legitimate manner. This is not an outlier opinion. It is the view of the parliament of Australia itself, which maintains a webpage that concludes,

> There was no constitutional crisis, other than the one that the Coalition created, that compelled a change of government. Even if all the Coalition's criticisms of Whitlam's Government were well-founded, there was no economic or international crisis that was about to bring Australia to ruin if Labor was allowed to remain in office until closer to the end of its three-year term. There was no imminent risk to Australian democracy, other than whatever risk emanated from the crisis that the Coalition provoked. Surely there was evidence of bungling, ineptness, incompetence, and remarkably unwise decisions. But democracies have survived worse—much worse.

In retrospect, many of the 'scandals' that embroiled the Whitlam government in its short time in office look groundless or exaggerated: its break with American President Richard Nixon, and refusal to support the carpet-bombing of North Vietnam; its attempts to raise overseas loans to buy back Australia's energy resources from foreign ownership; its view of ASIO as locked into an anti-communist mindset and blind to right-wing extremism; its vocal support for women's liberation and appointment of Elizabeth Reid to the newly created position of Advisor on Women's Affairs. These actions hardly seem like the stuff of revolution now. Yet they happened quickly and, given that Labor had not been in office for 23 years, often clumsily.

By contrast, the Coalition was distinguished by what Horne calls 'a belief in its divine right to govern' and smarted at being in opposition. Within 18 months of the 1972 election, its leader, Billy Snedden, was threatening to use his Senate majority to reject the government's budget bills ('block supply'). Whitlam's response was to call a double dissolution in June 1974 (elections of both houses of parliament, including a full Senate election). But though more Labor senators were returned, it did not give him control of the upper house.

After another 18 months the Coalition, now led by Fraser, tried the same trick again. This time Whitlam refused to be drawn. So the Coalition carried out its threat and blocked supply.

Slowly but surely the government ran out of money to run the country. Fraser's excuse for this questionable tactic—it was deliberately designed to bring Whitlam down—was that there were 'extraordinary and reprehensible circumstances' to justify it. Given these did not lie in the 'scandals' that so obsessed a prurient public and the sensationalist media that fed it, what were the causes for alarm? Was it only a belief in the Coalition's divine right to govern, or were there substantive factors that provided a context, if not an excuse, for their unscrupulous actions?

In fact, there were two, one economic, the other political. In respect of the first, 1973 is a significant date. In that year, the oil-producing countries of the Persian Gulf increased the cost of a barrel of crude oil by nearly 300 per cent. Through their peak body, OPEC, they controlled a substantial supply of a resource vital to the functioning of Western industry which had no option but to pay the higher price. The result compounded certain negative effects that had begun to threaten the stability of Australia's post-war prosperity and the Keynesian economic consensus behind it. Conspicuous was the phenomenon of 'stagflation' or 'slumpflation', a deadly combination of high inflation and high unemployment that, in theory, should not coincide, since one supposedly works as a trade-off against the other.

Though nothing the Whitlam government did precipitated the buckling of the world economy, it was nevertheless held responsible for the consequences—and they were dire. Australian Bureau of Statistics data shows an annualised inflation rate in the 1970s of over 10 percent (four times higher than the rate in 2020–21). The catcher's mitt that felt the worst of the impact was 1974. Tim Colebatch calls it 'The Year the Economy Went "Bung"' and writes,

> It began with unemployment at 2%, but ended with it heading for 5%... Consumer prices rose 16%, yet wages topped that, rising 28% as powerful unions came back for a second or third round of pay rises... Australia's

> current account slid into deficit, never to return. From a surplus of 1.5% of GDP… to a deficit of 3.2% by the end of 1974. It was the year when profits collapsed; industrial disputes escalated; and a housing boom gave way to the steepest bust on record… [T]he Commonwealth budget exploded. As the Whitlam government pressed on with its big-spending reforms despite Treasury pleas for restraint, Commonwealth spending surged 46% in 1974–75, dwarfing the 20% rise the year before.

The Treasurer, Jim Cairns, a politician of great intelligence but no particular financial skill, gave little indication he understood the emergency engulfing the country (he was, at the time, preoccupied by an extramarital affair with his principal private secretary, Junie Morosi). More importantly, nor did Whitlam. He had come to power with a social agenda not an economic one. The money was just supposed to be there. From Fraser's perspective, it was probably what the government *wasn't* doing that provided the 'reprehensible circumstances' for the Dismissal. Though tactically brilliant, in the end Fraser proved no more capable of dealing with a stuttering economy. His eight years as prime minister were marked by a combination of financial instability and industrial unrest.

In 1983, the nation turned to an unlikely duo to calm its troubled waters: a one-time head of the Australian Council of Trade Unions (ACTU), Bob Hawke, and an ex-pay clerk, Paul Keating. By then Western economies had begun to recover. But it came at a terrible human cost. In Britain, under Prime Minister Margaret Thatcher, and in the United States under President Ronald Reagan, whole industries were closed down as governments abandoned the postwar goal of full employment in an aggressive attempt to get inflation under control and profits flowing again. Thatcher drew a line in the sand for her allies and enemies alike when she coined the acronym TINA: There is No Alternative.

The political factors conditioning the Whitlam crisis are harder to parse because the atmosphere in which they pertained has largely dissipated. Neither the 's word' nor the 'c word' are used much when discussing the Dismissal now. Yet they should be. That the Whitlam government was socialist (near as), and sympathetic to communism (as shown by its withdrawal from Vietnam and lack of support for Nixon) was self-evident to many in the Coalition's ranks. The accusation was untrue in the sense that Whitlam, like Hawke later, spent much of his time wrangling with the left faction of his own party. But it reflected the bug-eyed paranoia coating the Cold War, when the Soviet Union looked, on occasion, to be doing better than the West. Even if the Soviet invasion of Czechoslovakia in 1968 had knocked the gloss off communism as a desirable ideological alternative, capitalism seemed everywhere under attack. This affected both those with a stake in the smooth running of the market economy, such as banks and the large corporations, and those doctrinally committed to it, such as the 'neo-conservatives' and 'neoclassical economists' making their first appearances in policy circles. The two perspectives were not mutually exclusive. Personal interest and principled belief are a powerful force when combined. Whitlam caught the global economy as it was running out of cash, but also faced the global polity as it was turning to the right. The tide of 'real existing socialism' (a popular catch-phrase at the time) had to be turned back by fair means or foul. For some people, the Labor government was part of that tide.

Macintyre does not discuss this aspect of the Whitlam years, probably because it existed only in the minds of conservative politicians. But he notes the new order making its appearance:

> Out of the turmoil in the world economy during the 1970s a new economic order would emerge. It involved the growth of finance markets, liberalisation of trade, an increased mobility of capital and a new division of labour as Asian countries embarked on industrialisation… The needs of business came to dominate national life as never before, and economists claimed an unprecedented authority. The vocabulary of the market served as the language of public policy and entered into almost every aspect of social life… A new orthodoxy arose—neoliberalism—and a distinctive Australian term for it: here it was called economic rationalism. It was remarkable not so much for

devotees' capacity to incorporate every form of human behaviour into its ambit as for the assumption that there could be no other way of reasoning than by the logic of the market.

The most recent account of the Dismissal is the ABC podcast series *The Eleventh*. A word much used by both journalist Alex Mann and the Whitlam-era people he interviews is 'dramatic'. With good reason. The tight, intensifying pattern of events (revelations and reversals); the interplay of larger-than-life characters (stereotypes and archetypes); the high-flown language that came out of the mouths of the major players (poetic and vernacular): it could have been the stuff of a New Wave play; one of the more serious, naturalistic ones, perhaps. By contrast, the Queensland premier, Joh Bjelke-Petersen was running his state as if he were following a script written by Michael Boddy and Bob Ellis. The system of entrenched police corruption, later exposed by the Fitzgerald Inquiry was literally called 'The Joke'. Bjelke-Petersen even had a bit part bringing down the Whitlam government in 1974. Then in 1985, topping the ambitions of even the most hubristic O'Malley-style politician, he made a tilt for Canberra in an ill-fated (but entertaining) 'Joh for PM' campaign.

Antics such as this, and they were numerous in the period, narrowed the gap between Australia's national drama and its national life by increasing the flow of traffic from the other direction. If the 1970s saw playwrights more conscious of their role as examiners of the collective psyche and soul, it also provided abundant evidence of why this was so crucial. 'There was the diffused shock of an affronted trust in which [we] felt that democratic decencies were not for Australia', wrote Horne in 1976, as he lay in hospital, symbolically recovering from an eye operation. 'The political system seems to have powerful devices available only to the opponents of reform. In a showdown the reformers could see the system was stacked against them.'

Just as Australian democracy faced unprecedented trials and changes, so did Australian theatre. As early as 1929, Michael and Joan Tallis write, 'the original JC Williamson model of the complete theatre company providing total and continuous entertainment was a dinosaur; a relic of a past age'. By 1975, the repertory theatres and New Theatres that had replaced the Firm as the leaders of the sector were themselves either going or gone. In their stead arose the industry we have today: one mainstream, government-supported theatre company in (nearly) every state; an inner ring of small-to-medium size organisations, of which Nimrod and the APG were the pioneers; and a diverse scattering of groups, ensembles, one-off projects and lone artists.

Of the mainstream companies, Melbourne Theatre Company was the first to be established (1952 as the Union Theatre Repertory Company); followed by the Old Tote Theatre (1963) which collapsed and was replaced by the Sydney Theatre Company (1979); Queensland Theatre (1971 as the Queensland Theatre Company and later Royal Queensland Theatre Company—the Queen attended its first show, the farce *A Rum Do!*, and as an assistant director there in 1989 I used to eat my lunch in the Royal Box); the State Theatre Company of South Australia (1976 as the South Australian Theatre Company, also known as Lighthouse, the State Theatre Company, and the State Theatre); and in Western Australia, the Black Swan State Theatre Company (1956 as the National Theatre Company, the most stop-start of the group, it collapsed and was reconstituted several times with different names). A rash of new performing arts centres across the regions complemented the appearance of these companies, so there were now more venues in which to tour their shows. In 1976, JC Williamson's collapsed, leaving the state theatres to take over whatever was left of the commercial market for live drama.

In retrospect, the late 1970s was as good as it got for public assistance to Australian theatre. Either because mainstream companies became too large, or because the Australia Council's annual allocation shrank in the shift to 'small government', after 1980 there was heavy pressure on budgets, and the stark financial realities that had overwhelmed the Firm confronted its successors also. If 'slots' for Australian drama did not reduce, cast sizes certainly did. Three-year contracts for actors went out with the passing of the Tote. Later, so did annual contracts, with actors now hired on a show-by-show basis. By contrast, marketing departments grew, as companies became conscious of what outside experts told them was 'their brand'.

After 1975 Australian theatre artists faced a double whammy: ructions in their own profession and upheaval in the world outside it. Justin Macdonnell gives a detailed account of these years in *Arts, Minister?* and I cover the same period in *Australian Theatre After the New Wave*. 'Heavily conflictual' is a fair summary of the endless, sometimes bitter wrangling in the sector at this time. The interwar Little and New Theatres did not go gentle into the good night of organisational eclipse, while the alternative and fringe ones resented the size, expense and (as they saw it) entitlement of the state companies. The issue of who was creating 'real' Australian theatre loomed in much the same way as the question of who constituted a 'real' Australian once did. The nationalism of the early 1970s acquired a puzzled look. This did not mean a return to Anglophone cultural dependency, but it meant a halt to the confident assumption that Australian theatre would progress into an unproblematic future without challenge or check. It meant the fading of the lucky-country optimism that marked the creative energies of the previous ten years. It meant a darkening of the compelling mood of Australian drama.

Stephen Sewell's *The Blind Giant is Dancing* (*Blind Giant*) premiered in 1983, Katherine Thomson's *Diving for Pearls* in 1990. Only seven years separate these two plays, and their content and political views are similar in many ways. Yet they might have come from alternate realities so stark is the contrast in their sensibilities. Though in part this comes from their different styles, it is their background assumptions that make them so distinct. In other words, they portray two radically different Australias. Is there another seven-year period in our history that presents such a fundamental shift in the nation and the national consciousness? Reading *Diving for Pearls* now it is easy to relate to its action and tone. Thirty years later, we are still living in the world of Thomson's play. By contrast, the world of *Blind Giant* has disappeared into oblivion. Not only does its story feel distant, so do the values that gave rise to it, and with which Sewell expected his audience to identify. This is a clue to the scale and significance of the changes. By 1990, not only was another kind of Australian play being written, another kind of Australian had appeared to watch it.

In this chapter, I first examine *Blind Giant* and *Diving for Pearls*, then look at *Inside the Island* and *No Sugar*. The phrase 'state of the nation drama' was coined to describe plays by writers such as David Edgar, David Hare, Howard Barker and Caryl Churchill grappling with the travails of modern Britain. It is also an apt label for these Australian plays. 'Australia', its complexion and history, is the chosen target. Social relations are explored in their widest possible extension—'the personal is political'. There is an epic sweep to the narratives and characters that pushes them towards parable and allegory. These are plays that deal with the nation on the nation's terms.

By contrast, *Call of the Wild* and *The Forty Lounge Café* offer more dreamlike experiences. While no less socially committed, the texture of that commitment is expressed in heightened theatrical aesthetics—'the political is poetic'. *Away* may be thought of as a moment of pivot (1986). *Brodie's Notes: The Complete Guide to Exam Success* informs its readers that this celebrated play is '*not* a study of Australian society' (emphasis added), though admits 'in its late sixties setting familiar social issues of that time emerge'. I take the opposite tack, reading *Away* into the history of the nation, but am aware that by the mid-1980s the assumption that stage plays can proclaim universal truths was being questioned.

As ideological 'grand narratives' suffered intellectual eclipse, especially on the left, the critical focus of Australian drama altered. It would be incorrect to say that 'it diminished', but one can perceive a reassessment of its function in both mainstream and alternative theatre. Some practical aspects of theatre production definitely did diminish though. *Blind Giant*, *Inside the Island* and *No Sugar* all demand cast sizes of between 12 and 20 actors. *Away* asks for only eight, *Call of the Wild* and *Diving for Pearls* for five, and *The Forty Lounge Café* for just four.

A nation-building state changes its mind

'The central difficulty in coming to terms with *The Blind Giant is Dancing*', says Stephen Sewell in his preface to the script, 'is that on the surface it appears to be "about" certain recognisable institutions and features of Australian society but its characters and action seem totally alien... the play is then dismissed as a laboured attempt to show that power corrupts in a context the author has no knowledge of' (vi). The truth of this observation depends on how *Blind Giant* is historically framed. If it is seen as part of New Wave drama, then its millennial negativity is certainly a break with that upbeat body of work. If it is viewed as kin to Douglas Stewart's *Ned Kelly*, however, then it marks the return of an Australian play dealing with shocking violence, pervasive corruption, and a struggle against state power with fatal consequences for those who wage it. Though *Ned Kelly's* dialogue is in blank verse and *Blind Giant's* has the point/counterpoint rhythm of political debate (with references to every major thinker of the modern era), the Old Testament atmospheres of both works, infused with fundamental questions about right and wrong, reveal their shared focus. Sewell and Stewart both occupy the same strain in Australian drama, constructing plays that grapple with the ethical values—or lack of them—of the Australian nation as a whole.

Blind Giant starts with an assassination and ends with a suicide. Themes of death and dying are constant throughout, not the pleasant (by comparison) life-fading of *A Cheery Soul*, but a coal-black horizon of hostility and murder. Allen Fitzgerald, the lead character, is a 1980s version of a 1870s bushranger: a socialist economist. He is involved in a no-holds-barred power struggle with Michael Wells, a kingmaker in the Labor Party (a state setting is presumed, either New South Wales or Victoria). Allen is leader of the left faction of the party, Wells of the right. As their manoeuvring plays out like a deadly game of chess, there is a chance for the left to 'get the numbers' and take control of the party executive. Allen could then replace Wells, who would be 'finished' (the play's most frequently fired epithet), and Labor forced to adopt a socialist policy agenda.

Over the course of two long acts the relationship between the men goes from personal dislike to satanic hatred. There seems to be no end to the anger Allen and Wells feel towards each other, or towards themselves. Yet their hyper-animation as they scheme, plot, deal and destroy, feels curiously devoid of agency, as if the two men are mindlessly obeying a rule that demands kill or be killed. 'Capitalism constructs us in its own image', Allen tells his wife, Louise, a feminist who, like *Crossfire's* Cilla Onslow struggles to escape her middle-class upbringing, with the added twist that she is a Jew carrying a heavy burden of inherited guilt.

At the core of *Blind Giant's* narrative is Austeel, a steel smelting factory. Allen's family is working class, and his father, Doug, and brother, Bruce, are employed there. There is a third brother, killed in the Vietnam War, and, along with the possible takeover of the factory by an American firm, these are examples of the 'recognisable features' that formed the background to the play when it premiered in 1983. Doug is a blue-collar patriarch, all male pride and bragging self-reliance ('I'm a man and man stands on his own legs. I'm not dependent on anyone' 100). He is also a bully, who forced his eldest son into the army, and now blames Allen for his death. Like Allen and Wells, capitalism brings out the worst in Doug. He is similar to Cox in *Ned Kelly*, so focused on his own self-interest he is blind to the oppression of the class to which he belongs.

Bruce, by contrast, changes for the better. From being a reflection of his father's anti-communist prejudices he achieves political awareness and becomes a union organiser. Other characters have a similar representative function: Bob Lang, a 'bourgeois economist' (it says a lot about the changes in Australia that this phrase is meaningless now); Sir Leslie Harris, who owns Austeel, and is described simply as 'a capitalist'; Ramon, an exiled Chilean socialist, abandoned by Allen; and Rose Draper, a financial journalist whose nihilism symbolises the despair of Australia's intellectual elite in the same way that Doug symbolises the cupidity of its manual workers (ROSE: All I want is to chronicle the last screams of a dying world 104. At the end of the play she suicides).

Reading *Blind Giant* is like stepping into a Hieronymus Bosch painting. The luciferous nature of the action—many of the scenes are at night—magnifies its dysphoric feel, supercharging the message that capitalism is in its death throes. The description of the steel mill is hellish: '*It is spectacular and terrifying... There are flames, torches, unbelievable noise. Men are directing a river of molten steel across the floor*' (37). The political positions of Allen and Wells will not be obvious to a contemporary audience. Austeel is an Australian company protected by tariffs and government grants. Although a Labor Party bureaucrat,

BHP Continuous Slab Caster, Port Kembla, Wollongong, 1987. Black and white photographs do no justice to the profusion of yellow, orange and red flame that is the interior of a smelting works. Though reduced in size during the waves of deindustrialisation that swept Australia after 1990, Port Kembla remains operational today.

Wells wants to privatise the factory as a way of winding back subsidies that are 'only an excuse for lining the pockets of titled bludgers' (41). Allen's left faction hopes not just to nationalise, but to socialise, the steel mill (give it over to worker control; again, few people now would know the difference), putting him on a collision course with both Wells and his father.

In the background is the crotaline figure of Carew, ostensibly an American Labour Hall functionary, actually an American intelligence agent. After the Dismissal many on the left, catching the paranoia of the right, were convinced that the CIA had a hand in bringing Whitlam down. There is a 'foreign interference' undertow in *Blind Giant*, but it is comparatively weak. None of the characters need to be corrupted by an outside power: they are more than capable of corrupting themselves.

Everyone betrays everyone else: Allen is unfaithful to Louise, and Louise to Allen; Wells is set up by Carew, and Allen takes the bait, manipulated by Rose. Doug betrays his family and his class, while Allen betrays his principles and himself. After Wells is thrown out of office because of a (fake) corruption scandal, Allen takes his place. His first action is to pave the way for the privatisation of Austeel. When Bob Lang visits Allen to tell him that Labor plans to 'import everything. We won't have a manufacturing sector left', Allen replies, 'That's capitalism' (112).

Blind Giant's dialogue is thick with ideas. Many of the scenes echo each other in shape and themes, however, so giving a taste of the overall style is easier. In the extract below, Bruce confronts his brother after Allen has abandoned his moral compass. Note the lack of subtext. Unlike a naturalistic drama—but very like *Ned Kelly*—Sewell's characters are super-articulate, moving easily across personal disclosure, social critique and existential statement. They speak their minds even when, like Allen, they are losing them:

> ALLEN: Did Ramon tell you the deal I had to make with Charlie Palmer to keep us in the Party?
> BRUCE: What deal?
> ALLEN: That any Party or criminal investigations against him had to be stopped. Do you know what that means, Bruce? That we'll be protecting him while he's pumping heroin into this State and putting fifteen-year-olds into his brothels for his elite fucking clientele—
> BRUCE: No.
> ALLEN: Capitalism's perfect, Bruce: there's no way you can overthrow it.
> BRUCE: You wouldn't do that!
> ALLEN: I did it. It was my socialist duty…
> BRUCE: Did you go to the brothel with him?
> ALLEN: Yes.
> BRUCE: I don't believe—
> ALLEN: I wanted it, Bruce. I wanted to feel everything—
> BRUCE: You didn't! Tell me you're lying!
> ALLEN: —that stinking deal meant! I wanted that degradation—
> BRUCE: Not you!
> ALLEN: —that horror.

BRUCE: How could you!
ALLEN: Because if I was going to do it, I wanted it all.
BRUCE: To poison your soul?
ALLEN: It's poisoned from the very moment it's born: that's what I finally realised, Bruce. The appalling beauty of capitalism is that it creates the illusion of our freedom; but it makes us think we can change it or alter it—that we create it. But that's not true. It creates us. It makes our desires and our thoughts—
BRUCE: That's bullshit. What's happening to you?
ALLEN: —it employs us to maintain and expand itself.
BRUCE: Have you gone mad?
ALLEN: That all we are, are momentary carriers of its power and what's finally real is capitalism; draining living things of their substance; a rapacious horror that'll never end until it's finally eliminated human life completely and replaced it with its own self-reproducing machines.
BRUCE: You're wrong.
ALLEN: I'm lost, Bruce. Get out before I burn you. (121–2)

Diving for Pearls is also set in a steel mill, this time in a specific place, Wollongong, though its name, State Engineering Works, feels less symbolic than Austeel. In fact, compared with *Blind Giant*, the play seems altogether more straightforward. Its leading male character, Den, has been employed as a 'shovel donkey' (23) in the fabrication department of the mill for 25 years. In the first scene, we see him try to hook up with an ex-lover, Barbara, who walked out on him a few months previously. The conversation between them borders on light banter, though it is Barbara who does most of the talking. Gone is *Blind Giant*'s umbrous sense of impending catastrophe and despair. The dialogue is bright and cheery, with a vein of tongue-in-cheek humour. After the nightmare world of Hieronymus Bosch, *Diving for Pearls* feels as playful and shadow-free as a Howard Arkley painting. The scent of recovery is in the air, the suggestion that an obliterating capitalist crisis may have passed Australia by after all.

Yet dramatic styles, like appearances, can be deceptive. *Diving for Pearls* is as full of betrayal and distrust as *Blind Giant*. Its outcomes are as nugatory and its politics just as rank. If anything, the underlying message is worse, in the sense that at least Sewell's characters know Australia is in trouble and they are letting themselves down. The socialism they hanker for is a clear goal, even if they can't achieve it, and the play ends with a rousing political occupation of Allen's office. *Diving for Pearls* finishes in a more disturbing way, as if its action were inherently irresolvable.

Like Austeel, the State Engineering Works is sold off to a private company. But in the years from 1983 to 1990 Australia has gone from downsizing to asset-stripping. The factory will be demolished for a housing development. As Ron, Den's brother-in-law and the management consultant brought in to reorganise the steel mill, tells him later, 'The bottom line is you were unlucky enough to work on a site that's got spectacular views' (68). *Blind Giant* ends with a battle, a losing one, but a fight nevertheless. *Diving for Pearls* ends with an entire life-world ceasing to exist. Its easy-on-the-ear comic tone masks an aftermath grimmer than anything in Sewell's play.

In the script, Thomson describes Barbara as 'close to 40. The years have taken their toll and she is going through a rougher patch than usual. She has worked in a clothing factory since the age of 14 and is accomplished at standing up for herself. While she eschews self-pity, there is a vulnerability to her, despite her brittleness' (xiv). Like Olive in the *Doll* and May Hallinan in *Brumby Innes*, she is somewhat self-delusional, aspiring to a way of life not available in reality. She gets back together with Den but harbours doubts about their relationship, thinking he is insufficiently 'entrepreneurial' (65). She then borrows a large amount of money from him to enrol in a deportment course ('Your colours done, that's the first thing. Where are you if don't know your colours?' 21), hoping to land a job at the new Resort Beach International Resort ('They're changing the name of the beach, to fit the hotel' 19).

Barbara is not an unattractive personality. She's funny and self-deprecating, and has what would now be called 'resilience'. But the values underneath the bubbly surface are less appealing. As she lurches from disaster to disaster—the grooming classes fail to work a *Pygmalion*-like makeover—she behaves in an increasingly destructive way. Her selfishness goes from being one aspect of her character to being its central trait. The cause is the same as in *Blind Giant*: the corrupting power of capitalism. Not only is Barbara oblivious to the changes happening around her, she believes the hype (hints of Peggy from *Fountains Beyond*, who also fails to understand the politics in which she is immersed). Some of her remarks might be lifted from Milton Friedman's 1962 work, *Capitalism and Freedom*. 'It's all a race', she tells Den early on; then, when talking about getting work at the hotel, 'You can do anything these days. Well, you have to' (12, 20).

Her greed intensifies as the action unfolds. 'Money's not to live on. It's just to use so you can get more', she says, when Den is talking about refusing his redundancy package, 'I do know. I have been thinking about money pretty solidly for most of my waking life' (65). At root, Barbara has the same Darwinian view of existence as *Blind Giant*'s Doug (and Margaret Thatcher): 'People have to look after themselves. That's the solution' (66). Throughout the play she emits a steady patter about the need for 'marketable skills' and a 'keep flying through, fuck you all and thanks for the memories' attitude (64, 66). She makes casually racist comments and disparages the working-class community from which she comes. Although expressing herself with honesty and humour, she writes it off nevertheless, just as she eventually writes off Den.

While *Blind Giant* ends with a suicide, *Diving for Pearls* begins with one. In the opening scene, Den and Barbara run into each other at the funeral of a mutual friend, Jacko, a union firebrand. Having fought to keep jobs safe at the State Engineering Works, Jacko was himself made redundant, and took his own life. The conflictual world of Sewell is thus symbolically buried to make way for Thomson's (seemingly) quietist one, with workers and management now a 'team'. 'I'm talking about empowering people', Ron tells Den, as his management consultancy gets underway, 'breaking down fucking hierarchies. Making the place more efficient. If I just announced we were going to start ripping off [people's] balls, I don't remember saying it' (30). Den is no Jacko, having stayed in the same house all his life and kept his head down at work. Personal fulfilment comes from a weekly public speaking class (unlike Barbara, he does improve) and the model railway set that occupies the spare bedroom of his house.

Barbara treats Den with a corrosive disrespect that never quite topples into open disdain. This is not true of her behaviour towards Verge, her disabled daughter, however, or Marj, her prim but not uncaring sister, to both of whom she is openly abusive. When Verge leaves her care home in Sydney to come and stay with Barbara unannounced, her mother does everything she can to be rid of her, seeing her as an impediment to the 'sophisticated' life she craves. In Act 2, she binds and gags Verge and locks her in a cupboard to stop her following her to a job interview. Verge escapes and appears just as Den is telling Barbara he will definitely refuse a payout ('It's the principle' 70). The argument that follows is ugly beyond anything in *Blind Giant* in large part because it runs counter to the comic tone that dominates the rest of the play. Barbara's physical appearance is an indication of her emotional disarray: '*a trail of pantyhose, make-up, beauty case, et cetera. She has been crying. Clothes and hair awry... She is savagely wiping make-up off her diploma*' (69). 'You're poison', she hisses at Den. 'Look at yourself', he responds. 'People have started staring at you in the street' (71).

The last scene takes place on the hill where Barbara and Den met in the first scene. 'You take back all those things you said about me', she demands, forgetting the many things she said about him. 'I can't', Den replies. Barbara then delivers a final speech that illuminates both the play's title and her own underlying motives:

> BARBARA: Anyway it's all in the past. Put it all behind me. Would never have worked. Certainly not for me. There's a bloody great world out there. I was just thinking about these ferry trips we used to get taken on to Manly. When we were little. I like boats. And how at the end of the wharf there used to be these boys, teenage boys, diving off the high part for coins. Silver coins. Sixpences and shillings. And how sometimes someone'd trick them. You know, throw in a penny. And one of them'd go in. Just as straight as if it was a shilling. Not me. I won't. Diving for dirty old pennies.
>
> DEN: We've both done a bit of that.
>
> BARBARA: When you think how we could have been... diving for anything... pearls... (76)

Blind Giant and *Diving for Pearls*, so close in time, highlight the changes sweeping over Australia in the late 1970s and 1980s. During this period, domestic manufacturing fell from 20 per cent of GDP to less than 13 per cent. At the same time, tariffs and government grants to industry (the 'effective rate of assistance') dropped from more than 25 per cent of revenue to less than 10 per cent. A 1999 federal Treasury report blandly notes, 'Many Australian manufacturers have moved their production offshore, to remain competitive in international markets... However they still contribute to the well-being of Australians as the profits from the manufactures accrue to Australian shareholders' (12). Not to people like Den and Jacko though, who lost their jobs in the process.

The argument that deindustrialisation was a 'cultural change' prompted by a new 'international outlook' in the manufacturing sector is not convincing. It was led by the government, intent on pursuing an economic doctrine of 'comparative advantage', where countries that could produce goods cheaply (that is, developing ones) compete with those with high labour costs (advanced ones) in open markets, causing the 'restructure' (downsizing or closure) of industries in the latter. In theory, this leads to a more efficient use of global resources, if new jobs are created of equal worth, and all nations play by the same rules (two big 'if's).

This radical shift in government policy is examined by Michael Pusey in his 1991 book *Economic Rationalism in Canberra*, whose subtitle, 'a nation-building state changes its mind', I have borrowed to headline this section. Interviewing high-ranking public servants in the Senior Executive Service in the 1980s, Pusey reveals how Australia's ruling elite abandoned the Keynesian trifecta of government intervention, progressive taxation and full employment, and embraced the neoliberal one of small government, flat taxation and a 'natural rate of unemployment'. *Blind Giant* and *Diving for Pearls* capture this shift in experiential terms, showing the human cost involved. It was Whitlam who began it when he established the Productivity Commission in 1973, accepting the argument of its first chair, Alf Rattigan (a Wells-like figure), that tariff protection was costing the government millions of dollars it needed for social programs. After Hawke and Keating were elected in 1983, they continued the process of 'reform', winding back government assistance in a range of policy domains in the belief that free markets and private firms were better allocators of resources than central planners.

As someone who originally trained as a political economist, I have a keen interest in the changes happening in Australia at this time. For the national repertoire, there are two things to note. First, unlike the United Kingdom and the United States, the shift to the political right was led by the Labor Party, especially the technocratic element in it, people like economist Max Corden (an Allen-like figure, who invented the concept 'effective rate of assistance'). This began the breakdown of ideological binaries along a left–right political spectrum that accelerated after the fall of the communist regimes of Eastern Europe in 1991. Thatcher's TINA became prophetically true. The free market economy replaced command and 'mixed' economies across the world, creating a new, supposedly integrated 'global economy'.

Second, while the political edge of Australian drama is no less incisive after 1990, it no longer takes the same form. The major policies of the two major parties merged, as they did in the 1950s, when Menzies adopted Chifley's agenda. Now Hawke and Keating adopted Fraser's agenda, accomplishing the 'structural adjustment' of Australian industry as completely as any conservative government. The volcanic anger in *Blind Giant* makes sense when seen from this perspective. The 1970s saw a Labor government betrayed by the Coalition. For some Australians, at least, the 1980s saw a Labor government betray itself.

A change in the nation's narrative presages a change in the characters who populate its drama. In moving from the corruption of Allen to the disintegration of Barbara, a different conception of 'an Australian' appears on stage. Shorn of her class affiliations and connections to community, the representative side of Barbara's character collapses. By the end of *Diving for Pearls*, she 'represents' nothing but herself. This is a reflection of the neoliberal outlook, where individual striving replaces collective struggle, personal fulfilment replaces social development, dreams of escape replace visions of progress. No wonder problems of identity preoccupy Australian playwrights after 1990!

The question of what Barbara stands for looms like the edge of a cliff at the end of Thomson's play, the bonds of collective belonging dissolved along with the way of life that produced them. Lest this seem an overly romantic view of an industrial past marked by poverty and grinding toil, it is important to point out that *Blind Giant* and *Diving for Pearls* contain themes running in the opposite direction. Work at Austeel is hard, relentless and soul destroying. If those slaving away in the factory lose their jobs, is that a bad thing? Likewise, is Barbara wrong to aspire to a better life? Den *is* boring and being the *de facto* of a man who plays with model trains is hardly a rewarding role. Den can only suggest to Barbara that she have a baby and shoulder the domestic drudgery that Eileen, Doug's wife in *Blind Giant*, meekly accepts. Barbara wants more. Even if her diving for pearls is ill-defined and self-serving, she is surely right to strive for an existence beyond the one to which society would consign her. Haunting both plays therefore is a question: 'What comes next for the lucky country?' If one kind of Australia was passing away, what kind of Australia was emerging to replace it? It is a question that shapes the nation's drama for the next 30 years.

Back to the future

Louis Nowra's *Inside the Island* and Jack Davis's *No Sugar* are plays of the early 1980s that belong to a Sewellian world of bleak politics, distrust of authority and a pervasive sense of loss. Like other plays in this book, they explore issues of race, class and power in the present by turning to the past. Two 'go to' periods provide the settings, the federation era for *Inside the Island* (specifically a few days in 1912, the year *On Our Selection* and *The Time is Not Yet Ripe* premiered) and the Great Depression for *No Sugar* (starting in late 1929 and running over a few months). If *Blind Giant* and *Diving for Pearls* are 'state of the nation' dramas that look for the causes of national discontent in the class struggles of their times, *Inside the Island* and *No Sugar* explore white impact on Australia's history to a similar end. There is a crucial distinction between plays that are, in a documentary sense, *about* the past, and those that *use* the past as a lens to explore the contemporary world. Nowra and Davis do both, but the eye of these writers is on

Australia now, even when—especially when—they portray events that happened long ago.

Inside the Island is like a hallucinatory version of *Here Under Heaven* in which the settler family at the heart of it, the Dawsons, not only fail to redeem themselves but sink further into moral decay. The action in the second act is especially lurid, but Nowra warns in his preface to the script that 'The scenes of madness should come out of the context of the play and not be played as if it were some sort of comment on the first half. It is always a mistake to believe that just because behaviour is extreme it is unreal' (14). This might be an observation on Australia's white history generally, with its litany of massacres and violent land clearings that in retrospect seem so incredible that for some people they cannot be true. Speaking about the revisionist history of which he was a pioneer, Henry Reynolds concludes *Why Weren't We Told?* with these words: 'It [is] time to throw back the veil which early generations [have] drawn over the brutal history of the frontier. Australians no longer need to cling to those comforting legends of the empty land, peaceful settlement, the heroic and bloodless conquest of the island, the unarmed frontiersmen singing to the cattle'. *Inside the Island* gives a glimpse of the Australia that lies behind the veil.

Lillian Dawson is the Edwardian matriarch at the centre of the play. Just as *Stretch*'s Monk O'Neill is the male apogee of the Awful Australian, so Lillian is the female. She is the opposite of Miss Docker. If honesty and blundering do-goodery define White's central character, duplicity bordering on evil animates Nowra's. She is the inheritor of a large property on the Australian plains. It is not the deprived life of the North, but it is remote enough, and her most frequent tone is one of weary complaint. Like Mrs Abbott in *Men Without Wives* or Barbara in *Diving for Pearls* she constantly wishes she were somewhere more 'civilised'. Her husband, George, is a well-meaning but useless alcoholic.

At the start of the play, a squad of newly recruited soldiers arrive on her land to undertake training ('a small outfit. Fifty men' 25). Their commander, Captain Henry, and his NCO, Sergeant Collins, ask Lillian for permission to set up camp, and in a gesture of self-conscious magnanimity she agrees. Life on the property is one of Chekhovian idleness for the Dawsons who own it, and backbreaking labour for those who work it. The question of how the farm was acquired hangs in the air at every point. Nowra deals with this theme obliquely, in hints, clues and metaphors, rather than making it part of the narrative in an explicit way. It is all the more effective for it. After Captain Henry compliments Lillian on her large and splendid house, she replies, 'My father built it forty years ago. He was a great man. When he first came here it was just bush—a huge plain of Aboriginals and gum trees. He got rid of the blacks, except for those whom he converted; removed the gum trees. His picture is on the wall. Painted by a very talented Aboriginal youth who died soon after' (24).

A cricket match is planned for the following day, with the squad's cook to make food for the lower ranks, but crucially not for Captain Henry or the Dawsons. He has run out of ingredients. In another florid display of generosity, Lillian donates four bags of flour ('It's a privilege to have you in the district. You can have the flour as a gift' 35). However, there is a problem. The flour set aside '[is] very grey' George warns Lillian, 'I'm telling you there's something wrong with it'. 'Soldiers have the appetites of horses', she brusquely replies, dismissing his concerns. 'You could feed them chaff and they wouldn't know the difference. Fix it up with Arthur before lunch. Bin Five' (35). At the end of Act 1, a soldier appears to collect the bags set aside for the army's consumption. At this point, the mood of the play is indeterminate. On the surface, all is serene and bucolic. Beneath, there is a darker current. A village girl has fallen pregnant to the local clergyman and committed suicide (or perhaps she was murdered). Susan, the Dawsons' daughter, is estranged from her father, thanks to her mother's unforgiving opinions, which she parrots in the same way that Bruce in *Blind Giant* parrots Doug's.

In the second act, all hell breaks loose. The flour turns out to be contaminated with a poison (Nowra identifies it as the fungoid parasite *Claviceps purpurea*), and the soldiers go mad. Hieronymus Bosch is provided further employment painting an extended canvas of carnage and terror, in which the infected men mutilate themselves, butcher each other and rape and murder Susan Dawson. Nowra is a master of the disturbing image, and the incidents that comprise the soldiers' delusional rampage have the quality of a never-to-be-forgotten nightmare. They resonate on two levels simultaneously. They are indicative of the insanity of white settler society, its repressed violence and capacity for destruction. But they are also a bizarre re-enactment of the killing of the Indigenous population, the blind fear overwhelming the Dawsons as they face an invasive horde not unlike that felt by the land's original inhabitants. The hands and the feet of the poisoned soldiers go black (*Ergotismus gangrenosus*), adding to the surrealism and the symbolism.

In the end, the house and mill are burnt to the ground, George dies in the fire, holding the body of his dead daughter, and the farm is rendered 'just ashes and dust' (89). Lillian is left contemplating the destruction she herself has caused. Without hesitation, she puts the blame on George. 'No doubt you have heard about my husband's behaviour on Saturday evening', she says to her foreman. 'He was mentally unstable. He should have checked the wheat before he gave it to the troops. Would you tell Captain Henry that, if he should ask?' (88). After a brief bout of remedial weeping, she gets ready to leave and 'live comfortably in England… as far away from this place as possible' (91). She has a final exchange with the Captain that, as with Barbara's last speech in *Diving for Pearls*, illuminates the theme of the play:

LILLIAN: How many men did you lose?
CAPTAIN: Nine.
LILLIAN What about the rest?
CAPTAIN: Sick and dazed… I'm sending them all back on the train… I hope they'll recover.
LILLIAN: They will.
CAPTAIN: I mean, inside their heads. Mentally. Can you go as mad as my men did and fully recover?
LILLIAN: Why not? Just as a drunk recovers from his binge.
CAPTAIN: No, it's not like drink… *yes*, it is. Alcohol releases what's inside of people… like the poison in the wheat. The only way I can understand it, Mrs Dawson, is that the terrible things were inside of them, like when people go crazy on drink.
LILLIAN: What?
CAPTAIN: It occurred to me while watching my men. What

was going on inside of them... it would be a mistake to believe that what they experienced—the hallucinations, the horror—wasn't a part of them. What they saw... the things that went on in their heads... Can they ever see the world the same way they saw it before? (90)

There is a special relationship with the past in *Inside the Island*, which is also found in *No Sugar*. History is not inert. It is not, as Arnold Toynbee once described it 'just one damn fact after another'. It is connected to the present by bonds at once flexible and strong. The more it is repressed, the more surely it returns to the collective consciousness. Both plays share this dynamic conception of memory, a commitment to understanding Australia's past in a larger frame of symbolic reference. In 1962, the first volume in Manning Clark's *History of Australia* was greeted by a reviewer as reprising 'dusty and overworked territory'. The remark shows both ignorance and concealment. Stage plays can lead the way by reopening questions that have too long been closed. The historical record is quite properly the domain of historians. Our *sense* of history, however, comes from a variety of sources, an important one of which is drama.

In *No Sugar* we are at the opposite end of the social spectrum to *Inside the Island*. The Mundays and Millimurras are two Indigenous families living on Government Well Aboriginal Reserve near the Avon Valley town of Northam, 95 kilometres from Perth. Times are hard for all Australians. They are especially tough for those who are 'protected' as part of the 'flora and fauna' of a land declared *terra nullius* by Governor Bourke in 1835, thus depriving its original inhabitants of any claim to ownership. The Reserve is a blend of *Fountains Beyond*'s mixed-blood shantytown, with some freedom of movement for those who live there, and *The Cake Man*'s mission, with meagre rations handed out in a regime of police-enforced penury.

The action of the play, based on historical events in 1933, involves the forced removal of the two families from Government Well to the prison-like Moore River Settlement, over a hundred kilometres away. The author, Jack Davis, was a member of the Nyongarah people of Western Australia, and Nyoongah words and phrases are used throughout the dialogue by all the Indigenous characters. A glossary of Aboriginal terms in the script notes that 'Nyoongah literally means "man" but has become a general term denoting Aboriginality in the South-West of Western Australia' (107). This wider resonance is crucial. The impact of the play comes not from showing the lives of the Indigenous characters in an exotic way, but from making them readily recognisable to anyone, including a white audience. Davis's choice of the strain of stage realism lends *No Sugar* a powerful, near-universal quality. In the words of the actor Ernie Dingo, 'we did it like we lived it' (153).

The history of Western Australia is an important context for the oppressive conditions the Mundays and Millimurras endure in the play. While forced assimilation was the general policy in Australia from Federation onwards, the Western Australian Government adopted a program of racial segregation (apartheid). In her invaluable account of the development and first productions of *No Sugar* Maryrose Casey comments,

> According to AO Neville, Chief Protector of Aborigines from 1915 to 1940, 'the native must be helped in spite of himself'. Neville was one of the foremost advocates for intervention to isolate 'part' Aboriginals, and the Moore River settlement was established under his administration. As Chief Protector he was the legal guardian of all Aboriginal people. The 1936 Native Administration Act gave the Department of Native Affairs unprecedented powers in relation to the daily lives of Aboriginal people in Western Australia... The power of the Acts was extended through the redefinition of Aboriginality to include all people of Aboriginal descent. Intercultural cohabitation was made a punishable offence and the Protector had the power to object to marriages between Aboriginal people.

Neville has a poor historical reputation. He is one of the white characters in *No Sugar*, where interestingly he comes across as a misguided, officious bureaucrat, rather than a malicious tyrant—a role reserved for NS Neal, the drunken, predatory superintendent of the Moore

River settlement. In 1936, a Royal Commission found conditions on the Settlement akin to those of a concentration camp, with separation of the sexes and generations, unhygienic conditions, poor nutrition and severely restricted liberty.

At the end of Act 1, the Mundays and Millimurras leave for Moore River because the WA premier, Sir James Mitchell, wants to improve his election chances by evicting Northam's Indigenous population (it didn't work, he lost the vote resoundingly). Casey's description of the treatment of Western Australian Aboriginal people during the Depression makes for grim reading, and many of these details are reflected in the play (the racism of the police, the endless search for food, the inequity of employment practices). It may seem odd to observe, then, that *No Sugar* is also a lot of fun. The depiction of Australian politics may provoke repugnance, but the liveliness of the Indigenous characters jumps off the page. If resistance in *Blind Giant* is a matter of factions and 'getting the numbers', in *No Sugar* it resides in small acts of defiance and backchatting authority to drive home the point that the families have agency over their own lives, however much the government tries to take it away. Nor is this liveliness an occasional feature. It is a tone throughout the action, infusing a spirit of hope into even its darkest recesses. No Australian play has about it less of a mood of defeat.

Jimmy Munday and Sam Millimurra are the elder men in their families, and Jimmy in particular is headstrong in his views and behaviour, a constant thorn in the side of the authorities. At the start of the play, he breaks the law by drinking two bottles of port wine, an offence for which he is sentenced to three months hard labour. The days of the Indigenous characters are taken up dealing with endless official procedures of one sort or another—appearing in court, collecting rations, undergoing medical examinations, complying with the specious edicts of the Department of Native Affairs. Davis skilfully captures a coercive system adept at hiding its real intentions in administrivia, at once self-justifying and opaque. Colonial rule as it applies to Indigenous Australians in the twentieth century (and arguably today) is shown as an all-pervasive bureaucratic power that everyone must obey but for which no-one seems accountable.

However, Jimmy never obeys, and speaks out in a way that asserts not only his autonomy, but his humanity. Backchatting Neville when he goes to his office to get a travel voucher, he says 'You know one thing about Fremantle Gaol? Even some of them screws are polite—not like this place. Native Protector, couldn't protect my dog from fleas' (39). To which Neville can only respond 'Cheeky, too bloody cheeky'. Jimmy is defiant, but also funny, intelligent and wry. In Act 3, after the families have carved out a restricted yet still viable life in Moore River, he dies of a heart attack, but not before passing on his self-determining attitude to his nephew, Joe. In the last scene, Joe, his wife, Mary, and their young baby leave the settlement for a life outside it—after signing an official undertaking 'not to domicile in the town of Northam, nor anywhere in the Northam Shire' (102), such written contracts being one of the ubiquitous instruments of white colonial power.

Though the dialogue of *No Sugar* is warm and sprightly, at the heart of the play is a chilling account of a mass killing of Indigenous people. Again, it is based on the historical record: the notorious, but until recently denied, Forrest River/Oombulgurri massacre of 1926, when 20 Indigenous Australians were murdered in cold blood by police and local farmers. Although a commission was set up to discover who was responsible for the atrocity, the case never went to trial 'with a preliminary hearing concluding that a jury would not be able to make a conviction'.

In the play, one of Moore River's camp guards is Billy, a spectral figure despised by both the Indigenous families he oversees, and the white administrators who employ him. He is a member of the Oombulgurri people. One night, he tells Jimmy and Joe the story of the massacre:

> BILLY: I bin stop Liveringa station and my brother, he bin run from Oombulgurri. [*Holding up four fingers*] That many days. Night time too. He bin tell me 'bout them *gudeeah*. They bin two, three stockman *gudeeah*. Bin stop along that place, Juada Station, and this one *gudeah* Midja George, he was ridin' and he come to this river and he sees these two old womans, *koories*, there in the water hole. He says,

what you doin' here? They say they getting' *gugja*. Midja George say, where the mans? ... He get off his horse and he bin belt that old man with the stockwhip... Then he break the bottle glass spear, and he break the *chubel* spear. And that old man, he was bleedin', bleedin' from the eyes, and he get up and he pick up that one *chubel* spear, and he spear that one *Midja George*...

JIMMY: Serve the bastard right.

BILLY: No, no, no bad for my mob. Real bad. That old man and his two *koories*, they do this next day. [*He indicates running away.*] Two *gudeeah* come looking for Midja George. They bin find him dead.

Silence

[*Holding up a hand*] Must be that many day. Big mob *gudeeah*. Big mob politjmans, and big mob from the stations, and shoot 'em everybody mens, *koories*, little *yumbah*... They chuck me on a big fire, chuck 'em in river.

They sit in silence, mesmerized and shocked by BILLY's *gruesome story.*

JIMMY: Anybody left, your mob?

BILLY: Not many, gid away, hide. But no-one stop that place now, they all go 'nother country.

JOE: Why?

BILLY: You go there, night time you hear 'em. I bin bring cattle that way for Wyndham Meat Works. I hear 'em. Mothers cryin' and babies cryin', screamin'. *Waiwai! Waiwai! Waiwai!*

They sit in silence staring at BILLY *who stares into the fire. Suddenly a night hawk screeches.*

SAM: Gawd, I'm getting out of here.

JIMMY: Me too! (62–3)

Casey observes, 'With *No Sugar* Davis was portraying life under the apartheid Acts of the 1930s and 1940s to audiences conditioned by the assimilation Acts of the 1960s and 1970s and undergoing a transition towards multiculturalism in the 1980s'. This is the activated knowledge space of live drama, the larger frame of reference to which it is attuned and that it sometimes transforms. Casey quotes *No Sugar*'s producer as saying that when she commissioned Davis in 1982, white audiences 'weren't going to go and look at an Aboriginal play. The older audiences would say, we don't understand the Aboriginal dialect and we don't know what it is about'.

The success of *No Sugar*, both in Perth where it premiered, then the following year in Canada, where it represented Australia at the World Theatre Festival, is triply significant. First, it attests to the work of a talented Indigenous playwright using a 'Western' form for his own creative ends. Second, it marks a point of take-off in what, over the next 35 years, became a distinctive body of work from a cohort of Indigenous theatre artists. Finally, and most importantly, after *No Sugar* it was harder for non-Indigenous Australians to claim 'they didn't know' about the historical treatment of Indigenous people. In its quicksilver shifts of mood and focus, its blending of humour, rage, resilience and tragedy, in its careful moral judgements, *No Sugar* provides a major means for the Australian nation to come to terms with its 'unmastered past'.

Internal worlds

The imaginative qualities of *Away*, *The Forty Lounge Café* and *Call of the Wild* make them an expression of the poetic strain in Australian drama. As with plays of the 1940s and 1950s, there is a shift away from cause-and-effect plotting, but taken much further, with *Call of the Wild* having no linear narrative of any kind. This is accompanied by a loosening of the concept of character similar to the chorus scenes in *A Cheery Soul*, where individual characters materialise when required, then merge back into a collective but powerful stage presence. The term 'meta-theatrical' has been applied to these plays, and it is true that they are self-conscious in their construction in ways that realist dramas are not. But such terms are exercises in *post facto* critical labelling. It is the *experience* of seeing them in the theatre that counts, and here two things stand out: they rely on advanced staging techniques to realise their full dramatic potential; and they make an inward turn, to explore the subconscious and unconscious realm. The kingdom of the Australian mind is shown to be as vast as Australia's physical landscape—and as complex as its history. These plays, short in comparison with some other dramas, feel like Dr Who's

TARDIS: bigger on the inside than on the outside, capable of travelling across time and space in magical ways.

Away is one of Australia's most popular plays (the AusStage database shows 90 separate event entries for it). *Brodie's Notes* describes it as,

> set in the summer of 1967–8 in a Sydney suburb and on the northern coastal beaches of New South Wales and the Gold Coast of Queensland. Events in the wider Australian community and the world at large shape the attitudes and behaviour of the characters. Situations which arise in *Away* are to be understood in their historical context.

True enough—though, as we have seen, 'historical context' is a flexible mental container.

The play follows three couples whose holidays and fates are intertwined. Meg and Tom are teenagers in their last years of high school. In the opening scene, they are performing in a cheesy school production of *A Midsummer Night's Dream*. References to Shakespeare's plays—to the storm scene in *The Tempest*, and the opening of *King Lear*—recur throughout the action. The children's families are very different. Meg's mother, Gwen, is critical and controlling, while her father, Jim, is a peace-at-any-price appeaser. Tom's parents, Harry and Vic, are happy-go-lucky 'ten pound Poms', immigrants from war-affected Britain. Although Meg and Tom grow close as a result of doing the school play together, Gwen's attitude towards Tom and his parents is hysterically snobbish. By contrast, Harry and Vic are the epitome of good cheer. But tragedy hangs in the air. Tom has terminal leukemia, and only just survived his last stay in hospital. As the two families prepare to go on holiday up the New South Wales coast, their contrasting lives and attitudes are on display. Gwen, Jim and Meg own a luxury caravan and plenty of material goods, but fight bitterly among themselves. Tom, Harry and Vic have only a tent and a few possessions, yet are content in each other's company, notwithstanding the fact this might be their last summer together.

The third couple is Roy and Coral. Roy is the headmaster at Tom and Meg's school and Coral is his wife. They had a son, but he was killed in the Vietnam War. The overwhelming grief of this loss is causing their marriage to fall apart. The past makes significant claims on the present. After Meg fights with her mother when she behaves deplorably, Gwen shouts: '[I've] [s]acrificed! Gone without. Gone through hardship so what happened to us will never happen to you. So you'll never know what we saw—never, never, never. Never see people losing jobs and never finding another one, never be without a home, never be without enough money for a decent meal, never be afraid that everything will fall apart at any second' (31).

Away is haunted by the memory of two historical events, the Depression and the Vietnam War. Thematically, it shares the preoccupations of plays of an earlier era. Aesthetically, it belongs to the drama of the future in its fluid structure, economical dialogue, and characters that blend stereotype and archetype. It is also conscious of its existence *as* a play. Some audiences will pick up on the repetition of 'never' in Gwen's speech, which appears in the last scene of *King Lear*, when Lear emerges holding the body of his dead daughter, Cordelia. The words come out of Gwen's mouth, but, given the allusive way *Away* works, poetically they attach to Tom.

Roy and Coral holiday in an expensive hotel on the Gold Coast, where their relationship crumbles further. Coral makes friends with Rick, a young honeymooner as lost and depressed as she is. Angry that his wife continues to blame him for their son's death (Roy's justifications for the Vietnam War are as pitiful as Henry McKay's in *Private Yuk Objects*), Roy threatens to have Coral committed ('Do you want me to send you to a doctor? Do you want me to arrange shock treatment? I can. I looked into it. It's very easy. I just have to take you to a doctor and they plug you in and that's that' 38). So Coral does a moonlight flit.

In Act 3, a storm descends—third acts always being decisive in Shakespeare's plays—and holiday plans go awry. Gwen and Jim's caravan is wrecked, but Meg persuades her parents to visit the quiet beach where Tom, Harry and Vic are safely camped. Coral is there too. 'Isn't she an interesting-looking woman?', Vic says, not recognising her from the start of the play. 'She just arrived one morning, all by herself. I think she might be an artist or something… She goes and sits on the rock ledge for hours and stares into the sea' (42). The last night of the trip involves all the campers watching an impromptu playlet by Tom and Coral about a drowned captain and his lover, a mermaid. At the end, she is granted legs by the god of the sea to 'return to [her] own world and [her] people' (56). Which Coral duly does, walking away from the beach, back to Roy.

The ending of *Away* presents images and tones of healing, forgiveness and reconciliation. Gwen sees the error of her ways, expresses remorse and makes amends. Coral reunites with Roy and their love is restored. Tom remains critically ill, but his condition is endowed with new existential grandeur. *Away* represents an important fusion in Australian drama. Its political themes of family life and Australian history parallel *No Sugar*, but its use of Shakespearean imagery invites a poetic level of response. Audiences can follow its swiftly moving realistic storyline while ingesting symbols that communicate the inner lives of the characters in a non-realistic way. No wonder the play is so often revived. Hilary Bell writes, 'When *Away* premiered at Griffin Theatre in January 1986 I was nineteen and just embarking on a career as a playwright… I clearly remember sitting in the audience with the growing awareness that this play was a game changer. The bar had been raised. We baby playwrights were being shown that Australian plays could still be, as they had been hitherto, comic, political and broad to the point of caricature, and at the same time elegiac, lyrical, nuanced, superbly crafted, local while referencing a bigger world'.

Yet, for me, an intriguing question remains. *How* exactly is the healing, forgiveness and reconciliation in the play accomplished? Lives are shown to be strained. Then a storm comes. After it has gone, the characters are miraculously whole again. As a dramatic event, the storm is brief (though *theatrically* it can be an all-stops-out moment for a director). Where are the middle scenes in which the tensions at the beginning are connected to the emotional relief at the end? Here we need a different conception of 'historical context', not the one *in* the play but the one *of* the play. *Away* is often discussed in terms of its 'universal themes'. *Brodie's Notes* comments, 'Healing, reconciliation and resolution occur through various actions'. Perhaps the most important of these is audience imagination. The middle of *Away* is a gap waiting to be filled with meaning by those watching it. Which is not to diminish Gow's achievement, only to observe that at the time of the play's premiere in 1986, the need of Australian audiences for a resolution with the past was so great that specific ways of arriving at it did not need to be shown.

Lack of explicitly stated meaning is a feature of *Call of the Wild* and *The Forty Lounge Café* too. In *The Doll's Revolution*, Rachel Fensham and Denise Varney discuss Jenny Kemp's unique body of work, saying

> Jenny Kemp's theatre is less about a political revolution in which the writer takes up arms against gender inequality and political injustice and more about a poetic revolution in which expanded conditions of possibility for the psyche, particularly for women, are the key to cultural transformation. The poetic revolution takes place first of all in the imagination where the association of images to words, in bodies and space, resonate… Kemp's theatre sets out to navigate between two worlds, the material everyday and the symbolic universe.

This observation is true of Tes Lyssiotis's stage work too. The two plays premiered within a few months of each other, *Call of the Wild* in September 1989, *The Forty Lounge Café* in March 1990. Both have predominantly female casts (there is one male role in *Call of the Wild*, and one male musician in *The Forty Lounge Café*). Both are about women's experience of the world, but as Fensham and Varney observe, what is at issue is less the social relations in which gender roles are embedded, than the miasma of female desires, dreams, hopes and memories that lie beneath the crust of perception we call 'reality'. The call in *Call of the Wild* is from this subcutaneous level of existence: the call from within. The lounge in *The Forty Lounge Café* is a mnemonic construction in which recollections of all kinds reside. Both plays are noteworthy for the distinctions they do not observe and the conventions they flout: the convention of individual characters; the distinction between past and present; the distinction between action that 'really happens' and action that is 'only imagined'. They are beautiful, deep-natured, elusive, poetic experiences. While they do not use the consciously modernist idiom of Patrick White, they share his

Rosie Lalevich, Evolskia Kahahanas, Mary Sitarenos and Carmelina Guglielmo in the Playbox 1990 production of The Forty Lounge Cafe, Tes Lyssiotis's play was the first in the newly-opened Beckett Theatre, at the Malthouse in Southbank, Melbourne. Playbox Theatre renovated this building, an old brewery, after it original Exhibition Street theatre burnt down in 1984. Photo: Jeff Busby

fascination with archetypes and the realm of truth lying beneath the appearance of the real. The visual design of these plays is key to appreciating their verbal dialogue. Critical summary can do faint justice to the impact they have in the theatre.

The Forty Lounge Café centres on Elefteria Tavlidis, an immigrant Greek Australian, her daughter Toula, and her three sisters, Aspasia, Marika and Irini. Scenes of Elefteria's life in 1960s Horsham, working in a delicatessen that she owns with her husband, Vasseli, are intercut with scenes from her childhood in Greece: living in an orphanage with her sisters, courting as a young girl, and journeying to Australia for an arranged marriage and an unknown future. Greek folk music, dance and song are constant throughout the action. The play is as much a musical and choreographic experience as a dramatic one. Drama is a type of understanding, however, not a list of structural traits. So *The Forty Lounge Café* is most definitely a play, but of the most liquid kind, where reverie, recollection, and real-time action constantly wash together. Shifts of mood drive the play forwards and turn its 34 short scenes into a panoptic image of Elefteria's life. The playfulness and hopes of Elefteria and her sisters at the start of the play—dumped in an orphanage while their mother sorts herself out—contrast with the scene at the end, where the siblings bicker over their inheritance. For a drama with no male characters in it, men are strongly present: as lovers (real and imagined), would-be lovers, husbands, fathers and uncles. They are a mixed lot, but by no means all oppressive figures. Sexual desire is a strong force, sometimes acknowledged, more often not. Neither Elefteria nor Vasseli marry the person with whom they are truly in love, or claim to have been in love with; feelings, like memories, being somewhat unreliable. When Vasseli dies, Elefteria's grief is all-consuming. Running through the play like a current of ice is the fear she has left one home in Greece but failed to find another in Australia. She is a stranger in two countries. When she returns to Greece to claim her portion of her mother's estate, her sisters treat her like a foreigner.

A conspicuous feature in both *The Forty Lounge Café* and *Call of the Wild* is the recounting of dreams. In Act 1, scene 17, approximately one third of the way through Lyssiotis's play, Elefteria, who is an expert seamstress, is fitting her sister-in-law, Sonia, for a dress. They have an exchange rich in suggestive meaning, but hard to pin down in a precise way:

> SONIA: I was walking between the orange trees on my father's orchard, from nowhere these two men dressed in white blood-stained coats appeared. They followed me slowly at first, then began running. I watched them slit the throats of my father's chickens. They pulled out their tongues and forced them down my throat. NO WANT. NO WANT. NO. I called out. Theo woke me up. I was punching him in the face.
>
> ELEFTERIA: I don't dream anymore.
>
> SONIA: I still look like I'm pregnant.
>
> ELEFTERIA: Don't keep eating the lollies in the shop. It's crooked, stand still. Κάνε ένα γύρω [*turn around*]
>
> SONIA: Do you know how many doctors we've seen in the city? Theo won't look at his son. Won't hold him. Just give me money to buy him things. It doesn't run in our family. Είμαστε από γερό σόϊ. [*we're from strong stock*]. Of course

> I don't know about his side. Theo wants everything to be perfect, neat. Especially his son. I don't want any more children.
>
> ELEFTERIA: Hold this. The hem should be up to here, it's the fashion. (28–9)

There is as much Greek language in *The Forty Lounge Café* as there is Nyoongah in *No Sugar*, and it functions in the same way: as an expression of a lifeworld that the play reflects and from which the playwright comes. But the emotional charge is in the opposite direction. In *The Forty Lounge Café* language and history are being lost rather than reclaimed. Toula is Elefteria's charming, but spoilt daughter. The fact that she cannot read Greek is evidence of the disconnection that comes with the diasporic life. The mood is one of soft-hued disappointment, though this is not constant. People feel different things about their choices at different times, and Elefteria's inner world is complex. What is certain is that her life was (is) a full one, a rich tapestry of experiences that Lyssiotis builds up, detail by detail, like the religious icon painting Elefteria keeps in her pocket, pulling it out at the very end, and kissing it for luck, laughing quietly (70).

'I have always been fascinated with the inner life of the psyche. And in particular its relationship with the ordinary, everyday world', Jenny Kemp writes in the preface to the script of *Call of the Wild*. 'As one walks down the street one sees the ordinary world, but experiences both the street and the inner world of memory, imagination, fantasy, emotion and dream. It is with this disjunction that my work attempts a dialogue. One could say it is an investigation into the psyche and its ability to function creatively in a modern world' (8). This statement of intention is important. Despite the surreal nature of the action in *Call of the Wild*, it is not a fantasy, an escape from the real world into one of pure imagination. That world has plenty of reality in it anyway, and Kemp makes use of this fact in taking her audience on a strange and compelling journey into the mental recesses of her characters. These have labels rather than names: the Woman in the Transparent Skirt; the Woman in the Green Skirt; the Woman in the Pale Hat; the Woman in the Short Skirt. One might use such phrases to describe figures seen in a painting. This is no coincidence. Jenny Kemp is the daughter of Australian abstract painter Roger Kemp, and the influence of the visual arts can be felt in the way *Call of the Wild* unfolds as a series of tableaux, each sufficient unto itself, yet taken together providing a deep dive into the female unconscious.

If music is the binding element in *The Forty Lounge Café*, then *Call of the Wild* coheres around visual images, in particular four paintings by Belgian surrealist Paul Delvaux, which title and frame the four sections of the play. *Call of the Wild* is the first work discussed in this book to use projection as a central dramatic device, an avatar of Kemp's own authorial imagination. From time to time, selected words and phrases from the text are projected 'above the actors' (8). There is no logical connection with what is happening on stage in these moments, but the impact is not entirely random. Short sequences of action appear and disappear like spume on ocean waves: a man directing a pornography film; a small boy talking about dinosaurs; a snippet from a witch trial; a snippet from the writings of Tertullian, an early Church father and anti-sex zealot.

The longest speeches are recountings of dreams and fantasies from the women. Typically, they are followed by enigmatic dialogue exchanges with another character. The example below is from Section 2, perhaps 20 minutes into the play. The only context for understanding the scene comes from the non-related scenes that occur before it. 'SLIDE' is the designation for the projected words:

SEXY DREAM

> WOMAN IN GREEN SKIRT: I dreamt I was with a man, he was running carrying me, very sexual. His hands were light, moving over my belly button. I was completely seduced. We stopped to rest on the nature strip. I was liquid, I was so turned on, ready to fuck. But stopped him because we were in the street, and I thought we should find somewhere inside, we went on, saw a huge park, but still it seemed too public. I was dying to fuck and I knew I would not get pregnant because my period was about to come. But then I started to worry about fidelity and AIDS and ended up not having the fuck. Although I realised in the dream that if this was a dream I could do anything I wanted.
>
> SLIDE: *'Tough enough'*

WOMAN SEDUCES MAN IN COAT

All the WOMEN *are speaking*

WOMEN: Come in. What would you like?
MAN: Coffee.
WOMEN: Good, I would too. What about a whisky with it?
MAN: Have you got some?

SLIDE: *'I am too big for my sitting room?'*

WOMEN: I have actually.
MAN: Okay. But not too much I've got work tomorrow.
WOMEN: What time do you start?
MAN: Seven o'clock.
WOMEN: In the morning?
MAN: Yes.
WOMEN: So how many hours did you sleep last night?
MAN: I need eight hours.
WOMEN: Do you? What every night?
MAN: If I can.
WOMEN: Here's your drink. You know you look different tonight.
MAN: Do I? How?
WOMEN: I don't know really, your skin's different.
MAN: Well how is it normally?
WOMEN: Maybe it's because it's night-time. I haven't seen you much at night-time.
MAN: Maybe.
WOMEN: I love your jacket.
MAN: It's Canadian.
WOMEN: Is it real fur around the collar?
MAN: I think so.
WOMEN: Can I try it on?

SLIDE: *'I feel a part of my sitting room and the garden outside and the wall'* (13–14)

In a drama like *Call of the Wild*, meaning operates like a quantum field. There is no causal direction to the action. Scenes can be read forwards or backwards; as happening consciously or subconsciously; as reflecting abiding obsessions or passing thoughts; as being remembered, imagined or 'really happening'. Yet, like *The Forty Lounge Café*, substantive themes emerge. Peta Tait writes that Kemp 'sets up a space for the spectators to wander around in with their minds, to roam in, amble through, fantasise about, get lost in, to daydream in… If her work infers a search for a feminine unconscious… this is because [she] wants to redress the social repression of inner experience beginning from her own gendered perspective'.

Men and masculinity are as much of an 'absent presence' in *Call of the Wild* as they are in *The Forty Lounge Café*, but in a more volatile and unsympathetic way. Sexual desire is more explicitly explored, and some scenes involve acts of patriarchal violence. Like everything else in the play, these are transposed into a surreal theatrical register. Kemp writes: 'Key visual factors for the production are the partial nakedness of the women (sometimes the man), the non-naturalistic setting, the use of natural elements of earth and trees, a small realistic sitting room above the stage area, and a skeleton' (9). As in a dream, the last moments of the play are both lucid and baffling:

> WOMAN IN PALE HAT: … Evil, what is it? Should I know or should I not know? I climbed out, my little boy ran up to my wet body seeing his Mum, he is happy, I chatted away to him, standing on a razor edge inside, fragile, gradually I became his Mum again. Am I tough enough? (24)

Away, *The Forty Lounge Café* and *Call of the Wild* are all concerned with internal states of mind and psycho-physical forces. They reflect the poetic strain in Australian drama, yet should not be thought of as apolitical in intent or impact. The shape of their politics is different from 'state of the nation' plays, however. They do not rely on the representative dimension of dramatic character being precisely delineated or stable, and do not erect a hard barrier between external and internal realms. They work with the disjointed sense of self shown by Barbara at the end of *Diving for Pearls* (indeed, she might appear in *Call of the Wild* as 'Woman with Bad Hair & Make-up'). There are more ways to resist an unjust social order than party activism, and other categories of oppression than Marxist ones.

The mood of *Away*, *The Forty Lounge Café* and *Call of the Wild* is sombre, but not unrelievedly so. There is the suggestion that the politics of personal liberation—the creativity of the individual—can compensate for the ideological grand narratives then passing away. From being an object of power, the individual becomes the site of it. A new 'politics of the self' arises, together with an expanded sense of the importance of subjectivity and subjective perception. The legacy of this poetic revolution is passed on to future Australian drama. The 1980s-style 'state of the nation' play does not disappear entirely, but after 1990 it becomes increasingly rare. Sewell's later work is smaller in scale and scope. Nowra switches strains, writing naturalistic plays of contained conflict.

There is also an impact on theatre practice. The fact that *Away*, *The Forty Lounge Café* and *Call of the Wild* rely so strongly on theatrical staging means that henceforward the line between text and performance, and concomitantly between playwright and director, blurs. Michael Gow and Jenny Kemp are both directors themselves. Kemp always directs her own work, and Gow sometimes does. During the 1960s, 1970s and 1980s Australia produced many fine theatre directors, with some, like Jim Sharman, becoming internationally renowned. After 1990, however, directors are more visible and rewarded as a professional cohort. This is not unrelated to the fact that the plays they have to stage require a greater degree of personal creative investment. In a practical sense, it becomes harder to say where the work of Australian playwrights ends and the work of Australian directors begins.

7
1991–2005: The End (yet the persistence) of History

The Woman in the Window **(1998)**. *Life after George* **(2000)**. *Honour* **(1995)**. *The Seed* **(2005)**. *A Property of the Clan* **(1992)**. *Stolen* **(1998)**. *Black Medea* **(2000)**. *Conversations with the Dead* **(2002)**.

> Good news has come. The most remarkable development of the last quarter of the twentieth century has been the revelation of enormous weaknesses at the core of the world's seemingly strong dictatorships... Liberal democracy remains the only coherent political aspiration that spans different regions and cultures around the globe.
>
> Francis Fukuyama, *The End of History and The Last Man*

> The old century has not ended well.
>
> Eric Hobsbawm, *The Age of Extremes: 1914–1991*

When I turned 18, I could not imagine being 50. Now I'm over 50, there are moments when I forget my youthful self has gone. Likewise, I sometimes fail to remember that the political world in which I grew up, one divided between Western liberal democracies on the one hand, and Eastern communist regimes on the other, has disappeared. I was born in 1962, the year of the Cuban Missile Crisis. As a boy, I heard the testing of London's civil defence sirens. In the garden of our home stood a gloomy World War II bomb shelter that my parents left standing because World War III seemed imminent. I learned about communism early, by observing the splits in my own family between left and right factions. In my first term at university, I saw a screening of *The War Game*, a 1966 BBC pseudo-documentary depicting the fallout of a nuclear bomb dropped on an ill-prepared British population. As I studied international politics, a fundamental question asked about each country was whether it was part of the West or the Communist bloc. The Cold War was an exercise in binary categorisation. I participated in countless arguments that took as a basic assumption that the world was organised into two opposing camps, and our opinions had to be drawn in relation to these, regardless of whether we agreed with the division or not. All this seemed as immutable as my young body. Yet between 1989 and 1991 the division ceased to hold as communist governments around the world collapsed. The binary thinking of the Cold War subsided and the nuclear crisis receded. So did the sense of needing to be ideologically committed. Politics, it felt, could now unfold pragmatically, rather than as an eschatological search for an ever-elusive social utopia.

The historical events of this era were large in scale and complex in consequence. But their broad outline is easy enough to discern. In the 1980s, while the armies of NATO and the Soviet Union glared at each other across a partitioned Germany, both with the capability of destroying life on this planet, protests in a Gadańsk shipyard began to white-ant the government in Poland. The unrest led to the creation of Solidarity, the first independent union in a communist country, headed by Lech Wałęsa, an electrician-turned-union activist in the Sewellian mould. Semi-free elections were held there in June 1989.

It was the crack in the dyke through which the flood waters of insurrection were to break. In November 1989, the Berlin Wall came down (in my bedroom, I listened to the radio, incredulous, as ordinary Germans dismantled it). The following year, East and West Germany were reunited. In Romania, the communist dictator Nicolae Ceaușescu and his wife were overthrown, and the couple tried and shot. In Czechoslovakia, the Velvet Revolution toppled the communist government of Miloš Jakeš, with the people electing the playwright Václav Havel as their president.

Still it was just the beginning. Under its new technocratically minded first secretary, Mikhail Gorbachev, the Soviet Union cut its troop commitments abroad and loosened its control over satellite states. Pursuing an internal policy of 'glasnost' (openness) and 'perestroika' (restructuring), Gorbachev inaugurated a process of liberalisation that led in December 1991 to the lowering of the Soviet flag over the Kremlin, and his own exit from office. The Soviet Union was officially dissolved and the 15 different countries that composed it—Russia, foremost among them—granted their independence. In 1992, Yugoslavia went down the same route, becoming five separate countries (then, in 2006, a further three). When George Bush senior became the forty-first American president in January 1989, he delivered an inauguration speech that was eerily prescient:

> I come before you... at a moment rich with promise... For a new breeze is blowing, and a world refreshed by freedom seems reborn; for in man's heart, if not in fact, the day of the dictator is over. The totalitarian era is passing, its old ideas blown away like leaves from an ancient, lifeless tree. A new breeze is blowing, and a nation refreshed by freedom stands ready to push on.

I remember these events, and the hope that captured people's hearts, particularly those in Eastern Europe. China remained recalcitrant. The Tiananmen Square student massacre in June 1989 seemed to buck the trend. But China was an isolated case and besides, it was turning to free market economics in an attempt to raise the dire standard of living of its vast population. A common assumption was that political liberalisation (Western-style democracy) would follow economic liberalisation (Western-style capitalism) as surely as day follows night. When Bill Clinton was elected in 1993, the new American president faced a global order unrecognisable from that of his predecessor four years prior. The Overton Window, the range of ideas considered politically acceptable at any given time, (named after American policy analyst Joseph P Overton) had been moving to the right since Whitlam. After 1991 it moved further right. And stayed there.

In 1989, a 38-year-old American policy analyst of Japanese background wrote an article for the conservative journal *The National Interest* called 'The End of History?' Three years later, he published a best-seller with the same title, but the question mark had disappeared.

Francis Fukuyama's *The End of History and The Last Man* (1992) is a book of its moment rather than a timeless classic. Similar books appear regularly, and some are of excellent quality. But their day passes and other writing holds sway. The fact that *The End of History* still provides a reference point for discussion today means that in some way we remain beholden to its view. What is this? If the dualistic world of West versus East disappeared in the early 1990s, what replaced it? This is Fukuyama's subject.

For those unfamiliar with the philosopher Georg Hegel, the book's title is misleading. 'The end' refers not to a cessation but a destination. It refers to 'ultimate purpose', to history conceived as a normative, civilisational project—which is why it gets a capital letter: History. For Fukuyama, liberal democracy in its capitalist mode is 'the end' (the purpose) of History, the destination for all political and economic systems of the past:

> Liberal principles in economics—the 'free market'—have spread, and have succeeded in producing unprecedented levels of material prosperity, both in industrially developed countries and in countries that had been, at the close of World War II, part of the impoverished Third World. A liberal revolution in economic thinking has sometimes preceded, sometimes followed, the move towards political freedom around the globe. All of these developments, so much at odds with the terrible history of the first half of the century when totalitarian governments of the Right and Left were on the march, suggest the need to look again at the question of whether there is some deeper connecting thread underlying them.

One might wonder, reading this, whether grand narratives were as dead as many assumed, or whether they had simply shuffled rightways along the political spectrum. The suspicion is confirmed when Fukuyama writes, 'All countries undergoing economic modernisation must increasingly resemble one another... [and] replace traditional forms of social organisation... with economically rational ones based on function and efficiency...[T]he logic of modern natural science... dictate[s] a universal evolution in the direction of capitalism'. 'Scientific capitalism' replaces 'scientific Marxism' in Fukuyama's version of History. *The Blind Giant is Dancing* had shown Australians a vision of the ruinous effects of laissez-faire individualism. It turned out its millennial mood was correct, but its target was wrong. It was socialism that had crumbled away.

The triumph of democracy as a political system gives Fukuyama a bit more trouble. Adopting Hegel's concept of the 'struggle for recognition' he argues that democracy meets people's need for this by 'establishing the principles of popular sovereignty and the rule of law'. There is a catch, however. Liberal democracy has an unwholesome levelling effect on people that leads to a loss of thymotic pride (from the Greek word *thymos* meaning 'spiritedness'). Universal recognition is not 'completely satisfying'. Here Fukuyama turns from Hegel to Friedrich Nietzsche to propose that 'the typical citizen of liberal democracy [is] [Nietzsche's] 'last man' who... [gives] up prideful belief in his or her own superior worth in favour of comfortable self-preservation... [yet] without such desire no excellence or achievement [is] possible'.

It would be wrong to think of Fukuyama as a political reactionary or social Darwinist, an upholder of the master–slave distinction that Hegel thought a major obstacle to human progress. But he does see the 'the last man' mentality as a threat to the long-term health of democracy. Fortunately, capitalism is the solution here too, because it ensures much-needed inequality by providing an economic realm in which the drive for superiority (*megalothymia*) can be usefully pursued. Liberal democracy can avoid being 'subverted' by 'the fanatical desire for equal recognition' (*isothymia*) by 'entrepreneurship and other forms of economic activity' that encourage thymotic striving. 'Capitalism does not just permit, but positively requires, a form of regulated and sublimated *megalothymia* in the striving of businesses to be better than their rivals', says Fukuyama.

Two themes thus emerge from *The End of History* that provide anchoring assumptions for the next three decades. First, that liberal democracy has proved itself the best (or, least worst) political system. Second, that if capitalism is necessary for liberal democracy, then capitalist inequality is an acceptable price to pay to maintain it. For

Fukuyama, the age of ideological alternatives was over, and the era of personal choices had begun.

All this had profound implications for our national drama. I know of no noteworthy Australian plays after 1992 that argue for a *revolutionary* change in Australian society in the way New Theatre plays do. The portrayal of rich and powerful characters shifts ground, from political critique to moral evaluation. Capitalist liberal democracy may be decried as ethically deficient, but it is not regarded as fundamentally unsound. The larger structures of society, and the relationship between them, are no longer a focus for playwrights in the same way. Drama as a mode of inquiry takes on a piecemeal look—addressing problems one by one, rather than assaying global drivers and causes.

A positive benefit of this is that there is no longer a single, privileged position from which to claim one story as more important than another. The cost is the eclipse of themes of universal transformation. It is as if the relationship of Australian plays to national life that widened in the 1960s and 1970s is now re-contained. Arguably, the *professional* quality of playwriting continues to improve. But its *cultural* capacity is circumscribed by a world where general truths can no longer be offered (unless you are Fukuyama).

Australian drama clearly expanded in the 1990s, with a growing diversity of artists and forms. Yet this pluralism was accompanied by a ceding of the high moral and political ground that companies like Nimrod and the APG had claimed as of right. In the eyes of the government, Australian artists increasingly looked like another 'elite'. In the policy domain, cultural activism was reframed as 'arts advocacy'. In the theatre, judgements became individualised. Instead of writing about what they could imagine, playwrights were expected to write about what they knew. Yet, as we shall see, this eclipse was far from complete. For a collective sense of the world, and a desire to offer general truths about it, continued to preoccupy Australian drama at every turn.

It is interesting to see how different historians characterise this period. For radical nationalist Manning Clark it is 'an Age of Ruins'. For democratic socialist Stuart Macintyre it is a time of 'Rectification', his optimism stemming from the 1992 High Court ruling to uphold native land title—the Mabo decision—and open the way to reconciliation between Indigenous and non-Indigenous Australians. For British Marxist Eric Hobsbawm, whose book *The Age of Extremes* (1994) is about the 'short century' of 1914–1991, it is 'a new era of decomposition, uncertainty and crisis'. He rebukes Fukuyama: 'Historians may wish to remind metaphysical speculators about "The End of History", there will be a future. The only completely certain generalisation about history is that, so long as there is a human race, it will go on'. For mainstream economists it is the 'Great Moderation', 'a period of economic stability characterised by low inflation, positive economic growth, and the belief that the boom and bust cycle had been overcome'. All of which suggests a curate's egg of positive and negative developments, and indicates that the hope my friends and I felt was not entirely misplaced, even if we had not yet reached a final Elysium.

It is important to remember what still lay ahead. In 1991, the first digital cellular network, the technology underpinning the widespread use of mobile phones, was two years away. Personal computers had not yet taken over the office environment, or social media the relational one. Climate change was a niche concern, wealth inequality was not egregious, and the average wage was still rising. House prices were affordable, and university HECS fees had only just been introduced. The belief that a better-educated workforce might replace jobs lost in deindustrialisation seemed reasonable enough (Barry Jones aspirationally dubbed Australia 'the Clever Country'). The destruction of the Twin Towers lay ten years in the future, the Global Financial Crisis 16 years away. If 1989–92 is not to be ranked next to 1945–49 and 1972–75 as a classic period of progressive change, it was, perhaps, a time of relief, the world letting out a long breath after a century of unparalleled violence.

For Australian theatre, the 1990s were a reprise of the 1980s, with one important exception. In 1994, the federal government, led by Prime Minister Paul Keating, launched Australia's first national cultural policy, *Creative Nation*. It had an immediate impact. For some, it ranks alongside Keating's Redfern speech and his *Working Nation* white paper, as a major intervention in a policy domain previously considered incidental to the main business of government. The

Paul Keating announcing Creative Nation. *Master of the one-line put-down, Keating once famously described the performance of the Coalition Shadow Treasurer, John Hewson, as 'like being flogged with a warm lettuce'.*

switch from an 'arts policy' to a 'cultural policy' was significant. The Arts portfolio and the Communications portfolio were joined together (and remain so today). This lent a grander sweep to cultural policy-making, announced on the first page of *Creative Nation's* tasteful, mauve-grey booklet:

> Culture arises from the community, even when the community may not be fully aware of it. It encompasses our entire mode of life, our ethics, our institutions, our manners and our routines, not only interpreting our world but shaping it. The most highly developed and imaginative aspects of our culture are the arts and sciences which are fed back to the community by the most talented individuals.

Creative Nation acknowledges the 'unique attributes' of Australian arts and culture, and the government's responsibility for maintaining an environment in which they can flourish. Encouraging diversity is a key policy goal, as is recognising the centrality of Indigenous Australian culture. There is repeated and strenuous assertion of the link between culture and the economy. 'Culture creates wealth… Culture employs… The level of our creativity substantially determines our ability to adapt to new economic imperatives. It is a valuable export in itself and an essential accompaniment to the export of our commodities. It attracts tourists and students. It is essential to economic success'. It concludes:

> The Commonwealth's responsibility to maintain and develop Australian culture means, among many other things, that on a national level: innovation and ideas are perpetually encouraged; self-expression and creativity are encouraged; our heritage is preserved as more develops; and all Australians have a chance to participate and receive—that we invigorate the national life and return its product to the people.

At last the relationship between Australian culture and Australian life seemed to have received proper acknowledgement. The question that Leon Brodsky first asked in 1907 found an eloquent answering call in 1994. Though Keating organised a committee to write *Creative Nation*, its writing style shows the masterly touch of Don Watson, the historian who crafted his greatest speeches. The appearance of *Creative Nation* should have been a moment of triumph for Australian artists. There are two reasons why it was not. First, only 18 months after it launched, the Coalition under Prime Minister John Howard was elected to office, and *Creative Nation* was consigned to the filing cabinet. The incoming government took a more incremental approach to cultural policy, one continued by Labor when it returned to power in 2007.

The second reason is more profound. In writing about the fervour for the 'new nationalism' that swept through government circles in the late 1960s, Stuart Ward argues that it was bad timing—that politicians wanted a national culture at the very moment when national cultures were dissolving in larger global structures. 'Australians were becoming aware of the threadbare trappings of their emergent nationhood at a time when nationalism itself had long since passed its prime', he argues. 'The new nationalism was an elusive, and ultimately illusory creed for a society not quite reconciled to the passing of empire, and not yet "at home" with its inherently derivative diversity'.

I do not agree with this view of the New Wave period, which focuses on government conceptions of Australian culture, not what

Australian artists were doing at the time to create it. But it is a good description of *Creative Nation* 20 years later, when the Whitlam legacy was all but over, and the Labor Party under Hawke and Keating had embraced economic rationalism and everything it implied. For it is not possible to champion the 'unique attributes' of Australian culture while pursuing neoliberal policies that favour an 'international level playing field' (which has turned out to be not so level). Arts and culture end up a means for securing other objectives, chiefly economic ones. Australia's first national cultural policy is superior in comparison with previous arts policies (though this is not a high bar). But it is a conflicted document, its fiscal preoccupations undermining its nation-building concerns.

Australian artists face the same impasse today. Politicians and their advisers may show sympathy to arts and culture on a personal level, depending on their interests, backgrounds and experience. But on a political level, there is no meaningful pursuit of the idea of a national culture, either holistically or in respect of how its constituent parts relate to one another. After *Creative Nation*, a disjunction sets in between creative arts practices and how these are framed in government policy that renders 'culture *qua* culture' as incidental to a collective life now seen mainly in economic terms. In the years since *Creative Nation*, many Australian artists have felt they have had no choice but to adopt this reductive point of view.

In selecting plays for this chapter, there is such a rich field that any choice feels indefensible. A few words on my method may therefore be helpful. Looking at plays individually is a good way to understand how they work as singular artefacts. Viewing them through a biographical lens also has benefits. Discussing the life of Patrick White, Dorothy Hewett or Jenny Kemp, for example, can show how an artistic *oeuvre* develops. Then there are *longue durée* histories, like John McCallum's *Belonging* or Geoffrey Milne's *Theatre Australia (Un)limited*, that tackle Australian drama over decades.

All of these perspectives are useful, and I draw on aspects of all of them for this book. But when plays are read *against* each other, and *in* the context they were first produced, they shed light on the deeper structures that underlie them. Here it is important not to be confined to examining just one strain of Australian drama, or to imagine that plays exist in stylistic segregation. History converges. Though playwrights may not be aware of it, they work with norms and forms bequeathed by the past.

It is especially valuable to bring two or more plays into critical alignment that may not have been considered together before, in order to pursue holonic relations across standard classifications. Such a method allows for diagonal moves and unusual groupings in an effort to defamiliarise the repertoire—to encourage fresh appreciation of its originality, contingency and strangeness. In answer to the charge that my play choices are arbitrary, therefore, I can say that I am not trying to write a comprehensive history of Australian drama, only generate different questions about its place in our public life.

Not only can the plays in this period be situated within the historical arc of the twentieth century, they are explicitly about that arc. They have characters in them—often young, often female—who we might call 'the inheritors'. Mothers and fathers are ubiquitous figures, as are family mysteries and secrets. While kinship relations are ubiquitous in Australian drama from *On Our Selection* onwards, the focus now swings 180 degrees. It is the young and their responses to the gifts and burdens of the past that is a focus, the questions hanging in the air: 'What is the nature of the bequest?' and 'What should be done with it?'. Sometimes the past is present as personal story (*The Seed*, *Stolen*), sometimes as intellectual legacy (*Honour*, *Life After George*), sometimes as gender expectations (*Black Medea*, *Property of the Clan*), and sometimes as spiritual communication with the dead (*Conversations with the Dead*, *The Woman in the Window*).

One observation that applies to all the plays: naturalistic settings have gone. All occupy a loose zone of theatrical depiction that allows their narratives and characters to move across times and locations in an effortless way. Stylistically, they are calmer than New Wave plays, and do not manically mix their genres or registers of address. But their internal movement, the dramatic forces they unleash as they unfold, come from the same cloud of imaginative potential. Thematically, they occupy the land of 'post'—post-ideological, post-industrial, post-modernist. This unstable territory lies on the other side of the ideological border marked by *The Blind Giant is Dancing* and *Diving for Pearls*. All have a questing, questioning feel to them, as if they were trying to retrieve or repair something lost or broken. Premiering in the lead-up to, or just after, the turn of the new millennium, the twentieth century operates as an object of study, to be prodded and probed until its enigmas are finally solved. Hobsbawm writes that, 'no-one who has lived through this extraordinary century is likely to abstain from judgement. It is understanding that comes hard'. No truer words could be written for these dramas, in which the century was not 'short' at all, but endless. While the events of this brutal epoch may have been over, the flinty task of uncovering their meaning was just beginning. It is a task we are engaged in still.

I tackle the plays in two groups. First up are *The Woman in the Window*, *Life After George*, *Honour*, *The Seed* and *A Property of the Clan*, all white Australian plays about latter-day family relations, though *The Woman in the Window* is set simultaneously in the Stalinist past and the dystopian future. The second group—*Stolen*, *Black Medea* and *Conversations with the Dead*—presage a significant increase in plays by Indigenous Australian writers. For the first time since the 1920s, female playwrights outnumber male writers. Interestingly, in three plays of the first group, the same actor—Julia Blake—created the roles of three mother characters. This heightens the impression of a shared territory, as if they were all about the same family, or different branches of it. Families are the focus for the second group too, but here the past has wrought devastating destruction. The plays of the first group end with gestures of hope. In the second, the final scenes are darker. They are not entirely without optimism, but history casts a long, chill shadow, and its harmful consequences continue long after the events precipitating them have passed away.

The inheritors—part 1

The Woman in the Window has a dual location similar to *The One Day of the Year*, a split time period like *Crossfire*, and a dystopian view of the future like *The Day Before Tomorrow*. Its central character is the famous Russian poet Anna Akhmatova, who, at the start of the play, is under house arrest in Leningrad, her life one of isolation, deprivation and 24/7 surveillance. It is 1951, and Stalin is in power, about to unleash another political purge. These waves of murderous hysteria, which had been portrayed before in Australian drama, most notably in Stephen Sewell's *Traitors* (1978), are a confronting theme to tackle.

Akhmatova, whose verse inspired the Soviet army when it was fighting the Nazis during World War II, has been forbidden to write any more poetry and her son imprisoned as a hostage. Twice a day she must show herself at her living room window, to be logged by two KGB thugs standing in the street below. She is *persona non grata* to all but a small circle of people who are themselves under suspicion for staying loyal to her. A disgraced teacher, Lilli Kalinovskya, dismissed for propping open a window with one of Stalin's books during a summer heat wave, lives with Akhmatova, helping her with everyday tasks. Those around Akhmatova do not last long, and halfway through the play Lilli is subject to a brutal interrogation and 'disappeared'. Other people are not who they seem to be, like Tusya, her neighbour, who is a police informer.

Stalin's objective is to stop Akhmatova writing poetry while appearing to tolerate her existence. He certainly appreciated the power of culture, which is why he killed or imprisoned so many artists. But in Akhmatova's case, he failed in his aims, as her friends take it upon themselves to memorise her new poems so they aren't lost after she destroys them to avoid detection.

Akhmatova is subject to continual harassment by a security force whose thinking is a surreal jumble of past, present and future. In Act 1, scene 12, her flat is turned upside down, while the officer in charge tells her:

> KORZH: If your poetry isn't being published any more, it's because it isn't useful. Comrade Stalin tells us life must be depicted as it should be, not as it is. Yes… we live in the present, but we look at it from our glorious future. During the war your poems were valuable, but most of your work… was too personal. There's no personal life any more. You wrote about nature too—
>
> AKHMATOVA: There's no nature any more?

KORZH: It's no way to turn us into a great economic power.
Poetry needs to pay its way like everything else. (19)

Korzh might be speaking for the Australian Productivity Commission.

The contemporary resonances are even more evident in the second strand of the play, set thousands of years in the future, where a managerial elite spend their time on luxuriously appointed space stations, while most people live deprived lives on Earth, underground, addicted to virtual reality games. A small number are allowed the 'privilege' of working. One of them is Rachel, a Conference Stress Consultant—effectively, a sex worker. Like Akhmatova, her existence is tightly policed. Even the expressions on her face are analysed to check whether she is 'really' smiling for her wealthy clients. Culture is confined to a giant digital archive that few people want to access, and fewer are allowed to. Music composers have just been 'delisted' (MAREN: They say computers do a better job now 13).

Rachel's latest assignment is Sandor, a poet, who has uncovered the plays of Shakespeare and is attending a conference on Earth to announce this discovery to his privileged peers. In Act 2, Akhmatova and Rachel connect across time, and a transference of thought commences, from the past to the future and vice versa. When Sandor learns that poets are to be delisted too, he asks for Rachel's help downloading poetry stored in the upper reaches of the archive. But, influenced by Akhmatova, Rachel wants to go deeper. 'Why aren't there any women in your list?', she asks him (17). 'There are billions of terabytes of data that haven't been accessed in no-one knows how long', Sandor replies. 'The authorities say history stirs things up.'

A recurrent theme throughout the play is art's capacity 'to scrape the skin of [one's] soul' (47). Rachel uncovers a poem by Akhmatova, and though it leads to Sandor's arrest, he has time to release an unstoppable virus that will henceforward randomly release poetry into people's computers. The act of suppressing art only makes it more potent. The play ends with Rachel exploring her new-found psychological freedom, and Tusya rejecting her role as a police informer and taking Lilli's place memorising Akhmatova's poems (TUSYA: They say the human body isn't worth much. Suddenly mine feels immensely more valuable 56).

If *The Woman in the Window* is about the power of art, *Life After George* is about the power of ideas. The comic tone of Hannie Rayson's play is very different from the sombre one of Alma De Groen's, but their preoccupations are the same: what the past owes the present; what the future should take from the past. At the start of the play, Peter George has died in a light plane crash. He was a charismatic, free-thinking (and even freer-loving) 50-something literary academic in the 1960s insurrectionist mould. By turns brilliant, charming and incorrigible, he leaves behind three wives and a daughter. Beatrix, his first wife and the mother of his daughter Ana, is a painter, living in Tuscany and happily remarried. Lindsay, the second wife, is a 'femocrat', a high-powered university administrator, once George's most radical student. Poppy is the third and much younger wife. Although not without political opinions, she is more emotional in her response to the world, and to George's unexpected death. When she learns that George was in the plane with a young woman at the time of the crash, she burns his correspondence with the great intellectuals of the age (which also keeps it out of the hands of the careerist Lindsay).

Character representativeness is key to both the fun and the meaning of *Life After George*. George is a New Left archetype, a fusion of many of the personality traits ascribed to this oppositional, usually male figure. Is he to be applauded or deplored? Held in high regard as the embodiment of progressive opinion, or dismissed as an old-style philanderer obsessed with his own importance? The question weighs heavily on Ana, who, like Rachel in *The Woman in the Window*, doesn't have a 'type' and seems lost without one. Now in her late 20s, she undersells her musical talent by playing nights in a piano bar to get by. The action begins with a funeral eulogy by Alan Duffy, a close friend to George and all the women, before moving back and forth from present day to remembered moments in the three marriages.

Unsurprisingly, 1968 emerges as a time of glorious change. Early in the first act, Beatrix addresses the audience:

> BEATRIX: When you tell people you were there in Paris during the events, this is greeted with amazement. It gave us a kind of credibility in Leftie circles—certainly in Australia—and George made the most of it. Naturally.

> If you run a course on the History of Revolutions and you were there when ten million workers went on strike, and it seemed as if everyone in Paris was taking to the streets, you could be excused for thinking it was one of the greatest movements of this century. There was a kind of delirium in the air. For a time there, they really believed they could down the de Gaulle Government. Mind you, no-one had any idea of what they would actually do if that happened. But for George, it was a defining moment. Being an actor, rather than a spectator, in history—that was his big thing. (7)

George's life was an ongoing drama, in which he played the lead character, at least in his own mind. In flashbacks, he is shown as feckless and careless, but not a fraud. This is the play's signal message, presenting George's legacy as one that needs to be reckoned with rather than valorised or dismissed. Like Mrs Hamilton from *Here Under Heaven*, George is capable of both good and bad decisions, and beneath its comedic language the play has forensic intent, a determination to judge carefully and fairly. The women are portrayed critically and their negative aspects are not spared. Beatrix comes across as often precious and self-absorbed, Poppy as uncontrolled and self-dramatising. Lindsay, the economic rationalist bureaucrat, receives the harshest treatment. The second act reveals that the woman who died with George in the plane was not his lover but his daughter. Lindsay hid an early pregnancy, and gave the child up for adoption without telling George he was the father. When this daughter wrote to Lindsay years later, asking to meet, she refused. She has betrayed both her political principles and the bonds of family in pursuit of career ambition. Lindsay is the modern version of Miss Kingsbury and her final speech, after she learns the truth of the crash from Duffy, has a *Morning Sacrifice* feel to it: 'That's it then. My husband and my daughter. Both dead. So that's all there is now. More of the same. More work. That's all there is. [*Beat.*] They've offered me the Chair of Global Studies'. To which Duffy can only reply, 'Congratulations' (71).

The final scenes of *Life After George* are resolved in a similar way to *The Woman in the Window*. Ana could be Rachel's sister (in fact, she is: Rachel is the name of George and Lindsay's daughter), and after communing with her dead father, just as Rachel communes with Akhmatova, Ana reconciles with her memories and embraces a more authentic life. What she takes from the past is summed up in the two words that best define George: moral courage. 'Every day, people like Lindsay are justifying their compromises. They say, "In principle I agree but the reality is I have no choice". But you do have a choice', George's ghost tells Ana. 'Ultimately the great leap of faith, the great expression of hopefulness—is to have a child' (79).

Honour was written five years before *Life After George* but is similar in its approach to its characters, who also have an archetypical feel to them. George becomes Gus, a literary critic of some standing, but not of the highest rank. Ana becomes Sophie, Gus's daughter, in her first year at university. George's three wives become one wife, Honor (played by Julia Blake in *Honour's* premiere, who went on to play Akhmatova and Beatrix). Unlike Beatrix, Honor's marriage to Gus has lasted. From the outside it seems a happy one.

At the start of this remarkable and remarkably disturbing play, Gus is interviewed by a cadet journalist, Claudia, described in the script as 'a striking young woman in her late twenties' (viii). The simplicity of the play's action belies the dazzling complexity of its implications. Gus 'falls in love' with Claudia and without warning leaves Honor to go and live with her. Honor, shell-shocked, tells Sophie, who is sympathetic, but also blames her mother for sacrificing her promising writing career to support her husband. In an early scene, Sophie defends Claudia as a victim of male power. Honor, by contrast, defends Gus as a dupe of middle-aged sexual delusion. Such twists are typical of the play's subtle argumentation, in which the characters (and therefore also the audience) constantly shift viewpoints. As Sophie leaves to confront her father, Honor warns her 'Don't *become* me, all right?' (29).

Honour has no physical setting, only 'an abstract, neutral design through which the characters float' (viii). As a play, it is all language. The clever patterning of the dialogue, its use of unfinished sentences, repeated phrases, of clauses without subjects, or objects, or both, and its seamless moving across tenses, generates an unnerving feel of past, present and future playing out simultaneously. At stake for Honor, but also for her daughter, are the meaning of their lives and how, as women, they are supposed to conduct it. 'You used her up', Sophie tells Gus in an exchange bursting with outrage at his treatment of her mother. 'I'm fighting for *my* life. I'm fighting for *my* future. I'm talking to you not as my father but as my husband. I'm telling you that in forty years I won't be standing in the wake of your weakness. I won't be weeping over you' (33).

In Claudia, shades of Mrs Dawson from *Inside the Island* are detectable. Like the Edwardian matriarch, she is a negative principle of entropy and disorder. The emotional tone of *The Woman in the Window* and *Life After George* is a warm one. Even their conflictual moments are treated in a manner sympathetic to human weakness. They are forgiving, if not all-forgiving. *Honour* is much cooler. Its judgments have an irrevocable quality to them reminiscent of *Blind Giant*. Murray-Smith's plays are sometimes seen as apolitical, concerned 'only' with middle-class manners and mores. In *Honour*, nothing could be further from the truth. Its politics are cold-branded into every word the characters speak, every action they take.

As the story unfolds, Claudia behaves like the Angel of Death, bringing an end to Honor's marriage, to Sophie's illusion of having happily wed parents, and to Gus's foolish belief that 'passionate' love with a young woman, based primarily on physical attraction, is his by right, and the damage done to others is irrelevant. Claudia is a cypher, a symbol of the emptiness at the heart of (post) modern relationships. On the surface, the play is about gender roles and expectations. Beneath this theme, or entwined around it like a strangling weed, is the whole mad history of the twentieth century. In scene 10, Gus tries to help Claudia understand its endless slew of 'isms':

> CLAUDIA: Okay, if that's *realism*—what's *naturalism*—?
> GUS: Naturalism is—just about presenting nature in a life-like way—
> CLAUDIA: But isn't it French or something?
> GUS: Well—yes—that too—It's a nineteenth century French literary style which—
> CLAUDIA [*impatient*]: Gus, *tell* me—Don't let me look foolish—
> GUS: Which reflected a *determinist* view of things—

CLAUDIA: It just gets more and more difficult! I've got these *gaps* everywhere.
GUS: You're an Honours student
CLAUDIA: So I know how to reduce great works of literature into text and subtext—
GUS: Right—
CLAUDIA: Can we go through the list then—?
GUS: What's on the list?
CLAUDIA: The Cold War [*Beat.*] I don't get it.
GUS: You don't get it.
CLAUDIA: The whole Korean War thing. And—and—Space—
GUS: Space—
CLAUDIA: I've tried, but I don't understand space—
GUS: I'm shaky on space myself—I do know it's expensive to get there—
CLAUDIA: Who are the Fauves? What was the Krushchev Report? Edmund Wilson. Wittgenstein—I just need to know—how they fit in—
GUS: To what?
CLAUDIA: Twentieth century thought. (37)

Like the endgame of a chess match, *Honour*'s scenes play out as a series of defined mathematical possibilities. All are two-handers, although Murray-Smith specifies that 'characters should be able to silently participate in scenes they "overhear"' (viii). Honor talks to Sophie; Sophie talks to Claudia; Claudia talks to Honor; Honor talks to Gus.

The close sees Gus and Honor divorced, and Honor rediscovering her writing. Claudia evaporates like a wraith, leaving Gus utterly alone. Sophie graduates from university, not with Honours but with 'honour'. This ancient ethical concept is the play's chief preoccupation, and ranks alongside that of 'moral courage' in *Life After George* and the 'power of art' in *The Woman in the Window*. What does it mean for *a woman* to live honourably? I stress the gender because 'honour' is often seen as the concern of the masculine life. *Honour* explores it from a different gender perspective, as a way of living with integrity and meaning, rather than being undone by the disorders of the twentieth century, as Gus is, and its remorseless stoking of human appetites.

The Seed is the only one of this group of plays to have a stable setting: a living room in Nottingham, England, in the present day. 'It is a hovel. *A small, dark, dank room filled with dated furniture and ornaments, photos and junk—and many, many boxes all taped securely*' (xiv). A moment's reflection shows this to be the antipole of the bush hut of early Australian drama, a depiction of everything British migrants might flee—a poetic inversion of the 'convict colony' (11).

Mulvany's three characters are from three different generations of one family. Danny and his daughter, Rose, who live in Geraldton, Western Australia, are paying a visit to Brian, Danny's father and Rose's grandfather. In keeping with the gallows humour of the play, all have the same birthday. Their different generational perspectives are not an incidental matter, but propel the action forwards, marking the extent of access each has to the family past. Brian, 80, knows the early history of his son, but not what happened after Danny migrated to Australia as a young man. For Brian, Danny is 'the little runt [who] ran away' (27) and he greets the prodigal's return with recriminations, sarcasm and threats. Rose, 30, knows her father's Australian history, including his time fighting in the Vietnam War, which left him with serious medical problems and her unable to have children, but nothing that happened to him earlier, in England. Until recently, Rose was a newspaper reporter. Later we discover she has secrets of her own.

For Rose, the trip to Nottingham is to uncover this chapter of Danny's past—symbolised by the taped-down boxes that litter Brian's living room—and she carries around a tape recorder for that purpose (DANNY: Don't talk to me like I'm one of your stories. ROSE: You are one of my stories, Dad. My most important story 6). Danny, in his late 50s, is the pin-hinge between the two generations, and in theory knows everything there is to know about the family. But he is traumatised by his war experience, and possibly by his childhood too, and the past is full of things he either cannot remember or does not want to. He has a number of older brothers who are clearly criminal hoods. Brian claims their arrival to 'pick a bone' (28) with Danny is imminent, but it never occurs. The past, when it comes out, is so much less impressive than imagined. But the *hold* of the past is a different matter.

Rose's family, the Maloneys, are Irish, and the anger, anguish and historical suffering of that oppressed nation runs through *The Seed* in similar fashion to Douglas Stewart's *Ned Kelly*. Brian brags about

Three generations of the Maloneys celebrate a shared birthday together, while unanswered questions about the family's past loom. Kate Mulvany as Rose, Danny Adcock as Danny and Martin Vaughan as Brian in the 2007 Mimmam production of The Seed *in Sydney. (Photo: Brett Boardman)*

having been an active member of the armed wing of the IRA, and the number of British soldiers his bombs have killed. Danny's time in Vietnam, 'fighting for the Crown' (45) is proof sterling for Brian of his son's lack of character and his desertion of the cause of a united Ireland. But no aspect of Danny's life in Australia is intelligible to him, really, and he remains as stuck in an anti-British past as he is in his dingy terrace (Nottingham is the poorest city in England, or as Brian colourfully puts it 'The rancid, rotten, hairy hole smack bang in the middle of this shitarse of a country' 9).

There are memory scenes in *The Seed* just as there are in *Life After George*. Rose recollects taking a boat out to sea with her father to check crayfish pots as a child, her job to throw back the smaller catch, 'the cackers'. Her description of hauling up the pots is a metaphor for hauling up the past. 'You never know what you're going to get when the pot bursts through the water. Some days it might be full of crays, clacking angrily and screaming. Sometimes an octopus that pisses ink all over our ankles… Or sometimes we'll get a baby shark glaring at us through the rungs of the pot' (34).

The rapport between Rose and Danny is one of the most beautiful depictions of a father–daughter relationship in Australian drama. Rose is like a mother to Danny when he's lost and broken; Danny is like a lover to Rose, who is grief-stricken at a broken engagement to a man she adored, and the children she will never have. Towards the end of the second act, she gives a speech about the unknown past that is crushing the life out of her:

> ROSE: I'm carrying this huge black box around on my back and it's heavy and it's weighing me down and it's full of things I need to know but I'm not allowed to just put it down and open it!…
>
> I'm your biggest war wound, Dad. I'm covered in your battle scars. I'm stuck in the middle of a war that ended six years before I was even conceived… So please, don't tell me to shut up about it. I need to believe this never-ending fucking fight is worth it. (55)

In different ways, *The Woman in the Window*, *Life After George* and *Honour* are all about reclaiming the past. *The Seed* is about letting it go. Brian turns out to be a hollow man. As the play climaxes, he is shown not to be a rebel and an IRA freedom fighter, but a drunk and a liar. When the boxes are torn open, they are empty.

The question of where Danny and Rose truly belong fills the air, as it does in Lyssiotis's *The Forty Lounge Café*. Rose describes her father as having 'English, Irish, Australian eyes' (53) as if he were a strange, unclassifiable fish hauled out of the immense ocean of the past. Ultimately, hope lies not in history, which cannot be changed, but in the future—and in Rose herself. Towards the end of the play, Danny speaks to his daughter in the same way as George does to Ana: 'People know my story', he tells her. 'They do. They just choose to ignore it. But your story's new, Rose… And so I will help you. But not here. Not like this' (61). So they depart, the past, like Britain, a country that must be left to its own devices. *The Seed* opens with an image of Danny as a boy, caught on a barbed-wire fence while trying to run from the police—an image of crucifixion; an image of history *as* crucifixion. The last scene reprises the image, but this time Rose untangles her father and gently takes him down saying, 'Time to come home, hey, Dannyboy?' (62).

A Property of the Clan (*Clan*) is the first play in this book written specifically for a young audience—for the Rachels, Anas, Sophies, and Roses of contemporary Australia, but also, crucially, for the young men with whom they share their lives. Chronologically, it was the first to premiere, at Freewheels Youth Theatre, in 1992. AusStage lists only seven professional productions since, but this ignores the many school and amateur stagings the play has undoubtedly received, as well as its full-length stage version, *Blackrock*, and the film of the same name, which screened in 1997.

Clan is not a documentary drama, but its starting point is a crime that occurred in Newcastle in 1989, when a 14-year-old schoolgirl was raped and murdered after attending a birthday party at which drugs and alcohol were present in large amounts. The media coverage of the killing was sensationalist, and is often cited as an example of 'blaming the victim'. The ensuing police investigation was murky, leaving behind a strong sense that justice was not served. More particularly, the issue of community attitudes to the behaviour of the young men involved escaped examination.

This is the territory that *Clan* explores. Like *Honour* it is a masterly braiding of short scenes and two-hander exchanges. The playwright Nick Enright, like Max Afford, died prematurely, at 52, and his loss to Australian drama is hard to overstate. He contributed to every part of the national repertoire, including mainstream musicals, studio plays, and film scripts. In the 1970s he ran the education program of the Melbourne Theatre Company and his work in young people's theatre was ongoing. *Clan* is what Bertolt Brecht would have called a *Lehrstück*, or 'learning play'. It is designed to instruct its young audience as well as entertain them. It demonstrates a sure balance of these qualities and a merging of them. *Clan* is at its most watchable when exploring the truth of its characters. This is how drama operates as a mode of inquiry. Its entertainment function is not separate from its educational role. *Clan* is a powerful example of how they can work together to generate a unified knowledge experience.

Rachel (that name again!) is a Year 11 student in an intimate relationship with Jared, a boy at her high school. They come from different social classes however, like Hughie and Jan in *The One Day of the Year*. Rachel is bookish, Jared a surfer. The surfing culture in Jared's working-class suburb of Black Rock is aggressively male and matey. His best friend, Brett Ricketson—'Ricko'—is older and a bit of a bum. At the start of the play, he has just returned from Queensland, where he was doing nothing much. It is Ricko who holds the party at which a young girl, Tracy, is sexually assaulted and killed. 'Saturday night, mate. I'm throwing myself a welcome home party... Spread the word', Ricko tells Jared (2). 'Spread the word? Everyone in the yard's heard about it', Jared responds. 'The yard', 'everybody', 'people', 'the guys', 'the word': these are all synonyms for the collective beliefs of the community in which Rachel and Jared live, where the rape and murder of a young girl is, if not excusable, then at least explainable by how young men 'just are'. Because their behaviour is hardwired, Tracy's death is seen as the result of her own unwise choices. By going to Ricko's party, she brought it on herself.

Clan is a 360-degree attack on these gender misconceptions. This is pursued on a number of fronts. Tracy's death occurs early in the action. The majority of the play is about its consequences, so when details of what happened on that fatal night are finally revealed, they are leached of melodrama and can be seen as the result of deeper social forces. The murder is not a one-off event, but part of an inherited pattern of sexist prejudice and violence. Gender roles are narrow and coercive, maintained by a peer group pressure every bit as brutal as the KGB in *The Woman in the Window*. 'People have to act the way they are', insists Ricko (46), after he has confessed to killing Tracy, and discovered she was not 'a real little cock-teasing whore' (45), but a helpless virgin. At the party, she was out of her depth.

Yet if the community tolerates bad male behaviour, it also fears the results, especially the mothers. They have had abusive experiences which they do not want for their daughters. A sense of cross-generational gender violence is accentuated by role doubling. The actor playing Rachel also plays Diane, Jared's mother; the actor playing her best friend Jade, Jared's sister, also plays Marian, Rachel's mother.

When the mothers get together in the latter half of the play, Diane tells Marian:

> I work at the nursing home down the bottom of the hill. And one old dear, she collared me, knew I was from over Black Rock, and she says what a terrible thing, but wasn't that kid asking for it, going to a party like that? And over home, it's the same, people saying how sad, how terrible, but I hear she was a real sleeparound. Not a bloody word about the boys. About why blokes grow up the way they do. And why nobody ever tries to change them. (40–41)

The thinking of adults, caught in snatches, is one line of attack in the play. A second involves the Year 11 students at school, who are completing assignments on 'prejudice and discrimination… based on… the value systems of power' (8). Periodically, we see their class presentations on issues that involve structural forms of discrimination, such as Australia's policy of forcing young Aboriginal women to become domestic servants, and Nazi Germany's race-based genocide of the Jews. When it is Rachel's turn to speak, however, she changes her subject 'to talk about women. Women and men. The last two weeks, there's been one topic of conversation around this school. Tracy Warner. And why she died… Why did she die? Or actually, because she didn't die, like grandparents die, why was she killed?' (20). Her teacher admonishes her, saying this is 'more of a personal development issue. Not a topic of history class'. Rachel's response is clear and unequivocal: 'This is history. Our history'.

Clan's third line of attack focuses on Jared and his personal journey as he tries to transcend the stereotyped thinking that no longer reflects the moral reality he faces. Soon after the killing, overcome by guilt, he tells Ricko that he witnessed Tracy's sexual assault on the beach. Ricko replies, 'Forget you ever saw it. Nobody knows you were there… It's just the way things happen… She was always a bloody moll' (30). After Ricko is arrested for the murder, Jared goes into angry withdrawal, wagging school and breaking off his relationship with Rachel. Crude though his prejudiced opinions are, they are hard to escape.

Rachel has a friend, Glen, with whom she is writing a piece for the school newspaper (more hints of *The One Day of the Year*). Glen is gay, and Jared's homophobia towards him, like all his attitudes, is a second-hand view, borrowed from others around him. His local community seems a bit like the one in *Diving for Pearls*, struggling with deindustrialisation and the accompanying social dislocation. Jared's father is estranged from the family, and it is hinted that he is violent towards Diane. 'There's so much anger inside you I think you are going to burst open', his mother tells Jared (48). 'You don't have to work it out on your own. You don't even have to work out why you're feeling what you're feeling. You can just share'. At the end of the play, Jared finds the courage to do so, telling Rachel that he saw the rape and Tracy stumble away afterwards. 'I could have taken her home. And then she would never have died… [but] I turned and ran the other way' (52).

History is a key theme in *Clan*, as it is for all the plays in this group. It has two meanings. On the one hand, it is a word used to consign past events to oblivion. This is how Jade understands it. In a manner reminiscent of *The Woman in the Window* and *Life After George*, she communes with Tracy's spirit in her dreams, and nurtures the tree planted to commemorate her. But it is uprooted by those who want to forget. 'This is over. This is history', (53) she says bitterly to Rachel in the final scene, as they stand by Tracy's grave. By contrast, Rachel's understanding is more positive. She writes in the school newspaper, 'When something as bad as this happens to a girl our age, I believe most of us think: I'm glad it's not me. But until we think, it is me, stand up and say what happened to her happened to all of us, then nothing is going to change' (48). History is precisely what must *not* be forgotten. In remembrance lies hope of renewal. The play gives a glimpse of this. The last line reads, 'JARED *appears at a distance, in a wind-cheater. He has a small bunch of flowers. The three look at each other in silence*' (53).

All dramas, like the world they engage, reflect the two forces sociologists call 'structure' and 'agency'—things that are given to characters as a set of constraints, and things it is possible for them to change. The plays written in this period are tightly focused on the line between them. They are preoccupied with acts of decision-making and, in that sense, all have a *Lehrstück* quality to them. Their characters face starting conditions that are historically and socially defined. Gradually, they become aware of their constructed nature. Acquiring this awareness is painful and involves coming to terms with the mixed legacy of the past. But if successfully entrained—and for the protagonists in these five plays, it is—then new choices appear. What seemed like immutable structures are shown to be open to human thinking and will. Perhaps this is the chief lesson of the twentieth century for those living in the twenty-first: that history sometimes repeats itself; but it doesn't have to.

The inheritors—part 2

When is history over? When should we hold on to the past, and when should we let it go? And how? What happens if some people cannot remember what others cannot forget? The past then splits in two, and 'history wars' erupt. At stake is not only the factual record, but the fate of what anthropologist Jan Assmann calls our 'cultural memory'. He defines it as 'a collective concept for all knowledge that directs behaviour and experience in the interactive framework of a society and that obtains through generations in repeated societal practice[s] and initiation'. For Assmann, time, history and memory are closely interwoven, almost synonymous. History defines our sense of time, and vice versa. Memory populates history, and divides time into epochs and eras, naming them, the simplest denominators being 'before' and 'after'.

What fateful consequences those two short words can signpost. *Before* 1788. *After* 1788. 'The first step in the creation of our white utopia was brutal and relentless', writes Julianne Schultz, reflecting on Australia's white history:

> It depended on the humiliation and elimination, by design and neglect, of the million First Nations people who in 1788 still called the continent home as they had done for countless generations with an elaborate, ancient patchwork of languages, social relations, trade and lore... [B]y the time the 3.7 million new arrivals became Australians in 1901, the First Nations' population had been reduced, systematically and deliberately, to about 90,000 people.

Some things do not get better with the passage of time, they get worse. As historians continue their work of constructing factually accurate accounts of Australia's colonisation, other domains deal with its moral, social and political implications. Drama is a serious register of collective address. It is not only an aid for a nation looking to speak of events in the past in a different way. It is often the only means by which a nation can speak of such events at all.

Stolen, *Black Medea* and *Conversations with the Dead* appeared as part of a growing number of Indigenous Australian plays during this period. These works include Jimmy Chi's *Bran Nue Dae* (1990), John Harding's *Up the Road* (1991), Deborah Mailman and Wesley Enoch's *The Seven Stages of Grieving* (1995), Tammy Anderson's *I Don't Wanna Play House* (2001) and David Milroy's *Windmill Baby* (2005). The companies involved in producing these and other First Nations' plays, particularly Ilbijerri Theatre Company in Melbourne, and Yirra Yaakin Theatre Company in Perth, are as crucial to the development of this body of work as Nimrod and the APG were to New Wave drama 20 years earlier. In retrospect, it looks like a creative contribution waiting to happen. At the time, it was a difficult struggle for recognition and resources.

Carl Jung, who pioneered the 'psychological archetype', also coined the term 'shadow self' to describe parts of our personality we excise from consciousness because they threaten our preferred identity. Encountering the shadow self is an important challenge for those who want to live an integrated life, and involves acknowledging aspects we have previously refused to accept. *Stolen*, *Black Medea* and *Conversations with the Dead* can be thought of in this deeper way. They are not simply additions to the national repertoire: they open up a new dimension of dramatic experience for Australian audiences. This dimension is painful to engage. In the case of *Conversations with the Dead*, about the trauma involved in investigating Aboriginal deaths in police custody, overwhelmingly painful. Here, the entertainment function of drama is necessarily secondary to its educational function, and it is no surprise that two of the plays, *Stolen* and *Conversations with the Dead*, connect to government inquiries. It is worth contrasting these reports with the plays. In the tonal range and power of their speeches and dialogue, their imaginative action, images and kinetic moments, the plays act as a shadow self to the official documents. The truths of a nation are not only to be found in its record-keeping, but in the cultural responses they provoke.

History dominates this second group of plays as it does the first, but in a different way. The past is not distant, but oppressively close, pressing down on the characters like the stormy skies that dominate the environments they inhabit. If making decisions is the main task facing characters like Rachel, Sophie, Ana, Rose and Jared, for those in *Stolen*, *Black Medea* and *Conversations with the Dead*, lack of choice is a main feature of their lives. Inherited trauma is a hurricane force, generations torn apart by events that have previously happened, and that threaten to occur again. This impacts not only at a narrative level—in stories that show the reproduction of racial and gender violence over time—but at the inner level of character. Jack, the central investigator in *Conversations with the Dead*, Jason and Medea in *Black Medea,* and the five institutionalised children-cum-adults in *Stolen*—are scarred by being treated for what, rather than who, they are, unable to escape the political implications of being Indigenous in a society that responds to them on the basis of race. As this view is coercive, constricting and abusive, it bequeaths a legacy of disempowerment far more negative than the 'lostness' of the characters in the first group of plays. There is sharp awareness of inheritance in this second group of plays too. The challenge is how to escape it.

Structurally, *Stolen*, *Black Medea* and *Conversations with the Dead* draw on the poetic strain in Australian drama; thematically, they draw on the realist strain. They continue the trend towards scenic fluidity. There are passages in all three plays that resemble *The Forty Lounge Café* and *Call of the Wild* where present actions and past memories commingle, and 'real' and 'imagined' exchanges achieve functional equivalence. However, their political messaging reaches a new intensity of purpose. Building on plays like *The Cake Man* and *No Sugar*, they assay events not previously seen on the national stage. The dialogue is light-touch in construction, but biblical in its feeling of ultimate reckoning. As in all encounters with the shadow self, there is a sense that what lies beneath the surface is coming out. Nothing can be repressed forever. Justice will be served. More than perhaps any others in this book, these plays leave audiences with the question about what they will do after they have left the theatre.

Tackling the three plays together reveals their homophonic qualities, the way they echo each other. *Stolen* premiered in 1998 after a long period of research and collaborative development. In May 1995 the Australian Human Rights and Equal Opportunity Commission began its *Inquiry into the Separation of Aboriginal and Torres Strait Islander Children from Their Families*. Almost two years later it handed down the *Bringing Them Home* report. Workshops for *Stolen*, it should be observed, started three years before this. Jane Harrison writes in her playwright's note,

> In 1992, when the project was begun, there was very little knowledge or understanding about the plight of the Stolen Generations outside the Aboriginal community itself. Despite my Aboriginal heritage, I for one, knew nothing about it, and found my new knowledge often difficult to deal with emotionally. What always impressed me though, was a lack of bitterness from the survivors of these policies and I've tried to mirror that attitude in the play. *Stolen* is not about blame, it is about understanding and acceptance (v).

Stolen is a seamless flow of action following the lives of five Aboriginal people put into a children's home. Jimmy, Ruby, Shirley, Sandy and Anne are social types condensed from the many people Harrison interviewed while researching the play who were forcibly removed from their birth families as children. The characters display a variety of responses to their experiences. Jimmy is assertive as a child, defeated as adult; Ruby is lost as a child, psychotic as an adult; Shirley, who has her own son taken from her, just as she was taken from her mother, never gives up on herself, or her child; Sandy is 'always on the run', a 'man in search of something' who 'finally finds... a sense of place' (vii); and Anne, adopted early by a white family, initially rejects her Indigenous history, only to rediscover it as an adult. The non-chronological narrative moves from scenes when the characters are young, both before their removal and in the children's home, to scenes when they are adults, and back again. Transformations of time and place are instant, as if (again) past and present are co-located and it is possible to access history simply by remembering it. Scenes of direct address mix with short exchanges of dialogue between the children, or the children and their families. White characters are rarely portrayed, and then in a satirical way. The bubbly tone of the dialogue is beguiling. The children are charming and charmingly vulnerable. Each scene has a name indicating its function in the story—The Chosen (Anne with her adopted parents); It Rained That Day (when Shirley's son is taken); Unspoken Abuse 3 (Jimmy's return from a day out with a visitor where *'he just hangs his head and goes slowly over to his bed and lies face down'* 25). Harrison's *pointillism* builds up a big picture, tale by tale, image by image, asking the audience to infer beyond the literal information provided, co-opting them as active participants in the drama. The transformation of general awareness for which *Stolen* aims, historically and politically, begins with watching the play itself. To be moved by *Stolen*, is to be persuaded by it. And to be persuaded by it, is to seek the change it seeks.

The hold of the past is evident at every point. In an early scene, Your Mum's Dead, the children, newly incarcerated in the home, collectively 'dream' their subordinate status:

> *All the children sleep. More 'dream' images (projected slides) circle around their beds. Jimmy whimpers in his bed.*
>
> JIMMY [*crying out in the dark*]: I wanna go home.
> MATRON [*voice-over*]: Quiet!
> JIMMY: When's my mum gunna come for me?
> MATRON [*voice-over*]: Your mother's not coming. She's dead.
> JIMMY [*muffled by the pillow*]: She's not dead, she's not.
>
> *Night-time lighting as each kid sits up on their own bed and chants in a dreamlike state.*
>
> CHILD: Nobody loves me.
> CHILD: Everybody hates me.
> CHILD: I think I should go and eat worms.
> CHILD: Big ones, small ones.
> CHILD: Fat ones, skinny ones.

CHILD: Worms and squiggle and squirm.
CHILD: Nobody wants me.
CHILD: Everybody hates me.
CHILD: I think I should go and eat worms.
They lie back down to sleep. (12)

Black Medea is a version of Euripides's *Medea*. It is not 'an adaptation' in the sense that the source material already exists in dramatic form, rather, it is a contemporary transposition in which surface details of the original text are changed but its compelling mood is retained. Such 'versions of' classic plays are more frequent in Australian drama from 1990 onwards. Not every 'version of' can be treated as a genuinely new play. But some can, and they make an impressive contribution to the national repertoire. Where *Stolen* follows five main characters, *Black Medea* has just two: Jason, of Argonauts fame, and Medea, who abandoned her native people, the Colchians, to help the man she loved, had children by him, then, when he cast her out, killed them in revenge. It was a confronting story in 431 BCE, and is no less so today. A mother's love for her children is usually seen as absolute. What can justify Medea's horrendous betrayal of maternal care? It is testament to the artistic subtlety and political resonance of Wesley Enoch's play that it illuminates the conditions whereby such an unthinkable action can be understood, without recourse to melodrama and the easy 'out' that Medea is just a 'bad person'.

Two moments in *Black Medea* hint at the dark themes buried in the action like underground volcanoes waiting to erupt. The first is the initial description of Jason by the Chorus as 'a blackfella in a suit. Working his way up the corporate ladder, a city black with his hair wavy, bleached with saltwater air. Carrying his briefcase and his jacket. Sweat marking his new shirt and his feet baking in his leather shoes. All the girls laugh at him' (66). Medea, however, sees him as her ticket out of the isolated desert community into which she has been born. She wants to live 'in a big house with a garden, in a place where the sand doesn't creep in under the door'. In the play, there is a Chorus figure who performs much the same functions as the Chorus in *A Cheery Soul*, though there is a sinister edge to its role in the story later on. In the early scenes, it is confined to scene-setting and delivering the backstory. 'He smells of soap and sweat', the Chorus tells the audience. 'She smells of ambition'.

The second moment is more mysterious. Medea and Jason both have scenes in which they recount their dreams. These are effectively communions with the dead, with Medea's matrilineal heritage and Jason's patrilineal one. The violence inherent in the play starts here: the past cannibalises the present, turning it into a version of itself:

> JASON: I had this dream. I'm following this man… I can't see his face but I know it's my father. I'm following this alley between two high walls… [It's] only wide enough for one… I'm following my father and I can see we're in a line of men all walking in the same direction down this thin alley. Then we stop like we reached the end.
>
> I'm staring into the back of my father's head and I look up. The sun's burning the back of my eyes… I look back down… and I see my father's face… He's now facing me… there's anger in his eyes… I turn around to face the other direction and see the empty alley stretching out to the horizon and realise I have to lead the line… In front of me, I see my son… I can hear him crying, I want to take him by the hand… I want to show him a way out… but I can't show him anything… so I put my hands on his shoulders and shove him to start walking. (75)

The desert wind is almost another character in *Black Medea*, a personification of Jason and Medea's thoughts that are infected with self-defeat from the beginning, like those of the children in *Stolen* (a play Enoch directed). The couple's cultural dislocation, the play implies, is a big reason for the domestic violence that overwhelms their lives. The Chorus accentuates Medea's worst fear: that her son will turn into Jason, and become another abusive male. 'CHORUS: And so the father becomes the son becomes the father becomes the son' (71). Medea reaches for an iron pipe while 'Jason is asleep at the table, a bottle of beer beside him' (76). One brilliant technique of *Black Medea* is its Jenny Kemp–like montages of visual images, allowing rapid glimpses into the home life of the couple: 'JASON holds a toy bulldozer box. / CHILD with bulldozer. / MEDEA is banging her head up against the leg of the table' (76). It accelerates the action, but also lends it a symbolic feel, as if Jason and Medea are emblematic of all dysfunctional Indigenous marriages, wrenched apart by a leprous past that just won't let go. The experiments in blending verbal and visual information that began in earnest with New Wave plays—and in getting the audience to extrapolate a world from the short snippets they are shown directly—continues here.

The ending of *Stolen* is equivocal. Some characters survive, some do not, some are left in limbo. The ending of *Black Medea* is calamitous. There is no question of a 'lack of bitterness... and blame' here. Bitterness and blame are the essence of the drama. Medea beats her son to death. 'Look upon this sight, Jason... and weep', she tells her husband in a last speech. 'I have saved him from becoming you. And if in my womb another of your children lies waiting, know this... that he will encounter the same fate as his brother... Whatever my hell, I will sleep pleased in the knowledge that my grief has yours as company. Wherever you go, bear witness that there are no gods' (80). This implacable note is a familiar one in Australian drama by now, almost a strain in its own right. It is the shadow self to the 'utopia' that white Australia imagined (and still imagines) itself to be. Whatever difficulties reckoning with the past might entail, denying it involves consequences that are infinitely more terrifying. 'MEDEA burns down the house. JASON carries the body of CHILD offstage' (80).

Conversations with the Dead begins where *Black Medea* ends: with a vision of unbearable suffering. Even to read the play is an ordeal, so relentless is its representation of grief, pain and loss. As with *Stolen*, a government inquiry provides the backdrop, while the drama shows what is at stake in human terms. Jack, the central character, is the alter-ego of Richard J Frankland. This gifted and polymathic playwright of the Gunditjmara people of south-western Victoria is also a filmmaker and musician. In 1998, he was the composer for *Stolen*. In 1996, he wrote and directed *No Way to Forget*, the first Indigenous film to win an AFI award. It is the basis for *Conversations with the Dead*, but also very different from it. The play is longer for a start, and the dead make an appearance. Indeed, they are the most talkative characters in it, while Jack struggles to find words to express his feelings. This leads to a strange reversal: the dead are alive and keen to communicate; the living are beset to the point of expiration, dying from the inside out.

In 1988 Frankland was appointed to the Royal Commission into Aboriginal Deaths in Custody that ran from 1987 to 1991, in part because of his army experience. The Commission was charged with investigating the deaths of Indigenous persons while under arrest, being pursued by the police, in pre-trial remand, in prison or in youth detention. The published script carries no author's notes, but Frankland dedicates it 'to anyone who has seen too much grief either through their own eyes and soul or through the dreaming path of others' (218). In the second scene of the play, Jack makes a declaration to the audience 'centre stage on a chair... sitting as if he is a bird':

> JACK: Imagine that you're a Koorie, that you're in your mid-twenties, that your job is to look into the lives of the dead and the process, policy and attitude that killed them.
> Imagine seeing that much death and grief that you lose your family, and you begin to wonder at your own sanity.
> Imagine when the job's over but the nightmares remain and that deaths keep on happening more than ever.
> What would you do? Where would you put the memories? What would keep you sane? Who do you think could understand what you carry inside you? (221–2)

Conversations with the Dead breathes with anger and violence, a significant part of which originates from Jack himself, overwhelmed by what he is required to do. Facts and statistics are embedded in the narrative like broken teeth. 'STATISTICS. In an 8-year period 124 deaths in custody, 99 investigated... No charges recommended overwhelming evidence of violence or negligence in some deaths' (242–3). Jack's job is to investigate these deaths for the Commission, to meet with family members, hear their stories, and make sense of what has happened. As the Commission's one Indigenous investigator, he is often the only person to whom the family will talk.

> JACK [*to the audience*]: Another fucking eulogy, saying goodbye to the dead again, honouring them, loving them, their families, in some cases my family, helping them to live one more time, washing away tears with love. (242)

Jack's experiences are tearing him apart, and what leaks out like blood from an eye socket is the most destructive and self-destructive behaviour imaginable. Next to the Irish Bushranger and the Socialist Economist, we may put the Indigenous Field Officer in Australia's pantheon of suffering archetypes. Each is aware of vast historical injustice, backed into a corner by political power, and placed under unbearable strain by the agony they see around them. But Jack is a rawer character than Stewart's Ned Kelly or Sewell's Allen Fitzgerald, perhaps because he can affect general conditions even less. Hence the courageous and utterly surprising leap of agency he finds himself engaging: talking to the dead.

Frankland uses all the techniques that Australian drama had by the 1990s claimed as its own: songs, poetry, direct address, silent images, snatches of realistic dialogue, sequences of surreal action, slide projections, and abrupt changes of time and location. The core around which this theatrical medley coheres is the journey of Jack himself, the descent into the hell of his own mind and memories. The cool judgements of *Honour* are replaced by burningly passionate ones. Jack spares nothing and no-one, including, most of all, himself. In its confessional intensity and ruthless honesty, *Conversations with the Dead* evokes Leslie Rees's description of Sydney Tomholt's plays as 'an electric wire stretched almost, if not quite, to breaking point'. The main pillars of the action are four conversations Jack conducts with deceased Indigenous men: the at-peace David (JACK: I stretch out my feelings to see what he feels like. To see if he is angry…I reckon he's more confused than anything else 225); the furious Peter (JACK: I stand silently, awkwardly trying to find my place in this conversation… Our environment is flicking from his deathbed, to the toilet where he stabbed himself in the eye, to his art room and to his cell 234–5); the infinitely sad Uncle (JACK: In the police watch-house book they said you were a 'good bloke for an Abo'… Didn't know that you were a gun rover, a stockman, a real man 247); and the apparently cheerful Joe (JACK: You didn't wear shoes or socks I heard… but they say you hung yourself with a footy sock. How did you hang yourself with socks when you had none? 250). The tone of these conversations is purgatorial, Jack trying to say sorry without knowing what he is sorry for.

It is not right to see David, Peter, Uncle and Joe as ghosts. They are what the ancient Greeks would have called the restless dead, *aōroi* (people who died in an untimely manner) and *biaiothanatoi* (people who died by violence). By contrast, Jack himself sometimes seems barely alive. He surrounds himself with ways of killing himself and starts each morning with a rope in his hands, scanning his house for possible hanging points. It is as if his job invests him with quasi-dead status. 'I see the faces of the dead, and I see the world through a mother's tears... I can see sadness in the streets, pain in people's faces, grief in their hands and the way they walk. I can see loneliness like a man sees a long-lost brother, I do see hope sometimes... and love, I see love, from pain and grief, this is what hurts most of all' (260).

Jack's journey does not resolve, either at the end of the play, or at any time during it. This is because it is symbolic of the history of Indigenous Australians under white law which has likewise not resolved. The play is not a factual lecture, but a cry of pain from the soul of a dramatist who has exposed himself to Fukuyama's History and become aware of its full social and political cost. A result is Jack's loss of individual identity. 'Your experience becomes mine and our lives become so intertwined', he tells David, 'that I don't know where one begins and one ends' (231). And to Peter, 'I don't know how I feel. I don't know who I am. Or even what I am... I think that somewhere in it all I became a part of you or you became a part of me'. Jack is the opposite of Barbara in *Diving for Pearls*, who loses the representative side of her character and is just herself (whoever that is). By contrast, the representative side of Jack grows disproportionately. He must be all things to all people:

> JACK [*to the audience*]: Time for the dinner party.
>
> *He walks to the table and raucous conversation and music is playing.* JACK *laughs. The honoured guest.*
>
> Yes, yes, yes, of course, Francis, of course. Aboriginal people have always been at one with the land.
> [*To the audience*] Here is where I get to be the lawyer, the politician, the doctor, the herbologist, the historian, the spiritual one, the mystical noble savage and, of course, the suffering wounded activist warrior.

> *He turns back to the table.* FRANCIS *taps the glass.*
>
> FRANCIS: Friends, friends, your attention please. We are gathered of course for our good friend Jack.
>
> LILLY AND MICHAEL: Hear hear, well done, Jack.
>
> JACK *is beaming modestly.*
>
> FRANCIS: Jack. Please do tell, Jack, how do your people die in jail... I mean why do they kill themselves in jail, Jack?
>
> LILLY: Yes, Jack, please tell us.
>
> MICHAEL: Come on, Jack, you know we love these stories...
>
> JACK: Well... well...
>
> LILLY, MICHAEL *and* FRANCIS *are leaning forward eagerly.*
>
> [*To the audience*] Wounded warrior activist time...
>
> It's an interesting question that you ask. I think the real question is: do my people kill themselves or are they killed? (262–3)

The racial forces that irradiate *Conversations with the Dead* and rend Jack's life are never directly named in the play—which is saying something, given the determination of the drama to be unswerving at every turn. 'Do you really want to know what kills my people?' Jack asks his dinner guests, who are being soaked from a rain of blood falling from the skies, before turning to the audience and saying, 'We know, don't we?' (264).

***

Of the eight plays discussed in this chapter, four contain passages in which the living talk to the dead directly, while the other four have scenes where characters commune with the past indirectly. This strongly suggests that far from being gulled by Fukuyama's claim that History has come to an End and no longer requires interrogation, Australian playwrights thought the opposite. In the professional, cultural and political scope of these eight plays there is renewed emphasis on drama's truth-revealing power, its capacity to offer general views of, and to, the nation. Australian drama's stylistic techniques continue to expand, reflecting the exploratory growth of different dramatic strains inherited from earlier periods. But its intellectual and emotional engagement becomes more concentrated. Drama's value as a mode of inquiry increases, even as its messages become harder to bear.

8
2006–2020: The return of the nation

When the Rain Stops Falling **(2007)**. *The Dark Room* **(2009)**. *SHIT* **(2015)**. *The Bleeding Tree* **(2015)**. *Black is the New White* **(2017)**. *Counting and Cracking* **(2019)**. *Hungry Ghosts* **(2018)**. *Triple X* **(2020)**.

> Not every narrative is an arc. The universe just keeps expanding. But from the universe's perspective, the expanding might barely have started. Or it might be almost finished.
>
> Sarah Manguso, *300 Arguments*

Anyone who has looked in the rear-vision mirror of a travelling car and been amazed as the world behind them becomes a rapidly diminishing image will appreciate the paradox of history: there is always more of it, yet it is always going or gone. For many readers of this book, my last period falls within the scope of personal memory and hardly qualifies as history at all. The car has not yet sped away. The mirror is a mass of details. What will be recalled from 2005–2020 in a century's time, as we look back on Federation now, remembering only a few features? Dates are boundary stones for constructing one story rather than another. Do the current years mark the beginning of an era or the end of one? Or are claims for an approaching utopia or impending catastrophe equally overblown? Living history is a poor position from which to judge it—or write about it.

A semi-random trawl of my bookshelf to provide background for this chapter reveals: Tony Bower's 2016 biography of Tony Blair, *Broken Vows: The Tragedy of Power*, on the British government's—and

Australia's—blundering Middle Eastern intervention in search of imaginary weapons of mass destruction in the Second Iraq War (2003–11); Jacqueline Kent's *Take Your Best Shot*, about Julia Gillard, whose last pages quote from her exit remarks as Labor prime minister, 'What I am absolutely confident of is, it will be easier for the next woman and the woman after that, and the woman after that' (121); and Adam Toose's *Crashed*, on the 'bait and switch' of the 2007–8 Global Financial Crisis when ordinary citizens were made to pay for the dysfunction of their financial sectors in years of counterproductive austerity. 'Though it is hardly a secret that we inhabit a world dominated by business oligopolies, during the crisis and its aftermath this reality… stood nakedly exposed', Toose writes. 'It is an unpalatable and explosive truth that democratic politics on both sides of the Atlantic has choked on' (13). Making the same argument but in a more academic way is Thomas Piketty's massive *Capital in the Twenty-First Century*, a 793-page historical trend analysis of income and wealth inequality in Western nations—trends that accelerated after it was published in 2014, prompting a sequel in 2020, *Capital and Ideology*, which is even longer (1150 pages). In *The Future of Everything*, Tim Dunlop discusses the problem of 'the commons' in an age of social media and the concentration of economic and political power. He writes, '[W]e are born into a world of cooperation and interdependence… Our ability to function as individuals and a species is enabled by interdependence. And that interdependence is enabled by the things we share in common'. *Just Cool It! The Climate Crisis and What We Can Do* by David Suzuki and Ian Hannington sees cooperation as key to the 'slow-motion catastrophe' of global warming. The authors issue a call to arms that is at once hopeful and urgent: 'If we summon the human ingenuity and intelligence that have propelled us as a species, this can become a time of great opportunity. But we must act now'.

The problems of the past 15 years are as diverse as their historical expressions. A list of significant events might add to the above: the vote for Brexit in the United Kingdom in 2015; the election of Donald Trump as the forty-fifth American president in 2016; the continued spread of casual employment and the rise of 'the precariat' as Guy Standing called them in 2011; and Trump supporters storming Washington's Capitol building in 2021. Hyper-partisanship has intensified in elite politics, while the Me Too and the Black Lives Matter movements have transformed politics at the grassroots level. Intellectuals in Australia, as elsewhere, self-evidently struggle with the challenges facing contemporary democracies, and would probably concur with Dunlop's remark that 'we have become incredibly good at analysing where our society has gone wrong [but] there are far fewer attempts to explain how we might fix it'.

Yet there is a convergence to the plethora of 'issues' that governments like to treat separately. Whatever problem one examines, the root causes feel similar. Peter Fleming's *Dark Academia*, discusses the plight of universities in an age of neoliberal corporatisation. Its central argument might come from any of the books I have mentioned: 'Capitalist realism continues to prime human beings as discrete economic units, ones that observe strict boundary lines between them and the world', Fleming contends. 'This artificial fetishisation of the individual is nearly pathological today… it is still difficult to openly confront'.

Australia may be forced to confront it soon. In the Asia-Pacific region an alternative political system has emerged. Communist China is the second largest economy and most populous nation on the planet. Right now, Australia and China seem bent on a mutually unhelpful collision course. The eminent Sinologist Linda Jaivin writes,

> The lesson of Trump is that the institutions of democracy are not invincible. If we are to rise to the challenges presented by global autocracy, they must be guarded and strengthened. The profound disruption caused by Covid is also an opportunity to rebuild. A clean and transparent political system and—crucially—a return to bipartisanship on foreign affairs as well as issues such as the climate crisis, a diverse media and a robust and accessible tertiary education system are as important in equipping Australia to deal with China's rise as are bolstered diplomacy and defence capabilities.

The importance of fully functioning democratic institutions for solving problems of diversity, diplomacy, inequality, polarisation and climate change is a concluding theme in Stuart Macintyre's *A Concise History of Australia*. The last chapter of this invaluable book is titled simply, 'Outcomes, 1997–2019'. In it, Macintyre offers scattershot insights into Australia 118 years after Federation: the major parliamentary parties dwindling in appeal; the economy over-reliant on primary resources (half selling to China!); reconciliation with Aboriginal and Torres Strait Islander peoples as elusive as ever; climate change avoided as a political hot potato; and a new mega-rich class negatively impacting 'a society that has taken pride in its egalitarian ethos'; though he adds, 'qualities of fortitude and compassion were less apparent when the coronavirus struck… and panic buying of toilet paper took hold'.

The pandemic has demonstrated to anyone still in doubt how interconnected the world is, and how tightly political, social, economic, cultural and medical factors are bound together. The 2005–2020 period feels like a riposte to confident predictions of the triumph of capitalist individualism. Across the world, 'the nation' has been returning as the cynosure of political power. Covid accentuated it, each country scrambling first to protect citizens from its ravages, then to vaccinate them against its recurrence. It is noteworthy that those who loudly proclaimed their support for neoliberal individualism before the pandemic—the United States, Britain, India and Brazil—performed the worst at managing it. Australia was more circumspect. Happy to be part of such an ideology when it suits, it has retained its capacity to act collectively in the face of disaster. Infections and deaths from Covid have been lower in Australia than in many other countries (though a slow vaccine rollout in 2021, and muddled communication around the Omicron wave in 2022, undid some of this good work).

The return of the nation as a unit of political action (exemplified by the intergovernmental National Cabinet), however, is not to be confused with its emotional correlative—a *sense of* the nation. This all-important cloud of shared views and values inheres the nation as a communally lived reality. To argue that 2005–2020 shows a resurgent awareness of nationhood leaves open whether this is a good or bad thing. I would argue that it *can* be good, because the nation is *potentially* a mechanism for inclusion, a way of balancing individual choices with common purposes and actions. Here, the relationship between Australia's national life and its national drama is one indicator of democratic health. When we look at our stage plays we should see this balance being actively explored. Our national repertoire is an integumentary system, a protective layer of public discussion that allows us to parse the individual and representative dimensions of our lives in useful ways. I return to this point in the Conclusion.

For Australian theatre, these years brought further problems but few solutions. Federal support for the cultural sector continued to decline, while the Australia Council for the Arts was 'reformed' by the Australia Council Act 2013 to make it less arm's length, and more responsive to ministerial decree. With the election of federal Labor to power under Prime Minister Kevin Rudd in 2007, debate about a national cultural policy restarted. For a short time, I was involved in this myself, as part of a Creative Australia Advisory Committee, when the musician Peter Garrett was Minister for the Arts. Matters proceeded at a glacial pace. *Creative Australia* did not officially appear until March 2013. As the Coalition won government in October, the document had an even shorter shelf life than *Creative Nation*, whose title it was designed to invoke. Its spirit is different, however, more technocratic than democratic, with an emphasis on 'investment', 'targets' and 'returns'. The language of the creative industries is evident, a framing of arts and culture as drivers of 'the creative economy' and post-industrial growth. It won no hearts with the new Tony Abbott–led government, and little favour with the new minister responsible for the arts portfolio, George Brandis. He ignored *Creative Australia* just as his predecessors had ignored *Creative Nation*.

Then in May 2015, Senator Brandis did a surprising thing. Without warning, he cut 16 per cent from the Australia Council's budget to establish his own, ministerially controlled, grant-giving body, the National Programme for Excellence in the Arts. This action sparked a backlash from the sector that dominated its interactions with the federal government for the next three years. While in theory (that is, legally) the minister can make executive decisions about the Council's annual allocation, in practice (that is, politically), it is a difficult power to exercise. In July, the Senate established an inquiry into the cuts that received an unprecedented more than 2000 submissions from practitioners around the country. By November, Senator Brandis was no longer Minister for the Arts. During 2016–17, the Council's budget was restored to previous levels. However, the cuts had a long-term souring effect on relations between the government and the sector. Ben Eltham's *When the Goal Posts Move* is an account of 'Brandisgate' and a reminder—if one is needed—of the influence artists wield when they act in a united way. But the fractured relationship with Canberra continues today. The widespread perception that the government's neglect of arts and culture in its Covid support packages—especially its JobKeeper program, which excluded artists on short-term contracts—is a reflection of this.

I deal with the eight plays in this chapter in chronological order. I saw the last, Glace Chase's *Triple X*, at Queensland Theatre in April 2021. But I continue my method of reading different plays into each other, and into the drama of earlier periods, rather than treating them in standard categories ('new stage voices', 'Asian–Australian drama', 'queer theatre' for example). Of course, approaching plays in this conventional way is illuminating, but my aims are more holistic. I am focused less on differences and claims to originality than on shared features and lines of continuity (holonic connections). I concur with Eamon Flack, the director of S. Shakthidharan's *Counting and Cracking*, a play about four generations of a Sri Lankan immigrant family, when he writes in the script's foreword that '[it] is an Australian story. It's not only an Australian story, but it is definitely an Australian story. Much of it takes place in Sri Lanka: the story of Australia is the story of many places, many people' (xi). No words could better express my understanding of our national repertoire as it becomes more diverse, or better illustrate the use of the term 'Australian' as an inclusive one.

The plays I have chosen are not even vaguely representative of the large body of work that is Australian drama in the period, but they show a good spread of authors. Andrew Bovell and Patricia Cornelius are established playwrights, their theatre work starting in the 1980s. Angus Cerini's first plays appeared in the 1990s, Angela Betzien's in the 2000s. S. Shakthidharan, Jean Tong, Nakkiah Lui, and Glace Chase are dramatists who have emerged in the last ten years. Taken as a group, the plays show a continuation of New Wave experiment but with a sensibility that Bovell calls 'post postmodern', defining it as one 'of great reflection from which we will emerge regenerated' (ix). This suggests an upbeat quality, and that is indeed the case with most (not all) of them. Darker tones are matched by lighter ones, often humorous, sometimes hopeful. Compared to plays of the 1980s, themes of millennial despair are far less present. Perhaps these playwrights sense the world now really is poised on the edge of catastrophe, and they must take care how they address audiences more fragile and perturbed than any since the 1930s. In this, they show an inimitable understanding of the Australians who will watch their plays.

There is no point at all trying to separate realist dramas from non-realist ones. All the plays blend techniques from the two strains continually, naturally and creatively. In doing so, they display a high level of professional skill, cultural capacity and political messaging. They operate as powerful engines of discovery on issues of public importance to Australians, broaching them directly and indirectly. They are critical, which is no surprise, but also sophisticated in their political, psychological and moral judgements. They create space around their stories, allowing audiences to reflect on the worlds they present, rather than filling the air with one-way messages. Sometimes they utilise 'new' forms, sometimes traditional ones. Their stylistic choices reflect their different purposes, rather than a pursuit of innovation for its own sake.

Plays in time

Andrew Bovell's *When the Rain Stops Falling* (*Rain*) premiered at the Adelaide Festival of Arts in 2008, with my friend, the actor Neil Pigot, in the lead role of Gabriel York. I flew down to see it on an unforgivingly hot night in March. The city was sweltering through ten successive days of temperatures over 35 degrees Celsius. One year later, the 'Black Saturday' bushfires burnt 450,000 hectares of Victoria, and claimed 173 lives. In 2019–20, the 'Black Summer' bushfires ravaged 18 million hectares of Queensland and New South Wales, and claimed 34 lives. News footage of these disasters provided a terrifying glimpse into a scorching Hades. *Rain* is not explicitly

Time and space unbent into a single zone of apprehension. Anna Lise Phillips as Gabrielle York (younger), Yalin Ozucelik as Gabriel Law, Michaela Cantwell as Elizabeth Law (younger) and Carmel Johnson as Elizabeth Law (older) in the 2008 Brink Productions, State Theatre Company of SA and Adelaide Bank Festival of the Arts production of When the Rain Stops Falling. *(Photo: Wend Lear)*

about climate change, but Bovell says that 'the idea of extinction was the starting thematic point and this naturally led to a conversation around global warming... More importantly, it led to the use of the weather as a metaphor for the emotional state of the characters and the background to the playing out of their stories. The weather stood for something that was shared across generations' (xiv). We have seen how the generational transmission of knowledge is a concern for many Australian plays. But between 2005 and 2020 this concept attracts even more interest. Positioning themselves *in time* is as important for the characters in these dramas as location *in space* is for characters in earlier ones. Families and family stories are examined not just for their historical details, but for precedents, patterns and prefigurations. The past is not just the past, or even a legacy to the present. It is prophetic, its concatenating consequences stretching into the years to come, shaping them. Shaping the future.

Rain occurs over four different generations of two different families: the Laws and the Yorks. The locations and times are: London in the 1960s and the 1980s; the Coorong and Uluru in the 1980s; Adelaide in 2013 (the future when the play opened, but the past now), and Alice Springs in 2039 (still the future now, but one day it won't be). The critic Murray Bramwell writes in his introduction to the script, 'it is not often we see a play that has its first scene in 2039 and features a fish falling from the sky' (xiii). Different actors portray the same character at different stages in their lives (young/old) or different generations of the two families.

Gabriel York is a withdrawn, middle-aged man living in a dank, one-room apartment in Alice Springs in a future when the world is disappearing under torrential rain and rising sea levels. He is alone and lonely. He abandoned his son as a small boy and is now estranged from him. The same actor who plays Gabriel York also plays Henry Law, his grandfather, an intelligent and seemingly happily married man in 1960s London, who likewise has a son that, under different circumstances, he likewise deserts. *Rain* is thus driven by two starter questions: why did Henry walk out on his wife and child in 1968, and will Gabriel find the courage to reunite with *his* son, Andrew, Henry's great-grandson, 71 years later?

Into this immense temporal river flows another narrative involving Gabriel York's mother, Gabrielle York, who, in the 1980s, has a brief, intense liaison with Gabriel Law, Henry's son. Gabriel Law is then killed in a car crash in the Coorong that Gabrielle York, pregnant with her dead lover's child, narrowly survives.

The blurring of character names is deliberate, part of the play's carefully constructed poetic architecture. What is hard to explain is easy to watch. Not only does the narrative move backwards and forwards across past, present and future in ways reminiscent of De Groen's *The Woman in the Window* and Lyssiotis's *The Forty Lounge Café*, but the action in different periods co-occurs, sometimes with two actors simultaneously playing the same character at different stages of their life.

Repetition and refrain are key to the momentum of the play. Certain words, phrases and ideas are reiterated by different characters, often in an effort to fathom what they meant when first spoken. The words 'There you are', when repeated across generations and places, become, by turns, a social greeting, a motherly rebuke, an existential insight and a historical memory. The plot of *Rain* is not composed of twists and turns in a classic sense—though there are a few of these—but Jenny Kemp-ish cut-aways, double-backs and overlays. Bovell explains,

> it wasn't the stories that mattered. I knew they would change and they did. It was the principle of how narrative would be organised… so that the stories would unfold across generations and time periods and that they would be told simultaneously and in parallel… we knew or discovered that the work needed to reach back into the past and deep in the future (xi).

The 'we' here refers to Bovell's collaborators, the designer–artist Hossein Valamanesh, the composer Quincy Grant, the director Chris Drummond and the actors of the Brink ensemble.

Without going into the details of *Rain*'s development, it exemplifies the tendency towards extended collaborative practice in Australian theatre. Bovell did not write *Rain* and bring it to Brink fully formed. Nor was Bovell commissioned by Brink in the conventional way. The play evolved from a cloud of shared ideas. The way this happened is similar to how *Rain* itself achieves dramatic coherence: through the accumulation of words, images and moments that by the ineluctable pressure of their repeated presence transmute into the white light of understanding.

The link between the Law and York families is both supremely hopeful and terrifyingly tragic. Henry Law is a paedophile. This revelation comes late in the play, by which time its consequences are the focus of the play's attention (thus avoiding melodrama). Henry's wife, Elizabeth, exiles him from the family, and he leaves for Australia, from where he writes his son six cryptic postcards that she unsuccessfully tries to hide. Years later, Gabriel goes to Australia to retrace his father's footsteps to Uluru, where he mysteriously disappeared. *En route* through the Coorong he meets Gabrielle York, whose parents committed suicide after their son, her brother, was abducted and murdered as a young child ('It's like your father', she says to Gabriel, 'I remember him because he wasn't there' 35).

Gabriel is killed in the car crash while they are trying to escape to a new life and Gabrielle names her son after him, though she can hardly bear to speak his name ('You made my life hell', her husband Joe tells her, 'but what's worse… you did the same to your son' 47). Heartbreaking secrets are buried under layers of generational silence, in what families do not say to each other because 'having nothing to say is just another way of having so much to say that you dare not begin' (50 *and* 56). In the middle of the play, while driving out of the Coorong, Gabriel and Gabrielle work out that Gabriel's father was there when Gabrielle's brother was abducted. It is this *peripeteia* (reversal) that causes Gabriel to crash the car.

Bovell calls the mood of *Rain* 'melancholic', which he says is 'not a state of sadness but [a] deep state of reflection out of which new thinking will arise' (ix). The scene that ends the play suggests that the past, no matter how awful—and in *Rain* it really is awful—can be recovered and the future resolved. Gabriel York meets his son, Andrew, and gives him lunch. With no money, nothing in the fridge, and seafood long extinct, a fish miraculously falls out of the sky to provide their meal. The stage direction reads, '*The* OLDER *and the* YOUNGER ELIZABETH, *the* OLDER *and the* YOUNGER GABRIELLE, GABRIEL LAW *and* JOE *enter. Each takes a plate from a pile and takes a place at the table*' (55). Gabriel brings out a number of family heirlooms—props used during the course of the play—and they are passed down by his 'ancestors' until they reach Andrew. The last lines read:

> GABRIEL *looks at* ANDREW.
>
> Forgive me. You let people go, Son, I have let people go all my life. I have run away from love… and now love seems to have found me, anyway. I don't know what all these things mean. It's not much. It's hardly anything at all. I can only tell you that somewhere at the end of this mess is where you belong. And now it's time to eat that fish before the world ends.
>
> *He leaves for a moment.*
>
> *The ancestors watch* ANDREW *as he wrestles with the weight of his mysterious past…*
>
> GABRIEL YORK *enters with the splendid fish on a platter. He lays it on the table and all the ancestors look at it with hunger in their eyes.*

ANDREW: It's beautiful.
GABRIEL: Listen…

They all look up… hearing the same thing in their own time and place.

The rain has stopped. (57)

All the horrors of the twentieth century, the painter Francis Bacon once observed, occurred in rooms. The sentiment suits Angela Betzien's *The Dark Room*, which is a play about a place as much as the people who inhabit it. It is described as 'A three-star motel room in the Northern Territory' (12), indicating that a) no more needs to be said about its seedy furnishings and atmosphere, and b) we are once again 'in the North', with all the complex feelings Australians have for this part of the country—its sadness, badness and abuse of colonial rule.

The deep background to the play, discussed by Betzien in her foreword to the script, is the 2007 'national emergency' intervention in the Northern Territory following the release of the *Little Children Are Sacred* report. This called for better support for Aboriginal children at risk of abuse or neglect. The federal government responded by suspending the Racial Discrimination Act, re-acquiring land controlled by First Nations peoples, and imposing mandatory 'income management' on targeted communities. By these and other actions the Territory became—and remains—a byword for racist police attitudes and the unjust incarceration of Indigenous Australian youth. This context hangs in the air of *The Dark Room* in the same way that global warming haunts *Rain*.

Three couples occupy *The Dark Room* at different times and at the same time. The notes read 'the action takes place in the same room with characters moving in and out of focus and time' (11). As with *Rain*, temporal co-occurrence is a feature, but the sequence of events is more restricted, taking place over weeks and months, rather than years and decades. Time bends around the characters like a quantum field. Without warning, the narrative shifts from what looks like present action, to memory or dream (or, more accurately, nightmare). These shifts are seamless, and the dialogue echoes and overlaps in unexpected ways. Lines said by one character in one time period, gather responses from another character in a different one.

The motel room has a bathroom and a cupboard. These provide exits and entrances, but are also physical objects via which the action abruptly advances or rewinds, so that suddenly the audience is seeing a different situation, studying a different problem. Unlike *Rain* there are no time markers, no indication of which events are 'before', which 'after'. Having read it, one might guess that *The Dark Room* begins in the past (or the present), shifts into the present (or the future), backtracks to the past (or the present), then ends in the present (or the future). But that imposes a directionality the action neither requires nor expects its audience to generate. *The Dark Room* is not a 'whodunnit' but a study in motives, morality and power. Its gothic feel arises from the interior landscape of the characters—from 'the dark room' wherein their own pain, anger and guilt reside. Technically, the play is similar to Compton's *Crossfire*'s 'kinetic stuttering'. Time loops rather than passes, with characters stuck in an endless cycle of rewind, review and remorse.

The three couples are: Anni, a youth care worker in her 40s, and Grace, her troubled teenage client; Stephen, a young cop, and Emma, his pregnant wife, both in their mid-30s; and Craig, an older policeman, and a cross-dressing Aboriginal youth who he bashed. The last is a ghost, another *biaiothanatoi*, haunting the imagination of Craig and Grace simultaneously. He appears in brief glimpses until a last extended exchange with the man who caused his death and now can't forget him:

> CRAIG *stands and approaches the wardrobe to reveal an* ABORIGINAL BOY *wearing a wedding dress and holding a dog's heart.*
>
> *The* BOY *is badly bruised.*
>
> BOY: Boo.
> CRAIG: You the one throwing rocks?
>   Out here
>   in the light.
>
> *The* BOY *steps out and walks towards the light.*
>
>   Who did that?
> BOY: Don't you know me?
> CRAIG: What do you want?
> BOY: Want to be with you. (83)

Grace is a difficult young woman. Anni brings her to the motel as a temporary respite while she tries to find her somewhere permanent to stay. Anni cares for Grace, but Grace challenges Anni's authority with her never-ending, impulsive demands. It is one of the achievements of the play that without diluting Grace's provocative behaviour, a context is revealed that not only changes our view of her character, but creates new understanding of what being 'a young person at risk' entails. At the beginning of the play, and periodically throughout, Grace wears a pillowcase over her head, with the eyes cut out and the corners tweaked, like the ears of an animal. She hides a knife under the mattress of the motel bed without Anni seeing. Given her aggressive demeanour, it is not unreasonable to think she might use it on Anni. At one point, she gives Anni a dog's heart. 'He was my favourite', she says. 'Smashed his brain with a hammer. Cut this out' (77). But it's all show. Grace is terrified out of her wits. When she does use the knife, it is on herself.

Stephen and Emma's marriage is breaking down. Stephen is a whistle-blower sent to the Territory for either protection or punishment, it is unclear which. It is the night of his best friend's wedding. He's drunk and looking to get drunker. As the couple fight, the toxic world of the North is illuminated: the abused schoolboy that Emma, a teacher, could not assist ('He yelled at me. Fuck off white cunt. I had to call for help' 58), and the AVOs, ODs, rapes and shootings Stephen must deal with on a daily basis ('Fuck off white cunt? That's good morning officer in my world' 59).

In the motel room, Stephen is a presence in all three time periods, quarrelling with his wife, conspiring (reluctantly) with Craig, and comforting Anni when it turns out she is remembering things that won't let her go. Later, it emerges that the 'best friend's wedding' is actually Craig's. Stephen is a Mrs Hamilton figure, torn between good choices and bad ones. Unlike Brand's *Here Under Heaven*, Betzien's play does not end with a moment of redemption. But the potential is there if Stephen can find a way to deal with Craig's corruption, and the horror of the Territory's streets. The suggestion of widespread domestic violence and patriarchal oppression boils in the background like a poisonous fog. It is infectious, passed from Craig's father to

Craig, from Craig to Stephen. 'It's tough in the Territory/no question', Craig tells the younger policeman. 'You can't be soft. Like my old man says/sometimes you have to drink a glass of cement and harden the fuck up' (67).

Like *Black Medea*, *The Dark Room* has passages of rapid-fire action, the silence of which contrasts with the sombre dialogue of its longer scenes. But the purpose is different. In Wesley Enoch's play they are a means of filling in the backstory, showing the family in a range of different domestic situations. In Betzien's play, they are used to wrench time periods out of orbit, to show damage and trauma spreading across them like a virus.

> *Darkness*
>
> *The* BOY *recedes into darkness.*
>
> CRAIG *is alone clutching his chest.*
>
> *Darkness.*
>
> *Light.*
>
> CRAIG *is gone.*
>
> STEPHEN *approaches* EMMA. *He touches her stomach.*
>
> EMMA *turns away from him and leaves.*
>
> *Darkness.*
>
> *Light.*
>
> GRACE *is staring at the mirror.*
>
> *She is wearing the dog mask.*
>
> *Darkness.*
>
> *Light.*
>
> GRACE *stares at the motel door.*
>
> *Darkness.*
>
> *Light.*
>
> GRACE *is sitting on the bed holding the knife.*

> *Darkness.*
>
> *Light.*
>
> ANNI: Grace.
>
> GRACE: You're calling them now.
> Aren't you Anni?
> You're gunna call the hospital now.
>
> GRACE *lifts the knife to stab herself.*
>
> ANNI: No.
>
> *Darkness.* (86–7)

Of all the plays in this chapter, *The Dark Room* is tonally the one most like *Ned Kelly*, *Blind Giant* and *Conversations with the Dead*. But despite the grim world it portrays, its characters all have an air of fragility. Even Craig, the worst of them, is seen wrestling with his sexuality. Like *Rain*, the play moves towards, but stops short of, final judgement. The end is a horrendous description of the murder–suicide of Grace's parents. The last lines are Anni's: 'I saw her out there/Grace's mother/She was up by the shed./She was waving at me./Maybe she didn't know she was dead' (91). It isn't hope, and it certainly isn't forgiveness. But Anni's continuing to care is a hint of positive change.

SHIT and *The Bleeding Tree* share a number of thematic and structural similarities. They premiered within six weeks of each other in 2015 before transferring to state theatre companies after successful seasons in smaller venues. Reading the plays together allows for some useful generalisations, the most important of which is that verse drama is not dead! Angus Cerini writes in his script note to *The Bleeding Tree*, 'I am hoping the reader will engage with the work more as a poem or a stream of consciousness' (xiv). The remark applies equally to *SHIT*.

Both published scripts are solid dialogue. There are few stage directions, and little indication of what setting, physical or projected, should be used. Both plays are premised on the expectation their directors will take creative decisions to realise them in stage terms. *SHIT* was co-produced by Patricia Cornelius and her long-time collaborator, Suzie Dee. Its sparse stage directions provide scope for Dee's directorial imagination rather than dictating to it. *The Bleeding Tree* takes this a step further. There are no named characters at all, or lines assigned to one actor rather than another. 'I tend to think such practicalities get in the way of the thrust of the piece', Cerini writes. 'Least of all by giving these characters names' (xiv–xv). But the plays are intensely visual in another way. Both SHIT and *The Bleeding Tree* show drama's capacity to generate vivid stage pictures by using image-laden language. In doing so, they range further, on a more epic scale and with greater impact than if they represented those images literally. What audiences see in their heads can be more compelling than what they see with their eyes. A picture may be worth a thousand words. But a few words can summon a whole world into existence.

Let us briefly sample the language of the plays. Here is the much-celebrated opening speech of *SHIT*, delivered by Billy, a member of a so-called girl gang, and below that, a speech from *The Bleeding Tree* that probably belongs to the wife who has just clubbed and shot to death her abusive husband:

> BILLY: And he goes, look at you, fuck look at you, what the fuck you done, you fucking done nothing, you never fucking going to do something, you fucked-up waste of space, what fucking contribution you made, nothing, nothing at all, you fucked-up nothing, fucking nothing you are, a big fucking nothing, he goes, the biggest fucking nothing, the biggest fucking nothing I know, and I think, who's this fucking fucked-up fuck telling me I'm fucked up, who's he, and I go, who are you to fucking tell me I'm fucking nothing, you fucking fuck, you're the fucking nothing, never going to fucking do nothing fuck, what contribution you and you're fucking telling me I'm fucking nothing makes you fucking way more fucking way more, way way more fucking nothing. (113)

> — That stink you stink never made such a sweet smell as this one come wafting from your dead heart. Flimsy show-body up there in the sky. All or nothing up against the wall so often had me. With time on our side this place was green. Had character, hope, future-making here with the fences all strong like rope. Never believe in dreams come true before. (22)

The language of *SHIT* and *The Bleeding Tree* is glorious, a dramatic event in itself. Poetry in plays can take many forms, but the oldest rely on alliteration, sprung-verse, half-rhyme and switches of cadence, line length and subject matter, to achieve sometimes consonant, sometimes discordant effects. Similar techniques can be seen in ancient Greek drama, as well as in plays like *Ned Kelly*, *Stretch of the Imagination* and *Stolen*, all of which rely on a juxtaposition of vernacular and poetic terms. 'Fuck', 'cunt', 'shit' and 'prick' may be profanities outside the theatre. In it, they are plosive sounds deployed for their expressive qualities. So, to make an obvious point, both these speeches are great fun to hear, not despite their blue language, but because of it. The two plays are laugh-out-loud funny as a result.

SHIT and *The Bleeding Tree* are all-women plays, three characters apiece. We are back in a world without men, though not a world unaffected by them, any more than are the women in Dymphna Cusack's *Morning Sacrifice*. *SHIT's* Billy, Bobby and Sam are three delinquent youths who form a criminal gang, mugging wealthier women in an unspecified urban location. In the character notes, Cornelius describes them in brutal terms: 'There's not a single moment when the three young women transcend their ugliness. There's no indication of a better or in fact any inner life… They love no-one and no-one loves them. They believe the world is shit, that their lives are shit, that they are shit' (112). *The Bleeding Tree*'s characters are described as 'Three women play[ing] a mother and her two daughters' while the action 'occurs in a farmhouse some distance from a rural town' (xviii).

SHIT ends with a murder, *The Bleeding Tree* begins with one, and they are opposite in moral valency. When *SHIT*'s characters attack their final victim it is described as 'a glimpse of SAM, BOBBY *and* BILLY committing an horrendous act' (146). By contrast, after the unnamed husband in *The Bleeding Tree* is killed, the women exclaim, 'Thank Christ the prick is dead' (5), a view undoubtedly shared by the audience. The domestic violence in the background in *The Dark Room* is front and centre in Cerini's play. Grace might be one of *The Bleeding Tree*'s two daughters, in an alternative universe where her battered mother fights back, with satisfyingly terminal results. The violence that is so shocking in *SHIT*, and asks for some explanation, is a relief in *The Bleeding Tree*, and requires none. The thrust of the two plays are thus toward different ends. In *SHIT* we undergo a journey where the unjustified is justified, in *The Bleeding Tree* one where the justified come to terms with what they have done—and see that it is justified.

One way of looking at both plays is to see them as 'chorus dramas' reminiscent of Patrick White's *A Cheery Soul* or *Black Medea*. The functions of a chorus, it will be recalled, are to narrate backstory, provide ongoing commentary and deliver warnings from the gods. The collective presence of a chorus is what matters most, and in this respect their personality is entirely a 'representative' one. In ancient Greek drama, they are the voice of the city, in *A Cheery Soul* of aging and forgotten women, in *Black Medea*, of Australia's destructive colonial past.

Bobby, Billy and Sam are representative of a certain kind of abused young woman, raised in a string of unspeakable foster homes, spoken down to, treated worse, attacked verbally, physically and sexually. They are made to feel at every moment of their lives that they are 'shit', until they internalise this as an unshakable self-belief and behave accordingly. Although they are three characters they might be one. Their experiences impose upon them a uniformity of suffering and distress. Despite what Cornelius says about 'no indication of a better or in fact any inner life' the action shows their feelings cannot be extinguished. As in a Greek tragedy, no violence is shown directly. The scenes in *SHIT* are filled with talk. But in the stories the women share about their broken families, cruel carers and dashed hopes, the lives they would like to lead, and the people they would like to be, stand out in negative relief. That they never admit to them explicitly, does not mean they are not there every moment of the play:

> *A room.*
> SAM: Do you think anything could save us?
> *Pause.*
> BILLY: No.
> BOBBY: Like God, do you mean?

Pause.

BILLY: No.

BOBBY: Like someone puts their hand in and pulls you out before you drown?

BILLY: Like someone says, you're right, you're right, I got you.

BOBBY: Like someone shoots a crocodile just before it gets you.

BILLY: Like a doctor cuts out the rot before it infects you.

BOBBY: Like when you jump someone's going to catch you.

BILLY: Like someone puts their mouth on yours and blows air in you.

BOBBY: Like someone says, keep away from her or I'll kill you.

BILLY: Like when a boulder comes pounding down and Superman scoops you up in his arms.

BOBBY: Like someone grabs you just before…

SAM: Alright, alright.

BILLY: Sam, nothing's going to save us.

BOBBY: Too late to save us.

BILLY: Way too fucking late.

BOBBY: We're past saving.

BILLY: Way past saving.

SAM: Maybe someone could've saved us when we were little.

BILLY: Doubt it…

BOBBY: From the moment I came out nothing could save me…

SAM: Nothing at all?

Pause.

BILLY: A bedroom with a lock on the door.

They laugh. (120)

The allusion to God and a sense of biblical decree—of a world divided into the damned and the saved, the sheep and the goats—is not accidental. It is even more evident in *The Bleeding Tree*. It puts both plays in the harsh school of judgement occupied by *Conversations with the Dead*, with its note of stern, retributive justice. Unjust societies provoke acts of resistance to injustice. Some of these, in *Ned Kelly* fashion, will be violent. What is unleashed is not good in an absolute sense, but is preferable to the abjection that preceded it. In her introduction to the script, Diana Simmonds writes of *The Bleeding Tree*:

[In Australia] one in three women have experienced violence perpetrated by a person known to them. One in five women over the age of 18 have been stalked. Over 12 months, on average, one woman is killed every week by a current or former partner. Domestic and family violence is the principal cause of homelessness for women and children… These bland numbers and the neutrality of the language… make relatively benign a national disgrace… [T]he violent deaths of Australian women [in] 2016 was 71. Already, by end of January 2017, five more have been murdered. We can expect a quarter of our children to be exposed to domestic violence. And overwhelmingly there is one basic cause… [as] Cerini [says]: 'White men run the world so if the world is crap, well it's white men we have to look at'. (ix)

It is a depressing testament to what Cerini assumes his audience already knows that he does not need to mention the theme of domestic violence directly in the play. It is simply 'there', less the elephant in the room than the room itself. After killing the husband, the three women are interrupted by a stream of visitors to their poverty-stricken farmhouse. The first is a neighbour Mr Jones. 'Jones, the nice one./Not his son?/His old man, nice one./If he comes in, he comes in' (8). He does come in, and sees the body of the murdered man lying under a blanket. 'Shit, he see it, the old man's peg?' (11). But rather than report the murder, Mr Jones gives coded instructions on how to dispose of the body by stringing it up on a tree used to hang animal carcases, where weather, rodents and insect life will strip it to the bone in three days (another biblical allusion). And so it continues. Each visitor offers practical help and advice about the corpse, until the women can boil up the remains and tip them onto the rose garden that, when he was alive, the husband destroyed.

– You grow a new garden Ma?
– I grow one for you.
– What colours you after?
– Any'll do.

– Any?
– Yeah, any but his.
– The colour of his gaping hole where all hell pokes through.
– Just three days it takes, to be rid of his spell.
– Patience and good luck, some the universe sends.
– The dead hole where his place was, makes its own amends.
(43–4)

One could argue that *SHIT* and *The Bleeding Tree* are 'anti-morality tales'. But there is no 'anti' about them really, despite the fact they involve criminal acts. All six women are victims who take matters into their hands and achieve a degree of agency. *SHIT* has the darker ending, and its message is grimmer—that violence and abuse leads only to violence and abuse, and there is little that is positive in this. Billy, Bobby and Sam, after all, attack other women, not the people who made their lives hell. The finale of *The Bleeding Tree* is more hopeful. It has a witty, urban legend feel to it, where people get back what they have given out, and if they have given out nothing but pain and hurt then they end up chicken feed like the husband (literally, though the postie's dog also gets a good meal).

There are no entrances and exits in *SHIT* or *The Bleeding Tree*, no intervals, or shifts of scene beyond the most functional. Time, a slithery beast in *Rain* and *The Dark Room*, slows down, almost stops. The sense is of moments expanding to an age, rather than years collapsing to a moment. Both plays fulfil the Aristotelian unities of time, place and action. They focus on a single chain of related events, with an emphasis on motivations and consequences. For ancient Greeks, the purpose of drama was not to tell audiences a new story, to surprise us with novelty or keep us guessing what might happen next. It was to investigate territory we already have opinions about. Playwrights can then challenge these by presenting alternative views, revealing aspects not previously considered, or casting their meaning in a different light. Both *SHIT* and *The Bleeding Tree* perform this ancient role of drama. They do not tell us something we do not know. They show us something we know all too well, but have been too reluctant, afraid or complicit to openly admit.

At this point, it is worth noting how much being a member of the working class diminishes as a desirable status in our national drama in the 1990s, and especially after 2000. This does not mean that working-class characters cease to appear in Australian plays. But their social background has more negative connotations to it. The characters in SHIT and The Bleeding Tree are the opposite of the confident, aspirational manual workers in the Doll and The Shifting Heart, or the politically articulate ones in Blind Giant. The working class is now more like an underclass, defined by what it has lost or had taken away. As such, it is a set of circumstances to escape from, à la Barbara in Diving for Pearls, rather than an identity to acknowledge, à la Hughie Cook in The One Day of the Year. Certainly, the idea of the working class as the carrier of an emancipative vision for Australian society as a whole is nowhere to be found.

To be clear, Cornelius and Cerini write compelling working-class characters; but not even they can render positive a representative identity that has been so heavily eroded. In celebrating—as we should celebrate—the fact that race, gender and sexuality expand as topics for dramatic investigation post millennium, we should also ask where the concept of class has gone. The last four plays in this chapter grapple with this question, and its implications for a multicultural nation seeking to escape the grip of 'white men [who] run the world'. In 1963, HG Kippax complained that Australian playwrights were obsessed with 'the slums… the criminal half-world… the world of the race track… [and] seedy Bohemianism' which were 'not typical of a modern, middle-class nation'. After 2000 the boot is on the other foot. Where are the working-class characters in Australian drama today and, most vitally, what do they represent when they step on stage?

Intersectionality—and beyond

In 1989 the American legal and social theorist Kimberlé Crenshaw coined the term 'intersectionality'. It is a complicated and contentious set of ideas about how 'the personal' and 'the political' influence each other in a world where ideological grand narratives no longer supply off-the-peg explanations for every social conflict. YW Boston, an organisation dedicated to 'eliminating racism, empowering women, and promoting peace, justice, freedom, and dignity for all' explains that

> intersectional theory asserts that people are often disadvantaged by multiple sources of oppression: their race, class, gender identity, sexual orientation, religion, and other identity markers. Intersectionality recognizes that identity markers (e.g. 'woman' and 'black') do not exist independently of each other, and that each informs the others, often creating a complex convergence of oppression.

This is not the place to discuss intersectionality in detail. But it provides an intellectual backdrop for Australian drama in the twenty-first century in much the same way that Marxism and liberalism provided one for Australian drama in the twentieth. Post-millennial plays embody intersectional ideas in the dilemmas they put on stage, observing the results in human terms. Drama has always done this. As a mode of inquiry, it is both attuned to the wider political realm and supremely disruptive of it. Its symbolic offerings provide what ancient Greeks called *eikos muthos* ('probable myths'), situations and stories designed to capture the contingencies, ironies and slip-ups of life that *logos* (logical thinking) leaves out. Drama thus supplies the disciplined creative dimension that a well-functioning society needs, enabling it to grasp the full consequences of its actions. 'Silence is first broken by art', writes Radhika Coomaraswamy, a former UN Under Secretary General, in her introduction to *Counting and Cracking*. 'It captures the sentiments and the nuances. It gives first expression to the rainbow of emotions. Through the work of [its] artists a country expresses its pain and suffering… but also lightness and hope' (xviii).

The next four plays demonstrate Australian drama's capacity to change while sustaining meaningful continuity. *Black is the New White* and *Triple X* are romantic comedies in the Max Afford–cum–David Williamson mould. But Nakkiah Lui is a Gamilaroi/Torres Strait Islander woman, and the central family in *Black is the New White* is Aboriginal. Glace Chase is a transwoman playwright and *Triple X* a love story between a New York investment banker and a transgender performance artiste. *Counting and Cracking* is a generational family saga reminiscent of *No Sugar* and *Rain*. But the family is Tamil and more than half its scenes occur in Sri Lanka. *Hungry Ghosts*, with its spare text, absence of named characters and narrative equivocality, belongs to the cool tradition of New Wave playwriting. But its author is 'Queer–Chinese–Malaysian Australian' (vii) and its subject matter blends postcolonial critique with Buddhist reflections on dying and death.

Thematically, these plays overlap like a row of roof tiles. The need for compromise and agreement occurs in *Black is the New White* and *Counting and Cracking*; a sense of diasporic yearning in *Counting and Cracking* and *Hungry Ghosts*; the overriding call of love in *Triple X* and *Black is the New White*; the corrupting power of wealth in *Hungry Ghosts*, *Black is the New White* and *Triple X*. Each occupies a slot excavated by past Australian plays, while taking that slot in a new direction. They are thus both unique creative works, and directly connected to the larger body that is our national drama.

A politician father with an independent-minded daughter. A wealthy family with partisan views. A fiancé from the opposite camp. A comedic sweetness that does not preclude sharp social observations. Tensions resolved by mutual understanding and marriage. Politics satirised. Family life celebrated. Love affirmed. That this description applies equally to *The Time is Not Yet Ripe* and *Black is the New White*, attests to something monumental: a rediscovery of a tone of innocence in the Australian repertoire not heard so clearly since before World War I. It is easy to imagine that plays of political significance are invariably polemical, bursting with outrage and heartfelt denunciations of wrongdoing. But comedy has a long reach. It also has a facility denied even to the greatest tragic dramas: a ready capacity for humour and hope.

So when an Indigenous Australian playwright chooses this compelling mood for a play about black–white relations in Australia in 2020, it has all the force of a political intervention. In her introduction to the play, Nakkiah Lui writes:

> I looked at the census and discovered a surprising statistic: 74 per cent of Aboriginal people who get married marry non-Aboriginal people. We are the community most likely to marry a race outside of our own. I found this really interesting… primarily because I was one of them… That led me to investigate how my own family had shifted over the last two generations, and how this had affected their definition of class. I was really interested in how we identify ourselves in terms of racial and cultural backgrounds, and how that intersects with class. What does it mean to be successful?… I… wanted to present a family of Aboriginal people that hasn't been seen before, not just on stage, I would say, but within the canon of Australian artistic works… An Aboriginal family who have money, who are not necessarily oppressed, but are culturally quite strong. (x–xi)

As with *Rain*—and again in *Counting and Cracking*—two families dominate *Black is the New White*: in this case, the Gibsons and the Smiths. Ray Gibson, '[a] handsome, charismatic Aboriginal politician with a great head of hair' (87) is in his late 50s, once touted as a possible leader of the federal Labor Party. Dennison Smith, 'the dour, conservative social services minister for the Liberal Party' (87) was his detested Coalition rival. Although both men have now left parliament, they spend their days rubbishing each other on Twitter. Charlotte is Ray's 20-something daughter, legally trained and destined for a life in the political spotlight, if she wants it (RAY: You are an Aboriginal person with a platform… Use it! 40). But does she want it? (CHARLOTTE: Why me? Because I'm your daughter? 40). Running over Christmas Eve and the following morning, the action involves Charlotte introducing Francis, her new fiancé, to her startled family. For the Gibsons, Francis is problematic in three ways. First, he is white; second, he is an experimental classical music composer (read useless); and third—though this discovery is made only when the play is underway—he is Dennison Smith's son.

The three-word refrain in *Rain* 'there you are' has its equivalent in *Black is the New White*: 'here we go'. Characters say it under their breath when other characters start rolling out their pre-decided opinions. It applies almost every time Ray or Dennison speak, but also, on occasion, to Francis and Charlotte, as well as Rose, Charlotte's sister, a successful fashion designer. Rose has decidedly race-based views and disapproves of Francis because of the colour of his skin. The phrase 'black is the new white' therefore has an ironic edge to it, particularly given the fact that the Gibsons are exceedingly rich. The play is set in '[their] sprawling expensive holiday home… located in the bush on ancestral land' (xv).

The juxtaposition is intentional. Ray's political career was of the 1990s 'Third Way' variety, when Labor was embracing neoliberalism. 'I'd rather have nothing than have everything if it costs other people', Charlotte tells her father. 'You built [your career] on the back of a community and have managed to create a fortune off… The community hates you. They hate you' (128). In true Christmas spirit, everyone fights with everyone else. But family is family, and people must find a way to get along in spite of it all. So when Ray's intelligent and empathetic wife, Joan says the words, 'welcome to the family, Francis' (102) halfway through the play, the significance of the utterance is masked by the persiflage around it. By accepting Francis as Charlotte's husband, the Gibsons and the Smiths *have* to now accept each other, and this emerges as the major theme of the play.

Like David Williamson before her, Lui is an equal opportunity satirist. No character in *Black is the New White* escapes unmocked or without enduring suitably humiliating actions (my favourite is the disco dance-off between Ray and Dennison where 'each [dance move] is more outdated and preposterous than the other [and] they both start to sweat and turn red' 109). As with *The Time is Not Yet Ripe*, political rhetoric is lampooned without being dismissed altogether. *Black is the New White* is neither an anti-political nor an apolitical play. But it is focused on the *limits* of politics and when it should give way to less categorical ways of thinking.

Another way of saying this, in keeping with the analysis I am presenting in this book, is that a new balance is sought between the representative side of the characters and their individual side, such that they can escape the broad social identities imposed upon them. For example, Sonny, Rose's husband, is a successful banker and ex-football star: 'many say the most famous Aboriginal football player to date' (58). He is going to appear on the TV program *Celebrity: Where Do You Come From?* which involves tracing his family history. But the last scene reveals that he is Tongan, not Aboriginal. This not only changes Sonny's self-identity, but Rose's too, intent on having 'big Black babies' who 'know about their culture and their history because it's what both their parents are' (151).

Politics are important but, as it turns out, not all-important. At some point even the most committed must find a way to compromise if a viable future is to be envisaged. How? In scene 7, Charlotte and Francis quarrel. They plan to live in New York together, but Dennison cuts Francis off from the small allowance on which he subsists. So Francis scotches the move abroad, and insists Charlotte take up a lucrative TV job she doesn't want (FRANCIS: It's a TV job, Charlotte. Not a limb! CHARLOTTE: Is this what you really want: to stay in Australia? To fight to not have a job? 143).

Suddenly, the wedding is off. It is left to the two semi-useless dads to put things to rights. In the middle of this stock comedic situation—one that might be found in Menander or Plautus—Lui installs an exchange of compelling relevance to a contemporary Australian audience:

> DENNISON: Maybe we can make things better, get the kids back together. What about some kind of agreement… between us… over them.
> RAY: Like a… like a treaty?
> DENNISON: Like a treaty! How about we make a treaty!
> RAY: … That's not a half bad idea.
> DENNISON: Bet you never thought you'd hear that word coming out of my mouth. Treaty. Treaty. Treaty.
> RAY: I sure didn't.
> DENNISON: Where do we start?
> RAY: So: 'We, Ray Gibson and Dennison Smith, the fathers of the respective parties, hereby give our permission… blah… blah'.
> DENNISON: This remind you of something?
> RAY: Of the good old days?
> DENNISON: It does, doesn't it? Making laws, disagreeing. Agreeing.

> RAY: Making change.
> DENNISON: Feels good.
> RAY: I'll go get my iPad and we can write it up. (171–2)

It is a matchless piece of playwriting craft. It should be stressed that exchanges such as this—and there are a number of them in *Black is the New White*—are *more* rather than *less* politically resonant because they are delivered with a light touch. Choice of comic tone allows Lui not only to engage with intersectionality's complex ideas about race, gender and class in a deft and funny way, but to insist on the overriding need for love and shared understanding. *Black is the New White* is both a statement of this need and a vehicle for actioning it. No Aboriginal politician like Ray Gibson existed in Australia's federal parliament during the 1990s; but they might in future, if they can be *imagined* to exist. *Black is the New White* imagines it. Ray is thus part of a predictive dramatic vision of hope. Joan offers this Christmas toast for the two families:

> As I look around this table I see the past and I see the future. I see four young people who are changing the world around them in their own unique way… with passion and heart… [T]here is a multitude of histories but with that comes the potential for a clean slate. Conflict isn't always a bad thing; we all have beliefs and reasons for why we believe them. With conflict there is hope for change and growth; in our beliefs and in ourselves… But, remember, it's so much easier to judge those who are closest to us because we know their love is unconditional. We have love at this table in all different ways and forms. And that is invaluable. (116)

Counting and Cracking and *Hungry Ghosts*, like *SHIT* and *The Bleeding Tree*, are complementary plays. Both involve diasporic transgenerational inheritances—how other countries, cultures and histories are remembered (or not) by people who count themselves Australian, at least in part. A repeated line in *Hungry Ghosts* is 'How long is a piece of string if you tie one end to your home country and the other to your heart?' (9). Jean Tong's country of origin is Malaysia, S. Shakthidharan's Sri Lanka. Their connection to their familial lands is a source of both anguish and wonder. That mix of feelings is not new. It exists for many Greek, Italian, Irish and indeed British migrant characters in Australian drama. But the twentieth century has swept on, and family trees are more extended. Memories are now inherited, epigenetically passed on to second, third and fourth generations.

Marianne Hirsch uses the word 'postmemory' to describe situations where collective trauma is so significant it recurs across age groups in 'idioms of remembrance' (one of which, I would argue, is drama). She explains:

> We certainly are still in the era of 'posts', which continue to proliferate: 'post-secular', 'post-human', 'postcolony', 'post-white'. Postmemory shares the layering of these other 'posts' and their belatedness, aligning itself with the practice of citation and mediation that characterize them… Like them, it reflects an uneasy oscillation between continuity and rupture. And yet postmemory is not a movement, method, or idea; I see it, rather, as a structure of inter- and trans-generational transmission of traumatic knowledge and experience. It is a consequence of traumatic recall but (unlike posttraumatic stress disorder) at a generational remove.

As with intersectionality, there is no room to explore this important idea further. But naming it gives a sense of how *Counting and Cracking* and *Hungry Ghosts* differ from earlier migrant plays. Next to the issue of remembering and the status of memory is its flipside: what should be forgotten or challenged by a different version of the past. Memories enrich our lives. But they hold us back if we cling to them too tightly, and do not see the present moment as an opportunity for positive change. Memory is both alluring and paralysing, and *Counting and Cracking* and *Hungry Ghosts* show great courage in tackling this theme. Like *Black is the New White*, it makes them political, regardless of any specific message that can be read into them. They say to their audience, 'these things can be spoken of now'. They are public

Radha regards Rahda. Vaishnavi Suryaprakash as young Rhada, is observed by Nadie Kammallaweera as her older self in the Belvoir/ Co-Curious production of Counting and Cracking. *Photo: Brett Boardman.*

avowals of knowledge. 'Universality is the bottom line of *Counting and Cracking*', writes Coomaraswamy. 'It is a cast of mostly heroes clutching important values. They are thrown about in different directions, constantly being tested. Yet they retain their common humanity' (xix).

Counting and Cracking has a generational span identical to *Rain*'s: from great-grandfather, Apah, to great-grandson, Siddhartha, though the key figure is Radha, Apah's granddaughter and Siddhartha's mother (as in *Rain*, she has both 'old' and 'young' versions of herself, who sometimes appear together). *Hungry Ghosts* has a form similar to *The Bleeding Tree*, with three non-designated actors speaking directly to the audience in only nominally assigned lines of dialogue (though Tong specifies 'casting *must* be diverse' xii, original emphasis). Also like *The Bleeding Tree*, *Hungry Ghosts* has a hyper-compressed, 'expanded moment' feel, with lines echoing and adjusting to each other, in an effect akin to the sharpening of a pencil. By contrast, extended cause-and-effect chronology is central to *Counting and Cracking*, the action running from 1956 to 2004, during which time Sri Lanka is polarised into opposing religions and races, in a tit-for-tat cycle of provocations and reprisals, until civil war is eventually unleashed. Corruption rather than conflict is the theme of *Hungry Ghosts*. It measures the size of the bribes rather than the sum of the body count. But the question of where the characters truly belong is the same.

In the last act of *Counting and Cracking*, Siddhartha, an arts and media student conceived in Sri Lanka but born in Australia, and unable to prise the details of his family history from his tight-lipped migrant mother, says to his girlfriend, a Yolngu Matha Indigenous Australian,

> SIDDHARTHA: Something happened to my Amma [mother] in Sri Lanka in 1983 and so now I'm here. But if whatever that was in 1983 had gone a little bit differently I could be living in a house in Colombo. Or in a refugee camp in India. But I'm not. I'm in Sydney… In Amma's apartment in Pendle Hill there's a balcony where Ammamma used to sit and teach me thevarams. Like these Tamil lullabies. So I can't speak in Tamil but I can sing in Tamil. It's like an almost-connection. And I'm pretty sure that the chair Amma sits in isn't from Australia… and when I sit in it I feel almost connected to… something, and every time I go there the place smells like mustard seeds and curry leaves, and here this place smells like salty air and beer and I love it, I love it Lil', but it's not me…. And if I stay here I think I'm going to become something else… I need to return to those almost connections before they're gone, and trace them back to where they came from,

and actually I'm not sure of any of this at all, I could be completely wrong… I think I need to go… home.
LILY: Which means?
SIDDHARTHA: Pendle Hill. (96)

Hungry Ghosts is composed of three discontinuous, reported-action narratives, wound tightly round each other, like the yarns of a rope. The first involves the 2014 aviation disaster, Malaysia Airlines flight 370, in which 12 crew and 227 passengers (including six Australians) vanished, and neither aircraft nor bodies were ever recovered. We are back in the realm of *biaiothanatoi*, although Chinese Buddhism's ghosts are ravenous rather than restless, as in life they have been 'false, deceitful, greedy people, and their karma is an insatiable hunger' (viii).

The second involves the IMDB scandal, a high-level corruption saga, where public funds were siphoned off by the Malaysian prime minister, Najib Razak, and his son-in-law Riza Aziz. In a weird case of life imitating art imitating life, Aziz's film company, Red Granite Pictures, was the main funder of *The Wolf of Wall Street*, the 2013 movie about Jordan Belfort, the American 'pump and dump' stockbroker and convicted felon.

The third narrative is more personal, and reflects Tong's attempts to balance the competing claims of her Malaysian heritage and her Australian lifestyle, while coming to terms with the meaning of sudden death, and the corruption of Malaysian politics. But we do damage to the ethereal power of her writing if we describe the play too literally. Tong uses words like a surgeon probing a wound. The theme of identity as it emerges from this forensic process remains unresolved. If anything, doubts are deepened and contradictions intensified. Yet loss of certainty kindles acceptance of complexity. Petra Kalive, the director of *Hungry Ghosts*' premiere, writes in her introduction to the published play, that the text is:

> a collection of scenes, events and monologues using multiple languages, modes and tones, which all refract and relate to its central idea of what it is to be unexplained, forgotten, to exist in the liminal—to be 'ghosts'. The lack of a traditional narrative allows the audience to make

their own meaning from the disconnected scenes and moments. The specificity of the material does not push its audience away—quite remarkably it grounds the work and makes it relatable on so many levels (ix).

On the face of it, this is a paradox. How can narrative openness and specific detail not pull in opposite directions? But think of finding a portrait photograph in the street. The fact that it is undoubtedly *someone* and at the same time could be *anyone* creates an intense yet open-ended connection. It shows a small fragment of a story. But others can be imagined that spiral off in all directions. Specific detail clothes infinite possible worlds. Below is a sample of Tong's dialogue towards the end of the play. The fractured narrative has swung back to the MH370 flight. Line assignments are indicated by numbers. The effect is similar to the dialogue in *The Bleeding Tree*, but with threshold images and syncopated rhythms replaced by modulated repetitions and soft cadences:

> 1: After is
> 2: TWITTER: #MH370 thoughts & prayers please come home I love you be safe please
> 1: After is
> 2: FACEBOOK: thoughts and prayers #MH370
> 3: After is
> 1: YOUTUBE: devastated for the families affected by MH370, please add your thoughts and prayers to the comments
> 2: I wish I'd said it before they
> 1: After is
> 2: After is what didn't happen
> 3: Couldn't happen
> 1: Won't ever happen
> 2: After is everything I didn't get to say
> 3: After is everything you did say and wish you hadn't
> 1: After is not be able to think at all
> 3: After is dry eyes while everyone else manages to sob their numbness away
> 2: After is the relief you can't talk about, because no-one knew about the. and if you're the only one who remembers the. did it ever happen?

3: After is after
1: After is always *over*
2: But the problem with that is that we find the concept of finality
1: Really
3: Really
1: Really
3: Hard to grasp
2: So we make it up
1: Pause the moment in amber
3: Suspend it forever
2: Let it be something that will still be there After (35–6)

The plot of *Counting and Cracking* is large-scale, its resonance greater still. Apah, Siddhartha's great-grandfather, is an honoured politician, a brilliant mathematician, a committed democrat, and a believer in an inclusive national identity for all Sri Lankans, regardless of race, creed, caste or region. He is also a Tamil—'the *only* Tamil in the cabinet' (54). Just as Ray Gibson has Dennison Smith for a hated-but-not-really opposite number, so Apah has Vinsanda, a Sinhalese member of parliament as his 'PF/PE—personal friend, political enemy' (128).

The action of the play is anchored in 2004, but steps back in history to revisit three moments in Sri Lanka's past: 1956, when Apah's influence is at its height, with the country newly independent, the population not yet divided, and English (not Sinhala or Tamil) the national language; 1977, when Apah is out of power, and the country is suffering sectarian tensions, the Tamil Tigers are recruiting, and Sinhala is now the national language; and finally, 1983, on the day of the Black July massacres that convinced many Tamils that only a separate state could ensure their survival. Shakthidharan follows Sri Lanka at a time when an ugly convergence between race-based thinking and populist nationalism reduced the country to its component ethnicities; or, as Apah pithily expresses it, 'Two languages, one country. One language, two countries' (54).

Counting and Cracking is a drama about politics. Like *Black is the New White*, however, it has its eye firmly on its limits. In the play, there are four kinds of political talk. First, there is the high politics of

Apah, Vinsanda, and the other characters involved in the fate of the nation, before and during the civil war. The talk here is about what can be expected of democratic systems of government, and prompts Apah's comment that, 'Democracy means the *counting* of heads, within certain limits, and the *cracking* of heads beyond those limits' (112, original emphasis). The second kind is the diasporic identity talk of Siddhartha, Lily and Ismet, a Turkish–Australian tradie. 'Do you think you can have *two* homes?' Siddhartha asks Lily, before adjusting his thought in a *Hungry Ghosts* way: 'Okay maybe it's not two homes. Maybe it's still one, but just… a bigger one. It expands, you know?' (97). A third type of talk exists between the women characters, Aacha, Siddhartha's great-grandmother, Radha, his mother, and Nihinsa, the family's devoted Sinhalese housekeeper. The politics here focus on the primacy of family, friendship and the bonds of love.

In Act 2, scene 3, a wedding is held in Apah's Colombo home. It is a big, colourful event and involves politicians from all political parties. Apah, however, has been arrested for filibustering in the parliament at the orders of Vinsanda. When he is carried into the house handcuffed in the custody of the police, Radha has had enough. She chains herself to Apah's chair, and in words reminiscent of Joan admonishing Ray in the face of Charlotte's engagement to Francis, forces the two men to admit different priorities:

> APAH: Radha, darling, it's not a protest until you know your demands.
> YOUNG RADHA: Okay. [*Beat*] Weddings are more important than politics. Vinsanda Mama, say it.
> VINSANDA: Radha…
> YOUNG RADHA: Weddings are more important than politics!
> VINSANDA: You know that isn't true—
> YOUNG RADHA: It is true! We must live life first!
> VINSANDA: There is not life to live without politics.
> AACHA: Just shut and say it, man!
>
> *Beat.*
>
> VINSANDA: Weddings are more important than politics.
> YOUNG RADHA: Second. [*Thinks, then:*] Women run their families better than you run the country.
> VINSANDA: This is very silly.

YOUNG RADHA: Women run their families better than you run the country.
VINSANDA: Oh my God.
YOUNG RADHA: Say it. Apah. Say it.
APAH: Women run their families better than we run the country.
YOUNG RADHA: Visanda Mama
VINSANDA: Women run their families better than we run the country.
YOUNG RADHA: And third—I can marry who I choose.
APAH: I trust you to pick the right person, Radha.
YOUNG RADHA: Aacha?

Beat.

AACHA: Who are you in love with? (85)

The generosity of spirit of Shakthidharan's wedding is the same as Lui's Christmas. Characters are exposed in all their flaws but positive regard is mandated. It is this that *Black is the New White* posits as an achievable goal for modern Australia, and the loss of which *Counting and Cracking* charts in Sri Lanka.

The power of drama as a mode of inquiry is that it can show the actions, reactions, feelings and thoughts people have when trying to understand each other and find common ground. Or failing to. No other art form does this with the same combination of physical embodiment, intellectual clarity and emotional impact. Drama's capacity to vary its storylines and timelines, to individualise characters or blend them into a choral presence, to use languages of all kinds or its magnificent rival—silence—gives it the ability to move across the border of the 'real' and the 'true'. Documentary history and the creative imagination are not opposed. Drama treats them as complementary resources.

However, there is a fourth kind of political talk in Shakthidharan's play, less audible than the rest. Its equivalent can also be found in *Black is the New White*, *Hungry Ghosts* and *Triple X*. Its theme is class or, in the Tamil–Hindu/Theravada–Buddhist context, caste. In *Counting and Cracking*, it is symbolised by Radha's taking a poor Tamil engineer, Thirru, as her husband, rather than the well-born Hasa, Vinsanda's son. For all their open-mindedness, Radha's marriage to someone from a different ethnic group is easier for her grandparents to accept than marriage to a man of lower social status. During Black July, Thirru is arrested and imprisoned for 21 years. Pregnant with Siddhartha, Radha flees to Australia, believing Thirru dead (or needing to believe it), with a refugee visa her family's connections have secured. Over the course of the play, we see Thirru, unexpectedly released from gaol, make his way by boat to Australia as an asylum seeker. It is a slow, dangerous and frightening journey that only the desperate would attempt. *Counting and Cracking* ends with Radha, Siddhartha, Lily and Thirru meeting at Villawood train station. The resonances of this storyline are ones of poverty and social exclusion.

While the families in *Black is the New White*, *Hungry Ghosts*, *Counting and Cracking* and *Triple X* are diverse in their racial, gender and sexual traits, they are also, without exception, wealthy. They are the economic winners from the changes of the late twentieth century, and there is to my eye a strange reversal here. Australian plays in the decades after Federation have no problem tackling issues of class and class conflict directly, but treat issues of race, gender and sexuality in an oblique manner. Australian drama after 2005 does the opposite. Issues of race, gender and sexuality are dealt with more openly, but class is only indirectly referenced. It is most certainly *present* in these four plays, and impacts the narratives at important moments. But it is not separated out for dedicated dramatic investigation. When class issues surface in the dialogue, the characters seem uncertain in their views, as if the problem of inequality lay right at the edge of their social awareness. Just as racial, gender and sexual differences shadow mainstream Australian politics as the 'Other', so class shadows racial, gender and sexual differences. In post-millennial drama, class is the Other's Other.

Play no. 50

Of all the gaps in the coverage of Australian drama in this book, a lack of consideration of plays dealing with LGBTQI+ themes is one of the most egregious. The first openly gay character on Australian TV was *Number 96*'s Don Finlayson, who appeared in 1972. Mart

Crowley's ground-breaking play about gay life in New York, *Boys in the Band*, was produced by Harry M Miller in Sydney in 1968. Peter Kenna's *Mates*, which opened at the Nimrod Theatre in 1976, contains, I believe, the first depiction of a transvestite character in a realist Australian play.

But this ignores the hundreds of cabaret and vaudeville shows, especially at the Tivoli Theatre ('the Tiv'), that were always more diverse in their stage *personae*. The crossover with scripted Australian drama lies in the one-person plays of the extraordinary Reg Livermore, like *Betty Blokk Buster Follies* in 1975, *The Rocky Horror Show*, which Jim Sharman directed (and helped conceive) in 1974, and the mega-successful bisexual musical *Hair*, which opened in Australia in 1969, again directed by Sharman. Given that the first state to decriminalise homosexuality—South Australia—only did so in 1975, and the last, Tasmania, not until 1997, this puts theatre and drama at the forefront of challenges to heteronormativity in the 1960s and 1970s. But, of course, every conceivable type of interpersonal relationship had been indirectly portrayed in stage plays long before then.

Theatre, with its traditions of pantomime and burlesque, has always offered a safe space for the expression of what Sigmund Freud called 'polymorphous perversity'. In 2021, now that heteronormativity no longer exercises the chokehold it once did, it is possible to see the portrayal of LGBTQI+ characters as part of a broader opening up of discussion about gender and sexuality (two different concepts I will not attempt to distinguish).

Triple X is a play that sits within this tradition yet also takes it in a unique direction. It draws on the realist strain in drama and its setting, a 'luxury Fi-Di lofted two-bedroom apartment in Manhattan' (ii), strikingly parallels that of the *The Boys in the Band* ('a smartly appointed duplex apartment in the East Fifties' 5). In its whip-smart comic dialogue and character observations, there are echoes of Max Afford and Sumner Locke Elliott. Locke Elliott was gay, though did not declare his sexuality until 1990. He moved to New York in 1949 and became a leading script writer there. Glace Chase moved to New York in 2011. In 2021, she was described by the *Sydney Morning Herald* as 'a talent on the rise'.

I discuss no 'Covid play', and with good reason: the meaning of what some are calling 'the great pause' as yet remains unclear, even to playwrights. *Triple X*, however, is certainly a Covid-affected play. Due to premiere in Brisbane in 2020, it had two previews before closing in the first wave of nationwide lockdowns in March. It eventually had an opening night in April 2021, but the final part of its run was cancelled due to another lockdown in south-east Queensland. The play is thus one of the last to be written before theatre audience's assumptions radically changed. To illustrate what I mean: in the third scene of the play, the lead character, Scotty, is given a wedding present, two tickets for the World Cup soccer finals in Bulgaria (39). For spectators at the premiere who had been unable to travel abroad for a year, Scotty's line 'How the hell am I going to go to Bulgaria?' (40) had a particular impact. Even when international travel resumes, it will be in a society conscious that disease has shut it down once and can easily do so again. Yet the question lying at the heart of Chase's play—what kind of (moral and sexual) world do we want to live in?—has if anything amplified.

Scotty is a 30-something investment banker (an 'i-banker at Goldman' 58), living in a $3.5 million downtown New York apartment with great views, earning an annual bonus higher than the average wage. Hyper-intelligent and self-confident in the aggressive, alpha-male mould, he is one of Cerini's 'white men [who] run the world'. The play opens with banter between Scotty and his best friend, Jase, an African American, about barely legal sex (SCOTTY: Dude… you roofied her. JASE: Technically. But she asked for it 1).

It is the afternoon before Scotty's wedding, a high society event that will be the ultimate mark of his success. For this occasion his brittle mother, Deborah, with issues both medical and psychological, and his sister, Claire, a 'woke' lesbian who stands for everything her brother dismisses and derides, have flown into town. The action has a screwball feel. Wedding plans are going awry. Claire, who has travelled from Nepal, has the runs and is constantly dashing to the toilet. Deborah is the stereotypical, embarrassing mum, doting on her children and saying things that make them cringe.

Yet even at this early stage, the atmosphere is strained, as if everyone were playing a part in a pageant that might at any moment fall apart.

On the phone to the newspaper editor who has decided not to include the wedding in his sought-after section, Scotty turns nasty. 'Dude? What the fuck? What the fucking fuck? You need to focus on inclusivity? Diversity? Fuck diversity. How is a driver and a secretary—from the projects—an 'accomplished and interesting couple'?!... We're Wall St! We get into the Wedding Section!... Fucking run it next week or I'm gonna rain shit down on you so hard you'll be working for the Irish fucking Echo!' (13). The baked-in snobbery of the opening scene is disguised by the comic brio of the dialogue and situation. It is not far beneath the surface, though, lending the action a performative quality. We are not seeing, we suspect, the 'real' Scotty.

In its structure, *Triple X* steps back in time from a point in the present, like *Counting and Cracking*, but only ten months back. The action then runs forwards again, in scenes of remembered action, until the storylines converge, scenes from the past merging into ones happening in the present. The feeling is akin to watching a horse race where the horse behind gradually catches up with the one leading the field. As in *The Dark Room*, there is no overt indication of time period, and, as the setting remains the same throughout (the New York apartment), there is a similar blurring of remembered and present-day events.

This split approach to time—where one period is treated in an 'expanded moment' way, the other in more extended fashion—allows Chase to exploit her narrative in a highly original way. Details—both comic and serious—are planted in earlier scenes (either remembered or present-day), the pay-offs coming when they reappear in later ones (either remembered or present-day). The plot involves Scotty's affair with Dexie. In the play, Dexie is described variously as 'a stripper' (29), 'a tranny' (33), a 'drag queen' (61), a 't-girl' (78), and by Dexie herself, in typically colourful fashion, as 'a comedic go-go dancer' (JASE: That's a thing? DEXIE: I'm making it a thing 29). Scenes of past action focus on Scotty and Dexie as their romance develops. When halfway through the play, Claire discovers who Scotty has been seeing, she sums up the situation in one word, 'it is—so. So—so… [*mini beat*] SWEEEEET!!!' (97).

And it is. Scotty and Dexie's relationship is free of any base or ulterior motive. Like Charlotte and Francis, or Radha and Thirru, the disparity of their social positions and the certain community disapproval of their liaison, makes it attributable to one cause alone: genuine attraction. In past scenes alternating with ones involving the present-day wedding celebrations, we see their love affair evolve, from its beginning when Dexie carts Scotty home having found him lying dead drunk in the street, to the day before the marriage when there is a shooting at Candyland, the club where Dexie performs. Until the end of the play, it is unclear whether Dexie has been caught up in the shooting incident. Scotty is consumed with worry throughout, therefore, though desperately trying to hide it too.

Despite its deft deployment of rom-com conventions, however, *Triple X* is anchored in a very concrete social milieu. About Dexie, Chase writes, 'She is a real person in a real world, with a specific (and difficult) lived reality. It's the achievement of *Triple X* to communicate that lived experience. It is less a gay play (where good plays can go to die) or an expression of "true love conquers all" than a specific and truthful articulation of the personal mechanics behind trans realities.' And of Scotty, 'He is clearly attracted to trans women. This might be interpreted differently… and general audiences would not be aware of the complexities around trans realities. But it is embedded in a specific trans truth. These kind of relationships happen all the time.'

Triple X is two dramas, intertwined like a double helix. The first is a transgender rom-com, with Scotty and Dexie's love as its focus, a love that escapes every attempt to define it. 'I make a terrible trans,' Dexie confides to Scotty. 'I can't even remember to take my 'mones' (79). Then, more pointedly, 'I'm so sick of talking about it… There's this whole—politics of it all. I hate it. I mean I get it. But banging on and on about it. Some people just want to be angry. I don't want to be angry. I don't wanna talk about it all the time (80)'. Like *Black is the New White*, the action of *Triple X* focuses on the limits of politics, in this case sexual politics. Here the play is at its most subtle. Dexie's frustration is with a trans politics that gets in the way of her humanity. This isolates her from her trans community, but not from her trans identity—a vital distinction. Chase comments, 'It is not that gender politics are inaccurate, just that they don't hold the scope of Dexie's and Scotty's experience. Their relationship transcends these in a shared human connection.'

This fits. Both Dexie and Scotty seem uncertain about what their sexuality 'represents' but more importantly they don't really care. Their love defies all attempts to label it, while their scenes together are frank, funny and free of self-consciousness. This is all the more remarkable because the sexual talk and action in *Triple X* is of the most explicit kind. There is no coyness or innuendo. Everything is laid out in the open. But then none of the characters in the play has a moral problem with Scotty and Dexie's relationship—not even Deborah, when eventually she admits she has known about it for some time. It is the social acceptability of their love that is the problem. Which shades into the second drama contained in *Triple X*, the one about money.

Love and money are a long-established thematic doublet in stage drama. While Chase's play is ultra-contemporary in surface details, it sounds deep historical chords for a theatre audience. What is backgrounded in *Hungry Ghosts* is foregrounded in *Triple X*: the corrupting power of money. A defining feature of Dexie's love for Scotty, for example, a way in which we know immediately it is 'real', is that she will not take his money. In contrast, the family around him depend for their prosperity and well-being on the fact that he has a job that earns him obscene amounts of wealth. As the play continues, a backstory emerges of the grimmest kind, in which a childhood of poverty and domestic violence has led to a sense of overwhelming guilt, and a feeling in Scotty that he should support his mother and sister financially. He hates his job, and confesses to Dexie he has tried to kill himself three times, the last attempt only a few months ago:

> SCOTTY: I went to this cheap motel and I didn't write a note. I took my pants off and put a cock ring on—that way people would think I'd been jerking off and it was an accident. And I hooked myself up to the wardrobe railing. And when I went down—I hung there—like for a bit—and then the railing fucking broke. I guess I don't know my own strength… (83)

And about his impending marriage, he tells her:

> SCOTTY: I'm so—I lie in bed at night and I feel nothing. Absolutely nothing. I like her but I feel nothing and if she

touches me I seize up and I've said I don't like to touch while I sleep because it's—distracting. I don't like anyone touching me. So we sleep on opposite sides of the bed. Sometimes I think I might fall out. That can't be good. Is that right? There should be more—shouldn't there? I don't know. (84)

In plays of narrative revelation, as audiences learn more about the lives of the characters, a key question is 'who knows what, when?' Chase uses the uneven time spans of her double helix drama to maximise the impact of the answers. As *Triple X* is as yet unpublished, it would be a spoiler for its future productions to describe how this happens in detail. It involves a number of props that Alfred Hitchcock called 'Mcguffins', physical objects designed to draw audience attention to what is known, by whom, at any one moment in time. The results are, by turns, jaw-droppingly hilarious and chillingly disturbing. The genius of the writing—and I do not use that phrase lightly—lies in showing the prejudiced complicity of the characters even as they are presented in an empathetic way. Scotty's world is a horribly distorted one of extreme inequality, omnipresent gun violence, vicious gender and racial discrimination, and soul-destroying greed. It is as empty of genuine inner life as the sterile banking job to which he is chained. As the play heads towards its climax, Scotty faces a moral choice similar to that of Mrs Hamilton's in *Here Under Heaven*. Which will he choose? Which should he choose? Which do we, the audience, witnessing his decision-making, want him to choose? So far as I know, it is a romantic reality that has never been expressed on stage by a trans person before.

Like *Rain* and *Black is the New White*, Chase's *Triple X* also has its fateful words, though they are said only once, by Jase to Scotty, in the final scene: 'We're just not there yet' (168). Can there be greater condemnation of a society than that it would destroy true and real love not because of religious conviction or moral repugnance, but simply because 'it makes people self-conscious? And slightly uncomfortable' (167)?

Conclusion

> [Manning] Clark did not... present a vision of Australia that... has come to be known as the black armband view. What he did was recognise the need for a... critical reading of Australian history. [He] saw that Australians were 'ready to face the truth about our past, to acknowledge that the coming of the British was the occasion of three great evils: the violence against the original inhabitants of the country, the Aborigines; the violence against the first European Labor force in Australia, the convicts, and the violence done to the land itself.'
>
> Samantha Young 'Writing History to Understand the World We Live In'

You can learn a lot about a nation from reading its plays. In the modern era, every significant issue, tension and abiding preoccupation ends up on stage sooner or later. Drama is a medium for contemporary society to think itself *as* a society. It is an imaginative resource of ready availability, great flexibility and considerable real-world impact. Why then do Australians, and Australian governments in particular, treat it with scant interest and respect, dismissing its broad-appeal offerings as 'mere entertainment' and its challenging ones as 'elitist'? Every variety of specious argument is used to deflect the historically indisputable fact that drama is a serious mode of inquiry on a par with academic research, media journalism and public policymaking. We should celebrate it as an important pathway to collective self-knowledge. But we do not. Although we are instructed, moved and changed by what is shown in our drama, we close ourselves off to the implication that it plays a central role in shaping how we see the world around us, and how we interact with it.

The aim of this book has been to bring Australian drama into proper consideration of questions concerning the life of the nation. By 'proper consideration' I mean seeing drama as one of the sinews of public debate on the significant issues facing Australians. Drama is not an adjunct to our national life. It is a creator of it. In the words of the sociologist Charles Taylor, it is one of the 'repertory of collective actions' we use to construct our 'social imaginary'. Drama populates our social imaginary not only on a narrative level—the Australian stories that even governments recognise we need to tell—but in the deeper vault of shared symbols, shared emotions, and shared language, both poetic and vernacular. As stage plays travel through time and space, they craft our sense of history, eventually becoming, as social and artistic artefacts, part of the historical record themselves.

This book is about the past, but my concern is with Australian drama now and in the future. The meaning and value of a stage play is not a matter for one person to decide, not even its original creator. It is made manifest through collective expectations and responses. Plays do not have to conform to these, but they are most certainly affected by them.

As an art form, drama is a publicly minded, outward-facing, communal activity. The valorisation of the individual and the pursuit of private advantage that is central to the small 'l' liberal political tradition misrepresents what is involved in drawing on this resource of our shared life. Drama is not a 'market choice' in which 'sovereign consumers' make decisions that 'maximise utility' for a satisfaction that accrues only to them. No description could reflect drama's value less, or worse. Yet so indelible has the individualist perspective become, we accept it as simply the way modern Australia is. While some goals may be approached in this way, others are clearly beyond its scope—equitable immigration flows, urban regeneration, climate change mitigation, sustainable growth and disease prevention, to name just five. Seeing these as anything other than matters for the most inclusive debate and action is ethically questionable and politically disastrous. We *have* to act together in facing these challenges, whichever politicians happen to be in power.

Yet we are as beholden to the pre-eminence of individual choice as medieval cartographers were to the notion that Jerusalem lay at the centre of the earth. Talk of 'the community' is empty rhetoric if there are no vehicles to give it collective expression—if all we really mean by it is 'a community of individuals'. Such an atomised view reduces our social imaginary. It casts the inclusive debates we need to have as a nation—debates inseparable from *being* a nation—as a zero-sum struggle of each against each, special interest group against special interest group. The idea of a common good becomes remote. We struggle to know what we can achieve together, because we do not value what we can imagine together.

The individualist perspective suited both Federation liberal and post-1980s neoliberal Australia. In these periods, the country was able to ignore the question 'What kind of culture should Australia have?' Answering this involves honestly facing issues of history, class, race, faith, age and gender, as well as artform-related ones such as genre and style. Culture offers an important means of pursuing the common good. To abandon 'the culture question' to individual choice is to abandon a means of building a nation that is more than the sum of its competing differences. 'What kind of culture should Australia have?' is a question that can cope with any quantity of disagreement, but no amount of indifference. Australia's slighting of culture also arises from the dominance of a technocratic outlook in its ruling elite, as Michael Pusey identified 30 years ago. This reduces government support for culture to a bleak exercise in measuring 'inputs', 'outputs' and 'benefits'. This was (and is) the mentality of the Productivity Commission. Market thinking and technocratic hubris come together to demote the culture question to a low level of public concern. Drama seen in this instrumental way cannot contribute to issues requiring openness to a wide variety of views and experiences.

In the humanities and social sciences there are also problems. Postmodern and post-structural theories present a glittering array of paradigms, concepts and methods from which scholars can choose. The 'cultural turn' that began in Western scholarship in the 1960s has marched into every branch of academic research since. Once, 'culture' stood for a small number of artistic activities. Now it is an infinitely elastic dimension of social life with countless facets and features. It is a powerful, some would say all-powerful entity. But if this is the case, why the reluctance to admit the important role of cultural forms like drama, whose history and techniques offer such a rich form of *knowledge?* I stress the last word: drama is a way of *knowing* the world. It is not a 'preference' or a 'tool', but a mode of inquiry into our collective life. It critically assays public debate in ways equal to the humanities and social science disciplines.

What do I mean, though, when I say drama is a 'mode of inquiry' into our collective life? Let me briefly list six ways in which it can be said to be so, reflecting the points made about the different plays discussed in this book.

1. **Australia as narrative**. Drama as an inquiry into the events of the nation (documented or imaginative). *Australian plays explore questions of fact, memory, time and legacy through the stories, situations and actions they present on stage.*
2. **Australia as theme**. Drama as an inquiry into the meaning of the events of the nation. *Australian plays explore questions of politics, power, morality and choice by exploring the causes and consequences of the stories, situations and actions they present on stage.*
3. **Australia as character**. Drama as an inquiry into the social types and psychological archetypes of the nation. *Australian plays explore questions of human nature, nurture, perception and feeling through the range of characters they put on stage and the different ways they develop them.*
4. **Australia as word**. Drama as an inquiry into the speech of the nation. *Australian plays explore modes of collective communication by experimenting with different phrasings, rhythms, poetic and vernacular terms, and by the inclusion of different languages.*
5. **Australia as picture**. Drama as an inquiry into the imagery of the nation. *Australian plays explore images that are collectively symbolic by experimenting with different pictorial stagings, action sequences and kinetic moments in their visual representations.*
6. **Australia as lived experience**. Drama as an inquiry into the compelling mood of the nation. *Australian plays*

explore questions about the psyche and soul of the nation— the 'Zeitgeist'—by capturing in a holistic way something 'real' or 'true' about our collective experience in the worlds they put on stage.

As a mode of inquiry, drama offers a unique combination of proposition, criticism, embodiment, empathy, experience and reflection. It can state a point of view (*logos*), entrain it to a set of characters (*ethos*), make manifest an inner life (*pathos*), construct a course of action (*mythos*), and follow it through to a point where it can be evaluated in psychological, ethical, social and political terms (*phronesis*). It moves in two directions at once—it *analyses*, pulling apart situations and revealing their constituent parts; and it *synthesises*, joining the parts together again and showing how they relate to one another in a single field of apprehension. It is our most human-like art form. Even when it is not *lifelike* in its temporal and physical conditions, it is *like life*.

The twin engines propelling drama are human potency and human fragility, hence the masks of comedy (*Melpomene*) and tragedy (*Thalia*) that decorate many old-style theatres. Its value lies in its capacity to portray and interrogate human difference, division and conflict while presenting them in a unifying frame of understanding. This double movement can be seen from the earliest plays of the ancient Greeks, to the latest hybrid offerings of the contemporary stage. Drama contains both dynamics of change and continuity. Fixating on what is new in the art form does us no favours in appreciating the balance between them, which is also the balance between what we owe the past, in terms of awareness and respect, and what we owe our lives now, in terms of freedom and choice.

All this gives drama an important integrative function, and a capacity for summative judgment. This is not unique to the art form. Novels and poetry have it, and music too. But drama's temporal compression into a few hours, and its style of public address, lends the knowledge it offers special impact. The integrative function of drama is the result of its capacity to present narratives (or narrative-like structures) and characters (or character-like *personae*) and their contexts simultaneously.

This invokes what philosophers call 'the principle of charity', whereby an audience favours the most reasonable explanation when making sense of what is said and shown on stage.

This is the crucial difference between drama and melodrama, and lies at the heart of the former's capacity to illuminate the drivers of human behaviour. For example, one can argue that there are two main reasons why people act badly. First, that they are bad people; second, that there are factors in their lives that cause their censurable actions, some of which they control, some of which they do not. Bad people behaving badly is the stuff of melodrama (and superhero movies). People behaving badly for reasons that require further investigation is the matter of drama. The empathy we feel in the theatre is the result of engaging with drama in this deeper way. It is the emotional insight generated when we apply a principle of charity to the different perspectives and behaviours presented on stage. This does not absolve characters in a play from audience judgement. But it makes those judgements specific, and arriving at them harder work. In classic drama, Medea, Iago, Richard III, Hedda Gabler and Judge Danforth; in Australian drama, Ned Kelly, Miss Kingsbury, Allen Fitzgerald, Brett Ricketson, Henry Law and the young women in *SHIT*: all these characters do bad things. But though we condemn them, the plays in which they appear give us deeper insight into their actions.

How will we use the extraordinary gift of drama? This unmatched way of understanding each other and the world?

Reclaiming a sense of the nation (and a national drama)

I will conclude this book with some remarks on the issue of nationhood from the perspective of our national drama. 'The nation' is an important concept for achieving social cohesion, political cooperation and cultural inclusion, but our current view of it is too negative, especially on the left. The reasons for this negative view should be acknowledged so we can move forward with a renovated conception for today's pluralist, multicultural society. It may not be easy, but the game is worth the candle. Without a strong, positive sense of nationhood, not only can there be no real sense of its creative derivatives—Australian culture, Australian drama—there can be no holonic connection between 'parts' and 'wholes' in any sphere of public life. This is dangerous for two reasons. Firstly, it leaves the concept of nationhood to be manipulated by populist and reactionary forces—Australia's White Australia Policy is a dismal example of both. Secondly, it renders inoperative an important avenue whereby our understanding of the world can be shared through common signs and symbols. It is unlikely that political divisions in Australia are more intense now than in the past. But the weakness of 'the nation' as a felt idea, save at times of formal remembrance or extreme duress, means we are missing an important link in our collective thinking. A restriction on the concept of nationhood entails a restriction on our lives. It is not the term 'the nation' itself that matters. It is what we mean by it when we say it.

In my view, from the 1990s onwards, Australia gave up thinking about its nationhood in a deeper way. Pulled outward, towards a 'global village', and inward, towards 'local thinking', the associated meanings around the concept thinned out. It was unfortunate timing. Whatever benefits neoliberalism might be argued to confer as an economic system, even its supporters recognise it is destructive of the social fabric. If you are negatively affected, capitalism's endless 'creative destruction' is just destruction. Anyone who has lived in a deindustrialised city or a deserted regional town will have witnessed its catastrophic impact.

'The nation' stands as a rebuker and mitigator of neoliberalism. By treating it meaningfully, we can achieve common goals impossible to action in any other way. To give one example: it is impossible to realise the call in the Uluru Statement from the Heart for 'a fuller expression of Australia's nationhood', if the concept of nationhood does not resonate. The language of individual choice is inadequate here. We can disagree about what nationhood stands for. But we cannot dispense with a sense of it altogether if we are to respond to the Statement in a purposeful way. Our differences must be subsumed in a shared identity that permits us to relate to each other across them. The fate of one is the fate of all. It is here that a renovated idea of the nation is so crucial.

In 1762, Jean-Jacques Rousseau published his famous essay, *The Social Contract*. As with stage plays, it is helpful to recall the historical context in which influential political documents first appeared. In 1762, the American Declaration of Independence was 14 years away, Captain James Cook's 'discovery' of Australia eight years away, and its white colonisation 26 years away, and the French Revolution 27 years away. Global changes were afoot, both good and bad. But Rousseau wrote unaware of them. In effect, *The Social Contract* discusses nationhood before imperialism, colonialism and racism had terminally infected its associated meaning. This makes it a useful statement to return to when trying to uncover more positive connotations of the concept.

The essay is divided into four books that illustrate the two halves of Rousseau's mind, the Romantic (books 1 and 2), and the Classical (books 3 and 4). Together they form a devastating critique of non-democratic forms of government. But what makes Rousseau's argument so powerful, and an advance on the political theories put forward by his predecessors such as Hobbes, Locke and Hume, is that he grasps that it is a collectively shared *sense* of the nation which legitimates democracies on every level. Democratic institutions can, and do, vary widely. What is important is that they seek to articulate an all-important 'general will', which Rousseau distinguishes from the lesser article, the 'will of all', which today we would call the 'majority view'.

At heart, *The Social Contract* wrestles with one big question: 'the act by which a People is constituted as such'. For my purposes, the vital section of the essay is 'Of the Social Pact'. These four pages lay out the social and moral principles that must underscore any and all democratic institutions. Meaningful collective action is of the essence. 'Since people can by no means engender new powers, but can only unite and control those of which they are already possessed, there is no way in which they can maintain themselves save by coming together and pooling their strength', Rousseau argues. 'They must develop some sort of central direction and learn to act in concert'. The basis for coming together is not force, but 'agreement' the clauses of which 'must be everywhere the same, and everywhere tacitly admitted and recognised'. Thus, 'the resultant conditions are the same for all; and because they are the same for all, it is in the interest of none to make them onerous for his fellows'. The sense of collective identity that arises from this elegant, insightful and just conception of democratic politics is worth quoting in full:

> As soon as the act of association becomes a reality, it substitutes for the person of each of the contracting parties a moral and collective body made up of as many members as the constituting assembly has votes, which body receives from this very act of constitution its unity, its dispersed *self*, and its will. The public person thus formed by the union of individuals was known in the old days as a *City*, but now as the *Republic* or *Body Politic*. This, when it fulfils a passive role is known by its members as *The State*, when an active one, as *The Sovereign People*, and in contrast to other similar bodies, as a *Power*. In respect of the constituent associates it enjoys the collective name of *The People*, the individuals who compose it being known as *Citizens* in so far as they share in the sovereign authority, as *Subjects* in so far as they owe obedience to the laws of the State. (original emphasis)

Apart from being a wonderful description of democracy's coherence and strength as a type of government (no guff about 'thymotic striving' needed), Rousseau points to a system where pursuit of the 'general will' involves consensus-seeking through public debate and the provision of shared experiences, from whence arise vital expressions of a state's 'dispersed self'. No democracy has the right to say that they do this better than any other. There is no skewed sense in *The Social Contract* of a world divided into the West and the Rest, no sense (yet) of Europe's *superiority*. Interestingly for Australians, Rousseau has a short section, 'Of Real Property', where he discusses claims to 'first occupancy' of a land that a nation might make. He lays out three conditions for upholding such claims: that no-one is living on the land already; that only as much land is taken as is 'necessary for subsistence', and that '[it] must [be] take[n] possession of... not by empty ceremony, but by virtue of [an] intention to... cultivate it'. In debates about whether Australia was settled or invaded by Britain in

1788, it may be observed that none of these conditions for legitimate ownership were met. There were people already here, the whole continent was claimed, and it was used as a dumping ground for convicts.

'The bond of society is that identity of interests which all feel who compose it', says Rousseau. In observations like this, he makes a sense of nationhood key to the successful functioning of democracy. Seeking consensus and exploring shared experiences—debate and action towards common causes—is the chief expression of the indivisible soul of the body politic, and generates the moral will holding it together on a daily basis. While Rousseau only mentions culture briefly, in relation to censorship (he is all for it), by implication he describes a society in which cultural institutions and political institutions work together to strike an all-important balance between the rights of the individual on the one hand, and the needs of the collective citizenry on the other. In this way, diversity is preserved, while unity is pursued.

Where did Rousseau's vision come unstuck? After 35 years in the theatre, I am a better artist than social scientist, but disasters do not need experts to name them. As modern conceptions of the nation took shape in the minds of eighteenth-century *philosophes*, they were joined to race-based beliefs that emerged in earnest at the same time. This was, and is, a toxic marriage. It harnessed the resources of the industrialised state, in its military and productive might, to an irrational and dehumanising biologism. Perhaps fear of the Other is a feature of many societies. It is another matter to link suspicion of outsiders to what the sociologist Max Weber called 'monocratic bureaucracy', one 'superior… in [the] precision… stability… stringency… discipline, and… reliability' of its powers of 'imperative control'. The nation then emerges—as it did in the nineteenth and twentieth centuries—as an administratively sophisticated colonising machine, bent on using its new-found military and economic strength to pursue the non-idea of racial domination.

The extremes of this can be seen in Hitler's Germany, Hirohito's Japan and Miloševic's Yugoslavia. But white Australia made ample use of race-based thinking in its frontier wars against the Indigenous population after 1788. It is pervasive in the decades following Federation, and was institutionalised in the White Australia Policy. The policy was eventually overturned, but it has left an aura of justified scepticism around the concept of 'the nation' and an understandable belief that racist thinking continues to influence Australian politics today. This has two negative effects. First, it acts as a disincentive to collectively acknowledge Australia's historical record and deal with the legacy of our colonial past. Second, it discourages renovation of nationhood as a positive force, leaving it to be claimed by a paranoid national*ism*. A small-l liberal individualism may seem like a safer bet than engaging the concept of the nation once again. But many of the problems we now face cannot be addressed without it. By citing Rousseau, I hope to show that its intellectual origins are more inspiring than its later abysmal record suggests.

Let me return to the Uluru Statement from the Heart. Nation and nationhood is central to the language of this 439-word document. It addresses non-Indigenous Australians at a collective level, in respect of our 'dispersed self'. It seeks action based on three principles: 'voice', 'treaty' and 'truth'. Each of these principles speaks to, and can only be actioned by, the Australian nation as a whole. Constitutional and legislative change, treaty and the process 'of truth telling about Australia's history and colonisation' are matters for inclusive public debate. The agreement sought by the Statement is generally binding, across every Australian citizen–subject, now and into the future. In other words, the Statement is a common cause, and it is impossible to understand, let alone respond to what it is saying without a renovated sense of nationhood.

Our national life is key to this, since the associated meanings of the concept of the nation must be de-racialised if it is to be fit for purpose. In a radio interview, Noel Pearson, one of recipients of the 2021 Sydney Peace Prize, made it clear that the Statement is about culture, not race. He said these inspiring words: 'We need to move away from the language of race to the recognition of Indigeneity… Let us not hang the new garment of the "voice" [constitutional reform] on the old hook of race.' A main task for Australians now is disentangling our sense of nationhood from the non-idea of race, and rediscovering the real possibilities of Rousseau's 'general will'. In this respect, the Statement is one that all Australians, regardless of their political views, *can* and *should* uphold.

My argument is simple, and runs through this book like the red thread that in Chinese folklore brings true lovers together: the concept of the nation is key to the shared rights and duties of Australians of all backgrounds, faiths, classes, genders and ages, and the quality of our national life is key to our sense of nationhood. In turn, this relies on the breadth, depth and imaginative capacity of our national culture, a vital component of which is our national drama. I have tried to show, in detail, how our drama contributes as a mode of inquiry to the debates that comprise our national life, and how, at different times, it has reflected, challenged and changed our conception of nationhood as a result. Supported in the right way, drama is a practice of creative inclusion that can help us achieve the unity-in-diversity that is central to the flourishing of the modern democratic state that we call, with a mixture of pride, shame and exasperation, the Australian nation.

Last words

In Manning Clark's *History of Australia*, despite concerns about its accuracy, limits and omissions, there is holistic interest in the Australian nation and the drivers of its collective behaviour. Because these are murky, complex and hard to describe, Clark has been accused, among other things, of stepping beyond the scholar's brief and assigning to a mass of historical contingencies a historical purpose; of trying to tell a story that history cannot tell; of telling a myth. Again and again, Clark returns to the problem of Australia's national character, what makes up its nature, and how it has changed over time. How it failed itself in the past, but need not always fail itself. Perhaps Clark was ahead of his time. Any writer of what Robert Darnton would identify as cultural history might display the same flexibility in jumping between the factual record and its broader interpretation. This in no way obviates legitimate criticism of Clark's work, or licenses cultural historians to write whatever they like. It is to argue that Clark was concerned to investigate the inner meaning of Australia's national life, not just its event chronology. In this aim, the cultural historian and the historian of culture travel the same road.

The history of Australia after the British arrived is one in which terrible things happened, to the Indigenous population, to the convicts who were transported here, and to the country itself. The facts of the past must be owned in order to deal with their legacy today. More pointedly, Australian playwrights will go on talking about them, so they are sure to remain on our stages even as we argue about their place in the history books. Dramatists *remember things* that some people would like to forget. Perhaps this is one reason for Australia's slighting of culture. But it is enervating, as well as wrong, to live life in a bubble of contrived amnesia, to waste the energy of renewal shoring up the barriers of denial. Those who dismiss 'black armband history' might consider the cost that blotting out our past has on our understanding of the future.

Today, non-Indigenous Australians rightly pay their respects to First Nations' Elders past, present and emerging when they speak on the land traditionally held by their peoples, and recognise the importance of their culture. Where is the sense that we know what this means in terms other than individualistic ones? If we cannot understand the place of culture in our own lives, how can we respect it in those of others? As we reconsider the violence of Australia's white history and how to resolve it, drama can be a resource for helping us explore what this entails. In renovating our sense of nationhood, drama is engine, mirror, canvas and rite. In its origins it is the historical companion to democracy; in its contemporary forms it is ubiquitous. After 120 years of creative production, the diversity of Australian drama is clear. It is its unity as a body of work, its capacity to act as a societal binding agent while maintaining a critical edge, that is under-appreciated. Drama has the ability to *express* our differences, while *seeking* common understanding of them.

So it is with some feeling, and a life spent creating, critiquing and researching Australian drama, that I finish with this appeal: revive it. Do not neglect a matchless body of work because in the upgrade model of culture it is thought to be 'over'. As literary manager at MTC, every year I would face the unedifying task of frantically trying to fill the last 'slots' for the forthcoming season. Our new commissions were in place. Our classics had been chosen. Suitable British, American or

European plays had been found (we rarely roamed further afield). Yet a few slots remained stubbornly empty. I blush to recall the lengths I went to find suitable dramas. After a couple of years of this, I noticed that overseas theatre companies were doing something that Australian theatre companies were not: reviving plays from their own national repertoires. By my hasty calculation, this could be up to a third of their annual seasons. In 2011, under its artistic director Sam Strong, Griffin Theatre—a Sydney-based company dedicated to the production of new Australian drama—committed to one revival from the national repertoire a year. It is to be strongly hoped it has paved the way for more programming of the Australian repertoire in other companies.

Art, like life, is a conversation between past, present and future. When one temporal dimension drops out of sight, the others are diminished. What a privilege it has been to read and write about the 50 plays discussed in this book. In my time as a director, dramaturge, literary manager and theatre historian, I have read hundreds, probably thousands of plays. All of them have contained at least one memorable moment or line. I have never put down a play without being enriched by it in some measure, being stirred or surprised or invited into deeper consideration of myself and the society around me.

What makes drama such a bewitching form? I have touched on this, but it remains for me a deeply mysterious question, almost divine. Yet quintessentially human too. Drama's charged domains, however abstract or surreal, are always a version of our own, an experiment with reality or the construction of a space where reality can be something other than it appears. The live stage is at once pulpit, speaker's corner, confessional, dinner table, dreamscape, poetic reverie, prophetic vision and memory box. Everything we are, drama is also. Everything we fear, love, desire, detest and hope for, drama does too. It is the immediate artistic incarnation of the compounded predicaments of our shared, human existence. It is ever expanding in what it says, ever varied in what it shows, endlessly creative in the worlds it puts on stage, to delight, confound, challenge, instruct and profoundly move us, its audiences.

Appendix

The data in Figure 1 (opposite) was generated in August 2021 using AusStage event search with Primary Genre as 'Theatre–Spoken Word', Origin of Text 'Australia', Origin of Production 'Australia and events located in Australia'. The number of events represented is the annual total in search results.

Note that data includes adaptations by Australian writers, touring works (which may be listed multiple times), and remounted or new productions.

Note the reduction in frequency from 2012–2021 may reflect the pace of data entry; the impact of COVID-19 is yet to be realised in AusStage.

The figures also reflect the impact of particular research projects on the data set. The Australian Drama Project from University of Queensland and University of New England accounts for the increased number of events recorded in the 1930s, especially by one-act plays co-recorded in the AusLit Database (radio plays have been excluded, as well as one-act plays attached to play competitions, but one-act plays in Little theatre seasons are included). The Drama Project also accounts for a spike in the early 1980s.

One driver of the significant increase in events in the 2000s (especially from 2004 onward) reflects greater effort to record events at the Adelaide Fringe Festival, Melbourne International Comedy Festival, and Sydney Fringe Festival (events from the Short and Sweet 10-minute play competition have been excluded).

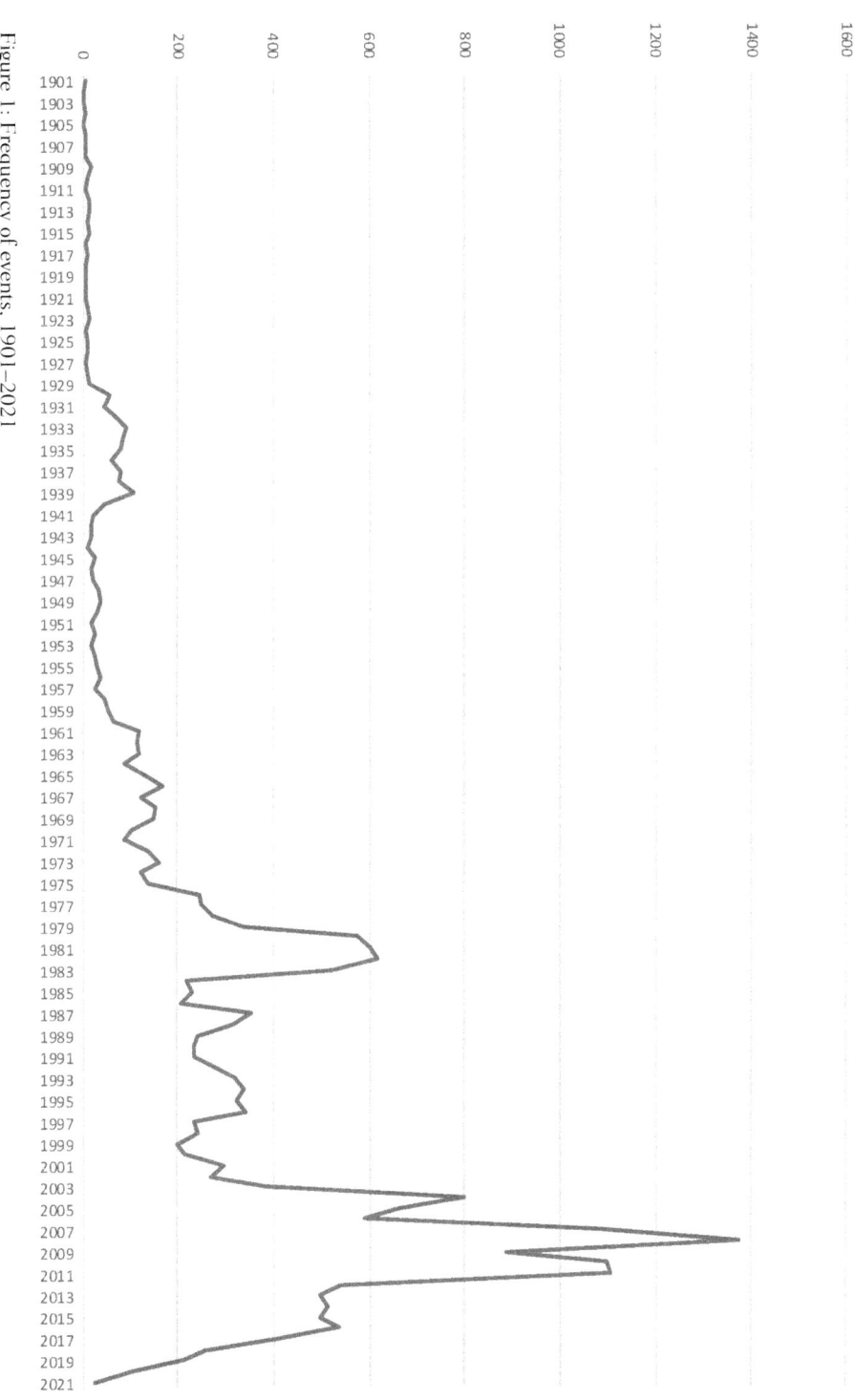

Figure 1: Frequency of events, 1901–2021

Appendix 297

Notes

Throughout the book, page references for play quotes and supplementary material published with playscripts are supplied in brackets directly after the quote. Play edition details are listed below, grouped by chapter. Full reference details for direct quotes from other sources are also given.

Introduction
Sources

page 1 'The relation of the theatre to national life!'. Leslie Rees. *A History of Australian Drama: The Making of Australian Drama from the 1830s to the late 1960s, vol 1.* (rev. edn). Sydney: Angus & Robertson, 1978, p. 101.

page 2 'first of the groups committed to a serious Australian drama', Margaret Williams. *Drama*, Melbourne: Oxford University Press, 1977, p. 5.

page 2 '… Australia which has given the world great novelists'. Allan Aldous. *Theatre in Australia*, Melbourne: Cheshire, 1947, p. 27.

page 3 'cultural strut', 'a relaxed erectness of carriage', 'cure for our disease', AA Phillips, *On the Cultural Cringe*. Melbourne University Publishing, 2006, p. 13.

page 3 'there is no short-cut', Phillips, p. 13.

page 3 'Between 1880 and 1911, The Firm employed leading international stars'. Elizabeth Kumm. 'Theatre in Melbourne, 1914–18: the Best, the Brightest and the Latest', 2016 p.8. <www.slv.vic.gov.au/sites/default/files/La-Trobe-Journal-97-Elisabeth-Kumm.pdf> (last accessed 19 August 2021).

page 4 'drama of poetry, drama of psychology', Rees. *The Making of Australian Drama from the 1830s to the late 1960s, vol 1*, p. 103.

page 4 'Australian in setting and mood', Aldous. *Theatre in Australia*, p. 48.

page 4 'The ideological weight of Shakespeare's legacy', Helen Gilbert

& Joanne Tompkins, *Post-Colonial Drama: Theory, Practice, Politics*, London: Routledge, 1996, p. 20.

page 5 'established enough for Rees to publish', Leslie Rees. *The Making of Australian Drama: A Historical and Critical Survey from the 1830s to the 1970s*, Sydney: Angus & Robertson, 1973; *A History of Australian Drama in the 1970s, vol. 2*, Sydney: Angus & Robertson, 1978.

page 6 '[the assumption that] one can distinguish levels in the past', Robert Darnton. *The Great Cat Massacre and Other Episodes in French Cultural History*, New York: Basic Books, 1984, p. 257.

page 6 'Anthropologists may have overworked the concept', Darnton. *The Great Cat Massacre*, pp. 260–1.

page 10 'for the first time I have enjoyed writing a novel'. Letter from Patrick White to John Sumner 25 October 1964. Copy in author's possession.

page 12 'Enter Gough, the Fertility God', Barry Andrews. 'The Federal Government as Literary Patron', *Meanjin*, 41:1, 1977, p. 9.

page 17 'By way of background', Stuart Macintyre. *A Concise History of Australia* (5th edn). Melbourne: Cambridge University Press, 2020; Manning Clark. *A Short History of Australia* (3rd rev. edn). New York: NAL Penguin, 1987.

1: 1901–1914: Ozziewood

Plays

Steele Rudd. *On Our Selection* (ed. R. Fotheringham), South Brisbane: Playlab, 2013.

Louis Esson. *The Time is Not Yet Ripe*, Sydney: Currency Methuen Drama, 1973.

Sources

page 20 'The first large float…', 'The Duke and Duchess Deeply Interested', *Argus*, 13 May 1901, pp. 6–7.

page 22 'Those plebiscites were all important'. Stuart Macintyre. *A Concise History of Australia* (5th edn). Melbourne: Cambridge University Press, 2020, p. 148.

page 22 '*Woman and Wine* is proving a big-draw', *Herald*, Melbourne, Vic, 20 May 1901, p. 5.

page 22 'On Saturday a number of 'chasers'', *Bulletin*, 18 May 1901, p. 8.

page 23 'In the activities of significant entrepreneurial "empires"', Veronica Kelly. *The Empire Actors: Stars of Australasian Costume Drama 1890s–1920s*, Sydney: Currency House, 2009, pp. 3–4.

page 24 'intractably regional', Kelly, p. 15.

page 25 'the only major professional Australasian company', Kelly, p. 157.

page 29 'a history of beginnings', Peter Fitzpatrick *After 'The Doll': Australian Drama Since 1955*. Melbourne: Edward Arnold, 1979, p. 17.

page 32 'wage levels were… to be based not on profits', Macintyre, *Concise History*, p. 160.

page 33 'a gang of cattle duffers', Kelly, p. 155.

page 33 'a crash course', Kelly, 156.

2: 1915–1929: Unknown knowns

Plays

Betty Roland. *The Touch of Silk*, Sydney: Currency Methuen Drama, 1974.

Katharine Susannah Prichard. *Brumby Innes and Bid Me to Love* (ed. Katharine Brisbane), Sydney: Currency Methuen Drama, 1974.

Arthur Adams. *Gallipoli Bill* (ed. R. Fotheringham), South Brisbane: Playlab New Vintage, 2013.

Sources

page 37 'the lamps are going out', Viscount Grey of Fallodon, Edward Grey. Twenty-Five Years, 1892–1916. London: Hodder and Stoughton, 1928, p.20.

page 37 'Bidding was very slack', 'Draught Stock Sales', *Argus*, 5 August 1914, p. 5.

page 38 'On 25 April 1915'. Australian War Memorial. 'First World War 1914–18', undated, np. <www.awm.gov.au/articles/atwar/first-world-war> (last accessed 24 October 2021).

page 38 'You could imagine nothing finer'. Keith Murdoch. Personal letter to Andrew Fisher, 23 September 1915, p. 18. <www.documentcloud.org/documents/2368309-keith-murdoch-letter.html> (last accessed 24 October 2021).

page 39 'For Bean, the archetypal Anzac', Sarah Midford. 'Bean's Anzac Book Shaped How Australians Think about Gallipoli'. *The Conversation*, 9 April 2015. <theconversation. com/beans-anzac-book-shaped-how-australians-think-about-gallipoli-38203> (last accessed 10 October 2021)

page 39 'Nearly five years ago'. 'War has Made Me a Pacifist', One Hundred Stories, 2015, np. <onehundredstories.anu.edu.au/stories/war-has-made-me-pacifist> (last accessed 24 October 2021).

page 39 'So far from strengthening a common purpose', Stuart Macintyre. *A Concise History of Australia* (5th edn). Melbourne: Cambridge niversity Press, 2020, p. 177.

page 39 'The cigarette replaced the pipe', Macintyre. *Concise History*, pp. 180–1.

page 40 '"Going out" usually meant', John Rickard. *Australia: A Cultural History* (3rd edn). Clayton, Vic: Monash University Publishing, 2017, p. 183.

page 40 'drinking now became primarily', Rickard, p. 175.

page 50 'shows insufficient theatrical technique', Leslie Rees. *A History of Australian Drama: The Making of Australian Drama from the 1830s to the late 1960s, vol 1.* (rev. edn). Sydney: Angus & Robertson, 1978, p. 148.

page 50 '*Brumby Innes* is not first and foremost about white exploitation', Margaret Williams. 'Natural Sexuality: Katharine Prichard's "Brumby Innes".' *Meanjin*, 32:1, 1973, p.42.

page 51 'Earlier humanitarians had', Macintyre. *Concise History*, pp. 145–6.

page 52 'Why didn't somebody produce this play?', Rees. *The Making of Australian Drama from the 1830s to the late 1960s, vol 1*, p. 148.

3. 1930–1945: The real Australia

Plays

Henrietta Drake-Brockman. *Men Without Wives*, South Brisbane: Playlab, 2012.

George Landen Dann. *Fountains Beyond*, South Brisbane: Playlab, 2012.

Cusack, Dymphna. *Morning Sacrifice: A Play in Three Acts*, Sydney: Currency Press in association with the Griffin Theatre Company, 1986.

Max Afford. *Lady in Danger*, South Brisbane: Playlab, 2012.

Douglas Stewart. *Ned Kelly* in Alan Seymour, Hal Porter and Douglas Stewart. *Three Australian Plays*, Ringwood, Vic: Penguin Books, 1963.

Sources

page 60 'through the 1960s'. Quoted in Caroline Lowbridge. 'Ladybird Books: the Strange Things we Learned', 6 March 2015, np. <www.bbc.com/news/uk-england-leicestershire-30709937> (last accessed 24 October 2021).

page 61 'consensus and common action', The Commonwealth Charter <thecommonwealth.org/about-us/charter> (last accessed 7 December 2021).

page 63 'the men who believed', Manning Clark. *A Short History of Australia* (3rd rev. edn). New York: NAL Penguin, 1987, p. 234.

page 63 'The method was simple', Clark, p. 235.

page 64 'Australia's unemployment rate'. 'Migration to Australia since Federation: A Guide to the statistics', Department of Parliamentary Services, 2010, pp. 1–27. <www.aph.gov.au/binaries/library/pubs/bn/sp/migrationpopulation.pdf> (last accessed 22 August 2021).

page 65 'If Australians had no more character', Vance Palmer. 'What is Significant in us Will Survive' in *The Words that Made Australia: How a Nation Came to Know Itself* (ed Robert Manne & Chris Feik). Collingwood, Vic: Black Inc, 2014, pp. 69–70.

page 67 'In play after play', John McCallum. *Belonging: Australian Playwriting in the 20th Century*, Sydney: Currency Press, 2009, p. 125.

page 71 'Australia looks to America', Stuart Macintyre. *A Concise History of Australia* (5th edn). Melbourne: Cambridge University Press, 2020, p. 200.

page 71 'you take care of the rear', Macintyre, *Concise History*, p. 201.

page 73 '[women] are more adaptable'. Quoted in 'The long, slow demise of the "marriage bar"'. Marian Sawer. *Inside Story.* 8 December 2016, np. <insidestory.org.au/the-long-slow-demise-of-the-marriage-bar/> (last accessed 22 August 2021).

page 73 'the horizontal hostility', Introduction, *Tremendous Worlds: Australian Women's Drama 1890–1960* (ed. Susan Pfisterer), Sydney: Currency Press, 1999, p. xii.

page 79 '[T]he commercial theatre and the embryonic nationalist drama', McCallum, *Belonging*, p. 7.

page 82 'an electric wire', Leslie Rees. *A History of Australian Drama: The Making of Australian Drama from the 1830s to the late 1960s, vol 1.* (rev. edn). Sydney: Angus & Robertson, 1978, p. 143.

page 82 'Without bothering to establish', Rees, p. 144.

page 83 'one of my sources of inspiration'. Manning Clark. Letter to Rosa Ribush. 18 March 1974. 'Ribush Papers', 9298. Box 996/9. Manuscript Section, State Library of Victoria.

4. 1945–1960: A step change

Plays

Sumner Locke Elliott. *Rusty Bugles*, Sydney: Currency Press, 1980.

Alan Seymour. *The One Day of the Year* in Alan Seymour, Hal Porter and Douglas Stewart. *Three Australian Plays*. Ringwood, Vic: Penguin Books, 1963.

Ray Lawler. *Summer of the Seventeenth Doll*, Sydney: Currency Press, 1978.

Mona Brand. *Here Under Heaven: Three Plays*, Sydney: Wentworth Press, 1969.

Oriel Gray. *Sky Without Birds* in *Plays of the 50s: Volume 1* (ed. Katharine Brisbane), Sydney: Currency Press, 2007.

Richard Beynon. *The Shifting Heart*. Sydney: Angus & Robertson, 1960.

Ric Throssell. *The Day Before Tomorrow* in *Plays of the 50s: Volume 1* (ed. Katharine Brisbane). Sydney: Currency Press, 2007.

Sources

page 90 'The Breakthrough', Leslie Rees. *The Making of Australian Drama from the 1830s to the late 1960s, vol 1.* (rev. edn). Sydney: Angus & Robertson, 1978, p. 254.

page 90 'the most famous Australian play', John McCallum. *Belonging: Australian Playwriting in the 20th Century*, Sydney: Currency Press, 2009, p. 77–8.

page 90 'Some Australians may have been chomping', Humphrey McQueen. *Social Sketches of Australia*, Ringwood, Vic: Penguin, 1991, pp. 214–5.

page 91 'The postwar settlement reconciled capitalism with democracy', Stuart Macintyre. *Australia's Boldest Experiment: War and Reconstruction in the 1940s*, Sydney: New South Publishing, 2015, p. 476.

page 93 'the women playwrights who rose to prominence', Michelle Arrow. *Upstaged: Australian Women Dramatists in the Limelight at Last*, Sydney: Currency Press, 2002, p. 6.

page 99 'the representative terms', Peter Fitzpatrick. *After 'The Doll': Australian Drama Since 1955.* Melbourne: Edward Arnold, 1979, p. 44.

page 101 'does not describe a reality', Jonathon Bollen, Bruce Parr & Adrian Kiernander. *Men at Play: Masculinities in Australian theatre since the 1950s* (Australian playwrights; monograph no. 11), Amsterdam: Rodopi, 2008, p. 5

page 101 'expos[e]... assumptions about Australian masculinity', Bollen, *Men at Play*, p. 7.

page 102 'respect for ordinary people', Review of *Summer of the Seventeenth Doll*. Kenneth Tynan, *Observer*, 5 May, 1957.

page 103 'Some strange conversion took place', 'Dawn of the Seventeenth Doll', *Age*, 18 December 1965.

page 107 'Yet it was Calwell who coined the term "new Australian"', Stuart Macintyre. *A Concise History of Australia* (5th edn). Melbourne: Cambridge University Press, 2020, p. 211.

page 107 '"Our aim", Arthur Calwell had laid down', Macintyre, *Concise History*, pp. 234–5.

page 111 'Till the Day I Die [was] an anti-Nazi play', Ken Harper. 'The Useful Theatre: The New Theatre Movement in Sydney and Melbourne 1935–1983', *Meanjin*, 43:1, 1984, pp. 58–9.

5. 1961–1975: Not better, just different

Plays

Patrick White. *A Cheery Soul* in Patrick White. *Four Plays*, Melbourne: Sun Books, 1967.

Alan Hopgood. *Private Yuk Objects* in *Plays of the 60s: Volume 2* (ed. Katharine Brisbane), Sydney: Currency Press, 1999.

Michael Boddy and Bob Ellis. *The Legend of King O'Malley* in *Plays of the 70s: Volume 1* (ed. Katharine Brisbane), Sydney: Currency Press, 1998.

Alex Buzo. *Norm and Ahmed* in *Plays of the 60s: Volume 2* (ed. Katharine Brisbane), Sydney: Currency Press, 1999.

Hewett, Dorothy. *The Chapel Perilous, or, The Perilous Adventures of Sally Banner*, Sydney: Currency Press, 1981.

David Williamson. *Don's Party*, Sydney: Currency Press, 1997.

Jack Hibberd. *A Stretch of the Imagination: A Play*, Sydney: Currency Press, 1973.

John Romeril. *The Floating World* (rev. edn). Sydney: Currency Press, 1982.

Robert J Merritt. *The Cake Man* (rev edn). Sydney: Currency Press, 1983.

Jennifer Compton. *Crossfire* in *Plays of the 70s: Volume 3* (ed. Katharine Brisbane), Sydney: Currency Press, 1998.

Sources

page 126 'the slithery snake dance of Australian theatre', Julian Meyrick. 'Patrick White, Spoiled Identity and Failure as a Logic of Use'. *Australasian Drama Studies*, 71. October 2017, p. 44.

page 126 'No doubt to pluck a message', HG Kippax, Introduction, Patrick White. *Four Plays*, Melbourne: Sun Books, 1967, p. 10.

page 126 'Miss Docker cannot be read only in her baleful aspect', Andrew

Fuhrmann. 'Patrick White: A Theatre of His Own', *Australian Book Review*, 356, November 2013. <www.australianbookreview.com.au/abr-online/archive/2013/108-november-2013-no-356/1695-a-theatre-of-his-own> (last accessed 10 October 2021).

page 132 'Australian casualties mounted', Stuart Macintyre. *A Concise History of Australia* (5th edn). Melbourne: Cambridge University Press, 2020, p. 240.

page 138 '*Norm and Ahmed* quickly became known in newspapers as "that word play"', Graeme Blundell, 'Triumph of the Censor's Art', *Australian*, 16 August 2009.

page 138 'Australia had always had one of the most rigid censorship regimes', Adam Carr. 'The Wowsers' Last Stand'. *Outrage*, June 1997, np.

page 139 'the symbolic beginning of alternative theatre in Australia', Julian Meyrick. *Australian Theatre After the New Wave: Policy, Subsidy and the Australian Artist*. Amsterdam: Brill, 2017, p. 13. I have also touched on censorship in 'Are You With Me? Offensiveness and Australian Drama in the 1970s' with Jenny Fewster. *The Routledge Companion to Australian Literature* (ed. Jessica Gildersleeve), New York: Routledge, 2021: pp. 85–98.

page 139 'Buzo's play dramatizes a late-night encounter', Blundell, 'Triumph of the Censor's Art'. *Australian*, 16 August 2009.

page 141 'the words are little labyrinths' Mark Fisher. *Ghosts of My Life: Writings on Depression, Hauntology and Lost Futures*. Winchester, Washington: Zero Books, 2014, p. 38.

page 142 'In a hierarchy, participants can be compared and evaluated'. David Spangler. 'Holon and Holarchy: Arthur Koestler'. 25 June 2014, np. <www.sociocracy.info/holon-and-holarchy/> (last accessed 4 October 2021).

page 153 'Whitlam extended the ambit', Macintyre, *Concise History*, pp. 247–8.

page 154 'a searching for liberty', Donald Horne. *In the Open*. Pymble, NSW: Harper Collins, 2000, p. 167.

6. 1976–1990: The compelling mood darkens

Plays

Stephen Sewell. *The Blind Giant is Dancing*, Sydney: Currency Press, 1985.

Katherine Thomson. Diving for Pearls, Sydney: Currency Press, 1992.

Louis Nowra. *Inside the Island; the Precious Woman* (with music score by Sarah De Jong), Sydney: Currency Press, 1981.

Jack Davis. *No Sugar*, Sydney: Currency Press, 1986.

Michael Gow. *Away*, Sydney: Currency Press, 1990.

Jenny Kemp. *Call of the Wild* in *Performing the unNameable* (ed. Richard James Allen & Karen Pearlman), Sydney: Currency Press in association with Realtime, 1999.

Katherine Thomson. *Diving for Pearls*, Sydney: Currency Press, 1992.

Tes Lyssiotis. *The Forty Lounge Café*, Sydney: Currency Press in association with Playbox Theatre, 1990.

Sources

page 159 'run mainly by second-rate people', Donald Horne. *The Lucky Country*. Melbourne: Penguin, 1964, p. 217

page 159 'This: The Governor-General secretly made a decision', Donald Horne. *The Death of the Lucky Country*, Ringwood, Vic: Penguin Books, 1976, p. 12.

page 161 'There was no constitutional crisis'. Stanley Bach. 'The Crisis of 1974-75', in *Platypus and Parliament: The Australian Senate in Theory and Practice*, 2003, np. <www.aph.gov.au/About_Parliament/Senate/Powers_practice_n_procedures/platparl/c04> (last accessed 24 October 2021).

page 161 'a belief in its divine right to govern', Horne, *Death of the Lucky Country*, p. 20.

page 162 'It began with unemployment at 2%', Tim Colebatch, 'The Year the Economy Went "Bung"', *Age*, 1 January 2005.

page 164 'Out of the turmoil in the world economy', Macintyre, *Concise History*, p. 255.

page 165 'There was the diffused shock' Horne, *Death of the Lucky Country*, p. 16.

page 165 'the original JC Williamson model', Michael Tallis & Joan Tallis. *The Silent Showman: Sir George Tallis, the Man Behind the World's Largest Entertainment Organisation of the 1920s*, Kent Town, SA: Wakefield Press, 1999, p. 255.

page 168 '*not* a study of Australian society', Heather Mitchell. *Brodie's Notes on Michael Gow's Away*, Sydney: Pan Books, 1988, p. 21.

page 180 'It [is] time to throw back the veil', Henry Reynolds. *Why Weren't We Told? A Personal Search for the Truth of our History.* Ringwood, Vic: Viking, 1999, p. 246.

page 183 'dusty and overworked territory', *Chronicle of the Twentieth Century* (John Ross editor-in-chief). Ringwood, Vic: Chronicle Australia, 1990, p. 889.

page 184 'According to AO Neville', Maryrose Casey. *Creating Frames: Contemporary Indigenous Theatre 1967–1990*, St Lucia, Qld: University of Queensland Press, 2004, p. 152.

page 186 'with a preliminary hearing concluding that a jury would not be able to make a conviction'. 'Forest Hill Massacre', Google Arts and Culture, undated, np. <artsandculture.google.com/entity/forrest-river-massacre/m02z3w_h?hl=en> (last accessed 24 October 2021).

page 187 'With *No Sugar* Davis was portraying life', Casey, p. 153.

page 188 'weren't going to go and look at an Aboriginal play', Casey, p. 147.

page 189 'the AusStage database' is the oldest and most extensive national dataset on live performance in the world. Selecting the 'event' search option on the homepage is best for precise results when using the database. <www.ausstage.edu.au/pages/browse/>.

page 189 'set in the summer of 1967–8', Mitchell, p. 12.

page 191 'When *Away* premiered at Griffin Theatre', Hilary Bell in Michael Gow, *Away*, Sydney: Currency Press, 1990, p. 59.

page 191 'Healing, reconciliation and resolution', Mitchell, p. 12.

page 192 'Jenny Kemp's theatre is less about a political revolution', Rachel Fensham & Denise Varney. *The Dolls' Revolution: Australian Theatre and Cultural Imagination*, Melbourne: Australian Scholarly Publishing, 2005, pp.64–5.

page 197 'sets up a space for the spectators', Peta Tait. *Converging Realities: Feminism in Australian Theatre.* Sydney: Currency Press, 1994, p. 86–7.

7. 1991–2005: The End (yet the persistence) of History

Plays

Alma De Groen. *The Woman in the Window.* Sydney: Currency Press, 1999.

Hannie Rayson. *Life After George*, Sydney: Currency Press, 2000.

Joanna Murray-Smith. *Honour*, Sydney: Currency Press, 1997.

Kate Mulvany. *The Seed.* Sydney: Currency Press, 2008.

Nicholas Enright. *A Property of the Clan*, Sydney: Currency Press, 1994.

Jane Harrison. *Stolen*, Sydney: Currency Press, 1998.

Wesley Enoch. *Black Medea* in *Contemporary Indigenous Plays*, Sydney: Currency Press, 2007.

Richard Frankland. *Conversations with the Dead* in *Blak Inside*, Sydney: Currency Press in association with Playbox Theatre, 2002.

Sources

page 202 'I come before you… at a moment rich with promise'. Inaugural Address of George Bush. 20 January 1989. <avalon.law.yale.edu/20th_century/bush.asp> (last accessed 24 October 2021).

page 203 'Liberal principles in economics', Francis Fukuyama. *The End of History and the Last Man*, London: Avon Books, 1992, pp. xiii–iv.

page 203 'All countries undergoing modern economic modernisation', Fukuyama, p. xv.

page 204 'establishing the principles of popular sovereignty', Fukuyama, p. xvii.

page 204 'Universal recognition is not "completely satisfying"', Fukuyama, p. xxi.

page 204 'the typical citizen of liberal democracy', Fukuyama, p. xxii.

page 204 "the fanatical desire for equal recognition, Fukuyama, p. 315.

page 206 'a new era of decomposition, uncertainty and crisis', Eric Hobsbawm. *The Age of Extremes: A History of the World, 1914–1991*, New York: Pantheon Books, 1996, p. 6.

page 206 'a period of economic stability'. Tejvan Pettinger. 'The Great Moderation', 21 February 2013, np. <www.economicshelp.org/blog/6901/economics/the-great-moderation/> (last accessed 24 October 2021).

page 207 'Culture arises from the community', Department of Communications and the Arts. *Creative Nation: Commonwealth Cultural Policy, October 1994.* Canberra: Department of Communications and the Arts, 1994, p. 1.

page 207 'unique attributes', government responsibility, encouraging diversity, *Creative Nation*, pp. 2, 5, 6.

page 207 'Culture creates wealth', *Creative Nation*, p. 7.

page 208 'The Commonwealth's responsibility', *Creative Nation*, p. 9.

page 208 'Australians were becoming aware of the threadbare trappings', Stuart Ward. 'Culture up to our Arseholes: Projecting Post-Imperial Australia'. *Australian Journal of Politics and History*, 51:1, 2005, p. 66.

page 211 'no-one who has lived through this extraordinary century', Eric Hobsbawm. *The Age of Extremes: A History of the World, 1914–1991.* New York: Pantheon Books, 1996, p. 5.

page 226 'a collective concept for all knowledge', Jan Assmann. 'Collective Memory and Cultural Identity' (trans. John Czaplika). *New German Critique*, 65, 1995, p. 125.

page 226 'The first step in the creation', Julianne Schultz. 'Facing Foundational Wrongs: Careful What you Wish For'. *Griffith Review*, 73, 2021, p. 13.

page 235 'an electric wire', Leslie Rees. *A History of Australian Drama: The Making of Australian Drama from the 1830s to the late 1960s, vol 1.* (rev. edn). Sydney: Angus & Robertson, 1978, p. 143.

8. 2006–2020: The return of the nation

Plays

Andrew Bovell. *When the Rain Stops Falling.* Sydney: Currency Press, 2011.

Angela Betzien. *The Dark Room.* South Brisbane: Playlab, 2009.

Patricia Cornelius. *SHIT* in Van Badham, Anna Barnes and Patricia Cornelius. *Muff, MinusOneSister and SHIT: Three Plays.* Sydney: Currency Press, 2017.

Angus Cerini. *The Bleeding Tree.* Sydney: Currency Press, 2017.

Nakkiah Lui. *Black is the New White.* Crows Nest, NSW: Allen & Unwin, 2019.

S. Shakthidharan. *Counting and Cracking*. Sydney: Currency Press, 2020.
Jean Tong. *Hungry Ghosts*. Sydney: Currency Press, 2018.
Glace Chase. *Triple X* (unpublished), 2020.

Sources

page 239 'What I am absolutely confident of is', Julia Gillard, quoted in Jacqueline Kent. *Take Your Best Shot: The Prime Ministership of Julia Gillard.* Melbourne: Penguin, 2013, p. 121.

page 239 'Though it is hardly a secret', Adam Toose. *Crashed: How a Decade of Financial Crises Changed the World.* London: Allen Lane, 2018, p. 13.

page 239 '[W]e are born into a world of cooperation and interdependence', Tim Dunlop. *The Future of Everything: Big, Audacious Ideas for a Better World.* Sydney: New South Publishing, 2018 p. 44.

page 239 'slow-motion catastrophe', David Suzuki & Ian Hannington. *Just Cool It: the Climate Crisis and What We Can Do, a Post-Paris Agreement.* Sydney: New South Publishing, 2017, p. ix.

page 239 'If we summon the human ingenuity', Suzuki & Hannington, p. xv.

page 240 'we have become incredibly good', Dunlop, p. 2.

page 240 'Capitalist realism continues to prime', Peter Fleming. *Dark Academia: How Universities Die.* London: Pluto Press, 2021, p. 95.

page 240 'The lesson of Trump', Linda Jaivin. 'Middle-Power Might: A Plan for Dealing with China'. *Australian Foreign Affairs*, 11, Feb 2021, p. 92.

page 241 'a society that has taken pride', Stuart Macintyre. *Australia's Boldest Experiment: War and Reconstruction in the 1940s*, Sydney: New South Publishing, 2015, p. 327.

page 260 'the slums… the criminal half-world', HG Kippax, Introduction to Alan Seymour, Douglas Stewart & Hal Porter. *Three Australian Plays*, Ringwood, Vic: Penguin, 1963, p. 19.

page 261 'intersectional theory asserts that people'. YW Boston. 'What is Intersectionality, and What Does it Have to Do With Me?', 29 March 2017. <www.ywboston.org/2017/03/what-is-intersectionality-and-what-does-it-have-to-do-with-me/> (last accessed 24 October 2021).

page 267 'We certainly are still in the era of "posts"', Marianne Hirsch. 'The Generation of Postmemory'. *Poetics*, 29:1, Spring, 2008, p. 109.

page 276 'a talent on the rise'. Daniel Penny. 'I am a worthy love interest: Glace Chase on her trans rom-com', 4 June 2021.<www.smh.com.au/culture/theatre/i-am-a-worthy-love-interest-glace-chase-on-her-trans-rom-com-20210521-p57u32.html> (last accessed 24 October 2021).

page 279 'she is a real person', Glace Chase, personal correspondence with author 1–2 December 2021.

page 279 'it is not that gender politics are inaccurate', Chase correspondence with author.

Conclusion
Sources

page 283 'repertory of collective actions', Charles Taylor. *Modern Social Imaginaries*. Public Planet Books. Durham: Duke University Press, 2004, p. 107.

page 288 'a fuller expression of Australia's nationhood', Uluru Statement from the Heart, <ulurustatement.org> (last accessed 24 October 2021).

page 289 'the act by which a People', Jean-Jacques Rousseau. 'The Social Contract' in Jean-Jacques Rousseau. *Social Contract, Locke, Hume, Rousseau*. Introduction Sir Ernest Barker. Oxford University Press, 1960, pp. 179.

page 289 'Since people can by no means engender new powers', Rousseau, p. 179.

page 289 'must be everywhere the same', Rousseau, p. 180.

page 290 'As soon as the act of association becomes a reality', Rousseau, p. 182.

page 290 'Of Real Property', Rousseau, pp. 186–89.

page 291 'The bond of society is that identity of interests', Rousseau, p. 190.

page 291 'superior… in [the] precision…', Max Weber (trans AM Henderson & Talcott Parsons). 'The Types of Authority and

Imperative Coordination' in *The Theory of Social and Economic Organisation*. New York: Oxford University Press. 1947, p. 337.

page 292 'of truth telling about Australia's history and colonisation'. 'Uluru Statement from the Heart', 2017. <ulurustatement.org> (last accessed 24 October 2021).

page 292 'We need to move away', Noel Pearson, ABC Radio National interview, 26 May 2021. <www.abc.net.au/radionational/programs/drive/uluru-statement-wins-sydney-peace-prize/13360650> (last accessed 28 November 2021).

Bibliography

50 Plays (in chapter order)

1. Rudd, Steele. *On Our Selection* (ed. R. Fotheringham). South Brisbane: Playlab, 2013.
2. Esson, Louis. *The Time is Not Yet Ripe*. Sydney: Currency Methuen Drama, 1973.
3. Roland, Betty. *The Touch of Silk* (ed. Jonathan Shaw). Sydney: Currency Methuen Drama, 1974.
4. Prichard, Katharine Susannah. *Brumby Innes and Bid Me to Love*. Sydney: Currency Methuen Drama, Sydney, 1974.
5. Adams, Arthur. *Gallipoli Bill* (ed. R. Fotheringham). South Brisbane: Playlab New Vintage, 2013.
6. Drake-Brockman, Henrietta. *Men Without Wives*. South Brisbane: Playlab, 2012.
7. Dann, George Landen. *Fountains Beyond*. South Brisbane: Playlab, 2012.
8. Cusack, Dymphna. *Morning Sacrifice: A Play in Three Acts*. Sydney: Currency Press in association with the Griffin Theatre Company, 1986.
9. Afford, Max. *Lady in Danger*. South Brisbane: Playlab, 2012.
10. Stewart, Douglas. *Ned Kelly* in Alan Seymour, Hal Porter and Douglas Stewart. *Three Australian Plays*. Ringwood, Vic: Penguin Books, 1963.
11. Elliott, Sumner Locke. *Rusty Bugles*. Sydney: Currency Press, 1980.
12. Seymour, Alan. *The One Day of the Year* in Alan Seymour, Hal Porter and Douglas Stewart. *Three Australian Plays*. Ringwood, Vic: Penguin Books, 1963.
13. Lawler, Ray. *Summer of the Seventeenth Doll*. Sydney: Currency Press, 1978.

14. Brand, Mona. *Here Under Heaven: Three Plays*. Sydney: Wentworth Press, 1969.
15. Gray, Oriel. *Sky Without Birds* in *Plays of the 50s: Volume 1* (ed. Katharine Brisbane). Sydney: Currency Press, 2007.
16. Beynon, Richard. *The Shifting Heart*. Sydney: Angus & Robertson, 1960.
17. Throssell, Ric. *The Day Before Tomorrow* in *Plays of the 50s: Volume 1* (ed. Katharine Brisbane). Sydney: Currency Press, 2007.
18. White, Patrick. *A Cheery Soul* in Patrick White. *Four Plays*. Melbourne: Sun Books, 1967.
19. Hopgood, Alan. *Private Yuk Objects* in *Plays of the 60s: Volume 2* (ed. Katharine Brisbane). Sydney: Currency Press, 1999.
20. Boddy, Michael and Bob Ellis. *The Legend of King O'Malley* in *Plays of the 70s: Volume 1* (ed. Katharine Brisbane). Sydney: Currency Press, 1998.
21. Buzo, Alex. *Norm and Ahmed* in *Plays of the 60s: Volume 2* (ed. Katharine Brisbane). Sydney: Currency Press, 1999.
22. Hewett, Dorothy. *The Chapel Perilous, or, The Perilous Adventures of Sally Banner*. Sydney: Currency Press, 1981.
23. Williamson, David. *Don's Party*. Sydney: Currency Press, 1997.
24. Hibberd, Jack. *A Stretch of the Imagination: A Play*. Sydney: Currency Press, 1973.
25. Romeril, John. *The Floating World* (rev. edn). Sydney: Currency Press, 1982.
26. Merritt, Robert J. *The Cake Man* (rev. edn). Sydney: Currency Press, 1983.
27. Compton, Jennifer. *Crossfire* in *Plays of the 70s: Volume 3* (ed. Katharine Brisbane). Sydney: Currency Press, 1998.
28. Sewell, Stephen. *The Blind Giant is Dancing*. Sydney: Currency Press, 1985.
29. Thomson, Katherine. *Diving for Pearls*. Sydney: Currency Press, 1992.
30. Nowra, Louis. *Inside the Island; the Precious Woman* (with music score by Sarah De Jong). Sydney: Currency Press, 1981.
31. Davis, Jack. *No Sugar*. Sydney: Currency Press, 1986.
32. Gow, Michael. *Away*. Sydney: Currency Press, 1990.

33. Kemp, Jenny. *Call of the Wild* in *Performing the unNameable* (ed. Richard James Allen & Karen Pearlman). Sydney: Currency Press in association with Realtime, 1999.
34. Lyssiotis, Tes. *The Forty Lounge Café*. Sydney: Currency Press in association with Playbox Theatre, 1990.
35. De Groen, Alma. *The Woman in the Window*. Sydney: Currency Press, 1999.
36. Rayson, Hannie. *Life After George*. Sydney: Currency Press, 2000.
37. Murray-Smith, Joanna. *Honour*. Sydney: Currency Press, 1997.
38. Mulvany, Kate. *The Seed*. Sydney: Currency Press, 2008.
39. Enright, Nick. *A Property of the Clan*. Sydney: Currency Press, 1994.
40. Harrison, Jane. *Stolen*. Sydney: Currency Press, 1998.
41. Enoch, Wesley. *Black Medea* in *Contemporary Indigenous Plays*. Sydney: Currency Press, 2007.
42. Frankland, Richard. *Conversations with the Dead* in *Blak Inside*. Sydney: Currency Press in association with Playbox Theatre, 2002.
43. Bovell, Andrew. *When the Rain Stops Falling*. Sydney: Currency Press, 2011.
44. Betzien, Angela. *The Dark Room*. South Brisbane: Playlab, 2009.
45. Cornelius, Patricia. *SHIT* in Van Badham, Anna Barnes and Patricia Cornelius. *Muff, MinusOneSister and SHIT: Three Plays*. Sydney: Currency Press, 2017.
46. Cerini, Angus. *The Bleeding Tree*. Sydney: Currency Press, 2017.
47. Lui, Nakkiah. *Black is the New White*. Crows Nest, NSW: Allen & Unwin, 2019.
48. Shakthidharan, S. *Counting and Cracking*. Sydney: Currency Press, 2020.
49. Tong, Jean. *Hungry Ghosts*. Sydney: Currency Press, 2018.
50. Chase, Glace. *Triple X* (unpublished), 2020.

Other plays cited

Bailey, Bert and Edmund Duggan. *The Squatter's Daughter* in 'Papers of Bert Bailey circa 1890–1952' [manuscript]. Bert Bailey. 1890. National Library of Australia.

Bedford, Randolph. *White Australia or, The empty North*. (ed. R. Fotheringham). South Brisbane: Playlab, 2013.

Cornelius, Patricia. *The Berry Man* in Patricia Cornelius. *Do Not Go Gentle... and The Berry Man: Two Plays* Sydney: Currency Press, 2011.

Edmunds, Albert [pseud. of Bert Bailey & Edmund Duggan]. *The Man from the Outback or, Stockwhip and Stirrup*. 'Papers of Bert Bailey circa 1890–1952' [manuscript]. Bert Bailey, 1890. National Library of Australia.

Gow, Michael. *Europe* in Michael Gow. *Europe / On Top of the World*. Sydney: Currency Press, 1988.

Gray, Oriel. *The Torrents*. Sydney: Currency Press, 2016.

Hewett, Dorothy. *This Old Man Comes Rolling Home* in Dorothy Hewett. *Collected Plays Volume I*. Sydney: Currency Press, 1992.

Hibberd, Jack. *White with Wire Wheels* in Jack Hibberd. *Selected Plays*. Sydney: Currency Press, 2000.

Shirley, Arthur and Ben Landeck. *Woman and Wine*. Manuscript 53575 in *The Lord Chamberlain's Plays*. British Library, 1895?

Inglis, Robert. *A Rum Do!* Brisbane: Arts Council of Australia (Queensland Division) & Queensland Theatre Company, 1970.

Keene, Daniel. *The Long Way Home*. South Brisbane: Playlab, 2015.

Nowra, Louis. *The Golden Age*. Sydney: Currency Press, 1985.

Odets, Clifford. *Waiting for Lefty*. In *Three Plays*. London: Gollancz, 1936.

Prichard, Katharine Susannah. *The Great Man*. In 'Papers of Katharine Susannah Prichard, 1851–1970 (bulk 1908–1969)' [manuscript]. Katharine Prichard, TH Prichard Hugo Throssell & Ric Throssell, 1851. National Library of Australia.

Roland, Betty. *The Touch of Silk* (1955 revision) in Betty Roland. *Granite Peak / The Touch Of Silk (1955)*. Sydney: Currency Press, 1988.

White, Patrick. *The Season at Sarsaparilla* in *Four Plays*. Sun Books, Melbourne, 1967; also published in *Patrick White: Collected Plays Volume 1*. Sydney: Currency Press, 1985.

White, Patrick. *Night on Bald Mountain* in *Four Plays*. Sun Books, Melbourne, 1967; also published in *Patrick White: Collected Plays Volume 1*. Sydney: Currency Press, 1985.

White, Patrick. *The Ham Funeral* in *Four Plays*. Sun Books, Melbourne, 1967; also published in *Patrick White: Collected Plays Volume 1*. Sydney: Currency Press, 1985.

Cited works

Aldous, Allan. *Theatre in Australia*. Melbourne: Cheshire, 1947.

Andrews, Barry. 'The Federal Government as Literary Patron'. *Meanjin*, 41:1, 1977: pp. 3–19.

Arrow, Michelle. *Upstaged: Australian Women Dramatists in the Limelight at Last*. Sydney: Currency Press, 2002.

Assmann, Jan. 'Collective Memory and Cultural Identity' (trans. John Czaplika). *New German Critique*, 65, 1995, pp. 125–33.

Australian Broadcasting Corporation. *The Eleventh* with Alex Mann, radio podcast. 17 February–24 March 2020. <www.abc.net.au/radio/programs/the-eleventh/> (last accessed 4 October 2021).

Australian Government. Royal Commission into Aboriginal Deaths in Custody 1987–1991. *Report* (Elliott Johnston Commissioner). 1991. <www.austlii.edu.au/au/other/IndigLRes/rciadic/> (last accessed 8 December 2021).

Australian Human Rights Commission. *Bringing them home: the 'Stolen children' report*, 1997. Australian Human Rights Commission. Sydney, 2010 <bth.humanrights.gov.au/sites/default/files/documents/bringing_them_home_report.pdf>

Bach, Stanley. 'The Crisis of 1974–1975' in *Platypus and Parliament: The Australian Senate in Theory and Practice*, 2003, np. <www.aph.gov.au/About_Parliament/Senate/Powers_practice_n_procedures/platparl/c04> (last accessed 24 October 2021).

Bollen, Jonathon, Bruce Parr & Adrian Kiernander. *Men at play: Masculinities in Australian theatre since the 1950s* (Australian playwrights; monograph no. 11). Amsterdam: Rodopi, 2008.

Bower, Tony. *Broken Vows: The Tragedy of Power*. London: Faber and Faber, 2016.

Brisbane, Katharine. *Not Wrong just Different: Observations on the Rise of Contemporary Australian Theatre*. Sydney: Currency Press, 2005.

Carr, Adam. 'The Wowsers' Last Stand'. *Outrage*, June 1997, np.

Casey, Maryrose. *Creating Frames: Contemporary Indigenous Theatre 1967–1990*. St Lucia, Qld: University of Queensland Press, 2004.

Clark, Manning. *A Short History of Australia* (3rd rev. edn). New York: NAL Penguin, 1987.

Comans, Christine A. *La Boite: The Story of an Australian Theatre Company*. Brisbane: Playlab Press, 2009.

Darnton, Robert. *The Great Cat Massacre and Other Episodes in French Cultural History*. New York: Basic Books, 1984.

Department of Communications and the Arts. *Creative Nation: Commonwealth Cultural Policy, October 1994*. Canberra: Department of Communications and the Arts, 1994.

Department of Regional Australia, Local Government, Arts and Sport, *Creative Australia: National Cultural Policy*. Canberra: Department of Regional Australia, Local Government, Arts and Sport, 2013.

Dunlop, Tim. *The Future of Everything: Big, Audacious Ideas for a Better World*. Sydney: New South Publishing, 2018.

Dutton, Geoffrey. *The Australian Heroes: A Rousing Roll Call of 47 of Australia's Greatest Heroes and Heroines*. Sydney: Angus & Robertson, 1981.

Eltham, Benjamin. *When the Goal Posts Move: Patronage, Power and Resistance in Australian Cultural Policy 2013–16*. Sydney: Currency House, 2016.

Fensham, Rachel and Denise Varney. *The Dolls' Revolution: Australian Theatre and Cultural Imagination*. Melbourne: Australian Scholarly Publishing, 2005.

Fisher, Mark. *Ghosts of My Life: Writings on Depression, Hauntology and Lost Futures*. Winchester, Washington: Zero Books, 2014.

Fitzpatrick, Peter. *After 'The Doll': Australian Drama Since 1955*. Melbourne: Edward Arnold, 1979.

Fleming, Peter. *Dark Academia: How Universities Die*. London: Pluto Press, 2021.

Fuhrmann, Andrew. 'Patrick White: A Theatre of his Own'. *Australian Book Review*, 356, November 2013. <www.australianbookreview.com.au/abr-online/archive/2013/108-november-2013-no-356/1695-a-theatre-of-his-own> (last accessed 10 October 2021).

Fukuyama, Francis. *The End of History and the Last Man*. London: Avon Books, 1992.

Gilbert, Helen & Joanne Tompkins. *Post-Colonial Drama: Theory, Practice, Politics*. London: Routledge, 1996.

Grey, Edward, Viscount Grey of Fallodon. Twenty-Five Years, 1892–1916. London: Hodder and Stoughton, 1928.

Halliwell, Stephen. *Aristotle's Poetics*. London: Duckworth, 1986.

Harper, Ken. 'The Useful Theatre: The New Theatre Movement in Sydney and Melbourne 1935–1983'. *Meanjin*, 43:1, 1984: pp. 56–71.

Hirsch, Marianne. 'The Generation of Postmemory'. *Poetics*, 29:1, Spring, 2008, pp. 103–128.

Hobsbawm, Eric. *The Age of Extremes: A History of the World, 1914–1991*. New York: Pantheon Books, 1996.

Horne, Donald. *In the Open*. Pymble, NSW: Harper Collins, 2000.

Horne, Donald. *The Death of the Lucky Country*. Ringwood, Vic: Penguin Books, 1976.

Horne, Donald. *The Lucky Country*. Melbourne: Penguin, 1964.

Horne, Donald. *Time of Hope: Australia 1966–72*. Sydney: Angus & Robertson, 1980.

Jaivin, Linda. 'Middle-Power Might: A Plan for Dealing with China'. *Australian Foreign Affairs*, 11, Feb 2021: pp. 71–92.

Kelly, Veronica. *The Empire Actors: Stars of Australasian Costume Drama 1890s–1920s*. Sydney: Currency House, 2009.

Kent, Jacqueline. *Take Your Best Shot: the Prime Ministership of Julia Gillard*. Melbourne: Penguin, 2013.

Kippax, HG. 'Australian drama since *Summer of the Seventeenth Doll*'. *Meanjin Quarterly*, No. 23, 1964: pp. 229–42.

Kippax, HG. 'Introduction' in Alan Seymour, Hal Porter, and Douglas Stewart. *Three Australian Plays*. Ringwood, Vic: Penguin, 1963.

Koestler, Arthur. *The Ghost in the Machine*. London: Hutchinson, 1967.

Kumm, Elizabeth. 'Theatre in Melbourne, 1914–18: The Best, the Brightest and the Latest' 2016. <www.slv.vic.gov.au/sites/default/files/La-Trobe-Journal-97-Elisabeth-Kumm.pdf> (last accessed 19 August 2021).

Macdonnell, Justin. *Arts, Minister?: Government Policy and the Arts*. Sydney: Currency Press, 1992.

Macintyre, Stuart. *A Concise History of Australia* (5th edn). Melbourne: Cambridge University Press, 2020.

Macintyre, Stuart. *Australia's Boldest Experiment: War and Reconstruction in the 1940s*. Sydney: New South Publishing, 2015.

McCallum, John. *Belonging: Australian Playwriting in the 20th Century.* Sydney: Currency Press, 2009.

McQueen, Humphrey. *Social Sketches of Australia.* Ringwood, Vic: Penguin, 1991.

Meyrick, Julian. 'Are You With Me? Offensiveness and Australian Drama in the 1970s' with Jenny Fewster. *The Routledge Companion to Australian Literature* (ed. Jessica Gildersleeve). New York: Routledge, 2021: pp. 85–98.

Meyrick, Julian. *Australian Theatre After the New Wave: Policy, Subsidy and the Australian Artist.* Amsterdam: Brill, 2017.

Meyrick, Julian. 'Patrick White, Spoiled Identity and Failure as a Logic of Use'. *Australasian Drama Studies*, 71, October 2017. pp. 42–67.

Meyrick, Julian. 'It's Not Simple Stupid: Re-Reading Margaret Williams on New Wave Drama'. *Double Dialogues,* 11 (Winter), 2009. <www.doubledialogues.com/article/its-not-simple-stupid-re-reading-margaret-williams-on-new-wave-drama/> (last accessed 10 July, 2016).

Meyrick, Julian. *See How It Runs: Nimrod and the New Wave.* Sydney: Currency Press, 2002.

Midford, Sarah. 'Bean's Anzac Book Shaped How Australians Think about Gallipoli'. *The Conversation*, 9 April 2015. <theconversation.com/beans-anzac-book-shaped-how-australians-think-about-gallipoli-38203> (last accessed 10 October 2021).

Milne, Geoffrey. *Theatre Australia (un)Limited: Australian Theatre Since the 1950s.* Amsterdam: Rodopi, 2004.

Mitchell, Heather. *Brodie's Notes on Michael Gow's Away.* Sydney: Pan Books, 1988.

Palmer, Vance. 'What is Significant in us Will Survive' in *The Words that Made Australia: How a Nation Came to Know Itself* (ed. Manne, Robert & Chris Feik). Collingwood, Vic: Black Inc, 2014: pp. 69–71.

Phillips, Arthur Angell. *On the Cultural Cringe.* Melbourne University Publishing, 2006.

Piketty, Thomas. *Capital in the Twenty-First Century* (trans. Arthur Goldhammer). Cambridge Massachusetts: The Belknap Press of Harvard University Press, 2014.

Piketty, Thomas. *Capital and Ideology* (trans. Arthur Goldhammer). Cambridge Massachusetts: The Belknap Press of Harvard University Press, 2020.

Pusey, Michael. *Economic Rationalism in Canberra: A Nation-Building State Changes its Mind*. New York: Cambridge University Press, 1991.

Rees, Leslie. *The Making of Australian Drama from the 1830s to the late 1960s, vol 1*. (rev. edn). Sydney: Angus & Robertson, 1978.

Rees, Leslie. *Australian Drama in the 1970s, vol. 2*. Sydney: Angus & Robertson, 1978.

Rees, Leslie. *The Making of Australian Drama: A Historical and Critical Survey from the 1830s to the 1970s*. Sydney: Angus & Robertson, 1973.

Reynolds, Henry. *Why Weren't We Told? A Personal Search for the Truth of our History*. Ringwood, Vic: Viking, 1999.

Rickard, John. *Australia: A Cultural History* (3rd edn). Clayton, Vic: Monash University Publishing, 2017.

Ross, John (editor-in-chief). *Chronicle of the 20th Century*. Ringwood, Vic: Chronicle Australia, 1990.

Rousseau, Jean-Jacques. 'The Social Contract' in *Social Contract, Locke, Hume, Rousseau*. Introduction Sir Ernest Barker. Oxford University Press, 1960.

Schultz, Julianne. 'Facing Foundational Wrongs: Careful What you Wish For'. *Griffith Review*, 73, 2021: pp. 11–25.

Standing, Guy. *The Precariat: The New Dangerous Class*. London: Bloomsbury Academic, 2011.

Sumner, John. *Recollections at Play: A Life in Australian Theatre*. Melbourne University Press, 1993.

Suzuki, David and Ian Hannington. *Just Cool It: the Climate Crisis and What We Can Do, a Post-Paris Agreement*. Sydney: New South Publishing, 2017.

Tait, Peta. *Converging Realities: Feminism in Australian Theatre*. Sydney: Currency Press, 1994.

Tallis, Michael & Joan Tallis. *The Silent Showman: Sir George Tallis, the Man Behind the World's Largest Entertainment Organisation of the 1920s*. Kent Town, SA: Wakefield Press, 1999.

Taylor, Charles. *Modern Social Imaginaries*. Public Planet Books. Durham: Duke University Press, 2004.

Toose, Adam. *Crashed: How a Decade of Financial Crises Changed the World*. London: Allen Lane, 2018.

Ward, Stuart. 'Culture up to our Arseholes: Projecting Post-Imperial

Australia'. *Australian Journal of Politics and History*, 51:1, 2005: pp. 53-66.

Weber, M. (trans AM Henderson & Talcott Parsons). 'The Types of Authority and Imperative Coordination' in *The Theory of Social and Economic Organisation*. New York: Oxford University Press. 1947.

White, Patrick. *Four Plays*. Melbourne: Sun Books, 1967.

Wild, Rex and Patricia Anderson. *Ampe Akelyernemane Meke Mekarle: 'Little Children are Sacred'*. Northern Territory Government. Board Of Inquiry Into The Protection Of Aboriginal Children From Sexual Abuse. 2007, <www.nt.gov.au/dcm/inquirysaac/pdf/bipacsa_final_report.pdf> (accessed 8 December 2021).

Williams, Margaret. *Drama*. Melbourne. Oxford UP. 1977.

Williams, Margaret. 'Natural Sexuality: Katharine Prichard's "Brumby Innes"'. *Meanjin* 32:1, 1976: pp. 91–93.

Williams, Margaret. 'Snakes and Ladders'. *Meanjin* 31:2, 1972: pp. 179–82.

Williams, Margaret. 'Mask and Cage'. *Meanjin* 31:3, 1972: pp. 308–13.

Williams, Margaret. 'Australian Drama—A Postscript: Some Comments on Recent Criticism'. *Meanjin,* No. 31, No. 4, 1972: pp. 444–8.

White, Patrick. Letter to John Sumner, 25 October 1964. Copy in author's possession.

Wolf, Gabrielle. *Make It Australian: The Australian Performing Group, the Pram Factory and New Wave Theatre*. Sydney: Currency Press, 2008.

Uncited works on Australian drama

Buzo, Alex. *The Young Person's Guide to the Theatre and Almost Everything Else*. Melbourne: Penguin, 1988.

Capelin, Steve (ed.) *Challenging the Centre: Two Decades of Political Theatre*. Brisbane: Playlab Press, 1995.

Carroll, Dennis. *Australian Contemporary Drama* (rev. edn). Sydney: Currency Press, 1995.

Fotheringham, Richard and James Smith. *Catching Australian Theatre in the 2000s*. Amsterdam: Brill, 2013.

Gilbert, Helen. *Sightlines: Race, Gender, and Nation in Contemporary Australian Theatre*. Ann Arbor: University of Michigan Press, 1998.

Glow, Hilary. *Power Plays: Australian Theatre and the Public Agenda*. Sydney: Currency Press, 2007.

Hamilton, Margaret. *Transfigured Stages Major Practitioners and Theatre Aesthetics in Australia*. (Australian Playwrights; Vol.14). Amsterdam: Rodopi, 2011.

Healy, Connie. *Defiance: Political Theatre in Brisbane 1930–1962*. Brisbane: Boombana Publications, 2000.

Hibberd, Jack (ed.) *Meanjin: Performing Arts in Australia* (special edition), March, 1984.

Holloway, Peter (ed.) *Contemporary Australian Drama* (2nd edn). Sydney: Currency Press, 1987.

Kardoss, John. *A brief history of the Australian theatre*. Sydney: Sydney University Dramatic Society, University of Sydney, 1955.

Kelly, Veronica (ed.) *Our Australian Theatre in the 1990s*. Amsterdam: Rodopi, 1998.

Kippax, Harry, *A Leader of his Craft: Theatre Reviews* (ed. Harry Heseltine). Sydney: Currency House, 2004.

McCallum, John. 'Studying Australian Drama'. *Australasian Drama Studies Journal*. 12/13, 1988: pp. 147–166.

McGuire, Paul, Betty Arnott, and Frances Margaret McGuire. *The Australian Theatre: An Abstract and Brief Chronicle in Twelve Parts*. Melbourne: Oxford University Press, 1948.

Meanjin Quarterly. Special drama edition. No. 23, 1964.

Murphet, Richard. *Acts of Resistance in Late-Modernist Theatre*. Amsterdam: Brill, 2019.

Parsons, Philip (ed.) *Companion to Theatre in Australia*. Sydney: Currency Press in Association with Cambridge University Press, 1995.

Radic, Leonard. *Contemporary Australian Drama*. Blackheath, NSW: Brandl & Schlesinger, 2006.

Radic, Leonard. *The State of Play: The Revolution in the Australian Theatre Since the 1960s*. Ringwood, Vic: Penguin Books, 1991.

Rees, Leslie. *Towards an Australian Drama*. Sydney: Angus and Robertson, 1953.

Varney, Denise. *Radical Visions 1968–2008: The Impact of the Sixties on Australian Drama*. (Australian playwrights; vol. 13). Amsterdam: Rodopi, 2011.

Index

Page numbers in *italics* refer to photographs.

Abbott, Tony 242
Aborigines *see* Indigenous Australians
Aborigines Progressive Association 76
Absurdism 122
Adams, Arthur 53–4, 130
Adcock, Danny 220
Adelaide Festival of the Arts 106–7, 122, 244–5
Adelaide Review 119
Adelaide Symphony Orchestra 62
Adelaide University Theatre Guild 122
Adeson, Lilias 26
Afford, Max 62, 79–83, 85, 222
After the Doll (Fitzpatrick) 90
The Age 119
The Age of Extremes (Hobsbawm) 206
Akhmatova, Anna 211–12
Aldous, Allan 2
alternative theatre 4, 139
America Hurrah! 138
Anderson, Maxwell 84
Anderson, Tammy 227
Anderson, William 23, 25, 33

Andrews, Barry 12
Anglo-Japanese Naval Treaty (1902) 34
anti-war protests 131–2
Anzac Day 98–101
ANZAC legend 38–9
Argus 38
Aristotle 106
Arrow, Michelle 93
Arts, Minister? (Macdonnell) 167
assimilation 74, 107
Assman, Jan 226
Auden, WH 84
AusStage 222
Australia Council 12–13, 92, 166, 242–3
Australia First 65
The Australian 119
Australian Aborigines League 76
Australian accent 102
Australian Broadcasting Commission 62, 83
Australian Broadcasting Corporation 117
Australian Council for the Arts 13, 92, 242
Australian Council of Trade Unions 163
Australian Elizabethan Theatre Trust 13, 90, 92
The Australian Heroes (Dutton) 85
Australian Human Rights and Equal Opportunity Commission 229

Australian identity 62, 293
Australian Labor Party 65, 135, 152–4, 160–1, 178, 206, 209, 242, 264
Australian Performing Group 11, 16, 135, 138, 144, 166
Australian theatre *see* theatre, in Australia
Australian Theatre After the New Wave (Meyrick) 139, 167
Australian Theatre Society 2
Awake My Love (Afford) 85
Away (Gow) 132, 159, 168, 188–92, 198–9
Aziz, Riza 270

Bailey, Bert 25, 26, 33, 53, 56
Baracchi, Guido 57
Barker, Howard 168
Barlow, WC 138
Barnes, Michael 97
Barry, Joan 122
basic wage 32, 73
BBC 201
Bean, CEW 37–9
Beckett Theatre 192
Bedford, Randolph 33
Bell, Hilary 191
Belonging (McCallum) 209

Index   325

Belvoir Street Theatre
10, 135, 268
Bennett, Gordon 89–90
Bentley, Eric 125
Berlin 121
Berlin Wall 201
Berrell, Lloyd 97
The Berry Man
(Cornelius) 53
Bertram, Arthur 26
Betty Blokk Buster Follies
(Livermore) 276
Betty Can Jump 136
Betzien, Angela 243,
249, 251–2
Bevan, Alfreda 26
Beynon, Richard 108
BHP Slab Caster *171*
bikinis 122
biopower 51
Bjelke-Petersen, Joh 165
Black is the New White
(Lui) 238, 261–7,
274–5, 279, 281
Black Lives Matter movement 240
Black Medea (Enoch)
200, 210–11, 227–8,
231–3, 252, 256
Black Swan State Theatre
Company 166
Blackrock (film) 222
Blackrock (play) 222
Blair, Ron 136
Blair, Tony 238
Blake, Julia 211, 216
The Bleeding Tree
(Cerini) 238,
253–60, 266, 269
*The Blind Giant is
Dancing* (Sewell)
159, 167–75, 177–9,
181, 204, 253, 260
Blundell, Graeme 138–9
Boddy, Michael 125,
136

Bollen, Jonathan 101
Bovell, Andrew 243–5,
247–8
Bower, Tony 238
Boyd, Arthur 61
The Boys in the Band
(Crowley) 138, 276
Bramwell, Murray 246
Bran Nue Dae (Chi) 227
Brand, Mona 108, 113,
115, 251
Brandis, George 12,
242–3
Brecht, Bertolt 122, 222
Brennan, Niall 102–3
Brexit 239
Bringing Them Home
229
Brink Productions 245,
247
Brisbane, Katharine
112–13, 119–20
British Empire 60–1
Broadway 79, 82
Brodie's Notes 168, 189,
191
Brodsky, Leon 1–2, 8,
208
Broken Vows (Bower)
238
Brumby Innes (Prichard)
37, 42, 46–53, 67,
78, 96, 155, 174
Bull, Hilda 29, 93
The Bulletin 22, 32
burlesque 276
Bush, George Snr 202
the bush, in theatre
66–70, 155
bushfires 244
Buzo, Alex 13, 125,
138–9

cabaret 276
Cairns, Jim 163
The Cake Man (Merritt)
119, 134, 148–9,
151–2, 155, 157–8,
183, 228
Call of the Wild (Kemp)
159, 168, 188, 192,
194–9, 228
Calwell, Arthur 107
Cantwell, Michaela 245
Capital and Ideology
(Piketty) 239
*Capital in the Twenty-
First Century*
(Piketty) 239
capitalism 164, 204–5,
239–40
Capitalism and Freedom
(Friedman) 175
Capitol building, storming of 240
Carr, Adam 138
Casey, Maryrose 184–5,
187
caste 274–5
Catspaw (Hewitt) 144
Ceau escu, Nicolae 201
censorship 8, 12–13,
111, 138–9
Cerini, Angus 102, 243,
253–5, 258, 260, 277
The Chapel Perilous
(Hewett) 119, 134,
143–4, *144*, 151–2,
155
Chase, Glace 243, 261,
276–81
A Cheery Soul (White)
10, 53, 85, 119, 122,
125–30, 155–6, 188,
231, 256
The Cherry Pickers
(Gilbert) 148
Chi, Jimmy 227

Chifley, Ben 91, 178
China 202, 240
Churchill, Caryl 168
Churchill, Winston 38
CIA 171
cinema 14, 41
Clark, Manning 18, 63, 83, 132, 183, 205, 282, 293
class 102, 110–12, 274–5
Clinton, Bill 202
Co-Curious 268
Coalition government 91, 121, 160–2, 178, 242
Cold War 117, 164, 201
Colebatch, Tim 162–3
colonialism 4–5, 60–1, 121
Comans, Christine 47
Commonwealth Literary Fund 12
Commonwealth of Nations 60–1
communism 111, 164, 201
Communist Party of Australia 50, 65, 92
comparative advantage 177
compelling mood, in plays 82–3, 87, 94
Compton, Jennifer 134, 250
A Concise History of Australia (Macintyre) 17–18, 107–8, 241
conscription 65, 131–2
Contemporary Art Society 61–2
Conversations with the Dead (Frankland) 200, 210–11, 227–8, 233–7, 253, 257

Coomaraswamy, Radhika 261, 268
Coombs, Herbert 'Nugget' 91–2
Corden, Max 178
Cornelius, Patricia 53, 71, 102, 243, 253, 256, 260
corruption 165, 269–70, 280
Council for the Encouragement of Music and the Arts 91–2
Counting and Cracking (Shakthidharan) 238, 243, 261–3, 266–70, 268, 272–5, 278
Country Party 91
see also Coalition government
Covid 18, 241, 243, 277
Crashed (Toose) 239
Creative Australia (cultural policy) 242
Creative Australia Advisory Committee 242
Creative Nation (cultural policy) 8, 206–9, 242
Crenshaw, Kimberlé 260
Crossfire (previously *No Man's Land*) (Compton) 119, 134, 149–52, 155–6, 158, 211, 250
Crowley, Mart 275–6
Cuba 121
Cuban Missile Crisis 200
cultural activism 204
cultural cringe 2–3, 61, 119, 159
cultural diversity 12

cultural history 6–7
cultural memory 226
cultural policy 8, 12, 92, 206–9, 242
culture 284, 288, 294
Currency Press 119
Curtin, John 65, 71, 91
Curtina, Frank 97
Cusack, Dymphna 61, 71, 79, 93, 113, 123, 155, 255
Czechoslovakia 164, 201

Dann, George Landen 71, 74–5, 77, 79
Dark Academia (Fleming) 240
The Dark Room (Betzien) 238, 249–53, 255, 259, 278
Darnton, Robert 6–7, 293
Darwin 71
Davis, Jack 183–5, 187
Davis, James 122
Davis, Susan 74
The Day Before Tomorrow (Throssell) 89, 108–12, 116–17, 211
De Groen, Alma 214, 246
Deakin, Alfred 2, 12, 56
The Death of the Lucky Country (Horne) 159–60
Dee, Suzie 253
deindustrialisation 177, 206
democracy 289–91
Democratic Labor Party 121
Dingo, Ernie 184
directors 199

The Dismissal 160–5, 171
Diving for Pearls (Thomson) 159, 167–8, 173–80, 182, 198, 225, 236, 260
The Doll's Revolution (Fensham, and Varney) 192
domestic violence 258
Don's Party (Williamson) 8, 119, 134, 144–6, 151–2, 155
Drake-Brockman, Henrietta 67, 70–1, 93
drama 7–8, 123, 282–8, 294–5
  see also plays; theatre, in Australia
Driscoll, Willie 26
Drummond, Chris 247
Duggan, Edmund 26, 33
Duncan, Catherine 93
Dunlop, Tim 239–40
Dutton, Geoffrey 85, 122

economic rationalism 164–5, 177, 209
Economic Rationalism in Canberra (Pusey) 177
Edgar, David 168
Eichmann, Adolf 121
The Eleventh (television series) 165
Eliot, TS 84
Elliott, Sumner Locke *see* Locke Elliott, Sumner
Ellis, Bob 125

Eltham, Ben 243
The Empire Actors (Kelly) 23
employment 239
The End of History (Fukuyama) 203–5
Enoch, Wesley 227, 231–2, 252
Enright, Nick 222
Entertainment Tax 8
epic theatre 122
Esson, Louis 24, 29, 31–2, 35, 42, 79, 123
Euripides 229
Europe (Gow) 53
Everage, Dame Edna 128
expressionism 122

Federation 1, 3, 5, 18–22, *21*, 61, 63, 138
Fellowship of Australian Writers 61
Fensham, Rachel 192
Fifield, Mitch 12
film 14, 41
Finlayson, Don 275
Fire on the Snow (Stewart) 25
The Firm *see* JC Williamson Ltd
Fitton, Doris 93
Fitzgerald Inquiry 165
Fitzpatrick, Peter 29, 90, 98–9
Flack, Eamon 243
Fleming, Peter 240
The Floating World (Romeril) 53, 119, 134, 147–8, 151–2, 155
Forrest River/

Oombulgurri massacre 185
The Forty Lounge Cafe (Lyssiotis) 159, 168, 188, *192*, 192–5, 221, 228, 246
Fotheringham, Richard 54
Foucault, Michel 51
Fountains Beyond (Dann) 60, 71, 74–9, 88, 101, 103, 155, 175, 183
Four-Power Treaty (1921) 34
Frankland, Richard J 233–5
Franklin, Miles 61
Fraser, Anne 102
Fraser, Malcolm 160, 162–3, 178
Frazer, Ronald 97
Freewheels Youth Theatre 222
Freud, Sigmund 276
Friedman, Milton 175
Fuhrmann, Andrew 126
Fukuyama, Francis 200, 202–6, 237
Fullers (entrepreneurs) 23
The Future of Everything (Dunlop) 239

Gagarin, Yuri 121
Gallipoli 38
Gallipoli Bill (Adams) 37, 53–6, 130
Garrett, Peter 242
gender 101–2, 112, 124, 151, 260, 275–6
gender pay gap 32
George V, King 37

328   Index

Germany 111, 201
The Ghost in the Machine (Koestler) 142
Gilbert, Helen 4–5
Gilbert, Kevin 148
Gillard, Julia 239
global economy 178
Global Financial Crisis (2007–8) 239
The Golden Age (Nowra) 10
Gorbachev, Mikhail 201–2
government policy *see* cultural policy
Gow, Michael 53, 192, 199
grant applications 11–12
Grant, Quincy 247
Granville-Barker, Harley 2
Gray, Oriel 90, 108, 123
The Great Cat Massacre (Darnton) 6–7
Great Depression 64, 104, 185
The Great Man (Prichard) 56
Greek drama 14–15, 256, 259, 261, 286
Grey, Sir Edward 37
Griffin Theatre 191, 295
Guglielmo, Carmelina 192

Hagen's Circus (radio serial) 62
Hair 138, 276
The Ham Funeral (White) 85, 122
Hamer, Sir Rupert 'Dick' 13
Hamlet on Ice (Boddy and Blair) 11, 136

Hannington, Ian 239
Harding, John 227
Hare, David 168
Harford, Alfred 26
Harris, Max 122
Harrison, Jane 8, 229
Harvester judgement 32, 73
Hastings, Guy 26
Havel, Václav 201
Hawke, Bob 163, 177–8, 209
Hawthorne, Nathaniel 18
Hegel, Georg 203–4
Here Under Heaven (Brand) 89, 108–15, 127, 215, 251, 281
Hewett, Dorothy 10, 134, 144
Hewson, John 207
Hibberd, Jack 71, 102, 134, 136
hierarchy 142
Higgins, Justice 32
High Court of Australia 78, 205–6
Hirsch, Marianne 267
Hirst, John 19
history 183, 226
A History of Australia (Clark) 83, 183, 293
A History of Australian Drama (Rees) 1, 50
Hitchcock, Alfred 281
Hobsbawm, Eric 200, 206, 211
holarchy 142
Hole in the Wall 16
Hollingworth, May 93
holons 142, 210
Holt, Bland 22, 56
homosexuality *see* LGBTQI+ themes
Honi Soit 99

Honour (Murray-Smith) 200, 210–11, 216–18, 221
Hopgood, Alan 125, 133
Horne, Donald 2, 137, 154, 159–60, 165
Howard, John 208
Hughes, Billy 34, 65
Humphries, Barry 128
Hungry Ghosts (Tong) 238, 262, 266–7, 269–72, 274–5, 280
Hunt, Hugh 90
Hutton, Geoffrey 119

I Don't Wanna Play House (Anderson) 227
I Love You 138
Ibsen, Henrik 2
Ilbijerri Theatre Cooperative 227
immigration 63–4, 107–8
independent theatre 4, 46–7
Independent Theatre, North Sydney 93, 97
India 61
Indigenous Australians
  decimation of 226
  displacement of 4
  federal intervention (2007) 249
  frontier wars 291
  in *Brumby Innes* 47, 50–2
  in *Conversations with the Dead* 233–7
  in *Fountains Beyond* 74–7
  in *Here Under Heaven* 113
  in *No Sugar* 183–8

in *Stolen* 227–31
in *The Cake Man* 148–9
in Western Australia 183–4
Indigenous playwrights 8, 148, 227, 233
Jindyworobak movement 62
Lui on Aboriginal identity 262–3
paying respect to 294
protest by 76
removal of children from families of 51, 229
Whitlam attempts to give vote to 121
individualism 204, 241, 283–4, 292
Inquiry into the Separation of Aboriginal and Torres Strait Islander Children from their Families 229
Inside the Island (Nowra) 112, 159, 168, 179–83, 217
intersectionality 260–1
Ionesco, Eugene 122
Iraq 239
irony 87, 101, 130
isolationism 64

Jaivin, Linda 240
Jakeš, Miloš 201
J&N Tait 23, 41
Jane Street Theatre, Sydney 135–6
Japan 33–4, 65, 71

The Jazz Singer (film) 40
JC Williamson Ltd (The Firm) 3–5, 8, 23, 41–2, 79, 92, 123, 165–6
Jindyworobak movement 62
JobKeeper 243
Johnson, Carmel 245
Jones, Barry 206
Jung, Carl 121, 128, 227
Just Cool It! (Suzuki and Hannington) 239

Kahahanas, Evolskia 192
Kalive, Petra 270–1
Kammallaweera, Nadie 268
Keating, Paul 8, 163, 177–8, 206–7, 207, 209
Keene, Daniel 53, 102
Kelly, Dan 85
Kelly, Ned 85, 87
Kelly, Veronica 23, 33–4
Kemp, Jenny 192, 195–9
Kemp, Roger 196
Kenna, Peter 276
Kennedy, JF 121
Kent, Jacqueline 239
Kerr, Sir John 160
Keynes, John Maynard 91
King Lear (Shakespeare) 190
King, Martin Luther 108
Kingsmill, John 97
Kippax, HG (Harry) 119, 122–3, 126, 137, 140, 260
Kisch, Egon 64
Knowles, Vernon 12

Koestler, Arthur 142
Kumm, Elisabeth 3–4

La Boite (Comans) 47
La Boite Theatre 93
La Mama Theatre 16, 135
Lady in Danger (Afford) 60, 79–83, 88, 101
A Ladybird Book of Travel Adventure 60, 88
Lalevich, Rosie 192
Lanseck, Ben 22
The Last Man (Fukuyama) 203
Laver, Rod 121
Lawler, Ray 8, 53, 70, 89–90, 94–5, 102–3, 106, 155
The Legend of King O'Malley (Boddy and Ellis) 119, 125–6, 134–8, 140
Lehrstücke 222, 225
LGBTQI+ themes 275–81
liberal democracy 203–5
Liberal Party 91
see also Coalition government
liberalism 283, 292
Life After George (Rayson) 200, 210–11, 214–18, 220–1
Lighthouse 166
Lindsay, Norman 83–4
literary managers 9–10
literature 61
Little Children Are Sacred 249
Little theatre 4, 46–7, 167

Livermore, Reg 276
Locke Elliott, Sumner 13, 62, 94–6, 98, 101, 106, 276
The Long Way Home (Keene) 53
Lorca, Federico Garcia 122
The Lucky Country (Horne) 159
Lui, Nakkiah 243, 261–6
Lyssiotis, Tes 192–4, 221, 246

Mabo decision 78, 205–6
Macarthur, Douglas 71
Macdonald, Fred 26
Macdonnell, Justin 167
Macintyre, Stuart
  as a source 17
  on a new world order 164–5
  on Federation 21–2
  on Indigenous Australians 51
  on postwar migration 107–8
  on regional Australia 70
  on the 1990s 205–6
  on the last 20 years 241
  on the post-war era 91
  on the Vietnam War 132
  on the Whitlam government 153–4
  on World War I 39–40
Macky, Stewart 29

Maeterlinck, Maurice 122
Mailman, Deborah 227
Malaysia 270
Malaysian Airlines flight 370 270–1
The Man from Outback (Bailey and Duggan) 33
Mann, Alex 165
Mannix, Daniel 65
manufacturing 177
Maralinga nuclear tests 117
Marlowe, Mary 26
marriage bar 72
Marvellous Melbourne (Hibberd and Romeril) 136, 138
Marxism 110–11, 204, 261
masculinity 58, 101–2, 198
Maslow, Abraham 6
Mates (Kenna) 276
mateship 96
McCallum, John 67, 80, 90, 209
Mcguffins 281
McIntosh, Hugh D 23
McMahon, Gregan 29, 46
McQueen, Humphrey 90–1
Me Too movement 240
Mead, Chris 9
Meanjin 50, 137
Medea (Euripides) 229
Melbourne Repertory Theatre 29, 42
Melbourne Symphony Orchestra 62
Melbourne Theatre Company 8–9, 89, 166, 222

melodrama 78–9, 287
memory 94, 267
men *see* masculinity
Men at Play (Bollen, Kiernander and Parr) 101–2
Men Without Wives (Drake-Brockman) 60, 66–71, 78, 82, 96, 103, 155, 180
Menzies, Robert 91, 178
Merritt, Robert 134
meta-theatrical plays 188
Metropolitan Theatre 93
Meynell and Gunn 23
Meyrick, Julian 8–9, 139
Midford, Sarah 39
Miller, Harry M 276
Milne, Geoffrey 209
Milroy, David 227
Mitchell, Sir James 185
Modernism 122–3, 140
monocratic bureaucracy 291
Moore River Settlement 184–5
Morning Sacrifice (Cusack) 60, 71–4, 78–9, 88, 96, 101, 155, 215, 255
Morosi, Junie 163
Mulvany, Kate 219, 220
Murdoch, Keith 38
Murray-Smith, Joanna 217–18
music 62
My Brilliant Career (Franklin) 61

National Institute of Dramatic Art 10

The National Interest
    202
National Programme for
    Excellence in the
    Arts 242
national theatre 91–3
National Theatre
    Company 166
nationhood 287–8,
    292–4
NATO 201
Nazi Party 111
Ned Kelly (Stewart) 60,
    83–8, 84, 102, 155,
    169–70, 219, 253,
    255
needs, hierarchy of 6
neoliberalism 164–5,
    177–8, 240–1, 264,
    284, 288
Netflix 118
Neville, AO 184
Nevin, Robyn 127
New Fortune Theatre,
    Perth 144, *144*
New Guard 65
New Theatre League
    57, 92–3, 108, *110*,
    110–11, 166–7, 205
New Wave
    beginning of
        119–21
    companies
        associated with 16
    diversity in creativity
        of 135, 158
    holarchic relations
        in New Wave plays
        142
    influence of Vietnam
        War on 133
    key examples of
        125, 135–6, 152,
        158
    Roy Rene's 'Mo'

becomes an icon
    for *41*
social and political
    backdrop to 154
use of stereotype as
    a dramatic device
    112, 137
view of the 'best'
    Australian drama
    124
New Zealand 21
Nietzsche, Friedrich 204
Night on Bald Mountain
    (White) 10, 122
Nimrod Theatre 10–11,
    16, 135, 166, 276
Nixon, Richard 161
No Sugar (Davis) 159,
    168, 179, 183–8,
    191, 195, 228
No Way To Forget
    (Frankland) 233
Nolan, Sidney 61, 84
non-commercial theatre
    4
Norm and Ahmed (Buzo)
    13, 119, 125, 138–41
Nowra, Louis 10,
    179–81, 199
Number 96 (television
    program) 275
Nureyev, Rudolf 121
Nyoongarah people
    183–4

O Calcutta! 138
Odets, Clifford 92
oil crisis (1973) 162
Old Tote Theatre 166
O'Malley, King 135–6,
    138
On Our Selection (Rudd)
    19, 24–8, 26, 31, 34,

52, 56, 155, 179
The One Day of the Year
    (Seymour) 89, 94–5,
    98–102, 104, 106,
    114, 128, 211, 223,
    260
OPEC 162
Operation Buffalo (documentary) 117
Ordell, Tal 53, 56
The Oresteia 15
Oswald, Debra 102
'Other', the 43, 107–
    118, 275, 291
Overton, Joseph P 202
Overton Window 202
Ozucelik, Yalin 245

painting 61–2
Palmer, Nettie 61
Palmer, Vance 29, 65–6
pandemic 241
Pankhurst, Adela 65
pantomime 276
Parkes, Sir Henry 20
Parsons, Philip 29, 119
Pearson, Noel 292
Peterson, Ralph 97
Pfisterer, Susan 73
Phillips, AA 2–3, 61, 83,
    86, 159
Phillips, Anna Lise 245
Pigot, Neil 244
Piketty, Thomas 239
Pioneer Players 29, 47,
    56
Playbox Theatre 192
plays
    characteristics of
        14–16
    characters in 53,
        260, 286–7
    cluster tendency
        118

comedy 286
compelling mood in 82–3, 87, 94
defined 14
dialogue in 15
LGBTQI+ themes 275–81
melodrama and beyond 78–9
meta-theatrical plays 188
narratives 285–6
performance of 123
programming of 9, 123–4, 166, 295
Poetics (Aristotle) 106
Poland 201
Post-Colonial Drama: Theory, Practice, Politics (Gilbert and Tompkins) 5
post-postmodernism 244
post-structural theories 284
Post-Traumatic Stress Disorder 44–6
postmemory 267
postmodernism 284
Pozières 55
Pram Factory 11, 135
Prichard, Katherine Susannah 42, 46–7, 50–3, 56–8, 61, 67, 93
principle of charity 287
Private Yuk Objects (Hopgood) 119, 125, 130–4, 138, 154, 190
pro-am theatre 4
Productivity Commission 177, 284
A Property of the Clan (Enright) 200, 210–11, 222–5

public service, exclusion of women from 72–3
Pusey, Michael 177, 284

Queensland 165
Queensland Symphony Orchestra 62
Queensland Theatre 166, 243
Queensland Theatre Company 166

race and racism 63–4, 112, 121, 184, 260, 275, 291
radio 41, 62
Rattigan, Alf 177
Rayson, Hannie 214
Razak, Najib 270
Reagan, Ronald 163
Reconstruction 91, 99
Redgrave, Roy 33
Reed, John 61–2
Rees, Leslie 1, 50, 52, 82–3, 90, 235
Reid, Elizabeth 161
Rene, Roy 'Mo' 37, 40, 41
repertory theatre 4, 46–7, 92, 166
Returned Serviceman's League 107
revelation, in drama 106
reversal, in drama 106
Reynolds, Henry 180
Ribush, Dolia 83
Ribush Players 83
Ribush, Rosa 83
Rickard, John 40
Rickards, Harry 23
Roberts, Laura 26

The Rocky Horror Show (O'Brien) 276
Roland, Betty 42, 46, 56, 57, 57–8, 62, 93, 123
Romania 201
Romeril, John 53, 134, 136
Ross, Freddy 75
Rousseau, Jean-Jacques 289–91
Royal Commission into Aboriginal Deaths in Custody 234
Royal Queensland Theatre Company 166
Royal Shakespeare Company 10
Rudd, Kevin 242
Rudd, Steele 24–5, 31, 35, 53, 79
A Rum Do! 166
Russia 202
Rusty Bugles (Elliott) 13, 89, 94–102, 97, 104, 106, 155

Schultz, Julianne 226
The Season at Sarsparilla (White) 10, 85, 122
Second Iraq War 239
sectarianism 65
The Seed (Mulvany) 200, 210–11, 218–22, 220
Sefton, Queenie 26
selectors 25
The Seven Stages of Grieving (Mailman and Enoch) 227
Sewell, Stephen 167–8, 174, 199, 212
sexism 72–3

Index 333

sexuality 50, 260, 275–81
Seymour, Alan 94, 101, 114
shadow self 227
Shakespeare, William 4–5, 189
Shakthidharan, S. 243, 267, 274
Sharman, Jim 199, 276
Shaw, George Bernard 2
Shaw, Jonathan 43
The Shifting Heart (Beynon) 89, 108–12, 115–17, 260
Shirley, Arthur 22
SHIT (Cornelius) 71, 238, 253–7, 259–60, 266
A Short History of Australia (Clark) 18
Simmonds, Diana 257–8
Singapore 71
Sisley, Barbara 93
Sitarenos, Mary 192
six o'clock closing (hotels) 40
Sky Without Birds (Gray) 89, 108–12, 115–17
slots, in theatre programs 9, 123–4, 166, 295
smelters 171
Smith, Frank Beaumont 25
Snedden, Billy 161
The Social Contract (Rousseau) 289–91
Social Sketches of Australia (McQueen) 90–1
socialism 110–11, 164
The Socialist 32
Solidarity 201
South Africa 121
South Australian Theatre

Company 166
Soviet Union 57, 121, 164, 201–2, 212
Spangler, David 142
Spender, Stephen 84
The Squatter's Daughter (Bailey and Duggan) 33
Sri Lanka 269, 272
The Stables 135
Staines, Norman 138
Stalin, Josef 212
Standing, Guy 239
state of the nation drama 168
State Theatre 166
State Theatre Company 166
State Theatre Company of South Australia 166, 245
Stewart, Douglas 25, 83–6, 123, 155, 169, 219
Stiffy and Mo 37
stock market collapse (1929) 64
Stolen (Harrison) 8, 200, 211, 227–31, 233
Stolen Generations 51, 229
A Stretch of the Imagination (Hibberd) 71, 119, 134, 146–7, 151–2, 155, 180, 255
Strindberg, August 2
Strong, Sam 295
suburbia 39
Summer of the Seventeenth Doll (Lawler) 8, 53, 71, 88–90, 94–5, 101–7, 122, 156, 174, 260

Sumner, John 90, 93, 126
surrealism 122
Suryaprakash, Vaishnavi 268
Suzuki, David 239
Sydney Harbour Bridge 40
The Sydney Morning Herald 119, 276
Sydney Opera House 10
Sydney Push 10
Sydney Repertory Theatre 29, 46–7, 51
Sydney Symphony Orchestra 62
Sydney Theatre Company 166
symbolism 122

Tait brothers 23, 41
Tait, Peter 197–8
Take Your Best Shot (Kent) 239
Tallis, Sir George 40–1
Tallis, Joan 165
Tallis, Michael 165
Taylor, Charles 283
television 14
Thatcher, Margaret 163, 175, 178
Theatre Australia (Un)limited (Milne) 209
theatre, in Australia
1901–1914 19–36
1915–1929 37–59
1930–1945 60–88
1945–1960 89–118
1961–1975 119–58
1976–1990 159–99
1991–2005 200–37
2006–2020 238–81

at Federation 1–2, 5, 16
complaints about lack of 1–3
perspectives on Australian drama 7–8, 123, 282–8, 294–5
pluralism in 205
politics of 13, 16
professionalisation of 93
see also plays
Theatre Workshop (UK) 10
This Old Man Comes Rolling Home (Hewett) 10, 144
Thomson, Katherine 102, 167, 175
Three Australian Plays 122
3LO (radio station) 41
Thring, Frank 41
Throssell, Hugh 39, 58
Throssell, Ric 58, 108, 116–17
Tiananmen Square massacre 202
Till the Day I Die (Odets) 111
The Time is Not Yet Ripe (Esson) 19, 24, 28–35, 52, 72, 155, 179, 264
Tivoli Theatre 276
Toller, Ernst 122
Tomholt, Sydney 82, 235
Tompkins, Joanne 4–5
Tong, Jean 243, 267, 270–1
Toose, Adam 239
The Torrents (Gray) 90
The Touch of Silk

(Roland) 37, 42–6, 52–3, 112
touring 23
Toynbee, Arnold 183
tragedy 286
Traitors (Sewell) 212
transvestism 276
Triple X (Chase) 238, 243, 261–2, 274–81
Troupe Theatre 16
Trump, Donald 239–40
Tucker, Albert 61
Tulloch (horse) 121–2
Tynan, Ken 102

Uluru Statement from the Heart 288, 292
Union Repertory Theatre Company 89–90, 126, 166
Union Theatre, University of Melbourne 83, 102
United Kingdom 239
universities 240
Up the Road (Harding) 227
Utopia (television program) 35

Valamanesh, Hossein 247
Varney, Denise 192
vaudeville 276
Vaughan, Martin 220
Vegemite 40
Velvet Revolution 201
Versailles Treaty (1919) 34
Vietnam War 46, 122, 125–6, 131–4, *133*, 161, 190

violence, towards women 258
von Brandenstein, Carl 47

Waiting for Lefty (Odets) 92, 111
Wałęsa, Lech 201
The War Game (film) 201
Ward, Peter 119
Ward, Stuart 208
Warner Brothers 40
Watson, Don 208
Weber, Max 291
Western Australia 184–5
Western Australia Symphony Orchestra 62
When the Goal Posts Move (Eltham) 243
When the Rain Stops Falling (Bovell) 238, 244–9, 259, 263, 281
White Australia, or, The Empty North (Bedford) 33–4
White Australia Policy 63–4, 66, 107, 288, 291
White, Patrick 10, 53, 85, 119, 122–3, 125–30, 155, 192, 256
White With Wire Wheels (Hibberd) 102
Whitlam, Gough 12, 121, 152–4, 160–1, 177
Whitlam government 160–5, 171
Why Weren't We Told? (Reynolds) 180

Wilhelm II, Emperor 37
Williams, Margaret 50, 137
Williamson, David 8, 134, 264
Williamson, JC (actor) 28, 40, 56
Williamson, JC (The Firm) *see* JC Williamson Ltd
Windmill Baby (Milroy) 227
Wolf, Gabrielle 135
The Wolf of Wall Street (film) 270
Woman and Wine (Shirley and Lanseck) 22
The Woman in the Window (De Groen) 200, 210–15, 217–18, 221, 223, 246
women
   discrimination against 72, 121
   violence towards 258
   women playwrights 93–4
working-class characters 260
Working Dog 35
Working Nation (white paper) 206
World Theatre Festival 188
World War I 37–9, 45, 55
World War II 34, 65, 71
Writers League 57

Yirra Yaakin Theatre Company 227

Young, Sam 282
Yugoslavia 202
YW Boston 260–1

Zeegan, Lawrence 60

www.ingramcontent.com/pod-product-compliance
Lightning Source LLC
Chambersburg PA
CBHW060929180426
43192CB00044B/2814